# Blocked by

G000155498

In recent years issues like caste discrimination and social exclusion have been discussed extensively in India. However, while the linkages between caste and society have been studied widely, the interface between caste and economy or economic development remains an under-researched terrain. *Blocked by Caste* explores contemporary patterns of economic discrimination faced by Dalits and religious minorities like Muslims and the underlying attitudinal orientations that contribute to inequality in various spheres of life.

This volume investigates empirical evidence of discrimination by focusing on the urban labour market as well as other markets in rural areas. It also analyses discrimination in non-market transactions like access to education, primary health care services, and fair price shops. Through detailed case studies, the essays examine the consequences of exclusion on unequal access to business, wage-earning, health status, and educational attainments and suggest possible remedies.

The introduction provides a conceptual framework and the foreword by Kaushik Basu underscores the importance of developing an interface between economics and social sciences in order to give greater visibility to research on discrimination.

This book will interest students and scholars of Dalit and subaltern studies, economics, sociology, and politics. It will be an invaluable resource for policymakers and activists.

**Sukhadeo Thorat** is Chairman, Indian Council for Social Science Research, and Professor of Economics, Centre for the Study of Regional Development, School of Social Sciences, Jawaharlal Nehru University, New Delhi. He is former Chairman, University Grants Commission.

**Katherine S. Newman** is James B. Knapp Dean, Zanvyl Krieger School of Arts and Sciences, Johns Hopkins University. She is former Malcolm Forbes Class of 1941 Professor at Woodrow Wilson School of Public and International Affairs and the Department of Sociology, and Director, Institute for International and Regional Studies, Princeton University.

# Blocked by Caste
# ECONOMIC DISCRIMINATION
# *in* MODERN INDIA

*edited by*

SUKHADEO THORAT

KATHERINE S. NEWMAN

*with a foreword by*

KAUSHIK BASU

**OXFORD**
UNIVERSITY PRESS

# OXFORD
### UNIVERSITY PRESS

Oxford University Press is a department of the University of Oxford.
It furthers the University's objective of excellence in research, scholarship,
and education by publishing worldwide. Oxford is a registered trademark of
Oxford University Press in the UK and in certain other countries

Published in India by
Oxford University Press
YMCA Library Building, 1 Jai Singh Road, New Delhi 110 001, India

© Oxford University Press 2010

The moral rights of the author have been asserted

First published 2010
Oxford India Paperbacks 2012
Third impression 2013

All rights reserved. No part of this publication may be reproduced, stored in
a retrieval system, or transmitted, in any form or by any means, without the
prior permission in writing of Oxford University Press, or as expressly permitted
by law, by licence, or under terms agreed with the appropriate reprographics
rights organization. Enquiries concerning reproduction outside the scope of the
above should be sent to the Rights Department, Oxford University Press, at the
address above

You must not circulate this work in any other form
and you must impose this same condition on any acquirer

ISBN-13: 978-0-19-808169-2
ISBN-10: 0-19-808169-3

Typeset in Adobe Garamond Pro 11/13 by Joჶy Philip
Printed in India at Shri Krishna Printer, Noida 201305

# Contents

NON-MARKET DISCRIMINATION: HEALTH, EDUCATION,
AND FOOD-RELATED INSTITUTIONS

DISCRIMINATION-INDUCED INEQUALITIES:
CAPITAL ASSETS AND POVERTY

# Tables and Figure

## TABLES

## FIGURE

# Foreword

There are very few topics in India that generate as much passion and policy debate as caste and group discrimination. India has for long grappled with the legacy of caste discrimination and social exclusion. These practices go back into the nation's distant history, certainly over two millennia, and mark and scar our society and economy even today. Somewhere during this long history, society got subdivided into *varnas*, four mutually exclusive endogamous groups, with a fifth segment getting added later—those who were considered to be beyond the pale of the caste system and were often called the Untouchables. Over the years, the varna system grew into a more complex and multilayered structure of *jatis*, and the Untouchables came to be called the Dalits, which is Marathi for 'oppressed'.

Soon after India gained Independence in 1947, the practice of untouchability was declared illegal by the founding fathers of the nation. But it is one thing for a practice to be declared illegal and quite another for it to go away. Though caste practices have been on the wane in recent decades, they continue to be a major characteristic of the nation, one that leaves its imprint on the labour market, the provision of education, indicators of health, and electoral politics. One way of trying to actually counter this age-old discrimination is to have some kind of affirmative action. India has tried many different versions of this, including direct reservations of jobs and seats in schools and colleges for the Dalits and other discriminated groups. But this has continued to be mired in controversy and the source of not just debates but rallies and even riots.

Despite the huge significance of economic discrimination and caste in the nation's economic life and development, the subject has received little formal attention. While there has been path-breaking work by Indian anthropologists and sociologists, which has enhanced our understanding of the role of caste in society, on the fluidity and rigidity of caste categories, on complex phenomena such as *sanskritization,* the interface between caste and the *economy* and *economic* development has remained a relatively under-researched field. As a consequence, important decisions, such as the design of affirmative action and reservations and the provision of education and health care to counter discrimination, have been left to the passions and machinations of lobbies and politicians.

This collection of essays edited by a distinguished economist and sociologist pair—Sukhadeo Thorat, Chairman of India's University Grants Commission (and Professor of Economics at Jawaharlal Nehru University), and Katherine S. Newman, Director of the Princeton Institute for International and Regional Studies (and Professor of Sociology), Princeton University, USA—is an attempt to make amends for this lacuna. The book brings together an impressive array of social scientists to inquire into some of the most pressing problems of our times in this field. Several of these chapters are exemplary scholarly work, using some of the best available methods of research in the social sciences on topics as diverse as caste; university education and post-university labour markets; public health services and discrimination; the correlations of health outcomes, on the one hand, and caste and religion, on the other; and the role of caste in the private sector. As such, the book can be invaluable not just to economists interested in the nature and impact of group discrimination, but to policymakers and politicians actually trying to design policy and interventions.

As in the case of India, the problem of group discrimination has been a subject of great practical and policy importance in the United States of America, with its history of slavery and race-based exclusion. This gave rise to some remarkable research in economics and, as a consequence, to some deep insights into the phenomenon. Without delving back to the long history of this research, one could mention the remarkable recent work of Marianne Bertrand and Sendhil Mullainathan.

In all these discrimination studies of the labour market, there was always the question of whether the employers were actually discriminating against some racial groups or whether their choice of workers of a certain race was influenced by the fact that these workers had some other indicators of higher productivity, such as greater education, more experience, and better grades. To crack this puzzle, Bertrand and Mullainathan designed a novel research experiment. They sent out fictitious résumés in response to actual advertisements for jobs in Boston and Chicago newspapers. Some of the résumés had names that are conventionally used by Whites—Allison, Anne, Carrie, Brad, Brendon, and Geoffrey, and some were given names associated with Blacks, such as Aisha, Ebony, Keisha and Darnell, Hakim, and Jamal. The aim was to find out how callbacks for job interviews vary by race even *when other characteristics of the applicants are the same or similar.* Since the résumés were created by the authors, they could control other characteristics, such as education and experience. The authors found that applicants with Black names needed to send out 15 applications to get one callback; White-named candidates needed 10. A Black needs eight years of additional experience to get the same number of callbacks as a White.

Thanks to the excellent control of the experiment, it firmly established the discrimination that Blacks face on the American labour market. The authors pointed out that, since the employers use race as a factor when choosing employees, even when it is not a correlate of some vital indicator of productivity, this fits the *legal* definition of discrimination.

The discipline of law and economics has always been prominent in this field. Another empirical finding that caught a lot of public attention in recent years is that of Richard Sander, who demonstrated that, in getting entry-level jobs in prestigious law firms, Blacks do not face any disadvantages but, when it comes to being partners, Blacks seldom make it. There seems to be the proverbial glass ceiling that thwarts Blacks in their career trajectory. Sander's own explanation of this striking empirical phenomenon is that firms use affirmative action when taking in Blacks, so that the average grades of Blacks getting these jobs is lower and their weaker long-run career and failure to rise to sufficient seniority reflects this.

Sander's analysis has come under some strong criticism. In a closely reasoned essay, James Coleman and Mitu Gulati point out that while Sander's data on the rarity of Black partners in top law firms are compelling, he does not have enough data to reach the *explanation* that he gives. They make an important technical point. Black associates are hired mostly from elite law schools and it is possible that even the Whites hired from elite schools may have weaker grades. Hence, minimally, one needs to put in control for this by, for instance, comparing the performance of Blacks and Whites from similar schools. While this will need statistical testing and so remains to be resolved, from my point of view, the more important criticism levelled by Coleman and Gulati is that Black associates receive little mentorship, lower-quality assignments, less client contact, and less interaction with their senior partners than White associates. It is not surprising that at the end of a period of such treatment, they appear to be less productive and often go away and usually fail to rise to more senior positions in the firm.

I give these examples only to illustrate the kinds of insights that can be generated through careful research in the interface between economics and other social sciences.

As with all major social questions, we will never have final answers. Especially on a problem as deep and historically rooted as caste and group discrimination in India, we will never have a definitive study that puts an end to the need for further inquiry. Yet, by giving this pressing problem our best effort, we can make large gains in our understanding and, through that, craft policy to hopefully bring such discrimination to an end. The present book is a commendable start towards such a research agenda and I hope that this will draw more Indian economists into this field, where anthropologists and sociologists have already made major contributions from the perspective of their disciplines.

KAUSHIK BASU
Professor of Economics and
Chairman of Department of
Economics, Cornell University, USA

# Preface and Acknowledgements

This volume brings together the findings of the research undertaken by the Indian Institute of Dalit Studies (IIDS), New Delhi, since its inception in 2003, on the theme of economic discrimination and inequality associated with the institutions of caste, untouchability, ethnicity, and religion in India.

The research undertaken by the IIDS came in stages, with support—academic and financial—from a number of researchers and organizations. The studies on labour market discrimination were undertaken with support from Princeton University, USA, and the International Labour Organization (ILO), Delhi. The four studies on labour market discrimination in the urban sector were undertaken in collaboration with Katherine S. Newman of the Department of Sociology at Princeton University, USA, and Paul Attewell, from City University of New York, USA. The studies used the methodology and techniques developed in the USA, with necessary modification to suit the Indian situation. The study on discrimination in rural markets covering labour and other markets was sponsored by the ILO.

The IIDS also undertook studies on the nature of discrimination faced by low-caste Untouchables in non-market transactions—in public provisions supplied by the state or by state-recognized public institutions. It developed a study with financial support from the United Nations Children's Fund (UNICEF), Delhi, on the issue of discrimination in public education and public health care services. This study unfolds the nature of discrimination faced by Dalit children in schools and public health centres, particularly in the rural setting. The IIDS on its own also did a study to examine the pattern of discrimination experienced by the Dalits in accessing meals in the mid-day meal scheme run by public schools, and also food items supplied by the public distribution system.

The IIDS undertook a study on the pattern of ownership of private enterprise by low-caste Untouchables, and tribals, bringing out the consequences of denial of property rights to Untouchables. The chapter that deals with ownership of business by Muslims was presented at a conference on 'Social Exclusion and Inclusive Policy', jointly organized by the IIDS and Princeton University. The remaining chapters, which deal with the status of Untouchables with respect to education, health, and poverty, were prepared and presented by the authors at the same conference. All the chapters in this volume are based on National Sample Survey data and fieldwork. The material in the book will be of immense use to policymakers, students, and researchers in educational institutions, as also to others interested in these issues.

The views expressed in the volume are of the respective authors and do not reflect the opinion of the volume editors or the publisher. They shall not be held accountable for the views expressed.

Many individuals and institutes have helped in bringing this volume to fruition. Princeton University's Institute for International and Regional Studies under the leadership of its director, Katherine Newman, supported four studies on urban labour market discrimination. Paul Attewell, Professor at the Department of Sociology, Graduate Centre of the City University of New York, provided intellectual leadership for several of these studies. We thank Princeton University for selecting the IIDS for collaboration and financially supporting the studies. We also thank Devah Pager of the Department of Sociology at Princeton University and other participants for contribution in the methodology workshop organized jointly by the IIDS and Princeton University in Delhi. Thanks are due to UNICEF for supporting two studies on discrimination in public education and public health. We are particularly thankful to Ramya Subramanian of UNICEF, Delhi, for her keen interest and academic input in these studies. ILO Delhi supported the study on discrimination in rural markets, and we particularly thank Coen Kompier and Sarah Webster for support to this research. Jimmey Rodger of ILO Geneva gave useful comments on the schedule prepared for the survey on rural market discrimination. We thank her for her suggestions.

This volume is based on studies undertaken by the IIDS independently and also in collaboration with other institutions. Over a period of five years, IIDS research staff played a major role in carrying out the research in one way or another. We thank all of them who have been a part of this endeavour. Nidhi Sadana, who is also co-author of some chapters in this volume, helped in its preparation. Thanks are due to her for doing the tedious work of fine-tuning the manuscript and related work. Narendra Kumar has helped in typing and preparation of the draft of this volume. We thank him for moulding the volume into shape.

Surinder S. Jodhka, Director of the IIDS, has helped in a number of ways, including arranging for the language editing of some chapters. We thank him for this constant support and encouragement. We have immensely benefited from the valuable comments of the reviewer, which helped improve the quality of some chapters as well as the volume overall. We also thank Kaushik Basu, Professor of Economics and Chairman of Department of Economics, Cornell University, USA, for writing a Foreword for this book. Finally, we are grateful to Oxford University Press, New Delhi, for undertaking publication of this book.

SUKHADEO THORAT
KATHERINE S. NEWMAN

# Abbreviations

| | |
|---|---|
| ASSOCHAM | Associated Chambers of Commerce and Industry of India |
| BPL | Below Poverty Line |
| CPIIW | Consumer Price Index for Industrial Workers |
| DE | Directory Establishment |
| DWACRA | Development of Women and Children in Rural Areas |
| FC | Forward Caste |
| FCI | Food Corporation of India |
| GoI | Government of India |
| HC | Higher Caste |
| HR | Human Resource |
| IHDS | India Human Development Survey |
| IIDS | Indian Institute of Dalit Studies |
| IIPS | Indian Institute for Population Sciences |
| IPS | Indian Police System |
| ISM | Indian Systems of Medicine |
| M&HC Survey | Morbidity and Health Care Survey |
| MDMS | Mid-day Meal Scheme |
| NCAER | National Council of Applied Economic Research |
| NCDHR | National Campaign on Dalit Human Rights |
| NCERT | National Council of Educational Research and Training |
| NCSCST | National Commission for Scheduled Caste and Scheduled Tribe |
| NDE | Non-directory Establishment |
| NGO | Non-governmental Organization |
| NSC | Non-Scheduled Caste |
| NSS | National Sample Survey |

| NSSO | National Sample Survey Organisation |
| OAE  | Own Account Enterprise |
| OBC  | Other Backward Caste/Class |
| OLS  | Ordinary Least Squares |
| PDS  | Public Distribution Scheme |
| SC   | Scheduled Caste |
| ST   | Scheduled Tribe |
| UP   | Uttar Pradesh |

# Introduction
## Economic Discrimination
## Concept, Consequences, and Remedies

*Sukhadeo Thorat and Katherine S. Newman*

Economic discrimination has received little attention in mainstream discourse in the social sciences in India. With the exception of gender, there are very few studies related to market and non-market discrimination associated with the institutions of caste, untouchability, ethnicity, religion, colour, and other group identities, and their differential market outcomes (Thorat *et al.* 2005). This applies to theoretical as well as empirical studies. The lack of systematic theoretical and empirical research on market and non-market discrimination has constrained our capacities to develop well-founded equal opportunity policies for production and business sectors, employment, education, housing, health, and other spheres for the discriminated groups.

However, market and non-market discrimination cannot be ignored due to its immense consequences for economic growth, income distribution, poverty, and inter-group conflict. In fact, the state, in recognition of the visible inter-social group disparities between the lower and higher castes (HC), male and female, and religious groups in Indian society, has developed selective policies—the government could not wait for academicians to come up with the optimal solution. Therefore, equal opportunity policies have often preceded the necessary research on theoretical and empirical aspects of market and non-market discrimination. This has also led to considerable debate, covering a wide spectrum of issues ranging from evidence on discrimination to alternative ways of overcoming its adverse consequences.

The chapters in this volume focus on the contemporary patterns of discrimination in various markets, particularly the labour market, and discrimination in the delivery of services supplied by public institutions in education, health, and foods. They also deal with the consequences of discrimination faced by groups as reflected in the inequality in access to income-earning capital assets, business, employment, education, and health services, and ultimately in poverty. This introduction presents the findings of the empirical studies that provide evidence on the contemporary forms of discrimination faced by Untouchables and religious groups, such as Muslims, in market and non-market transactions.

However, before presenting the insights of the empirical studies, we will first discuss some of the theoretical issues relating to social exclusion in general and economic discrimination in particular, to provide a conceptual backdrop and place the empirical studies in the necessary theoretical perspective. The theoretical discussion deals with some of the key questions surrounding economic discrimination. It specifically looks into the following issues: first, it discusses the concept of social exclusion and discrimination as developed in social science in general and economics in particular. Second, it applies the concept of economic discrimination to the Indian situation, with particular focus on the institution of 'caste'. Third, it discusses the likely consequences of discrimination, and finally, identifies the possible remedies for market and non-market discrimination.

## SOCIAL EXCLUSION AND ECONOMIC DISCRIMINATION

Rene Lenoir first developed the expression 'social exclusion' in the mid-1970s (Lenoir 1979) as a complement to the older framework of market discrimination conceptualized by Gary Becker (1957). Lenoir categorized the 'excluded' as mentally and physically handicapped, suicidal individuals, aged invalids, abused children, substance abusers, delinquents, single parents, multi-problem households, marginal and asocial persons, and other social 'misfits' (Sen 2000). Later studies added new categories to the group of excluded persons including those denied 'a livelihood, secure, permanent employment, earnings, property, credit or land, housing, consumption levels, education, cultural capital, the welfare state, citizenship and legal equality, democratic participation, public goods, nation or dominant race, family and sociability, humanity, respect, fulfilment, and understanding' (Sen 2000: 12–13). Today, we recognize a wide range of domains being affected by the processes of social exclusion.

Among social scientists today, there is general agreement on the core features of social exclusion, its principle indicators, and consequences. Buvinic summarizes the meaning of social exclusion as 'the inability of an individual to participate in the basic political, economic, and social functioning of the society', and adds that social exclusion is 'the denial of equal access to opportunities imposed by certain groups of society upon others' (Buvinic 2005: 5). This definition captures three distinguishable features of social exclusion— first, it effects culturally defined 'groups'; second, it is embedded in social relations (the processes through which individuals or groups are wholly or partially excluded from full participation in the society in which they live); and finally, it delineates the consequences of exclusion (Haan 1997; Sen 2000). Thus, the outcome of social exclusion in terms of low income and high degree of poverty among the excluded groups depend crucially on the functioning of social and economic institutions through a network of social relations and the degree to which they are exclusionary and discriminatory in their outcomes. Social exclusion has a sizeable impact on an individual's access to equal opportunities, if social interactions occur between groups in power/subordinate relationships. The groups' focus on social exclusion recognizes that people are excluded because of ascribed rather than achieved features beyond individual agency or responsibility (Buvinic 2005).

Sen (2000) draws attention to the various dimensions of the notion of social exclusion. Distinction is drawn between the situations wherein some people are being kept out (or at least left out) and wherein some people are being included (maybe even being forced to be included)—in deeply unfavourable terms. He describes the former as 'unfavourable exclusion' and the latter as 'unfavourable inclusion'. The latter, with unequal treatment, may carry the same adverse effects as the former.

Sen also differentiates between 'active and passive exclusion'. For casual analysis and policy response, Sen argues,

It is important to distinguish between 'active exclusion'—fostering of exclusion through deliberate policy interventions by the government or by any other wilful agents (to exclude some people from some opportunity)—and 'passive exclusion', which works through the social processes in which there are no deliberate attempts to exclude, but nevertheless, may result in exclusion from a set of circumstances. (Sen 2000: 28)

Sen (2000) further distinguishes the 'constitutive relevance' of exclusion from that of its 'instrumental importance'. In the former, exclusion or deprivation has an intrinsic importance of its own. For instance, not being able to relate to others and to partake in the community life can directly impoverish a person's life, in addition to any further deprivation it may generate. This is different from social exclusion of an 'instrumental importance', in which exclusion in itself is not impoverishing, but can lead to impoverishment of human life.

Within social science, a more precise elaboration of the concept of discrimination has come from the discipline of economics in the context of race and gender (Becker 1957; Darity 1995). Mainstream economics throws more light on discrimination that operates through markets and non-market transactions and develops the concept of market discrimination with some analytical clarity. In the market discrimination framework, the discrimination of a group may operate through restrictions on entry to markets and/ or through 'selective inclusion', with unequal treatments in market and non-market transactions, which is similar to Sen's concept of unfavourable inclusion.

Labour market discrimination can occur in hiring—for instance, when two persons with similar employment experience, education, and training apply for employment, but, because they differ in some non-economic characteristics, they face denial in hiring. The differences are, thus, correlated with certain non-economic (social origins such as caste, race, ethnicity, and religious backgrounds) characteristics of an individual.

## INDIVIDUAL EXCLUSION VERSUS GROUP EXCLUSION

Insights from the theoretical literature indicate that the concept of social exclusion essentially refers to the processes through which groups are wholly or partially excluded on the basis of group identities from full participation in the society, economy, and polity in which they subsist. It involves two crucial dimensions, namely 'societal relations' (causing exclusion) and their 'outcomes' (causing deprivation). Therefore, for understanding the nature of exclusion, insights into societal relations and institutions of exclusion are as important as delineating their outcomes in terms of deprivation for excluded groups.

More importantly, this concept of social exclusion clearly draws distinction between group exclusion and the exclusion of an individual. In case of 'group exclusion', all persons belonging to a particular social/cultural group are excluded because of their group identity, and not due to their individual attributes. Exclusion of an 'individual' is fundamentally different from the exclusion of a 'group'. Individuals (both from excluded and non-excluded groups) often get excluded from access to economic and social opportunities for various reasons specific to them (and not because of their group social/cultural identity). For instance, individuals may be excluded from employment due to the lack of requisite education and skills. Individuals may face exclusion in access to education due to the lack of minimum qualification and merit, or their inability to pay for costly education. An individual may also be excluded from access to input and consumer markets due to insufficient income and purchasing power. It is important to note that theoretically the exclusion of an individual has necessarily no connection with the social and cultural identity of a person. On the other hand, in case of the exclusion of a social group, variables associated with social and cultural identities— such as social origin like caste, ethnicity, religion, gender, colour, and race—become important, and exclude all persons belonging to a particular group from access to capital assets, businesses, employment, education, civil and political rights, and other social needs. Thus, the group characteristics of exclusion are based on social and cultural identity, and are irrespective of individual attributes.

This discernment has important policy implications. While in the case of 'individual exclusion' pro-poor policies will have to be focused on enhancement of individual capabilities and entitlement, in the case of 'group exclusion' the focus of equal-opportunity policy measures will have necessarily to be on the group as a whole, since the basis of exclusion is the group and not an individual. It is possible that all individuals within an excluded social group may be homogeneous with respect to their economic and educational status, or they may differ with respect to these characteristics. If they differ due to economic and educational position, there is likelihood that the capacity of economically and educationally better-off individuals from the excluded groups to overcome discrimination (or to become immune from discrimination) may be greater than that of worse-off individuals from the same group. This also means that the situation of individuals within the excluded groups may vary in respect to the degree and intensity of discrimination and, hence, their economic and educational status. Thus, while it will be necessary to have general safeguards against discrimination for all individuals in the excluded social groups (in the form of legal and other protection such as equal-opportunity policies), the policy of economic, educational, and social empowerment may vary depending on the economic, social, and educational status of the individual from the excluded groups. The confusion regarding drawing of a clear distinction between exclusion of an individual and group exclusion has created unnecessary debate in recent discussions on policies against discrimination for various groups in Indian society.

## CASTE SYSTEM, MARKET, AND NON-MARKET DISCRIMINATION

The insights from the preceding discussion on the concept of social exclusion are relevant for understanding the Indian situation. In India, exclusion revolves around societal institutions that exclude, discriminate against, isolate, and deprive some groups on the basis of group identities such as caste, ethnicity, religion, and gender.

The nature of exclusion associated with the institution of caste particularly needs to be conceptualized as it lies at the core of developing equal-opportunity policies, such as a reservation policy for the Scheduled Castes (SC), Scheduled Tribes (ST), and Other Backward Castes (OBC), which goes back to the early 1930s. Presently, there is growing demand, that utilizes the same justification as used in the case of SCs, STs, and OBCs, for extension of the reservation policy to religious minorities such as Muslims and low-caste converts to Islam and Christianity, and women.

Therefore, the insights from the discussion on caste could be used for other groups as well. There are very few theoretical attempts at economic interpretation of the caste system, but they do recognize that caste as a system of social and economic governance is determined by certain religious ideological notions and customary rules and norms which are unique and distinct (Akerlof 1976; Scoville 1991; Lal 1988; Ambedkar 1936, 1987a, 1987b, and 1987c). The economic organization of the caste system is based on the division of people in social groups (or castes), in which the social and economic rights of each individual caste are predetermined or ascribed by birth and made hereditary. The entitlement to economic rights is, however, unequal and hierarchical (graded). Economic and social rights are unequally assigned and, therefore, the entitlement to rights diminishes as one moves down the caste ladder. The system also provides for a community-based regulatory mechanism to enforce the system through the instrument of social ostracism (or social and economic penalties), and is further reinforced with justification from some philosophical elements in Hindu religion (Lal 1988; Ambedkar 1936, 1987a, 1987b, 1987c).

The fundamental characteristic of predetermined and fixed social and economic rights for each caste, with restrictions on change, implies 'forced exclusion' of certain castes from the civil, economic, and educational rights that other castes enjoy. Exclusion in the civil, educational, and economic spheres is, thus, internal to the system and a necessary outcome of its governing principles. In the market-economy framework, occupational immobility would operate through restrictions in various markets and may include land, labour, capital, credit, other inputs, and services necessary for pursuing any business or educational activity.

This implies that in its original form, unlike many other societies, the Hindu social order governed by the caste system does not recognize an individual and his distinctiveness as the centre of social purpose (Ambedkar 1936). In fact, for the purpose of rights and duties, the unit of Hindu society is not an individual—even a family is not regarded as a unit in Hindu society, except for marriages and inheritance. The primary unit in Hindu society is caste and, hence, the rights and privileges (or the lack of them) of an individual are on account of the latter's membership of a particular caste (Ambedkar, 1987b). Also, due to the hierarchical or graded nature of the caste system, entitlements to civil, economic, and educational rights of different castes become narrower as one goes down its hierarchical ladder. Various castes in their rights and duties get artfully interlinked and coupled with each other in such a manner that the rights and privileges of the HCs become the disadvantage and disability of lower castes, particularly the SCs and OBCs located at the bottom of the caste hierarchy. In this sense, a caste does not exist singularly, but only in plural (Ambedkar 1987c). Castes exist as a system of endogenous groups that are interlinked with each other in an unequal measure of rights and relations in all walks of life. Castes at the top of the order enjoy more rights at the expense of those located at the bottom. Therefore, the lower castes such as the Dalits and OBCs located at the bottom of the caste hierarchy have far fewer economic, educational, and social rights than the castes at the top.

Caste/untouchability-based exclusion is, thus, reflected in the inability of individuals from the lower castes to interact freely and productively with others and this also inhibits their full participation in the economic, social, and political life of the community (Bhalla and Lapeyere 1997). Incomplete citizenship or denial of civil rights (freedom of expression, rule of law, right to justice), political rights (right and means to participate in the exercise of political power), and socio-economic rights (right to property, employment, and education) is the key dimension of an impoverished life. Viewed from this perspective, the concept of caste- and untouchability-based market and non-market discrimination can be conceptualized in a particular way. Discrimination can, thus, be defined as follows:

i.    Complete exclusion or denial of certain social groups such as the lower castes by HCs in hiring or sale and purchase of factors of production (like agricultural land, non-land capital assets, and various services and inputs required in the production process), consumer goods, social needs like education, housing, health services, and other services transacted through market and non-market channels, which is unrelated to productivity and other economic attributes.

ii. Selective inclusion but with differential treatment to excluded groups, reflected in differential prices charged or received (different from market prices). This may include price of input factors and consumer goods, price of factors involved in production such as wages for human labour, price for land or rent on land, interest on capital, and rent on residential houses. This may also include price or fee charged by public institutions for services such as food items, water, electricity, and other goods and services.

iii. Unfavourable inclusion (often forced) bound by caste obligations and duties reflected, first, in overwork, loss of freedom leading to bondage, and attachment, and, second, in differential treatment at the place of work.

iv. Exclusion in certain categories of jobs and services of the former Untouchables or SCs who are involved in so-called 'unclean or polluting' occupations (such as scavenging, sanitary jobs, and leather processing). This is in addition to the general exclusion or discrimination that persons from these castes would face on account of being Untouchables.

## Consequences of Economic Discrimination

The theoretical literature has recognized the wide-ranging consequences of social and economic exclusion not only for the well-being of the excluded groups, inter-group inequalities, and resultant inter-group conflict, but also for the performance of the economy. The concern about discrimination is precisely because of its linkages with underdevelopment, inequality, poverty of the excluded groups, and inter-group conflict.

### For Economic Growth

The standard economic theory of discrimination implies that market discrimination will generate consequences that adversely affect overall economic efficiency and lead to lower economic growth. Market discrimination leads to failure of the market mechanism, which in turn induces inefficiency due to less-than-optimal allocation of labour and other factors among firms.

Factor immobility also brings in segmentation in the markets. In the case of the caste system, for instance, fixed occupations—

by not permitting mobility of human labour, land, capital, and entrepreneurship across castes—create segmented markets and bring imperfections in each of these markets. Thus, far from promoting a competitive market situation, it creates segmented and monopolistic markets. Labour and capital fail to shift from one occupation to another even if the wage rate and rate of return (on investment) are higher in the alternative occupation. Thus, factor immobility brings gross inefficiency in resource allocation and economic outcome (Ambedkar 1936, 1987b).

Economic efficiency is also affected by reducing job commitment and efforts of workers who perceive themselves to be victims of discrimination and by reducing the magnitude of investment in human capital by discriminated groups. In caste-based segmented markets, economic efficiency is thus lower than in the model of a perfectly competitive market economy (Birdsall and Sabot 1991).

Factor immobility also leads to unemployment, which is typically associated with the customary rules governing employment in various occupations (Ambedkar 1936, 1987a, 1987b, and 1987c; Akerlof 1956). By not permitting the movement of labour between occupations, caste becomes a direct cause of much of voluntary unemployment for the HCs and involuntary unemployment for lower castes. The HC Hindu would generally prefer to be voluntarily unemployed for some time than to take up an occupation that is considered polluting. For the lower castes, on the other hand, the restriction on taking up other castes' occupations will compel them to remain involuntarily unemployed. Thus, involuntary unemployment in the case of lower castes and voluntary unemployment in the case of HCs is one of the negative outcomes of the caste system.

The economic efficiency of labour also suffers severely in another manner. Since the division of occupations under the caste system is not based on individual choice, the individual sentiment, preference, and natural aptitudes have no place in it. Social and individual efficiency require us to develop the capacity of an individual to the point of competency to choose and make his/her own career. The principle of individual choice is violated in the caste system as it involves an attempt to appoint a task to an individual in advance, selected not on the basis of training or capacities, but on the caste status of the parents (Ambedkar 1936).

Further, some occupations are considered socially degrading, which reduces the social status of persons engaged in them. Forced into these occupations on account of their caste origin, people do not derive job satisfaction. In fact, such occupations constantly provoke in them aversion, ill will, and a desire to evade the work (Ambedkar 1936). The caste system also disassociates intelligence from work and creates contempt for physical labour. The dignity of physical labour is nearly absent in the work ethics of the caste system. The lack of dignity of labour, thus, adversely affects the incentive to work. This implies that the caste system (as an economic organization) lacks several elements that are required to satisfy the conditions for optimum use of resources and optimum economic outcome.

### For Inequality, Poverty, and Inter-group Conflict

This brings us to the consequences of discrimination and exclusion on income distribution and poverty. The consequences of the caste system for equity and poverty are more serious than for economic growth. Since access to a source of income and economic reward under the caste system is determined by unequal assignment of rights, the result is an income distribution generally skewed along caste lines. Lal writes, 'Much of modern abhorrence of the caste system is due to the legitimate dislike in my view of the system of economic inequality it perpetuates' (Lal 1988: 73).

Ambedkar argued that whatever may have been the purpose behind the origin of the caste system, later, as it evolved in its classical form, it certainly involved an economic motive, the purpose of which was income maximization through coercion rather than economic efficiency of any sort (Ambedkar 1936). The customary rules and norms regarding right to property, occupation, employment, wages, education, social status of occupation, and dignity of labour are framed and defined in a manner that involves denial of educational, social, and economic rights, and resultant deprivation and poverty of the lower castes. Disparities in economic and educational spheres in general and poverty of the lower castes like the former Untouchables and OBCs in particular, are a direct outcome of the unequal entitlement of economic rights under the caste system.

There is an additional social and political cost of caste-based social exclusion. By exacerbating current inequality between groups and by contributing to its perpetuation from one generation to the next, it also fosters inter-group conflict (Birdsall and Sabot 1991). Thus caste-based discrimination in access to sources of income and human development of subordinate groups has the potential for inducing inter-group conflict.

## Dynamics of Caste Economic Discrimination

As an institution of social organization of Hindus, the caste system has also undergone significant change from its original form. Only a few have ventured to explain the dynamics of the caste system. Akerlof's economic model of the caste system argued that the provision of social ostracism (with social and economic penalties involving social and economic boycott and isolation) measures against the violation of customary rules of the caste system which act as the main deterrent to change. The fear of being socially and economically boycotted and isolated acts as a powerful deterrent to change in the system. This implies that there are social costs associated with change that discourage the caste system from being dynamic in nature (Akerlof 1976). Scoville (1991) emphasized the role of the economic costs involved in the enforcement of the caste system. Enforcement of the system involves economic costs—transaction and enforcement—and these costs are too high for individual members to break the rules of the system. Scoville thus located the reasons for the rigidity of the caste system in the enormous economic costs which inhibit a change in the customary rules governing it. This implies that in a situation of low economic costs, the inefficient rules governing the caste system would change and make the system dynamic.

The 'cost and efficiency' explanation, however, remains silent about the other motives behind discrimination. Marxist explanations and those of Ambedkar go beyond 'cost and efficiency' and emphasize the role of social, educational, and economic gains of monopolization accruing to HCs as a reason for the perpetuity of the caste system.

The HCs will continue to support the caste system as long as it brings them gains in the social, economic, and educational spheres. The customary rules governing social and economic relations, and those relating to education under the caste system, would change if the alternative (or new) rules yielded higher economic and social profit to the HCs. Conversely, traditional rules would continue if the alternative rules (or new rules) yielded lesser benefits to the HCs. Ambedkar further added that a change in the ideas about human rights and equality also induces change in social relations, as the concept of human rights and justice involved under the caste system is contrary to the modern tenets of human rights and justice.

Thus the prevailing theoretical literature indicates that changes in the caste system will depend on the relative influence of social costs (in terms of social isolation/standing) and economic costs (transaction and enforcement costs), and the social and economic gains associated with change. It will also depend on the extent of acceptability of the modern ideas about human rights, justice, and equality. Lesser gains to the HCs in the existing system (as compared to the system governed by new rules) and low social and economic costs of change will induce such a change in the traditional social and economic relations of the caste system. Similarly, the recognition and pursuit of human rights and justice will also induce a change in the system. Conversely, if the gains to the HCs in the social, educational, and economic spheres in the traditional system are higher and the cost of change is high, and also the notion of human rights and justice as prevalent among the masses is against progressive norms of human rights, there will be less incentive for the HCs to opt for change.

## REMEDIES FOR ECONOMIC DISCRIMINATION
### Free Market versus Interventionist Policy

Given the adverse consequences of economic and social discrimination in multiple spheres, reducing discrimination is necessary, as it is likely to increase economic efficiency and growth, enhance access to economic and educational rights, and help reduce poverty and inter-group inequalities. How to overcome discrimination has been a central concern of economic theories. Two alternative solutions have emerged in the economic literature. One theoretical strand predicts that in highly competitive markets, discrimination will prove to be a transitory phenomenon as there are costs associated with discrimination to the firms/employers that result in a lowering of profits. Firms/employers who indulge in discrimination face the ultimate sanction imposed by the markets. This proposition sees the resulting erosion of profits as a self-correcting solution for eliminating discrimination. This view would suggest the promotion of competitive markets to reduce market discrimination.

However, other theories argue for an interventionist policy to overcome economic discrimination. This school of thought believes that there are several reasons why economic discrimination might persist over long periods. First, even if the markets are sufficiently competitive, exclusion and discrimination will persist. Discrimination may persist if all firms /producers practice discrimination, the possibility of which is quite high. Decades of labour market discrimination in high-income countries attests to the persistence of market discrimination. Second, in reality, not all markets are competitive. Indeed, in most economies, the markets are highly imperfect and are governed by oligopolistic and monopolistic market situations which often empower firms to discriminate at will.

The inherent limitations of the competitive market mechanism as a solution to the problem of market discrimination have been aptly summarized by Darity and Shulman:

The analytical stance of mainstream neo-classical economists is characterised as methodological individualism, and it presumes that economic institutions are structured such that society-wide outcomes result from an aggregation of individual behaviours. It is presumed that if individuals act on the basis of pecuniary self-interests, then market dynamics dictate equal treatment for equal individuals, regardless of inscriptive characteristics such as race. Consequently, observed group inequality is attributed to familial, educational, or other background differences among individuals who are unevenly distributed between social groups. The causes of a dissimilar distribution of individuals between social groups may be genetic, cultural, historical, or some combination thereof. The differences in cultural attributes include the value families and neighbourhoods place on education, attitudes, and work habits. The historical refers primarily to the impact of past discrimination on current inequality. In contrast, economists who may be classified as methodological structuralists do not accept this interpretation. Structuralism as an analytical method holds that aggregate outcomes are not the result of a simple summation of individual behaviours, but rather arise from the constraints and incentives imposed by organisational and social hierarchies. In this view, individual behaviour achieves its importance within the context of group formation, cooperation, and conflict. Economic and political outcomes are, thus, a function of the hegemony exercised by dominant groups, the resistance offered by subordinate groups, and the institutions that mediate their relationship. Discrimination, in this view, is an inherent feature of [the] economic system. Competition is either not powerful enough to offset the group dynamics of identity and interest, or it actually operates so as to sustain discriminatory behaviours. Discrimination is due to the dynamics of group identification, competition, and conflict, rather than irrational, individual attitudes. Market mechanisms, far from being relied upon to eliminate discrimination of their own accord, must be scrutinised and pressured to further the goal of equality of opportunity. (Darity and Shulman 1989: 105)

These two views have different policy implications for overcoming discrimination. The view that predicts discrimination to be self-correcting argues for strengthening competitive market mechanisms. The alternative view asserts that market discrimination will persist despite the presence of competitive market forces or for other reasons, and therefore interventionist policies will be necessary. According to them, correcting discrimination would require legal safeguards against discrimination and policies for facilitating fair access to discriminated groups in various spheres. It calls for state interventions not only in land, labour, and capital markets, but also in the product and consumer markets and social needs such as education, housing, and health. Central to this view is the exposition that discriminated groups face discrimination in transactions through market and non-market channels and, in that regard, their discrimination is multiple and plural in nature.

## Empowerment versus Equal-opportunity Policies

Current discourse in India is caught up in a conundrum of developing equal-opportunity policies (particularly in the form of reservation) for groups and communities that have suffered social, educational, and economic exclusion associated with caste, ethnicity, gender, and religious identities. Alternative policies for overcoming deprivation of discriminated groups emerged from the discussions particularly in the context of the initiative to extend reservation to the private sector for SCs and STs, and in public education for OBCs, and similar demands by low-caste converts to Islam and Christianity, and certain religious minorities such as Muslims. Two alternative sets of remedies, which can be grouped under 'social and economic empowerment' and 'equal opportunity', emerged from extensive discussions in early 2000. We, therefore, discuss the relative merit and relevance of these two policies.

The policy of social and economic empowerment is essentially directed towards improving the ownership of capital assets such as agricultural land and business, along with the educational levels and skills of discriminated groups. These measures are supposed to augment the capacities of discriminated groups to undertake businesses and to enhance their employability by improving their level of education and skill.

Generally, there is support for the policy of economic and social empowerment of the discriminated groups. These policies take the shape of pro-poor policies which involve measures to increase access to capital assets including agricultural land, employment, education, social needs like housing, and food. However, when it comes to providing equal opportunities in the form of reservation, particularly in the private sector, the policy does not find similar favour. It is argued that labour and other markets generally work in a neutral manner, and access to markets is determined by merit and efficiency considerations. As such, there is no need for safeguards against possible market and non-market discrimination. Thus, while policies for the general educational and economic empowerment of discriminated groups are favoured, those ensuring equal share and participation through reservations are marked by differences of opinion.

Why do we need equal-opportunity policies for the discriminated groups? Insights from the theoretical literature indicate that the problems of discriminated groups are different from those of other groups. The first problem is lack of access to income-earning capital assets like agricultural land and non-farm businesses, quality employment, and education due to denial of the same in the past for long periods of time, the consequences of which are visible in contemporary times in the form of inter-group inequalities in several indicators of human development. Second, and more important, is the continuation of discrimination in various market and non-market transactions in the present, in some forms if not all. Therefore, the problem of discriminated groups requires a dual solution—one set of remedies for improving their ownership of land and capital assets, quality employment, and augmenting their educational levels, as compensation for the denial of basic rights in the 'past', (which in fact are needed also for poor from non-discriminated groups) and another set of remedies to provide safeguards against discrimination in the 'present'. While the empowerment policies are based on the principle of compensation for denial of rights in the past (the consequences of which are visible in the present), the equal-opportunity policies are based on providing safeguards against discrimination in the present, in various market and non-market transactions, and ensuring due share and participation in employment, education, businesses, legislature, and governance.

These two set of policies are complementary. The policy of economic empowerment is expected to enhance the capacities of discriminated groups to take advantage of the ongoing social and economic progress. Improved access to income-earning assets will improve the capacities of the discriminated groups and enable them to partake in business activities. Educational and skill development is expected to increase employability and enable them to access jobs in both the private and public sectors.

However, the policy of economic empowerment needs to be supplemented by equal-opportunity policies to provide safeguards against discrimination in the present, which the discriminated groups may face. The reason for this is that even if they gain access to income-earning assets, education, and skills through empowerment measures, due to the practice of discrimination in various markets—particularly the labour market and non-market transactions—they may fail to get their due share and participation in ownership of assets, employment, social needs like education, health, and housing. In the absence of equal-opportunity policies in the form of reservation, and similar measures, the excluded and marginalized groups may continue to face denial. For this reason equal-opportunity policies are supplemented by the policy of general economic empowerment (pro-poor policies), which includes reservation policy—and similar policies in many countries—to ensure a fair share to discriminated groups. The complementary nature of these two policies will ultimately help the historically discriminated groups not only to improve their capabilities, but also to receive their due share in the economic and social progress of the country.

## GRADED INEQUALITIES, MULTIPLE GROUPS, AND INCLUSIVE POLICIES

Currently, in India there is a discussion on developing alternative policies not only for those groups who suffered caste discrimination in Hindu and non-Hindu folds, but also for those who have suffered discrimination associated with gender and religion. Indian society is characterized by multiple forms of exclusion associated with group identities like caste, ethnicity, gender, and religion in various spheres of society, polity, and economy. Therefore, addressing such forms of exclusion requires inclusive policies to overcome deprivation faced by each of these groups. The development experience of the last fifty years or so possibly makes some groups believe that the gains of social and economic development have not been fairly shared by them. Therefore, those who have experienced exclusion or derived limited benefits from social and economic development are now seeking solution to their group-specific problems. It is in this background that various new groups have begun to demand group-specific policies to ensure due share to them. The SCs and STs seek extension of reservation to the private sector, the OBCs demand reservation in public education institutions, and women are seeking reservation in the central legislature; and similar demands have come from low-caste converts to Islam and Christianity, and also from religious minorities such as the Muslims.

The lessons from the theoretical and empirical literature imply that equal-opportunity policies for various discriminated groups will have necessarily to be guided by the nature of exclusion and discrimination faced by discriminated groups in the Hindu and non-Hindu communities within Indian society. It will require the use of the both—policies of economic and educational empowerment and of equal opportunity in the form of reservation and similar forms.

This also means that the nature of reservation and/or similar measures for various discriminated caste groups within the Hindu fold and similar social groups in the non-Hindu fold, as well as religious minorities and women, may require us to take into consideration the specific features of the caste system, and institutions related to religion and gender in terms of their exclusionary character, with wider social and economic ramifications.

As regards Hindu society, we need to recognize the unique feature of the caste system. As discussed earlier, the core governing principle of the caste system is not inequality alone, but 'graded inequality', which implies 'hierarchically unequal entitlement' of rights to various castes. With the entitlement to rights being hierarchically unequal, every caste (except the HCs) suffers a degree of denial and exclusion. But all suffering castes do not suffer equally. Some suffer more, and some less. The loss of rights is not uniform across caste groups. As one moves down the caste hierarchy, rights and privileges also get reduced. By implication, castes located at the bottom of the caste hierarchy, such as the Untouchables, suffered the most. The OBCs followed closely. The OBCs have probably not suffered from the practice of untouchability, or from residential and social isolation, as much as the SCs, but historically, they too have faced exclusion in education, employment, and certain other spheres, reflected in their lower educational and quality employment level.

The system of graded entitlement to rights results in disparities in the social, economic, and educational conditions, which vary across different caste groups. The lesson we ought to learn from this is that, given the differential impact on each caste, policies against discrimination and deprivation need to be group-specific and governed by the specific social, economic, and educational conditions of each caste. By implication, equal-opportunity policies will have to be necessarily different for different caste groups, depending on the nature of discrimination faced by them and their social, economic, and educational situation.

In the case of non-Hindu religious communities, some elements of the Hindu caste system seem to have been carried along through a

spillover effect in the case of low-caste converts to other religions such
as Islam, Sikhism, and Buddhism. Such lower-caste converts also face
discrimination, though not in the same forms and manifestations
as the Hindu low castes. Therefore, their group-specific problems
need to be addressed. In fact, in the case of the former Untouchables
converted to Sikhism and Buddhism, and of the OBCs converted
to Islam, the reservation policy has been extended in selective
manner. But the problems of the former Untouchables converted to
Christianity and Islam have not yet been addressed.

As regards religious minorities, some among them, particularly
the Muslims, possibly face discrimination as a religious group in a
number of spheres, reflected in their poorer performance with respect
to the relevant human development indicators (although there are
extremely limited studies on discrimination against religious groups
in various spheres). Similarly, women too face gender discrimination,
though the extent of the discrimination varies with their caste, class,
and religious backgrounds. Some groups such as the STs and the
semi-nomadic tribes suffer isolation and exclusion due to their ethnic
backgrounds.

It thus becomes apparent that due to variations in the forms and
spheres of discrimination, the consequences of deprivation and poverty
across various discriminated groups vary. Unlike in the case of the former
Untouchables, there are limited studies on other discriminated groups
regarding the forms, nature, and manifestations of discrimination.
However, the visible presence of inter-group inequalities among
low caste–high caste, male–female, minority–majority religious
groups, and tribals–non-tribals with reference to various indicators
of human development points toward the consequences of historical
discrimination. This is reflected in differential access to income-
earning assets, property, businesses, employment, education, and
civil rights, and in participation in legislature and governance. Equal-
opportunity policies for the different discriminated groups would
differ in spheres and forms of intervention depending on the nature
of discrimination faced by each of these excluded groups, and their
present social, educational, economic, and political position.

The features of equal-opportunity policies for various discriminated
groups need to be comprehended in their unique context. Generally,

three components characterize equal-opportunity policies. First, they incorporate 'legal safeguards' against discrimination faced by certain social groups in multiple spheres of society, polity, and economy as a first remedial step. This generally takes the form of enactment of laws against discrimination, such as the Civil Rights Act in the United States of America (1964) or the Protection of Civil Rights Act in India (1955) (formerly known as Anti-Untouchability Act, 1955, and the Scheduled Caste and Scheduled Tribe Prevention of Atrocities Act, 1989). These Acts are necessary to provide legal safeguards so that in the event of discrimination, an individual could take recourse to these legal provisions. Second, although legal provisions are a necessary precondition to overcoming discrimination, they alone are not enough, as laws have their limitations in overcoming the consequences of historical exclusion through the denial of rights to education, income-earning assets, employment, civil rights, and other rights to some social groups. Therefore, equal-opportunity policies generally include specific measures in the form of reservation or similar means to ensure due share and participation of the discriminated groups in various spheres of society, polity, and economy.

Third, besides the above, the participation of the discriminated groups in governance at all levels—from legislature to the drafting policies, their execution and monitoring—is also crucial. Representation and participation of the discriminated groups in governance is a central element of inclusive policy and building an inclusive society. It is also imperative that provisions with respect to equal rights and protection against violation of rights are embodied in the Constitution. If a society practices discrimination, the impetus for change should come from the state. Private initiatives by civil society and the private sector in the form of reforms in society for ensuring equal human rights are equally necessary.

In sum, equal-opportunity policies will have some necessary elements. First, they will incorporate laws against discrimination in various spheres. Second, policies will need proactive measures in the form of reservation or similar measures to ensure a fair share of income-earning capital assets, employment (public and private), and social needs like education and housing. Third, participation in governance through a fair share in the legislature, executive, and administration, with necessary provisions in the Constitution and laws, is also required. It is necessary to recognize that there will be some common features of equal-opportunity policy cutting across all discriminated groups. However, its dimensions will vary across various discriminated groups (such as SC, ST, OBC, semi-nomadic and denotified tribes, the differently abled, women, and religious minorities), depending upon the nature and form of their discrimination and deprivation. Therefore, the equal-opportunity policy in the Indian context will be group-specific. It is only when the polity, society, and economy are more inclusive and participatory that democracy as a means of governance can become meaningful for everybody.

## PATTERN OF ECONOMIC DISCRIMINATION: AN OVERVIEW

We will now focus on the empirical evidence from the chapters in this volume on market and non-market discrimination and on its consequences for the human development of discriminated groups in Indian society.

The focus of the essays is on the empirical dimensions of economic and other types of discrimination. They provide empirical evidence on three main aspects of market and non-market discrimination. The first section includes essays examining empirical evidence on the forms of discrimination faced by low-caste Untouchables (or Dalits) and Muslims in various markets, with particular focus on the labour market. While the focus in urban areas is on the labour market, in rural areas, besides the labour market the analysis also deals with markets in agricultural land, inputs, and consumer goods. The second section includes discussions on the nature of discrimination faced by Dalits in non-market transactions, that is in accessing social needs such as education, health services, and food supplied by the government or government-approved public institutions. This includes government schools, public primary health centres, mid-day meals in schools, and food items supplied through the government-approved public distribution system. The third part provides empirical evidence on the consequences of exclusion for unequal access. Thus these essays deal with exclusion-linked inter-group inequalities in access to business, employment, wage earning, educational attainment, health status, and food.

In terms of empirical evidence and the methods used, the volume is possibly a first of its kind in the Indian situation, and is a benchmark in studies on economic and social discrimination experienced by discriminated groups in various market and non-market transactions in Indian society.

## Market Discrimination: Labour and Other Markets

The five chapters in this section deal with the nature of discrimination in labour and other markets in urban and rural areas. While the chapter on rural areas covers all market transactions, the four chapters on urban areas are confined to empirical evidence on labour market discrimination. The four chapters that capture the various dimensions of urban labour market discrimination, presented in part one of this volume, were conceived as tests of the proposition that discrimination is no longer an issue in Indian labour markets, particularly in the formal private sector. They make use of research techniques pioneered in the United States to measure discrimination in quantitative terms and to identify attitudes and beliefs through qualitative means that contribute to discriminatory patterns of hiring on the part of participants in the matching process (employers and job seekers). In order to focus clearly on discrimination and screen out the most vexing inequalities in human capital, the chapters focus on the formal labour market and the most highly qualified job seekers— graduates of the most prestigious universities in India. Admittedly, this does not cover the entire universe of questions that should be raised about discrimination in modern India. Yet these essays pose the questions in the context of the most advantaged applicants—those who should (in theory) face the lowest barriers to entry to favoured occupations since they possess formidable qualifications.

What these four chapters establish is serious evidence of continued discriminatory barriers in the formal urban labour market even for highly qualified Dalits and Muslims. Chapter 1 by Sukhadeo Thorat and Paul Attewell provides the results of a field experiment that found that low-caste and Muslim applicants who are equally or better qualified than HC applicants are significantly less likely to pass through hiring screens among employers in the modern formal sector in India. What explains this outcome? Chapter 2 by

Surinder S. Jodhka and Katherine S. Newman attempts to answer the question by contributing a qualitative, interview-based study of human resource managers responsible for hiring practices in twenty-five Indian firms. This research suggests that managers bring to the hiring process a set of stereotypes that makes it difficult for very low-caste applicants to succeed in the competition for positions.

In Chapter 3, Ashwini Deshpande and Katherine S. Newman focus on the experiences of equally qualified Dalit and non-Dalit cohorts from three major universities, who are moving out into the labour market at the same time. This longitudinal project shows that despite similar qualifications, the two groups expect and—true to form—experience divergent outcomes in the labour market. Dalit students bring weaker connections to the task and are far less likely to find jobs in the private sector. Hence, what we see as a discriminatory screen among employers, is also experienced by the most highly qualified Dalit students whose ventures into the labour market confirm what we learn from interviews with human resource managers about preconceived notions of 'merit'.

Such an outcome is costly in terms of discouragement, but it also impacts the bottom-line. Indeed, as S. Madheswaran and Paul Attewell show in their econometric analysis of National Sample Survey data in Chapter 4, SC and ST respondents experience a 15 per cent wage penalty compared to otherwise equivalent HC workers.

Together these four chapters constitute an argument that, far from fading as India modernizes, the problem of discrimination remains a serious one, even at the very top of the human-capital hierarchy. They cast some doubt on whether the natural operation of the market will be sufficient to correct this inefficiency in labour allocation.

This is not to suggest that investments in levelling the playing field are of no value. Clearly, Dalits who lack educational opportunities in childhood and adolescence will be greatly disadvantaged compared to those who have them (Dalit and non-Dalit). Dalit students who reach the best of India's universities, but are at a financial disadvantage because they bear the continuing burden of supporting their families, would benefit from additional financial aid so that they can concentrate on their studies just as more advantaged students do.

Yet, reaching the pinnacle of what Indian education has to offer is not sufficient to create full and open opportunity. The occupational and wage differentials that the research documents reflect the accumulated benefits of family connections that enhance the matching process for high-status students, while making it harder for their low-status counterparts who are otherwise well-qualified students. These studies also point to continuing attitudinal barriers that subject low-caste applicants for jobs in major companies, and people from remote tribal regions, to negative stereotypes that may overwhelm their formal accomplishments in the eyes of employers.

These observations—coupled with the shrinking size of the public sector—have prompted some to advocate extending reservations or some form of affirmative action to the private sector. As Chapter 2 by Jodhka and Newman makes clear, this is firmly opposed by private sector leaders, partly because they prefer to avoid any form of regulation over hiring, but also because they are convinced that there is no problem of caste or religious prejudice in modern India. The insights from the studies reveal that the debate over policy remedies should proceed in the light of empirical evidence, and the results from the chapters on the working of the urban labour market present themselves as a first step in that direction.

Reservation policy is aimed primarily at the formal sector of India's urban labour markets. As Sukhadeo Thorat, M. Mahamallik, and Nidhi Sadana point out in Chapter 5, other remedies will be necessary in order to wipe out the stain of caste discrimination from rural areas in the labour, land, inputs, and consumer goods markets. The chapter on rural areas provides empirical evidence on discrimination in farm and non-farm employment, wage earning, and work relations. In other markets, Dalits faced discrimination in the form of complete exclusion and/or inclusion with discriminatory terms and conditions. This has taken the shape of price discrimination in the purchase and sale of agricultural land and in the land rental market and of refusal to purchase some consumer goods put on sale by Dalits. Lower-caste individuals face the pressure of old prohibitions driven by the notion of pollution, and untouchability still holds sway. The necessary safeguards against discrimination in the form of policy measures, thus, will have to be extended beyond private labour markets so as to cover the agricultural land market for purchase and lease, input market, and the product and consumer goods market. Positive interventions will be necessary for overcoming the inefficiencies in the working of various markets by ensuring fair access for Dalits in the rural areas.

## Non-market Discrimination: Public Service Provision

Since the pathways to the market are paved with public services that either equip people to compete or deprive them of the means to develop themselves into effective job applicants or university students, we cannot limit our attention to market-based discrimination. Public services lay the groundwork for human capital accumulation, health, nutrition, and well-being. They are public goods supplied by the state or state-supported/recognized public institutions that are intended to be accessible on an equitable basis.

Social exclusion has significant consequences for morbidity and mortality, as Vani K. Borooah makes clear in Chapter 6. Here, too, poverty alone is not the central question, for Borooah shows that in the case of 'group independent' factors such as education, access to health care, and household living conditions, Adivasis, Dalits, and Muslims have markedly higher levels of morbidity and significantly lower life expectancy than 'forward caste' Hindus.

In Chapter 7, Sanghmitra S. Acharya turns our attention to problems in the health care system that subject social and religious groups to exclusion from health education programmes and discourage the equitable use of medical services. Aiming derogatory language at Dalit children, refusing to touch their bodies in the course of examinations or provide full information about health conditions to their parents, and insisting that they perform sanitation work that subjects them to 'unclean jobs' reinforce pollution taboos and contribute to health inequalities. Doctors who are unwilling to enter Dalit homes or hand out medicines, or who subject Dalit families to inordinate delays in the provision of care relative to non-Dalit patients, are instrumental in producing the inequitable outcomes described by Acharya.

Where Dalit and Muslim children go to school with young people from HC backgrounds and majority religions, they often face subtle forms of discouragement and ostracism that make school a painful place to be. When the exclusionary practices detailed by Geetha B. Nambissan in Chapter 9 are widespread, they can easily become catalysts for the kinds of drop-out patterns that plague Dalit children. Moreover, they contribute to inequalities in the mastery of basic skills discussed previously at length in Chapter 8 by Sonalde Desai, Cecily Darden Adams, and Amaresh Dubey.

Access to sufficient calories and nutrition is critical for human development. The Indian government clearly recognizes the importance of an adequate diet for any further form of engagement in social institutions, from schooling to the world of work. Yet, as Sukhadeo Thorat and Joel Lee show in Chapter 10 on food security programmes, locating the delivery of services such as mid-day meals and fair-price shops in HC settlements results in inadequate access and discriminatory pricing practices. Intimidation prevents lower-caste families from putting adequate food on the table.

## Discrimination-induced Inequalities

Two chapters deal with issues relating to ownership of business by Dalits and Muslims. Chapter 11 by Sukhadeo Thorat, Debolina Kundu, and Nidhi Sadana looks at the historical consequences of customary restrictions on ownership of business by Dalits. Using the Economic Census data for 2005 and 1998, the chapter indicates that denial of property rights has resulted in much lower ownership of enterprise and business by Dalits as compared to the HCs. Chapter 12 by Maitreyi Bordia Das brings out the consequences of possible discrimination in the labour market faced by post-primary-educated Dalits and Muslims, leading to a minority business enclave. They skirt discrimination in the primary labour market by resorting to self-employed ventures leading to minority enclaves, particularly in the case of Muslims. In the case of Dalits, due to lack of both financial and social capital, they fall back upon wage labour in much greater magnitude than Muslims. Thus, in the face of possible restrictions in hiring, self-employment ventures for Muslims and wage labour for Dalits serve as a residual activity of last resort. The chapter provides evidence of the concentration of Muslims in self-employed economic activities as a consequence of discrimination in the organized labour market.

The lack of access to capital assets, employment, education, and health care due to complete exclusion and/or inclusion with discriminatory treatment induced high levels of poverty among the discriminated groups. In Chapter 13, Smita Das examines patterns of poverty over the 11-year period 1993–2004, and captures the nature of exclusion-induced poverty and deprivation. Consonant with the Indian experience of high growth, Das shows that the risk of poverty dropped for most socio-religious groups. But for the most deprived groups—SCs, STs, and Muslims—the risk of poverty actually grew over this time period. Das's conclusion takes us back to a fundamental question that must be posed about the optimism associated with the modernization theory—and the assumption that growth would provide across-the-board improvements in the social conditions of India.

The empirical evidence presented contends that discrimination is not merely a problem of the past or an incidental force creating inequality, but an active agent in the growing gaps between those at the top and those at the bottom of Indian society. It unfolds the role that systemic discrimination plays to explain low- and high-caste gaps in educational attainment, occupational segregation, access to capital assets and employment, and income polarization. It provides evidence of discrimination-induced/linked deprivation and poverty of the excluded social groups. However, to claim this is the case and to demonstrate empirically that discrimination is a source of deprivation of excluded communities, and that it is a serious problem, are two different things.

This volume develops empirical evidence of this in urban and rural labour markets, as well as other markets, in education, and in the provision of food and health care services provided by public institutions. It relies on traditional survey and interview-based research, as well as innovative techniques involving experimental field studies. The evidence is overwhelming that discrimination by caste and religion plays a powerful role in creating the 'bottom-line' outcomes discussed in the final chapters on educational attainment, access to income-earning capital assets, morbidity, mortality, and poverty. This is not to say that contemporary discrimination among eligible or qualified job applicants, students, or citizens seeking access to universal benefits is the only problem. India also faces a profound legacy of historic discrimination that has placed the lower castes, tribals, religious minorities, and women at a tremendous disadvantage in developing the human capital needed to compete on an equal footing with the best-prepared members of society. Investment in quality schooling, availability of clean water and adequate sanitation, distribution of food, and transportation infrastructure that will reach all the citizens are critical challenges in a society developing at a rapid rate.

Yet, unless the problem of discrimination is addressed, these investments will not level the playing field. The fact that discrimination remains even under conditions of high growth reveals that this is not a problem India can expect to simply outgrow as it develops economically. The insights from theories on remedies for discrimination clearly indicate that market competition on its own, as the neoclassical economists seem to believe, will not eliminate economic discrimination; on the contrary, positive intervention in various markets will be required to correct the market failure associated with discrimination and ensure fair access for the discriminated groups—lower-castes, women, religious minority groups, and other similar groups. Interventions are also necessary to address the problem of discrimination in the provision of essential public services such as education, health care services, housing, and food supplied by public institutions. Growth with inclusiveness requires a concerted effort, backed by legal protection against discrimination in the form of law, and specific measures to remove the barriers that prejudice generates on a daily basis.

## REFERENCES

Akerlof, George (1956), 'The Theory of Social Customs of Which Unemployment may be One of the Consequences', *Quarterly Journal of Economics*, vol. 94, no. 4, pp. 749–75.

—— (1976), 'The Economics of Caste, the Rat Race and Other Woeful Tales', *Quarterly Journal of Economics*, vol. XC, no. 4. pp. 599–617.

Ambedkar, B.R. (1936), *Annihilation of Caste*, Jallaunder: Bhim Patrika.

—— (1987a), 'Philosophy of Hinduism', in Vasant Moon (ed.), *Dr. Babasaheb Ambedkar: Writings and Speeches*, vol. 3 (first published in 1936), Education Department, Govt of Maharashtra, pp. 1–94.

Ambedkar, B.R. (1987b), 'The Hindu Social Order: Its Essential Features', in Vasant Moon (ed.), *Dr. Babasaheb Ambedkar: Writings and Speeches*, vol. 3, Education Department, Govt of Maharashtra, pp. 96–115.

—— (1987c), 'The Hindu Social Order: Its Unique Features', in Vasant Moon (ed.), *Dr. Babasaheb Ambedkar: Writings and Speeches*, vol. 3, Education Department, Govt of Maharashtra, pp. 116–29.

Becker, Gary S. (1957), *The Economics of Discrimination*, Chicago: University of Chicago Press.

Bhalla, A. and F. Lapeyere (1997), 'Social Exclusion: Towards an Analytical and Operational Framework', *Development and Change*, vol. 28, no. 2, pp. 413–34.

Birdsall, Nancy and Richard Sabot (1991), *Unfair Advantage: Labour Market Discrimination in Developing Countries*, Washington, DC: World Bank Sectoral and Regional Studies, World Bank.

Buvinic, Mayra (2005), 'Social Inclusion in Latin America', in Mayra Buvinici and Jacqueline Mazza (eds), *Social Exclusion and Economic Development*, Baltimore: The Johns Hopkins University Press, pp. 3–32.

Connelly, Dalton (1999), *Being Black, Living in the Red: Race, Wealth and Social Policy in America*, Berkeley: University of California Press.

Darity, W. (Jr) (1995), *Economics and Discrimination*, vols I and II, Elgar Reference Collection, USA.

Darity, W. (Jr), and S. Shulman (1989), *Questions of Discrimination Racial Inequality in the US Labour Market*, Middletown, Connecticut: Wesleyan University Press.

Dirks, Nicholas (2001), *Castes of Mind: Colonialism and the Making of Modern India*, New York: Princeton University Press.

*The Economist* (2007), 'Untouchable and Unthinkable', 4 October, p. 16, see also http://www.economist.com/research/articlesBySubject/displaystory.cfm? Subjected=6899464&story_id=9905554.

Haan, Arjan De (1997), 'Poverty and Social Exclusion: A Comparison of Debates on Deprivation', Working Paper No. 2, Poverty Research Unit at Sussex, Brighton: University of Sussex.

Jodhka, Surinder and Katherine S. Newman (2010), 'In the Name of Globalization: Meritocracy, Productivity and the Hidden Language of Caste', in Sukhadeo Thorat and Katherine S. Newman (eds), *Blocked by Caste: Economic Discrimination in Modern India*, New Delhi: Oxford University Press, pp. 52–87.

Lal, Deepak (1988), *Hindu Equilibrium*, vol. I, *Cultural Stability and Economic Stagnation*, Oxford: Clarendon Press.

Lenoir, Rene (1979), *Les Exclus: Un Franscais sur Dix*, Paris: Editions du Seuil.

Oliver, Melvin and Thomas Shapiro (2006), *Black Wealth/White Wealth*, 2nd edition, New York: Routledge.

Pager, Devah (2003), 'The Mark of a Criminal Record', *American Journal of Sociology*, vol. 108, no. 5, pp. 937–75.

Scoville, James G.L. (1991), 'Towards a Model of Caste Economy', in James G. Scoville (ed.), *Status Influences in Third World Labour Markets: Caste, Gender and Custom*, New York: Walter de Gruyter, pp. 386–93.

——— (1996), 'Labour Market Under-pinnings of a Caste Economy Failing the Caste Theorem', *The American Journal of Economics and Sociology*, vol. 55, no. 4, pp. 385–94.

Sen, Amartya (2000), 'Social Exclusion: Concept, Application, and Scrutiny', Working Paper, Social Development Paper No. 1, June, Asian Development Bank, Bangkok.

Thorat, Sukhadeo, Aryama, and Prashant Negi (2005), *Reservations and Private Sector: Quest for Equal Opportunity and Growth*, New Delhi: Rawat Publications.

Thorat, Sukhadeo and Narender Kumar (2008), *B.R. Ambedkar: Perspective on Social Exclusion and Inclusive Policy*, New Delhi: Oxford University Press.

——— (2008), *In Search of Inclusive Policy: Addressing Graded Inequality*, Jaipur: Rawat Publications.

Weisskopf, Thomas (2004), *Affirmative Action in the United States and India: A Comparative Perspective*, New York: Routledge.

# MARKET DISCRIMINATION
## LABOUR AND OTHER MARKETS

# 1

# The Legacy of Social Exclusion[*]
## A Correspondence Study of Job Discrimination in India's Urban Private Sector

*Sukhadeo Thorat and Paul Attewell*

Current patterns of socio-economic inequality within nations are often intertwined with much older systems of stratification and social exclusion. In most nations, however, groups at the bottom of the stratification order have either won or have been granted rights of equal citizenship. Nowadays, modern constitutions and legal codes outlaw the more violent or oppressive forms of social exclusion that were common in the past. In some countries, lawmakers have gone further to offer group-specific rights and privileges intended to redress past wrongs (Darity and Deshpande 2003).

Ironically, the existence of these rights and protections lead many persons in the social mainstream—those not from a stigmatized or economically disadvantaged group—to conclude that discrimination is a thing of the past (Pager 2007). The fact that certain social groups remain disproportionately poor, despite these legal safeguards, is often attributed to their low levels of education, or to their concentration in economically backward sectors. When continuing discrimination is acknowledged, it is frequently viewed as a fading survival from the past, an aberration that is antithetical to a modern capitalist economy. Consequently, advocates for stigmatized groups face an uphill battle in persuading their fellow citizens that discrimination remains a powerful ongoing force that explains the persistence of inequality even in the modern sectors of society (Thorat *et al.* 2006).

* We wish to thank Devah Pager, who pioneered the methods used here, for her help in planning this project.

Field experiments provide a useful tool for determining the extent of present-day discrimination (Fix *et al.* 1993; Massey and Lundy 2001; Bertrand and Mullainathan 2004; Pager 2003; Blank *et al.* 2004; Quillian 2006). In this chapter, we apply one of these methods—a correspondence study of job applicants—to college-educated members of the lowest castes in India (ex-Untouchables or Dalits) and upon similarly college-educated individuals from the Muslim religious minority in India.

We study what happens when highly educated Indians from different caste and religious backgrounds apply for jobs in the modern urban private sector, encompassing multinational corporations as well as prominent Indian companies. This is the part of the Indian economy where supposedly caste and communal discrimination are things of the past. Yet our findings document a pattern of decision making by private sector employers that repeatedly advantages job applicants from higher caste (HC) backgrounds and disadvantages low caste and Muslim job applicants with equal qualifications.

## PREVIOUS RESEARCH AND THEORY
### Caste and Communal Exclusion in India

There is a huge scholarly literature about caste in India that spans disciplines from history to sociology, from anthropology to economics. There are many thousands of *jati*s within India; they have names and are usually associated with a certain regional or geographic base.[1] Sometimes, members of a caste share a distinctive surname. Castes are endogamous descent groups: most people marry within their own caste, and there are strong social norms against cross-caste marriages. Castes also have a hierarchical dimension. Each caste claims or is viewed by others as being located within a hierarchy of caste described in the Hindu scriptures: Brahmins or scholars, Kshatriyas or warriors, Vaisyas or traders, and Shudras or cultivators. Below these four is a very large group of people whom those scriptures describe as spiritually impure and defiling. Once known as Untouchables, members of this lowest stratum, which contains many sub-castes, are today called Dalits, a non-pejorative term connoting oppressed or downtrodden.

Historically, because Dalits were viewed by HC people as physically and spiritually polluting, they were not allowed to live close.

to HC persons, or to use the same water supply, or to enter into temples. They could not own land or be educated and were excluded from many occupations. Even their presence was polluting; in public places they had to keep physical distance from HC persons.

Many Dalits worked in stigmatized occupations that handled 'impure' materials such as human waste, dead animals, and hides. Tanning, scavenging, sweeping, and cleaning jobs remain distinctively Dalit occupations in modern India. In the 2001 Census, 167 million Dalits were landless or near-landless labourers in agricultural production or in the lowest paid kinds of manual labour (Thorat and Umakant 2004). They constituted 16.2 per cent of the Indian population in the 2001 Census.[2]

In the modern period Dalits have won important legal rights, including a 'reservation' system that provides a quota of positions in government and the universities, though not in private sector businesses, that are reserved for Dalits and for Other Backward Classes. This has led to the emergence of a stratum of university-educated and professional Dalits. The great majority of Dalits remain in or close to poverty, with rates of illiteracy and malnutrition that are substantially higher than for the rest of the Indian population.

Within India there is intense contention over the reservation system, with some commentators claiming that it is unfair to HC persons and/or that it allows less competent individuals to rise to higher occupational positions. Within this context, a debate has been underway over whether reservation should be extended to private sector companies. Dalit advocates claim that employer discrimination continues to prevent low-caste applicants from accessing any but the lowest-level jobs in the modern private sector, while business spokespersons claim that discrimination is a thing of the past and that reservation would be inimical to efficiency in the modern private sector, since they currently hire the best qualified applicants for jobs, irrespective of caste and communal background (Thorat et al. 2006).

This chapter examines the relationship between caste (and minority religious identity) and labour market discrimination in today's urban India. Akerlof (1976) and others have developed theories to explain why an economically irrational phenomenon such as caste discrimination might persist in a modern economy (cf. Scoville

1991, 1996; Deshpande 2005).[3] Jodhka (2002) and colleagues have shown that multiple identities (caste, religion, migrant status, gender) together affect patterns of employment and exclusion in Indian cities. Darity and Deshpande (2003) have drawn parallels between Dalits and disadvantaged groups in other countries. Thorat (2004) provides a compilation of data from Indian government surveys, contrasting Dalits with HC Hindus on indicators such as earnings, unemployment, education, and health. Thorat and Umakant (2004) compile articles that debate caste and discrimination against Dalits, in the context of the United Nation's World Conference against racism in Durban in the year 2002.

Prior research relies on four kinds of data: (a) descriptive statistics from surveys of the standing of Dalits relative to other groups in India on social indicators; (b) government accounting of 'atrocities' against Dalits (the term encompasses a variety of discriminatory behaviours penalized by Indian law that range from harassment to violence); (c) qualitative fieldwork and community studies; and (d) media descriptions of incidents against Dalits. There is similar material regarding discriminatory treatment of Indian Muslims (Perry 2003).

However, previous research has certain limitations. The qualitative studies often highlight caste oppression in rural contexts, strengthening the impression that caste inequality is a survival in traditional parts of India. Much of the quantitative evidence is not multivariate, thus there are few studies that separate human capital differences from job and wage discrimination. Important exceptions are Banerjee and Knight (1985), Lackshmanasamy and Madheswaran (1995), and Madheswaran (2004), who rely on data from 1981 or earlier. Even the econometric studies are not well suited to separating current discrimination from the legacy of past discrimination. By contrast, the correspondence methodology employed in this chapter is designed to assess the extent of present-day discrimination in the modern urban economy.

## Hiring, Favouritism, and Social Exclusion

The Weberian perspective on social stratification emphasizes the enduring importance of status groups within capitalist societies: communities that enjoy different amounts of social honour. Status groups may encompass racial, ethnic, or religious groups but can also involve strata such as 'gentlemen', 'the educated classes', the working class, and castes. Communities that constitute status groups share a certain lifestyle and maintain their solidarity through rituals, shared tastes, and social activities on the one hand, and through social closure on the other, reducing their intercourse with social inferiors (Weber 1968).

One important element in this Weberian conception is that status groups seek to monopolize valued economic opportunities. Collins (1979) has detailed how, in the US context, educational credentialism allows status groups to claim that lucrative occupations require certain degrees, thus limiting competition for privileged positions. Certain jobs come to resemble sinecures and social monopolies; their high earnings reflect the kinds of people who occupy them, rather than objective skills, according to Collins. Residential segregation of status groups by education and income, along with differences in child-rearing practices and in familial cultural capital, produces differential access to superior schooling opportunities and to elite universities, reproducing status group inequalities across the generations (Domina 2006; Lareau 2003; Massey and Denton 1993).

People who hold privileged positions within large organizations develop a sense that a certain kind of person is especially effective in their roles, leading many managers to favour potential recruits who are socially similar to themselves, a process that Kanter (1977) has termed 'homosocial reproduction'. Conversely, employers hold stereotypes about certain out-groups as being unsuitable for employment (Holzer 1999; Kirschenman and Neckerman 1991). One corollary is that a person's social networks prove important for finding jobs in the US, both at the professional end (Granovetter 1974) and at the blue-collar end (Royster 2003) of the labour market, because social networks often run along status group lines, sponsoring people who are 'like us' (Elliot 2001; Smith 2003).

This macro-sociological view of stratification and employment opportunity is paralleled by an extensive social psychological literature about the cognitive processes of prejudice and stereotyping that underlie both in-group preferences and social exclusion (see Fiske 1998, and Massey 2007 for overviews). An additional body of research charts the consequences of social exclusion for groups at the bottom of the status order (Hills *et al.* 2002).

Taken as a whole, this literature implies that social favouritism in hiring is not a matter of aberrant or unfair individuals, but rather a consequence of widespread in-group out-group dynamics. Favouritism only recedes when bureaucratic practices limit the discretion of those who hire. A reliance on exams or tests, reporting to superiors about applicant pools and hiring outcomes, and formalized collective decision making enhance universalistic hiring (Moss and Tilly 2001). In the absence of these mechanisms to ensure fairness, favouritism and discrimination are likely to proliferate.

## METHODS AND DATA

Beginning in October 2005 and continuing up to November 2006, we collected advertisements announcing job openings from several national and regional English-language newspapers, including *The Times of India* (New Delhi and Mumbai editions), *Hindustan Times*, *The Hindu* (Mumbai, Delhi, and Chennai editions), *Deccan Herald* (Bangalore), and *Deccan Chronicle* (Hyderabad).

From these we chose only advertisements for openings in private sector firms. There are important government-owned enterprises in India—including some banks, steel companies, and railways—but we deliberately excluded public enterprises from this study. We also avoided advertisements for positions that were highly specialized or that required many years of on-the-job experience. Our aim was to select jobs that a university graduate might be eligible for within the first few years after graduation: entry-level or near entry-level positions.

These job advertisements specified the educational credentials and the on-the-job experience (if any) desired from the applicants. The adverts sometimes indicated the degree subject as well as the level of degree, for example an MBA, a Bachelor's degree in Pharmacy or Science, a Bachelor's in Engineering. There was a bifurcation: some adverts asked for applicants with a Master's or higher degree, while others required a Bachelor's degree. In the Indian labour market, higher degrees are frequently required for better-paid administrative and sales jobs in large corporations, even for entry-level positions that in the US would be filled by employees with BA degrees. In the private sector in India, Bachelor degrees tend to be required for lower-paid white-collar positions.

However, job titles often overlapped at both credential levels. Many advertisements sought management trainees, branch managers, and marketing managers. Accountants, account managers, account executives, and sales officers were another large group found at both credential levels. Advertisements seeking engineers, assistant engineers, and engineer/sales were also common, but tended to require only a Bachelor's degree. Service, sales, and administrative jobs predominated.

The companies whose advertisements we responded to included the following: securities and investment companies; pharmaceuticals and medical sales; computer sales, support, and IT services; manufacturing of many kinds; accounting firms; automobile sales and financing; marketing and mass media; veterinary and agricultural sales; construction; and banking.

The correspondence methodology we adopted involved submitting by mail several artificial applications to each job advertisement. (All our applicants were young men; the issue of gender discrimination in Indian labour markets was beyond the scope of our study.)

The research staff prepared sets of three 'matched' application letters and résumés (in English) for each type of job. These experimental applications were carefully constructed to have identical educational qualifications and experience. For example, we prepared a set of three résumés, each of which indicated a BA degree and major from a university of similar prestige, with the same class of degree,[4] and that listed equal amounts of sales experience, in order to respond to advertisements for a sales officer. Another set of résumés and cover letters was prepared for managerial trainee openings, and so on. All the experimental résumés and cover letters were prepared so that they presented strong applicants for the job opening: they claimed suitable degrees from reputable universities, and (where indicated in the advert) appropriate job experience and skills. This was done to maximize the likelihood that an applicant would be contacted by the employer to proceed to the next stage of hiring, typically the interview stage.

For each advertised job, we constructed a set of matched applications which differed only in terms of the *name* of each male applicant.

No explicit mention of caste or religious background was made in the application. However, in each matched set, one application was from a person who had a stereotypically HC Hindu family name. A second job applicant had an identifiably Muslim name. A third applicant had a distinctively Dalit (low caste) name. In India, Muslim names are very distinguishable from Hindu ones; one can immediately tell who is a Muslim from name. Some Hindu family names also clearly signal the family's caste, although many other Hindu names are ambiguous in this respect. We, therefore, chose both Dalit and HC names that were very distinctive in terms of their caste origins.

To ensure that there were no effects of very minor differences in format between applications, the résumés and application letters were rotated after each job application. So the résumé and letter that were used for a Dalit for the first job advertisement were used for a Muslim in a subsequent job application, and for an HC applicant in the next application, and so on.

A record was kept of each job advertisement applied for. Over the course of the study, we sent at most two sets of applications to any particular employer: one set in response to an advertisement from that employer for a higher-credential job, and one set for an advertisement from the same employer for a lower-credential job. Thereafter we ignored any additional job advertisements we encountered from that employer.

Each experimental application listed a home address and a cellphone number where the employer could contact the applicant. Employers usually made contact by phone. Research staff answered these cellphones or read mail responses and recorded employers' replies to the job applications. The most common answer to an application was no response whatsoever. Rejection letters were rare: only 17 applications (one-third of 1 per cent) resulted in rejection letters. In other cases, those we classified as positive outcomes, employers either phoned or wrote to certain applicants asking to interview the person (or in some cases requesting the applicant to appear for a written test). There were 450 positive outcomes of this type (9.4 per cent of all experimental applications).

We reiterate that a successful outcome as defined in this study involves simply being admitted to the second stage of the job selection process: being contacted for an interview or for testing. The type of discrimination being assessed is whether some kinds of college-educated applicants are disproportionately successful, and others disproportionately unsuccessful, at this earliest stage in seeking employment.

On those occasions when employers did contact an experimental applicant to schedule an interview, the applicant always declined the interview, saying that he had already found another job. Thus we sought no data on the ultimate decision of who was offered the job.

The core of the correspondence method involved three identically qualified applications for the same job: one a Dalit, one an HC Hindu, and one a Muslim. However, we added one 'discordant' application to these three. For jobs that requested a higher degree, we sent in one additional application from a person with an HC name who only had a Bachelor's degree. In other words, this discordant applicant was an academically underqualified person but from a socially high-ranking group. For jobs that demanded BA degrees, we added a different kind of discordant application, from a person with a Dalit name who had a Master's degree. In other words, this second type of discordant applicant was overqualified in academic terms, but had a socially lower status. The purpose of these two kinds of discordant applicants was to act as yardsticks, to determine whether, in the application process, the effect of caste might outweigh or overcome that of academic qualifications or vice versa.

Throughout the study we submitted job applications to employers in sets of four: three identically qualified plus one discordant applicant. When the research began, we sent one group of four applications in answer to each job advertisement. However, after we discovered that positive responses were relatively rare, we shifted to submitting three sets of four applications for each job advertisement: 12 applicants per opening. The current chapter presents analyses of applications sent out during the first 66 weeks of the study starting in October 2005.

## FINDINGS

Table 1.1 provides simple descriptive statistics for the job applications. A total of 4808 applications were made in answer to 548 job advertisements over 66 weeks.

### TABLE 1.1: Descriptive Statistics

| Variable Name | N | Mean | SD | Minimum | Maximum |
|---|---|---|---|---|---|
| Muslim | 4808 | 0.25 | 0.43 | 0.00 | 1.00 |
| Dalit | 4808 | 0.25 | 0.43 | 0.00 | 1.00 |
| HC | 4808 | 0.25 | 0.43 | 0.00 | 1.00 |
| Overqualified | 4808 | 0.13 | 0.33 | 0.00 | 1.00 |
| Underqualified | 4808 | 0.12 | 0.33 | 0.00 | 1.00 |
| Outcome | 4808 | 0.09 | 0.29 | 0.00 | 1.00 |

*Note*: N = Number, SD = Standard Deviation

Our analytical goal was to determine whether the likelihood of receiving a positive response from an employer differed according to whether the application was made with an HC, Muslim, or Dalit name. Since applications were clustered within jobs, multi-level or hierarchical models are appropriate. Since outcomes were dichotomous (either a positive response or not) we employed a random effects logistic regression model. In this kind of model, there is a random effect of the particular job on the likelihood of receiving a positive outcome. The effects of caste and religion are represented in the model by two dummy variables—Muslim and Dalit, with HC Hindu as the reference category. Two additional dummy variable predictors are included in the model: one indicates whether the applicant was underqualified (the anomalous HC person with a BA applying for an MA position) and the last dummy variable indicates whether the applicant was overqualified (a Dalit with an MA applying for a lower-level job).

This model may be written as:

$$\text{Log}\,(p_{it}/(1-p_{it})) = \alpha_i + \beta D_{it} + \gamma M_{it} + \delta O_{it} + \lambda U_{it} \qquad (1.1)$$

where $D_{it}$ is a dummy variable for an appropriately qualified Dalit applicant, $M_{it}$ is a dummy variable for an appropriately qualified

Muslim applicant, $O_{it}$ is a dummy variable for an overqualified Dalit applicant, and $U_{it}$ is a dummy for an underqualified HC applicant. The subscript $i$ refers to the job applied for (i=1, ....., 548), such that $\alpha_i$ is a random effect for each job. The job effect $\alpha_i$ implies a correlation among applications for the same job and reduces the standard errors.

The results are reported in Table 1.2. The logistical regression model (on the left) was estimated using STATA's xtlogit procedure with a random effect for job. This procedure fits the data and calculates estimates using an adaptive Gauss–Hermite quadrature algorithm. (STATA Corp 2005: 161–9.) The effects are reported as odds ratios. Table 1.2 provides two different significance levels for each predictor in this model. The first is the default method in STATA and assumes clustering. The second used a jackknife method involving 250 replications, and calculated the standard error from this distribution.

TABLE 1.2: Modelling Differences in Job Outcomes

| | Random effects logistic regression | | | Bernoulli HLM unit-specific model | | |
|---|---|---|---|---|---|---|
| | Odds ratio | SE | p value | Jackknife p value | Odds ratio | robust p value |
| Predictors: (Compared to HC) | | | | | | |
| Dalit | 0.6724 | 0.1202 | 0.026 | 0.014 | 0.6835 | 0.013 |
| Muslim | 0.3318 | 0.0649 | 0.000 | 0.000 | 0.3475 | 0.000 |
| Underqualified HC versus: | | | | | | |
| Qualified HC | 0.5711 | 0.1409 | 0.023 | 0.033 | 0.6028 | 0.037 |
| Qualified Dalit | 0.8493 | 0.2134 | 0.516 | 0.538 | 0.8819 | 0.609 |
| Overqualified Dalit versus: | | | | | | |
| Qualified HC | 0.7818 | 0.1689 | 0.255 | 0.193 | 0.7718 | 0.146 |
| Qualified Dalit | 1.162 | 0.2571 | 0.495 | 0.435 | 1.129 | 0.503 |

*Note*: SE = Standard Error

As Table 1.2 indicates, there are statistically significant effects of both caste and religion on job outcome. Appropriately qualified applicants with a Dalit name had odds of a positive outcome that were 0.67 of the odds of an equivalently qualified applicant with an HC Hindu name. Similarly qualified applicants with a Muslim name had odds of 0.33 of an otherwise equivalent applicant with an HC name.

A second model (on the right-hand side in Table 1.2) was estimated using the programme HLM6 (Raudenbusch *et al.* 2004). It reports a two-level hierarchical non-linear Bernoulli model, with applications nested within jobs, fitted using a Penalized Quasi-Likelihood estimator. The coefficients are reported for the level-1 effects in a unit-specific model with robust Huber–White standard errors that correct for heteroskedasticity. The estimated effects are quite close to those from the random effects logistic regression in the previous model. For a positive job outcome, Dalits had a 0.68 odds ratio outcome of an otherwise equivalent HC applicant. Muslims had an odds ratio of 0.35 compared to an HC applicant. Both coefficients were statistically significant.

In sum, both models yielded consistent findings that job applicants with a Dalit or Muslim name were on average significantly less likely to have a positive application outcome than equivalently qualified persons with an HC Hindu name.

The two 'discordant' application types provide additional insights into the likelihood of gaining a positive job outcome. The odds of a positive outcome for an underqualified HC applicant applying for a higher-level job were statistically significantly lower than the odds for an HC applicant with an appropriate qualification (an odds ratio of 0.57). The odds of success for an underqualified HC applicant were not significantly different from the odds of success for an appropriately qualified Dalit. Having an HC name considerably improves a job applicant's chances of a positive outcome, but if an HC applicant lacks the requested credentials, his chances of success are considerably reduced.

The odds of a positive outcome for an overqualified Dalit applicant (a Dalit with an MA applying for jobs that required only a BA) were larger than the odds for a qualified Dalit but were smaller than the odds ratio for a BA qualified HC applicant. Although the effects were substantial in size, neither of these differences in odds was statistically significant, probably due to insufficient statistical power. This leaves us unable to draw any firm conclusions about the relative importance of qualifications versus caste in this specific context.

## DISCUSSION

This field experiment study of job applications observed a statistically significant pattern by which, on average, college-educated lower-caste and Muslim job applicants fare less well than equivalently qualified applicants with HC names, when applying by mail for employment in the modern private-enterprise sector. The only aspect of family background that was communicated in these applications was the applicant's name, yet this was enough to generate a different pattern of responses to applications from Muslims and Dalits, compared to those from HC Hindus. These were all highly-educated and appropriately qualified applicants attempting to enter the modern private sector, yet even in this sector, caste and religion proved influential in determining ones job chances.

These discriminatory outcomes occurred at the very first stage of the process that Indian university graduates go through to apply for a job. We did not collect data on who was ultimately hired for these particular jobs. Nor is it possible to determine the employment composition of private sector enterprises in India, because corporations are not obliged to report the caste and religious composition of their workforces to the government. (By contrast, US law requires companies of a certain size to report the gender and racial composition of their workforces to the federal government, and these data are monitored by the Federal Equal Employment Opportunity Commission.)

We speculate that if caste and communal discrimination are evident even at this early phase of the application process in India, then final hiring decisions are unlikely to be equitable. In a separate study, our colleagues have been collecting accounts of job interviews and hiring experiences from both high- and low-caste job applicants that suggest that caste biases also affect later stages of the hiring process. Those data will be the subject of a separate essay.

Our study examined one route by which Indian job seekers apply for jobs. In addition to applications to newspaper advertisements, some university graduates are employed through a process of on-campus job interviews held at the more prestigious universities towards the end of the final year at university. These are known as 'hiring cells'. This second method of hiring will be studied in a related project.

Our findings suggest that social exclusion is not just a residue of the past clinging to the margins of the Indian economy, nor is it limited to people of little education. On the contrary, it appears that caste favouritism and the social exclusion of Dalits and Muslims occur in private enterprises even in the most dynamic modern sector of the Indian economy.

## NOTES

1. The most current list of Scheduled Castes is available on the Indian Census website: http://www.censusindia.net/scstmain/SC%20Lists.pdf accessed in October 2007.

2. The Indian government refers to Dalits as 'Scheduled Castes', a term dating from the colonial period when an official list or schedule identified certain jatis as Untouchables. In many current government reports, Scheduled Castes are combined with Scheduled Tribes (SC/ST) who are indigenous tribal groups, most of whom are very poor. The figure of 166,635,700 was the count of SC persons in the 2001 India Census, constituting 16.2 per cent of the nation's population. The ST population is about 84 million or an additional 8.2 per cent of the Indian population. See http://www.censusindia.net/t_00_005.html. Accessed in October 2007.

   In recent legislation, an additional category 'Other Backward Classes' (OBCs) has been granted certain rights under the reservation system. OBCs are not Untouchables, but they are the second most poor category in the Hindu social hierarchy. The number of persons in the OBC category, which does not include the SCs/STs, is a matter of great contention, with official estimate being 27 per cent of the Indian population.

3. These scholars draw upon economic theories that argue that discriminatory hiring may be economically rational in situations where employers have few ways of evaluating the quality of job applicants. Employers, therefore, undertake statistical discrimination, using past experiences with employees from certain groups as a basis for selecting individuals (cf. Arrow 1972, 1998). This approach differs from sociological theories, reviewed below, that emphasize discrimination as an outcome of competition for jobs among status groups.

4. Based upon performance in final examinations, an Indian university student receives a certain class of degree that is noted on the diploma: first class, second class, etc. Our experimental applicants had degrees of the same class.

## REFERENCES

Akerlof, George (1976), 'The Economics of Caste and of Rat Race and Other Woeful Tales', *Quarterly Journal of Economics*, vol. XC, no. 4, pp. 599–617.

Ambedkar B.R. (1936), *Annihilation of Caste*, Jallandhar: Bheem Patrika.

—— (first published 1987), 'Philosophy of Hinduism', in Vasant Moon (ed.), *Dr. Babasaheb Ambedkar: Writings and Speeches*, vol. 3, Education Department, Govt of Maharashtra, pp. 1–94.

Arrow, Kenneth (1972), 'Models of Job Discrimination', in A.H. Pascall (ed.), *Racial Discrimination in Economic Life*, Lexington, MA: D.C. Heath Publishers.

—— (1998), 'What has Economics to Say about Racial Discrimination?' *Journal of Economic Perspectives*, vol. 12, pp. 91–100.

Banerjee, B. and J.B. Knight (1985), 'Caste Discrimination in the Indian Urban Labour Market', *Journal of Development Economics*, vol. 17, pp. 277–307.

Bayly, Susan (1999), *Caste, Society and Politics in India from the 18th Century to the Modern Age*, Cambridge, England: Cambridge University Press.

Bertrand, M. and S. Mullainathan (2004), 'Are Emily and Greg More Employable Than Lakisha and Jamal? A Field Experiment on Labor Market Discrimination', *American Economic Review*, vol. 94, pp. 991–1048.

Blank, R.M., M. Dabady, and C.F. Citro (2004), *Measuring Racial Discrimination*, Washington, DC: National Academies Press.

Collins, Randal (1979), *The Credential Society: An Historical Sociology of Education and Stratification*, New York: Academic Press.

Darity, William and Ashwini Deshpande (2003), *Boundaries of Clan and Color*, New York: Routledge.

Deshpande, Ashwini (2005), 'Do Markets Discriminate? Some Insights from Economic Theories', in Sukhadeo Thorat, Aryama, and Prasant Negi (eds), *Reservation and the Private Sector: Quest for Equal Opportunity and Growth*, New Delhi: Rawat Publishers, pp. 4–10.

Domina, Thurston (2006), 'Brain Drain and Brain Gain: Rising Educational Segregation in the United States 1940–2000', *City and Community*, vol. 5, no. 4, pp. 53–68.

Dudley-Jenkins, Laura (2003), *Identity and Identification in India: Defining the Disadvantaged*, New York: Routledge.

Elliot, James (2001), 'Referral Hiring and Ethnically Homogeneous Jobs', *Social Science Research*, vol. 30, pp. 401–25.

Fiske, Susan (1998), 'Stereotyping, Prejudice, and Discrimination', in Daniel Gilbert, Susan Fiske, and Gardner Lindzay (eds), *The Handbook of Social Psychology*, New York: Oxford University Press, pp. 87–100.

Fix, Michael, George Galster, and Raymond Struyk (1993), *Clear and Convincing Evidence: Measurement of Discrimination in America*, Washington DC: Urban Institute Press.

Granovetter, Mark (1974), *Getting a Job: A Study of Contacts and Careers*, Cambridge, MA: Harvard University Press.

Hills, John, Julian Le Grand, and David Piachaud (2002), *Understanding Social Exclusion*, New York: Oxford University Press.

Holzer, Harry (1999), *What Employers Want: Job Prospects for Less-Educated Workers*, New York: Russell Sage.

Johdka, Surinder S. (2002), *Community and Identities: Contemporary Discourses on Culture and Politics in India*, Thousand Oaks, CA: Sage Publishers.

Kanter, Rosabeth (1977), *Men and Women of the Corporation*, New York: Basic Books.

Kirschenman, Joleen and Kathryn Neckerman (1991), 'We'd Love to Hire Them But…: The Meaning of Race for Employers', in C. Jencks and P. Peterson (eds), *The Urban Underclass*, Washington DC: Brookings.

Lackshmanasamy, T. and S. Madheswaran (1995), 'Caste Discrimination: Evidence from Indian Scientific and Technical Labour Market', *Indian Journal of Social Sciences*, vol. 8, no. 1, pp. 59–77.

Lareau, Annette (2003), *Unequal Childhoods: Race, Class, and Family Life*, Berkeley CA: University of California Press.

Madheswaran, S. (2004), 'Caste Discrimination in the Indian Labour Market: An Econometric Analysis', Mimeo, Institute for Social and Economic Change, Bangalore.

Massey, Douglas S. (2007), *Categorically Unequal: The American Stratification System*, New York: Russell Sage Press.

Massey, Douglas and Garvey Lundy (2001), 'The Use of Black English and Racial Discrimination in Urban Labor Markets: New Methods and Findings', *Urban Affairs Review*, vol. 36, pp. 452–69.

Massey, Douglas and Nancy Denton (1993), *American Apartheid: Segregation and the Making of the Underclass*, Cambridge MA: Harvard University Press.

Mendelsohn, Oliver and Marika Vicziany (1998), *The Untouchables: Subordination, Poverty, and the State in Modern India*, Cambridge, UK: Cambridge University Press.

Moss, Philip and Chris Tilly (2001), *Stories Employers Tell: Race, Skill, and Hiring in America*, New York: Russell Sage Press.

Pager, Devah (2003), 'The Mark of a Criminal Record', *American Journal of Sociology*, vol. 108, no. 5, pp. 937–75.

—— (2007), *Marked: Race, Crime and Finding Work in an Era of Mass Incarceration*, Chicago: University of Chicago Press.

Perry, Alex (2003), 'India's Great Divide', *Time Asia*, http://www.time.com/time/asia/cover/501030811/story.html

Quillian, Lincoln (2006), 'New Approaches to Understanding Racial Prejudice and Discrimination', *Annual Review of Sociology*, vol. 23, pp. 299–328.

Raudenbusch, Stephen, Anthony Bryk, Yuk Fai Cheong, Richard Congdon, and Mathilda du Toit (2004), *HLM6: Hierarchical Linear and Nonlinear Modelling*, Lincolnwood, IL: Scientific Software International.

Royster, Deidre (2003), *Race and the Invisible Hand*, Berkeley: University of California Press.

Scoville, James (1991), 'Towards a Formal Model of a Caste Economy', in James G. Scoville (ed.), *Status Influences in Third World Labor Markets: Caste, Gender, Custom*, New York: Walter De Gruyter, pp. 386–93.

—— (1996), 'Labour Market Underpinnings of a Caste Economy', *The American Journal of Economics and Sociology*, vol. 55, no. 4, pp. 385–94.

Searle-Chatterjee, Mary and Ursula Sharma (1994), *Contextualizing Caste: Post-Dumontian Approaches*, Oxford: Blackwell.

Sharma, Ursula (1999), *Caste*, London: Open University Press.

Smith, Sandra (2003), 'Exploring the Efficacy of African Americans' Job Referral Networks', *Ethnic and Racial Studies*, vol. 26, no. 6, pp. 1029–45.

Srinivas, M. N. (ed.) (1996), *Caste: Its Twentieth Century Avatar*, New Delhi: Penguin Books.

STATA Corporation (2005), *Stata Longitudinal/Panel Data*, Reference Manual Release 9 College Station, Texas: Stata Corporation.

Thorat, Sukhadeo (2004), *Caste System in India: Economic Exclusion and Poverty*, New Delhi: India Institute of Dalit Studies.

Thorat, Sukhadeo and Umakant (2004), *Caste, Race, and Discrimination: Discourses in International Context*, New Delhi: Rawat Publications.

Thorat, Sukhadeo, Aryama, and Prasant Negi (2006), *Reservation and the Private Sector: Quest for Equal Opportunity and Growth*, New Delhi: Rawat Publications.

Weber, Max (1968), *Economy and Society*, edited by Guenther Roth and Claus Wittich, New York: Bedminister Press.

# 2

# In the Name of Globalization
## Meritocracy, Productivity, and the Hidden Language of Caste

### Surinder S. Jodhka and Katherine S. Newman

More than a decade ago, Joleen Kirshenman and Kathryn Neckerman interviewed Chicago area employers to try to understand the role they played in the production of unequal employment outcomes by race and gender. Recognizing that young black men, in particular, were plagued with high levels of unemployment, these sociologists sought to understand how hiring managers viewed the landscape of job applicants, and how the stereotypes they employed affected their judgements about the qualifications of those who sought work.

In their oft-cited paper, 'We'd Love to Hire them, But...' Kirshenman and Neckerman (1991) discovered that employers believed black men were unreliable, unruly, poorly educated, and low skilled. Coupled with evidence from audit experiments, like those conducted by the Urban Institute and Princeton sociologist, Devah Pager (2003, 2007), employer interviews contribute to the view that prejudice remains a problem in the distribution of jobs. Low skill and educational deficits are, to be sure, also implicated in the high unemployment rates of black men. But even those, who are qualified, will face suspicion on the part of employers who, the paper showed; begin with negative views of the urban minority labour force.

The example of Kirshenman and Neckerman has seldom been followed,[1] even in the US, much less elsewhere in the world. But the same goals that led them to study the social attitudes of employers and hiring managers in Chicago animated the present study of Indian employers in the formal sector.

## BACKGROUND

India is a country with a huge unemployment problem, one so vast that it is hard to estimate with confidence its real contours. Like many developing countries, the growth of the informal sector—particularly pronounced among the low skilled, rural migrants to large cities—has been enormous. Even so, the high growth of the formal sector in India's mega-cities has brought the issue of labour market discrimination in this domain to the forefront.[2] We have little research to rely on in understanding patterns of employment that differ by caste, religion, and region of origin in this domain and, hence, it is to the formal sector that we devote our attention in this chapter.

We note at the outset that one cannot extrapolate from our data that the un- and under-employment of stigmatized groups in India results from the actions of employers can be said to be entirely due to discriminatory actors, acting either consciously or unconsciously on stereotypical expectations to overlook or eliminate qualified workers. Our interview data cannot address the question of whether managers act on their preconceptions. It does not tell us whether clear statements, to the effect that 'merit is the only thing that matters', are the real watchword of employment decisions either.

For that, we have to turn to more persuasive experimental data.[3] But because that experimental data turns up fairly persistent evidence of discrimination under controlled conditions, researchers have turned to the study of employer attitudes as one ingredient that contributes to the pattern of unemployment that plagues minorities in the US and religious or caste-based minorities in India.

This chapter presents the results from a qualitative pilot study based on a convenience sample of 25 human resources managers in large firms based in New Delhi, but with satellite offices, manufacturing plants, and retail outlets all over the country. While this is a small sample, worthy of replication on a much larger scale, the firms involved are generally large, established, and responsible for a significant number of hiring decisions in any given year. We have employment totals for 22 of the 25 firms and together they employ over 190,000 'core' workers (meaning they are on direct payroll), and data on contract or temporary employees for only eight firms, usually hired via outsourcing, for another 63,000 workers.[4]

Lengthy on-site interviews were conducted in 2005–6 with the heads of human relations or managers holding equivalent responsibilities for hiring and employment policy in each firm. They were told that the purpose of the study was to explore employer perceptions of the Indian labour force and challenges involved in hiring policy. Our informants were first asked to describe the firm's history, size of the workforce, categories of employees, and labour search practices. They were then asked if they had any views on why members of the Scheduled Caste (SC) population display high levels of unemployment. Finally, we asked for their opinions on the 'reservations policy', the longest standing quota system in the world. In particular, we wanted to know their views on whether this policy instrument, which is legally required in public higher education, public employment, and the legislative branch of government, should be extended to the private sector. This became a matter of considerable controversy in India when the central government proposed a system of job quotas for the SC and Scheduled Tribe (ST) in the private sector, with business groups rallying to make their positions known. This is one of the first pilot studies to assess, in a formal fashion, the views of industry human relations leaders on this issue.

## Modernism and Merit

The most striking finding in our data was the view, expressed in virtually every interview, that workers should be recruited strictly according to merit. That this has not previously been the case in Indian industry was both clear and easily acknowledged. India has a very long commercial history and for most of it, jobs were doled out in a nepotistic fashion, according to personal ties first, village ties second, and caste affinity third. These traditional practices served India well for centuries, and the notion that a precious resource, a job opportunity, should willingly be handed over to a complete stranger—no matter how well qualified—was baffling.

Instead, the most natural practice of all was to trade jobs along the lines of personal networks, much as other resources would be exchanged. With labour in plentiful supply, competition for scarce employment prospects was severe enough on the inside of these networks to guarantee at least some level of competence.

Of course, India is not alone in this history. In most Western industrial countries, the same practices were followed, and whatever inequalities emerged as a result was simply accepted as the norm. It was not regarded as unfair or unfortunate; it was simply the way things worked. The rise of the professions in the West, with their elaborate systems of credentialism, interjected a different conceptual framework and corresponding practices. Qualification was now important and competition built up at the gateway to the institutions that certified the most desirable would-be businessmen, lawyers, doctors, teachers, accountants, and so forth. To be sure, nepotism and other forms of preferential selection played a role in the admission to credentialing institutions, but the concept of merit took hold as a public declaration in opposition to the old tradition of inherited privilege or I-scratch-your-back cronyism.

This attitude received a powerful shot in the arm with the invention of the civil service, a reform intended to break the back of corruption and distribute jobs more fairly. Civil service employment was coveted in Western states and, throughout the colonial period, in India as well. Stable jobs, relatively well paid, respected (to a degree) by authorities, these jobs and the pathways that led to them were the essence of modernism in the marketplace.

The fact that written exams often functioned to exclude minorities unfairly remained and still operates in many domains. But the concept of merit as the sole legitimate basis for employment was built into the foundation of what Western employers see as modern. Indian employers outside of the public sector did not leap on that bandwagon until the country began to move more decisively toward a self-conscious modernism.

Indian employers speak about the past—which was dominated by localism and favouritism—as a period best left behind. The more India takes its place as an economic powerhouse in the modern world, they explain, the more it must operate strictly in accord with meritocracy and utilize hiring practices that will achieve this goal. To do otherwise—either in the service of a potentially laudatory goal, like the advancement of SC or ST, or goals that no one would admit to in public, the exclusion of these groups from employment—is to stick the country (and the firm in question) in the mud.

A good example of this view is found in our interview with a
hiring manager at Global Productions,[5] which is a major media
company with its publishing headquarters in Delhi and bureaus in
16 Indian states. The firm is about 80-years old, and has a workforce
of 3,000 core employees and another 800 who are hired through
outsourced contracts. They recruit new employees on a national
level for their main news staff and locally for their auxiliary bureaus.
It is a publicly listed company, though the majority of the shares
belong to the Indian family that purchased the firm after Indian
Independence.

When asked about whether particular groups compose the
workforce, the manager responded that 'our workforce is quite
diversified. No concentration on caste, creed and colour...talent and
merit does not go with one particular caste or creed.' Pressed about
whether popular stereotypes of castes or religious groups influence
hiring, he was adamant that prejudice plays no role. 'No, things have
changed', he explained.

This was the perspective of the 1980s [before liberalization]. Today when you
are casting your own future in an unknown market, the internal flexibility is
very important.

We don't put any kind of template on any individual....We focus completely
on merit. As our main goal is standardization....We also have defined what
merit is....We need people who are more exposed [to the world]. We believe
power of imagination comes with exposure. Exposure makes you observe
certain things and this stimulates the power of the imagination. If you have to
be part of global culture, your leadership should be...defined by your capability
of redefining...the company. And this can be...made possible only through
the power of imagination.

For Global Productions, which relies on projecting a cosmopolitan
image as part of its market appeal, there is a bottom-line value to
recruiting people who are worldly, sophisticated, and well educated.
In principle, individuals with this kind of cultural capital could come
from any background. In practice, the institutions and experiences
that produce cosmopolitanism are rarely accessible to SCs. Nowhere
in the discourse of Global Productions' hiring practices, do we see
antagonism or exclusion toward the least favoured members of Indian
society. Indeed, quite the opposite. Throughout the interview, we see

consistent pronouncements about talent and merit, without respect to 'caste, creed and colour'. But the production of merit is itself a highly unequal business and, hence, the linkage of modernism with merit, and merit with cultural capital, effectively eliminates Dalits, for example, from the competition.

Perhaps this is to be expected in a media company where image is so critical to the bottom line. Let us turn, then, to a manufacturing firm where this pressure is less evident. Food Futures, a twenty-year-old company that sells processed agricultural products, is a small family-owned firm, launched some forty-five years ago. It has a total workforce of 150 people, some of whom work in the Delhi headquarters, while others work in an industrial town in Punjab. As a fairly new firm, they embrace management practices that they believe are consistent with modern techniques. As the human resources director explained, he saw no relationship between the quality of one's work and background characteristics such as caste:

I haven't seen any kind of correlation between the religion of a person and his work. It is basically his calibre, attitude, and commitment that are seen. I have seen people from various castes. Some hailed from the so-called BIMARU states,[6] but they are very active and committed towards their work....So, I never thought about caste and creed.

He acknowledges that not everyone shares his enlightened perspective and that some actively practise an affirmative form of caste discrimination:

Some owners of Indian companies come from a particular caste and the people, who belong to this community, may have some kind of positive discrimination. For example, a person who is a thriving businessman is always helped by people from his own caste or community, or the kind of friends he has also belong to the same caste.

Yet, from his perspective, this is not a modern attitude and it is fading quickly. It is more likely to be found outside major cities or in rural areas. 'Such things are not very strong today', he explained.

About the impact of these stereotypes in recruitment, I don't think it works. No one recruits anyone on the basis of his caste or the region he comes from if he is not going to be useful.

Even so, he notes that 'caste is a politically sensitive issue and there are people who are very particular about caste'. They would tend to be people in smaller organizations who are more likely to 'belong to the caste of the person who set up the company'. But these practices are going the way of the past because globalization creates competitive pressures that wipe the conservative or backward practices of the past out of the way:

I do see among my colleagues a kind of bias against these communities, stated or unstated. But now because of the competition being intensified, the corporations have started to overcome these issues. These things may be carried in small organizations...as [they] are run by one single individual. Also, in family owned organizations, there are these people who recruit people from their families, relatives, and villages. In professional organizations, these things have gone.

Hence, it is not that casteism or its cousin, in-group preference, has disappeared completely. As this manager sees the matter, an evolutionary trend is in progress. Firms that are most exposed to international competition and modern management have abandoned these vestiges of discriminatory tradition, while the smaller firms, that cater to local markets or rural employers who are far from the influences of large markets, are slower to accommodate. It is there, and only there, that these retrograde practices will persist.

The language of merit, the morally virtuous credo of competitive capitalism, subtracts from the conversation the many forms of institutional discrimination and disinvestment that prevent all members of a society from competing on a level playing field. It assumes that we begin from the same starting point (regardless of the evidence of deprivation), enter equally efficacious credentialing institutions (despite the clear inequalities in schooling that take a heavy toll on the poor and low castes), and come out ranked objectively in terms of sheer quality.

## FAMILY MATTERS

The American language of meritocracy similarly relies on the subtraction of institutional inequality, as well as the ability to over-look the persistent impact of historical discrimination that has left deep tracks in test score gaps, and differential educational attainment by race and class. Whatever the consequences of these handicaps, the American variant nonetheless clings to the principle that the only thing that matters is individual capacity.

For Indian employers, there is no contradiction between an emphasis on individual merit and the notion of valuing 'family background', which, virtually every hiring manager emphasized, was critical in evaluating a potential employee. Americans would view this notion as a contradiction in terms. The whole concept of the 'American dream', rests on the notion that rising above one's station at birth, one's family of origin, is essential to the very notion of merit. On this theory, it is no more legitimate to 'dock' a job candidate for characteristics of his family then it is to reject him on the grounds of race, age, or gender. This does not mean that background plays no role in the production of qualifications, for it surely does, but as explicit criteria for hiring, family characteristics would be beyond the pale.

What kind of information is an Indian hiring manager seeking when she asks about a candidate's family background? For some, the concept is amorphous and would stretch to include virtually anything that was not directly related to educational credentials or work experience. For others, the idea is quite specific.

The human resources (HR) manager of the India Shoe Company, a firm employing 10,000 core workers and 2,000 casual workers, focused on a variety of qualities entirely beyond the control of applicants. 'In family background', he said, 'we look at…'

1. Good background
2. Educated parents
3. Brother and sister working
4. Preference for those from urban areas

The ABC firm employs more than 20,000 people in over 60 locations throughout India. It has been an important corporation for over a hundred years, selling agricultural manufactures, clothing, and paper goods, among other diversified products. The 45-year-old Brahmin manager of ABC's HR department was clear that family background and/or the kind of setting in which a candidate was raised makes the difference between success and failure in a job applicant.

'We ask them about family background', he noted, 'depending upon the position applied [for] and the kind of task allotted with the position'. The need to prove one's worthiness through family characteristics is most important for managerial workers, he explained. For lower level workers, the assumption is that they would not measure up on these grounds. Instead, they want to know whether a potential janitor (for one of the firm's hotels) has the same standards as those that the company wants to promote:

Say for example, in housekeeping, we generally avoid keeping people from slum areas because his appreciation for cleanliness will be different from us. For him, a dusty room would also be a clean room. If he is trainable, then there is no problem of taking him in the company. But in front office, we go for trained and professional people and they all belong to higher castes.

Whether or not someone appears to be 'trainable', is going to be judged according to the interviewer's estimation of how far away from an assumed list of traits, born inexorably out of the 'neighborhood characteristics' of his upbringing, the applicant can be coaxed to come. There is a barrier to be overcome, rather than a blank slate on which to build.

Why does family background matter so much? It seemed unnecessary to explain for nearly all of our informants; it is so important a part of the hiring system that the question seemed surprising. But when asked for more detail, respondents answered with a theory of socialization: 'merit' is formed within the crucible of the family. The HR manager of Food Futures provided the most coherent expression of this theory:

Personal traits are developed through the kind of interaction you have with society. Where you have been brought up, the kind of environment you have in your family, home, colony, and village—these things shape up your personal attributes. These determine a person's behaviour and working in a group with different kind of people. We have some projects abroad, and if a person doesn't behave properly with the people abroad, there is a loss for the company. Here, family comes in between whether the person behaves well and expresses himself in a professional way for a longer term and not for a short term. This is beneficial.

What one sees on the surface—credentials, expressed attitudes—is shaped in the bosom of the family. For the hiring manager, who cannot delve more deeply into the character of the applicant than surface characteristics, the successes of the rest of the job applicant's family stand in as proof that the individual before him is reliable, motivated, and worthy. If the answers do not come back in a desirable form, the surface impressions may be misleading. Doubt is cast on the qualities of the individual.

Mr Soames, the hiring manager of a major manufacturing firm that employs over 2,800 people to produce some of the finest jewellery in India, echoed this sentiment in explaining what he learns from answers to questions about family background:

We also ask a lot of questions related to family background: questions like how many family members are there, how many are educated, etc. The basic assumption behind these questions is that a good person comes from a good and educated family. If parents have good education, the children also have good education. Some questions about their schooling, such as what type of schooling and where did they [grow up].

The HR manager of the Cool Air Corporation, a family-run manufacturing firm that produces air conditioning units, echoes the same idea, 'A good culture comes from a good family, good parenting. The person is also then stable. Not like people who come from workers background.'

As these managers see it, background characteristics of this kind are the source of 'soft skills' that are an asset for the firm. The person who can manage adroitly in the organizational context of a firm hierarchy in India and abroad is going to contribute to the bottom line; the person who has trouble in these interactions will detract. But the surface evidence of soft skills is difficult to judge in an interview and, by the time it matters, managers seem to believe, it would be too late if the judgement of the hiring manager at the outset had been faulty. Hence, they search for corroborating information to short up their estimation of an applicant's personal qualities and find it in the 'data' on family background.

In Erving Goffman's (1959) terms, the employment or educational status of family members is a source of discrediting or corroborating information that either undermines or reinforces a job applicant's impression management. One could create a smooth persona, projecting the ability to work well in a corporate environment, but if the rest of the family does not line up with this projected self, the manager is alert to the cracks in the façade.

This is as close as we can come to pinpointing the underlying rationale behind questions on family background. A more compelling explanation for the practice, however, probably lies in the history of recruitment over the long run in which a scarce commodity like a job would rarely be given over to a stranger, but would become a gift in a reciprocal exchange system. One's status as a member of a family was (and still is, in many places) an integral part of personal identity and, in many respects, is only fully understood within the social coordinates of local society as a representative of the family, the village, or the caste. A firm is, therefore, not hiring an individual but, in some sense, is employing a representative of a larger social body: the family, the village, the tribe, the caste.

Regardless of the origins or the contemporary purpose of screening applicants on family background, the practice, almost by definition, will eliminate Dalits, Other Backward Castes (OBCs), and others for whom historic (and contemporary) patterns of discrimination have made it difficult to assemble the necessary credentials in employment or education. While there are Dalit families that have managed, through the reservation system, to overcome caste bias and find jobs that are respectable enough to help launch the careers of the next generation, the odds are against them. Of the 160 million Dalits in India, the majority are rural, landless labourers. Unemployment among them is high, and the occupations they hold will not lend credence to the efforts of an educated job applicant looking for work in the formal sector in India today. Urban Dalits are largely relegated to the informal sector and, if employed, are more likely than not to be in low prestige positions. While pollution taboos have faded in the large urban centres, social exclusion remains pronounced and limits the mobility of Dalit families. The fortunate few, who manage to get an education, are far less likely to be able to produce the kind of evidence of sterling family background that an employer seeks.

Thus it would be safe to surmise that invoking family background in hiring decisions will act as a barrier to low-caste Indians in their search for employment. Ironically though, HR personnel point out that it will effectively put the brakes on the prospects of the well-to-do as well. If Dalits are considered too lowly, the scions of rich families are deemed bad material for employment for the opposite reason. As the HR managers see it, they are pampered and lazy and accustomed to getting jobs on the basis of connections alone. In the competitive world of global capitalism, this will not do either.

Security Services Inc. (SSI) is an enormous firm of over 100,000 employees. SSI provides security guards, training, and protection of everything from private firms to ATM machines. They operate in all the major cities of India and can brag of over 500 client firms. Typically, they hire guards from rural areas, recruited for their physical strength and imposing stature. Their employees are 'mostly from interior places where the state doesn't provide them jobs', the HR manager explained. '[There is] no availability of jobs and poverty is more....They generally come out [of the hinterlands] and join us.'

When the firm first began, Mr Smith explained, it recruited workers informally and made heavy use of nepotism, tribalism, and local connections to address the almost chronic labour shortage. 'Many people came up through references, children of earlier employees, people from the neighbourhood.' As time progressed, this was deemed 'not professional' and now recruitment is done from regional colleges and 'B grade institutes' as well as the armed forces as sources of labour. Family background, however, continues to play a role. What the manager tried to weed out, though, were people from families that are too elevated:

Somebody from a high profile family—for him, the job is not very exciting. For example, a chartered accountant, he has to do a lot of work in the company. That kind of professionalism is not there [in a high profile person]. So, that kind of person we may not like.

A car-manufacturing firm, employs 3,800 workers in one plant alone. It is in the process of building another and, hence, has been recruiting new workers of late. What do they look for in a new employee? 'First is the qualification and relevant background', the HR manager explains. 'If the person frequently changes jobs, he is not preferred.' But this is not sufficient. One must be willing to work hard and that is a quality this manager believes is absent from those at the top of the social structure:

We judge and prefer a person who is humble, not aggressive, and open to all....
We see the family background. People who come from high profile families
are not preferred as they have an inner pride within them, which makes them
arrogant. People from middle class are preferred.

Of course, the cost of exclusion for someone from the upper
classes is not nearly so punishing as it is for those at the bottom.
Nonetheless, it is important to recognize that the meritocratic model,
which places 'family background' in a central position, favours the
industrious members of the middling classes/castes and makes life
harder for those at the very top and the very bottom.

## REGIONAL STEREOTYPES

Americans are familiar with the stereotypical reputations assigned
to our regional cultures and the workers who come from them.
America's southern states are often deemed languid and slow.
Northeastern residents—particularly New Yorkers—are described
as brusque, fast paced, and almost genetically rude. Californians
are characterized as laid back and informal, superficially friendly,
and obsessed with physique. Midwesterners are sober and plain,
befitting the Scandinavian and German heritage of so many of them.
Relatively little research has been done on the impact of these regional
stereotypes on hiring patterns, at least compared with what we know
about racial bias in employment decisions. Nonetheless, region is
certainly in play as a background characteristic that, like height or
weight, may play a role in determining an individual's life chances.

While India is known for its hierarchical caste system, our interviews
suggest that equally pronounced regional stereotypes inhabit the
minds of HR managers, particularly those whose firms hire a large
part of the workforce from outside of large urban centres. Not only do
they have firm ideas about the qualities that different regions inculcate
in their residents, but they also worry about the social consequences
of either throwing workers together in unbalanced combinations of
antagonistic local groups or, about the opposite, endangering solidarity
within the workforce, based on caste, tribe, or village membership, in
the service of opposition to management.

The Kilim Chemical Company is a family-owned business,
founded decades ago to supply caustic soda to the aluminum

manufacturing industry. The company runs manufacturing firms in remote regions of India where the raw materials are extracted and refined. One family owns 65 per cent of the shares, but the firm is 'professionally managed', meaning it employs managerial staffs that are not beholden to the family. Kilim has over 1,000 core workers on the payroll and, in addition, employs thousands of seasonal workers who are involved in salt manufacture, an essential element of caustic soda production. The HR manager, an economist employed by the firm for two years, tells that the firm is very stable. 'We have extremely good industrial relations', he explained. 'We have never had workers going on strike.'

The firm is 'widely recognized for [its] generosity…there are people who have been working here for 20 years, 25 years and 50 years'. As is typical of many family firms, a paternalistic relationship obtains between the owners and the community surrounding the manufacturing plants.

[The owner] has a bungalow in [the township where the plant is located]. He goes there every two, three months and visits, and, then, goes around the place. So, everybody knows who he is. He is a Mai–Baap [mother–father], but in terms of welfare.

Though described as a shy man, the owner nonetheless makes a habit of turning up at village weddings to make contributions to the bride's father. In this respect, the firm is a kind of family, with obligations that stretch beyond the work world to the private sphere of kinship and households. Given this kind of integration, it is perhaps not surprising that the professional management can rattle off images of local ethnic groups that are strikingly categorical. 'Are there any kind of stereotypes about labour?' we inquired. 'I understand what you're talking about', the HR manager replied.

Now it is a little impolite thing to say it on a tape recorder. There is a great deal [of stereotyping] about Uttar Pradesh people. There is a constant mimicking of Bihari labourers. Lazy guys, come in, drop in without work, you know, but we have no choice, we have to work with those kind of people, rather than people from Gujarat and Maharashtra….

I can manage with these people, but in casual [conversation] we say he is so laid back. We have to adjust. The work I expect to be done in three minutes would probably take an hour and a half, but it will get done.

National Airlines, a fairly new transportation company, serves 45 cities in India and a variety of international destinations. 8,400 workers are employed by it, including those on regular and contract hiring agreements. Its core workforce tends toward management and high-level jobs, including pilots, airhostesses, and the like. Low-level jobs like loaders, cleaners, data entry operators, and sweepers are almost entirely contracted out, a common practice in Indian firms. A self-consciously modern firm, National Airlines maintains a web site for employment applications, its preferred recruitment method.

When asked about the kinds of workers they employ with respect to background, region, or religion, the HR manager was completely open about the fact that they select on appearance, fluency in English, and cultural sophistication. 'This is a service providing industry', Mr Gupta explained. 'We need good people, people who have some style and looks'.

A stylish guy, who also communicates well, speaks good English, who is very much educated, well grown, and who comes from a particular 'class', is preferred. So, we do not recruit anyone and everyone. We have identified some regions and communities from where we get out people. Say in north India, Punjabi culture is very much open; their faces have glow.

But that is not the same case with Haryana culture, Uttar Pradesh, or Bihari culture. They are not good for us. Their cultures, their way of speaking and dealing with others would not work in our company or in this industry. They don't have that openness.

A majority of airhostesses come from Punjabi families, as they are open. They can speak or communicate well. Some of them are from the Northeast.

Mr Gupta went on to explain that National Airlines likes to recruit 'sardar' (Sikh) girls who are also well spoken. But they are not interested in just any sardar. Instead, they specifically seek out 'those who come from good families....'

Sardar girls won't speak well if they come from Himachal Pradesh. They may not be cultured.

Physical appearance is integral to Gupta's image of the right kind of employee for National Airlines. He has very definite ideas about whether one finds people with the right features, the requisite 'glow on their faces'.

Frankly speaking, people from urban areas are preferred more than those coming from a rural area in this company, because rural mentality does not suit us and the company.

He is of the view that girls, whose fathers are in the military, are a particularly good bet for jobs in the airline industry. 'People who come from this particular culture', he notes, 'have a tendency to come together and work for the company.'

SSI, discussed earlier in the context of family background, combines views about the appropriateness of particular regions as a source of employment, with straightforward caste bias. Recruiting in rural areas, where labourers move in and out of agricultural labour and seasonal employment with firms like this one, they have come to know the ST in the region. They know that when the harvest season arrives, their workforce will disappear for a month or two. But this varies by region, and the HR manager has developed very strong views of who will work out and who will flake out:

If we go down to the South, say Chennai, Bangalore…that part of the country has a different attitude and they work much better. Basically, it is the culture of the area. The feedback from the customer is that the service in those regions is much better.

If I go to Noida area (in Uttar Pradesh), the social system is not balanced. If I go to Gurgaon, it is the most horrifying because of the concentration of Jats there. They are very arrogant. In India, this is the community, which is the most unsophisticated. The roughest community is the Haryanvi community. They don't understand logic; their blood starts boiling fast. In terms of discipline, commitment, and confinement to rule, I find it is least in these people.

Hiring managers who are themselves from urban areas, are particularly uneasy about rural and tribal peoples, and are prone to regard them in terms of group characteristics. They see tribals moving *en masse* into employment niches where they multiply through personal networks and, then, become a source of trouble. Urban dwellers are generally regarded as less troublesome, even if they descend from rural populations that fall under suspicion. The tempering influence of a heterogeneous urban environment reduces tribal affiliations, or so the managers seem to view it. Hence, as long as these communities mix with others and appear less as a block, they are more acceptable targets for recruitment. Nonetheless, underlying stereotypes prevail, as SSI sees the matter:

In Delhi, they have a mixed background. There are Biharis, Oriyas, Gadwalis, Pahadis (Nepalese). So, these people behave well with high profile people. If a group of Gadwalis [from the hills of north India] come together, then their behaviour changes. Same is the case with Biharis. If they are one, one each, then there is no problem. If they come in masses, there is a problem.

India Motors, an automobile manufacturer based in Punjab, is now a multinational firm, jointly owned now by one of the major Japanese firms. Two production firms—one in Gurgaon and one in Dharuhera—have been in operation for more than twenty years. 4,500 workers are listed on the India Motors payroll, but the actual workforce is nearly double that number, since contract employees are brought on as temporary workers. The senior HR manager, Mr Vincor, who had been with the firm for fifteen years, explained that the workforce that mans the plants is drawn from nearby areas and, hence, is dominated by the indigenous peoples of the area:

The social profile of labour varies significantly in the two plants. The first plant in Dharuhera is dominated by the labour from nearby villages, which means they are mostly from Haryana. Since they were recruited from available labour locally, they are not very educated. In fact, most of them were trained by us.

Caste plays an important role in organizing the rural labour force. As Mr Vincor explained, even the unions are structured by caste:

Nearly 450 workers [in the first plant] belong to the local dominant caste of Jats and another 250 to 300 come from another dominant caste of Ahirs. Around 100 to 150 would be from different backward castes. Our workers are also organized on caste lines. Trade Union elections are mostly on caste lines....

Jat group is arrogant. It does not listen to any one. Ahirs are tamed. Brahmins are more learned and they speak well, and the SCs are not vocal.

These are not neutral observations. The social organization of caste provides a platform for collective grievances, and the firm has been on the receiving end of labour actions that can be more easily organized, given the caste lines in the workforces. 'At times they are very aggressive', Vincor complained. 'We have seen a lot of bad phase, strikes and lock outs.'

The firm tries to temper the power of ethnic/caste-based organizing in two ways. First, the firm's owner maintains a paternalistic relationship that they hope will cut through these solidarities and engender loyalty to the firm. As part of its civic relations, India Motors builds hospitals, schools, and tube wells, and holds eye camps, and health camps. In this, they resemble the 'company towns' of the American past. Between the personal gestures to family members and the infrastructure the firm provides, the link between worker and firm tightens into a dependency.

The plant is everything for them, their *mai–baap*. They are loyal to the [owner's family]. Middle level officers directly communicate with the chairman. The chairman also patronizes them. There are some occasions when workers can meet the chairman directly. The chairman also attends the employees' weddings or their children's weddings.

Second, they try, where possible, to 'divide and rule' by limiting the number of like-caste individuals in any given part of the production process

If we recruit 50 people, not more than 10 to 12 Jats are recruited and the rest should be from diverse background. We need loyal and obedient workforce: people who will listen to us and work religiously.

India Motors relies on hiring practices that promote a mix of castes rather than permitting the dominance of a single group. And they avoid those groups that management regards as oppositional in character, likely to refuse management dictates and threaten labour actions instead.

The company's second plant is described in very different terms. Here labour relations are more professional and less personalistic. Mr Vincor regards the second plant as more modern, closer to the rest of the world economy in part because of its more impersonal labour practices. The language of globalization, which equates patrimonial bureaucracy and ethnic or caste-based hiring with the past, and advocates formal mechanisms for hiring rather than personal networks, meritocratic principles (albeit in the context of 'family background'), and national rather than local recruitment, represents a self-conscious effort to align India with international business culture, rather than traditional, customary, and ancient local practice.

The flip side of caste prejudice is a preference for specific groups, regional ethnicities, and religions, based on the view that they are particularly suited to a given occupation. Fitness Health Corporation, a relatively new firm owned by 'an upper caste Sikh family', employs about 4,000 people in northern India, while another 1,800 workers— ranging from 'ward boys to nurses, cleaners, and receptionists'—are contract workers. Fitness is a new industry of private health providers that caters to relatively wealthy families. They are particular about the people they hire because they are serving an elite clientele.

The majority of our employees are local, most North Indians. We have peoples who have migrated from Noida and Ghaziabad. However, most of our nurses are females coming from south India, especially from Kerala (Mallu Christian girls)...they are better in knowledge than other girls and this is because they are doing the job from generation to generation and the knowledge is passed from one...to another.

Higher caste people are reluctant to send their daughters in this nursing profession. They think that this is not a good profession, looking after the patients, cleaning them, and other things. The nurses [we hire] are mostly Christians, must be converted (from low caste [Hindus]) or born Christians. They generally don't belong to SC. People coming from north India are mostly Punjabis, an average Punjabi girl.

As the HR manager—an upper caste Hindu woman—makes clear, there are channels of recruitment in operation that have been, if not restricting, then at least providing insider advantage to a regionally based religious groups. These preferences are based in part on traditional views of who will be willing to come into physical contact with patients, and whom patients will accept in that role. One could argue that this manager is merely describing a labour migration flow, rather than unveiling a preference that affects who the firm will hire among those who present themselves as applicants. There hardly seems to be a difference in practice. Fitness Health searches among the groups it sees as 'fit' for the job and neither looks for nor entertains others easily.

Such a preferential policy often exists side by side with a bright line that excludes those who do not fit these stereotypical expectations. For Fitness Health, this clearly includes Dalits, who need not apply. 'Among SCs', the manager explains, 'there is a lack of technical skills.

And their attitude is unmatchable for the company'. Is this unfair, an example of bigotry? No, she insists.

We have no prejudices about SCs and Muslims. This is a mind set issue.

A 'mind set issue' echoes a global language of 'psychological fit', often determined through the use of psychometric tests that have become popular among modern managers in multinational firms. These multiple choice personality assessments are considered scientific instruments that will assist employers in matching the needs of the firm with the intrinsic qualities of applicants. Only a few of the firms we studied employ them, but the ones that do tend to be in the most globalized industries, particularly communications.

## RESERVATIONS

The constitution marking India's founding as an independent nation was passed on 26 November 1949 in the midst of fierce political battles over the religious and ethnic composition of the country. Dalits, or Untouchables as they were then termed, seeking to gain some leverage during Independence, agreed to remain inside the Hindu fold if they were guaranteed quotas in the public sector, especially higher education, employment, and in Parliament itself. Today 22.5 per cent of public university seats, including those in the most elite institutions, are set aside for SCs and STs who are primarily rural landless labourers whose standard of living is abysmally poor.[7] In the little over sixty years since the creation of this 'reservation' policy, a small (though impossible to measure with any certainty) proportion of these traditionally shunned groups have been able to claim places in public education, the civil service and, finally, in the government itself.

These opportunities are vital to the upward mobility of the Dalit population. Even though only a small proportion ever gets this far, it is a right that is fiercely protected. Indeed, other groups (including the so-called 'OBCs') have lobbied to extend the policy to themselves, arguing that an additional 27 per cent of seats in high education be set aside for them.[8] The proposal sparked riots across India in 2006, as medical students and doctors took to the streets and fought pitched battles with the police, insisting that merit should be the only criterion for entry into these coveted programmes and medical professions.

As eye-opening as these protests were, they are but the tip of a larger iceberg. The Indian economy has been gradually opening itself up to international competition, trade, and foreign investment. Pursuing a liberalization strategy, the state has been contracting in size while the growth of the private sector has been significant. By the middle of the first decade of twenty-first century, India had emerged as the third largest economy in the world, behind only the United States and China.[9] It is a matter of some controversy as to whether or to what extent the nation's poor have benefited from these trends. In any case, the ground is slipping out from under public sector workers as the government continues to pursue the liberalization strategy and the future increasingly seems to lie with private employment.

This trend, in turn, has turned the attention of legislators and advocates concerned about continuing discrimination against lower castes to suggest that the reservations policy be extended to the private sector. They argue that only if the private sector commits to affirmative action through quotas will the rights guaranteed in the constitution be protected.

Reservation in the private sector was uniformly opposed by the HR managers interviewed for this study. Not one in the entire portfolio of research subjects had anything positive to say about quota-based hiring. Ultimately, their objections trace back to the first topic raised in this chapter: the relationship between modernity and meritocracy. The future of the Indian economy, they argue, lies in increasing productivity and this, in turn, requires that each firm permits the 'creamy layer' to rise, while the incompetent fail and disappear. There should be little need to justify this perspective, as the employers/managers see the matter: it is the natural way of Adam Smith's hidden hand, the only means to achieve the greater good.

From the perspective of HR managers, reservations policy inserts ascriptive criteria into the hiring process and short circuits the competitive processes essential to the market. This they believe, would lead to the ruination of India's economy and, hence, the policy must be stopped dead in its tracks. Interference in the name of social engineering will ultimately defeat the purpose of national growth, and the loss of international investment that would accompany quota regulations would strip the whole country of the capital it needs.

Beyond this general attack on reservation, there were a variety of sub-themes worth exploring for the images they throw off of the underlying nature of low-caste workers. The first is the view that discrimination is not a problem at this stage in the development of India's labour market. It might have been an issue in the past, but India has turned a corner and as a modern nation, no longer thinks in terms of caste at all.

The most surprising example of this view came from the founder of an organization dedicated to reforming the occupation most often populated by Dalits, the urban scavengers. This firm runs public waste facilities in urban areas and provides employment, ostensibly to members of any caste, but in practice heavily subscribed by Dalits. The firm's birth was inspired by Gandhi's 1917 campaign to de-stigmatize the ex-Untouchables by insisting that every caste Hindu should clean his own toilets, a principle adopted by the Congress party and promoted by the government in the late 1950s. Waste Management Corporation was founded as a response to a public health initiative started in the late 1970s that was ideologically compatible with the de-stigmatization campaign, and has spread all over India as an industry intended both to improve sanitation and provide employment for those without more appealing options. Given this background, one might imagine the leadership of the firm would be acutely aware of employment discrimination. Not so.

'I haven't come across anywhere where a SC has been denied a job because he is a SC,' the director explained.

Nobody can do it, even in the private sector. Private sector is more concerned about its profit and production. If someone is an asset, he or she is accepted....If a Scheduled Caste person comes to me and he is brilliant, I will employ him.

Confidence in the basic fairness of the employment system was echoed in our interview with Mr Palin, the manager of a large retail firm established in recent years to supply the growing Indian market with household products. Today, the firm has 3,500 workers all over India and competes for workers who are not from the top universities and institutes, since the wages in retail are modest, but rather the graduates of less prestigious training programmes. When asked whether reservations were a good idea or a necessary practice, he answered, 'if a person is capable enough, he or she doesn't need reservation. There are enough jobs in the market; one can easily achieve what he wants....'

What matters—according to those who believe that opportunity is ample and, therefore, reservations are unnecessary—is talent. Those that have it will find work, regardless of their caste background, and those who do not, lack the necessary qualities and deserve to fail. As Mr Sunasi, the HR manager of a large transportation firm, emphasized, the cream rises:

We don't hire people based on their caste and creed. The company sees only one thing and that is merit and that is the only one criteria....I don't think there should be reservation on the basis of caste. Talent should be talent and should not be manipulated....

There should be no reservation in the private sector. No company will allow it. They need educated people and recruit only on the basis of merit....

Virtually every interview we collected includes a statement to the same effect. Yet, managers are aware that inequality is persistent, that low-caste individuals have less opportunity than others in the labour market. Few would argue that this state of affairs comes about just because talent is differentially distributed. Instead, they suggest that a human capital problem, created by an educational system that disadvantages Dalits and OBCs, is producing a talent deficit in this population. The hiring manager for Global Productions insisted that unequal education is the root of the problem. When asked why it was that Dalits are virtually never employed in top private sector jobs, she responded:

I haven't thought [about] it that way. I don't think that it is true [that discrimination is at work]. I think it could be a lot to do [with] the way our society is developed. There could be [the] possibility that because Dalits are economically weaker, so they haven't gone to [the] best schools and colleges. That could be a reason. But if you have a level and a degree, no one can stop you.

Hence, the explanation for poverty and disadvantage in the lower castes has shifted away from the pollution taboos and enforced exclusion toward the institutions that certify talent. Almost to a person, the view among employers is that education—not affirmative action—is the key to uplifting the low-caste population.

And here, some would admit, India lags behind. It has not invested as heavily in education as it needs to do and should feel some obligation to remedy the problem. Dalit students attend inferior schools and this, business leaders agree, needs to be addressed. Pradeep Wig,[10] the Owner of Kwality Ice-Creams, is the author of an important report from the business community that was submitted to the Prime Minister of India in July 2006.[11] Wig is concerned that the government would even contemplate the idea of extending reservation to the private sector and likens the idea to the confiscation of private property.

What, then, is the appropriate diagnosis and remedy? 'Frankly, corporations have no solution to the problem', he explained.

We cannot progress in this regard [equal hiring] unless there is integrated schooling in India. In countries like USA, where you have integrated schooling, the young people grow up together. For 15 to 20 years of their life, they have been together in the school despite the difference of colours....Industries have little role to play. One should not have more expectation from industry. (Personal interview)

Hence, investment in education and encouraging integration to break down barriers that divide Indians by caste will pay off in levelling the playing field. Then, and only then, can business be expected to show equal hiring rates, because it will be choosing from among equally qualified applicants.

Business elites express confidence in the notion that once a greater investment has been made, the playing field will be level and the natural, market driven, sorting devices will be able to operate as they should. Yet, it was striking in our interviews, how often HR managers argued that the business community should forge ahead in hiring as if equality of educational opportunity was already a reality. Hence, Mr Sunasi suggests:

Instead of reservation, provide them free schooling and, then, let them face the competition. If talent is there in them, it will come out. I am personally against reservation even in colleges and jobs.

His counterpart at Global Productions agrees. 'Reservation', she told us, 'this is a bad move'.

The caste or a particular social background does not qualify a person for any specific job. Why is a person getting into academics? A person gets in to perform, to achieve. So, you are killing the very purpose by letting people enter through reservation. You are killing your own institution.

She believes that investment in education for the poor will pay off as long as it is earned through hard work. Scholarships for the economically disadvantaged represent a sound response to the problem of under-representation of SCs in the formal sector:

See [a lower caste person's] economic situation, if you have to help him. Let him study well, let him get his marks and then wave off his fees. Do a favour! Yes, do a favour, wave off his fees and do that for any other, not for a particular caste, but that can be for anybody who provides the proof of income.

The fact that primary education is so weak in India, according to the manager of SSI, puts the SC and poor children at a disadvantage from the very beginning. 'In my perspective', he explains, 'elementary education has to be strengthened'.

Any parent who doesn't send their children to school—the roadside beggars, the street children—they should be provided with primary schooling and it should be strengthened. They should be rigorous at the primary level; there should be standardization of education. Instead of giving them reservation in jobs and compromising merit, provide them elementary education....Give them extra slots in schools for their personal grooming, overall personality development, and personal education. But [if we go] beyond this point, the country will go to hell.

His counterpart at the India Shoe Company echoes the same notion:

We do not support reservation. Productivity will suffer and the company will suffer. The SCs should be given opportunities in education and after that; they should compete on their own....There should be no reservation for any category of population in education either.

What are the pitfalls of insisting on reservation for the moment? Here, a litany of problems emerges. First, employers argue, acquiring a job through a reservations policy destroys the incentive to be productive. The HR manager of Kilim Chemical Company is certain that anyone who gets a job as a consequence of government-induced social engineering will behave as if there is no relationship between performance and his ability to hold on to the job, and that he will take the position for granted and underperform. 'In a corporate environment', he explained, '[reservation policy] is disastrous because people use it as a trick.'

People take advantage and do not do any work....This guy, like he says, because I am a SC, I will get away with anything that is not acceptable and it happens. That's number one.

This manager worries that grievances will follow if a SC person is passed over or not hired, not unlike the problems he encounters with trade unions, which he thinks, make trouble when they do not get what they feel is their due. The trouble brings production to a halt and costs the company on the bottom line.

See, *main chamar hun is liye muj ko nahin* select *karte* [because I am a Chamar (SC), that's why I am not selected]. That kind of thing is bad. In the private sector, if you reserve, they will bring productivity down.

Americans familiar with the debate over welfare reform will recognize the language here, though it is oddly transposed into a work context. Charles Murray, Lawrence Mead, and other critics of the US system of public assistance argued that it was fundamentally flawed, because it removed all incentives to work, and recommended dismantling non-work related benefits in order to drive recipients into the labour force where they would have to sink or swim. Murray's and Mead's complaints had to do with what they saw as incentives to avoid the labour market altogether. Indian employers complain that reservation will incline low-caste workers not to work as hard as they would if they had to 'earn' their job and worry about whether they can retain it. Multiply that times the millions of workers who would come into their organizations by virtue of quotas and, they argue, the productivity of their firms would collapse.

The assumption at work here is that the purpose of reservation is not to level the playing field or permit a deserving Dalit to gain a job he would otherwise be denied for reasons of prejudice. Instead, reservation represents a political victory that enables the unqualified to game the system, forcing firms to permit indolent time-servers into a labour force that is scrambling to meet production targets.

The hiring manager for SSI says that he sees this problem at work when he recruits new employees from universities that practice quotas for Dalits in higher education. Their qualifications are simply not equal:

In terms of calibre, competence, and delivery, these people are far lower than their batch mates [non-reservation classmates]. I had an engineer from [SC] background. We had to take this person because the salary structure was not so good and, hence, the lower rungs of IIT [Indian Institute of Technology] graduates will come in the company.

He terribly disappointed me. No discipline, no competence, and no confidence. The person did not understand the basic rules and fundamentals.... He was looking for small personal benefits, cutting corners, low comprehensiveness, losing the character of the company because of low job delivery.

I have experience of five to six people coming from such background. These people were from SC background, only carrying the tag of IIT, but no way compared to their batch mates.

The outcome of the experience, he explained, was that the firm raised wages to avoid being left with the dregs of the technical institutions.

For further proof of the damage reservation would do to firms' competitiveness, employers point to government organizations in their own fields. India has had public hospitals for many decades. The employment manager of Fitness Health, a private health care firm that operates hospitals for paying customers, looks upon his 'competition' with contempt and believes that if his firm were forced to comply with the reservation policy, they would end up in similar condition:

If there [were] reservation in this company, nurses and ward boys won't work and pay less attention to patients. See what is happening in government departments. Incapable people are pushed in and, ultimately, we all lose. These people do not work hard. They enter with low [grades]. Our job is very technical and incompetent people cannot be relied upon to [do] such work. There is no place for poor education and technical skills in our institution. Our company will resist any kind of caste-based reservation.

According to these employers, not only does reservation policy let the SC beneficiaries off the hook, but it has also the potential to spread a watered-down work ethic to others or so, the manager of

Global Productions explains. 'What has the reservation system done to India's education system?' we inquired. 'Somewhere, it affects the people who work hard. It de-motivates them.'

Dalits fail under reservation, we were told, in part because they have internalized the negative expectations that underlie the policy. Here employers reflected an acquaintance with the position taken by some American black conservatives that affirmative action casts doubt on the capabilities of its beneficiaries, as well as race-mates who compete and succeed without any assistance from social policies. This view posits that white students or employees in American schools/firms will come to see any black person as sub-standard and able to gain entry to an elite institution only with the special help of a selection system that gives them preference for ascriptive reasons. Conservatives like Ward Connerly[12] go on to argue that these preferential admissions policies undermine the self-confidence of minority students who come to believe that they are not really good enough to be in elite institutions. If the policy is dismantled, the only people who will be admitted are those who meet universal standards.

Pradeep Wig, the author of the report from the business community to the Indian Prime Minister on the subject of inclusive employment, is inclined to extend this diagnosis to the Indian case as well. 'The lower caste people are scared', he insists.

They have already accepted that they are smaller [less capable] than the high-caste people….They have a low confidence level. I had one person from SC background; he is a scared fellow. He doesn't even speak with me. They are so much oppressed that he doesn't even question me.

Reservation exacerbates the problem, he claims, because it reinforces the view that absent a special boost, the SC employee would never hold the job he has. What is more, Wig worries, reservation will increase rather than decrease 'casteism' in Indian firms. It will 'increase the divide in companies' as positions are doled out via background characteristics rather than personal qualities. Groups will form to protect their positions within the private sector and the result will be division everywhere.

Trouble will follow as groups align themselves in opposition to the privileges extended to some. Employers can see that something

of this kind has already happened in higher education, as upper caste
students rally outside the medical schools to protest the claims of
OBCs to a reservation quota for themselves. They fear similar forms
of disruption in their own organizations if reservations are imposed
on the private sector.

Finally, we see in some interviews arguments for fairness that see
in reservation the creation of unfair advantage and inherited rights.
On this account, reservation is itself unequally distributed. The
Jodor Steel Company is 30 years old and has production facilities all
over India. The firm produces pipes that supply gasoline and oil, and
employs 12,000 core employees and an equal number of temporary
workers. Owned by a *Baniya* family, traditional traders from
northern India, the Jodor Company is a powerful manufacturing
firm that employs tribal peoples in the hinterlands all over India.
The manager, who participated in this project, had experience of
working in both the private and public sector. He was of the firm
opinion that reservation policy is a disaster because it has become
the preserve of one class of Dalits:

It is high time we should get out of [the quota system]. We must stop this.
No one should avail of such a facility. It has become a privilege for them.
Father was taking it; then his son and now his great grand son. It then becomes
institutionalized. Government should stop it. Only the urban Dalits take the
benefit of it and [the] rural class is kept deprived.

Readers familiar with William Julius Wilson's argument in *The
Truly Disadvantaged* will recognize a common theme here. Wilson
argued that race-based affirmative action, while beneficial in many
ways, ultimately would do little for the poor. Middle class African-
Americans would be best able to compete under these conditions,
while the poor would be unable to benefit. For this reason, Wilson
argued for economic disadvantage as the basis for affirmative action.
Both for reasons of political appeal to colour blind policy and
because the poor are the most likely to need recognition of special
barriers, Wilson argued in favour of more universal policies with
targeted benefits.

In the end, though, it would appear that the reservation policy is a
complete 'no go' from the corporate perspective. In the 25 interviews

we had, there was not a single supporter of the idea. At the most, hiring managers were willing to support policies of educational investment, scholarships to reward deserving students, as a means of encouraging meritorious behaviour and the future benefits that are presumed to go with high achievement.

As the HR manager of security systems summed up the situation, nothing in the Indian experience of reservation policy since Independence inspires confidence that it is a viable or desirable route for the private sector. Instead, it should be dismantled everywhere else:

Why should we need reservation after 60 years of [it]? We have not done our jobs, as corporate ventures, as politicians. It is just a waste of the country. Sixty years and every 10 to 15 years, their generations have changed and there is no material change at all. Sixty years and that's enough. No more reservations are required.

India's success in the international market place provides ample justification, as this manager sees it, for the wisdom of promoting competition, meritocracy, and investment in the best. The least well off will receive the trickle-down benefits of high growth if the country avoids fettering itself with anti-competitive policies.

All our Indian universities have tied up with foreign universities, and now what for we need reservation? Today it has reversed; foreign companies are coming and tying with us. Indian Institute of Managements [IIMs] are opening up campuses outside [of India] because they have intellect to cater to others. Why can't people from SCs come up?

We have spoiled the country and played with the people for 50 years....It is people like us who are paying for these people.

## IN THE NAME OF GLOBALIZATION

The language of meritocracy has spread around the globe along with the competitive capitalism that gave birth to it. The notion that patrimonial ties, reciprocal obligations, and birthright should guarantee access to critical resources like jobs is largely gone. That ascriptive characteristics continue to matter—now dressed up as 'family background' rather than caste—hardly causes the managers we interviewed to skip a beat. They are convinced that modernism is the future of their firms and the future of the country. It calls for the adoption of labour market practices that the advanced capitalist world embraces and a blind eye to the uneven playing field that produces merit in the first place.

What are the consequences of this cultural shift, of the spread of a common language that resonates with moral precepts of fairness and level playing fields? Can one argue against meritocracy in the modern world? Two responses come to mind. First, as suggested in this chapter, the belief in merit is only sometimes accompanied by a truly 'caste blind' orientation. Instead, we see the commitment to merit voiced alongside convictions that merit is distributed by caste or region, and, hence, the qualities of individuals fade from view, replaced by stereotypes that, at best, will make it harder for a highly qualified low-caste job applicant to gain recognition for his/her skills and accomplishments. At worst, they will be excluded simply by virtue of birthright. Under these circumstances, one must take the profession of deep belief in meritocracy with a heavy dose of salt. Anti-discrimination law is required to insist on the actual implementation of caste-blind policies of meritocratic hiring and, we submit, to question common and accepted practices of assessing family background as a hiring qualification, for it may amount to another way of discovering caste.

Second, the findings in this chapter return us to the question of how merit is produced in the first place. The distribution of credentials, particularly in the form of education, is hardly a function of individual talent alone. It reflects differential investment in public schools, health care, nutrition, and the like. Institutional discrimination of this kind sets up millions of low-caste Indians for a lifetime of poverty and disadvantage. As long as the playing field is this tilted, there can be no real meaning to meritocracy conceived of as a fair tournament.

This is not to suggest that a commitment to competition is, in and of itself, a bad idea or a value to be dismissed. It is a vast improvement over unshakeable beliefs in racial, religious, or caste inferiority, for it admits of the possibility that talent is everywhere. Until the day that institutional investments are fairly distributed, policy alternatives will be needed to ensure that stereotypes do not unfairly block the opportunities of low-caste Indians and rural job applicants.

## NOTES

1. An exception would include Philip Moss and Chris Tilly (2003). For a perspective of employer attitudes based on survey research, see Harry Holzer (1999).

2. The official unemployment rate among the SCs in urban India is 10.5 per cent as against 8.2 per cent for the OBCs and 6.8 per cent among upper caste Hindus. It was 8.1 per cent among Muslims and 10.9 per cent among other minorities. Unemployment for the entire urban population was 8.3 per cent. These figures are based on the 61st round of the National Sample Survey carried out in 2004–5. Prime Minister's High Level Committee (2006), 'Social, Economic and Educational Status of the Muslim Community of India: A Report'.

3. See especially Sukhadeo Thorat and Paul Attewell, in this volume. It is more likely the case that employers and hiring managers understate the degree to which bias influences hiring than overstate it. As Pager and Quillian (2005) show in a comparison of results from an audit study and a telephone survey of the same employers, those who indicate an equal willingness to hire black and white ex-offenders actually display large differences by race in audit experiments where they are given an opportunity to consider matched pairs differentiated only by race.

4. Hiring managers often do not know exactly how many contract or temporary workers their own firms employ, particularly if they are spread out all over the country. Hence, it could easily be the case that the total workforce of these firms is closer to 300,000 than the 210,000 we can total up. But the data on the demographics of contract labour is less reliable by far than what we have on the core labour force and, in any case, the hiring managers, who participated in this study, are not responsible for actual hiring decisions where contract labour is concerned. This is an important limitation, though, because for many low skilled Dalits, the opportunities provided by contract positions are undoubtedly more important than the positions that are at issue for the core labour force.

| Firm Type and Size | | |
| --- | --- | --- |
| *Firm Type* | *Core employees* | *Contract employees* |
| Construction | 8000 | |
| Hotel | 550 | (100) |
| TV and magazine | 700 | |
| Auto manufacturer | 4500 | (3500) |
| Shoe manufacturer | 10,000 | (2000) |
| Daily newspaper | 3000 | (800) |
| Chemical company | 1100 | |
| Tobacco manufacture/hotels | 20,000 | |
| Health care | 4000 | (1800) |
| Steel manufacturer | 11,000 | (10,000) |
| Food processor | 150 | |
| National airways | 6000 | (2400) |
| Security firm | 100,000 | |
| Alternative medicine | 3000 | |
| Air conditioning manufacture | 300 | (700) |
| Courier/cargo | No data | |
| Public toilet placement/cleaning | 3500 | |
| Retail home furnishings/clothing | No data | |
| Hotel | 1000 | (100) |
| Automobile manufacturing | 7000 | (42,000) |
| Watch manufacturing | 2800 | |
| Hotel/restaurant/food processing | 2000 | |
| Ice-cream manufacturer | No data | |
| Communications/video | 800 | |
| E-commerce | 135 | |

The smallest of the firms has only 135 core employees, while the largest has approximately 100,000. They range from manufacturing—still heavily represented in the city of Delhi—to service firms, especially hotels and restaurants. Many of the firms were founded as family enterprises and some still are. A number of them began as British owned production companies in the colonial era, transferred to Indian management after independence, and have now been absorbed into multinational firms. Most were family-run firms that have now transitioned to what interviewees refer to as 'professional management', by which they mean that network-based hiring has declined in favour of more formal sources of recruitment, including websites, newspaper advertisements, on campus interviews, and 'headhunters'. These avenues do not entirely preclude the exercise of personal ties, as we shall see below, but it has become a matter of pride to move away from total reliance on 'in group' recruitment as the former is regarded as too traditional, while more formal and open routes have been deemed more modern.

5. All company names have been changed and identifying details modified slightly to protect the privacy of the firms and our interview subjects.

6. BIMARU is an acronym coined by demographer Ashish Bose to refer to India's less developed states of Bihar, Madhya Pradesh, Rajasthan, and Uttar Pradesh. The word *Bimaru* in Hindi means someone who is perennially ill.

7. Having long suffered from pollution taboos that forbid the higher castes to associate with them, Dalits were confined to jobs (often no more than forced labour) as 'scavengers', responsible for cleaning latrines, dealing with dead bodies or animals, and working with leather, which must be cured in urine. All of these traditional occupations are regarded with disgust by other castes. Gandhi famously insisted that his fellow Brahmins clean their own toilets and for this, he was regarded as a turncoat by millions of high-caste Hindus.

8. http://select.nytimes.com/search/restricted/article?res=F7 last accessed on January 2007. OBCs pushed for an additional 27 per cent of positions in higher education to be reserved for them.

9. See Walker (2007).

10. This is the only participant in our project whose real name is being used here because he is speaking as a public figure, the author of a major government report, rather than as a business owner whose hiring practices are at issue.

11. ASSOCHAM report on *Concrete Steps by Indian Industry on Inclusiveness for the Scheduled Castes and Scheduled Tribes*, submitted to the Prime Minister of India, 27 July 2006.

12. The former regent of the University of California who has sponsored successful ballot initiatives to make affirmative action by race or ethnicity illegal, on the grounds that it diminishes the confidence of minority students, causing them to question the legitimacy of their own achievements, as well as the illegitimacy of policies that are not 'colour blind'.

# References

Carter, Stephen (2005), *Reflections of an Affirmative Action Baby*, New York: Basic Books.

Coate, Steven and Glenn Loury (1993), 'Will Affirmative Action Policies Eliminate Negative Stereotypes', *American Economic Review*, vol. 83, no. 5, pp. 1220–40.

Goffman, Erving (1959), *The Presentation of Self in Everyday Life*, New York: Doubleday.

Holzer, Harry (1999), *What Employers Want: Job Prospects for Less-Educated Workers*, New York: Russell Sage Foundation.

Jencks, Christopher and Meredith Phillips (1998), *The Black-White Test Score Gap*, Washington, DC: The Brookings Institution Press.

Jencks, Christopher and Paul Peterson (eds), *The Urban Underclass*, Washington, DC: The Brookings Institution Press.

Kirshenman, Joleen and Kathryn M. Neckerman (1991), '"We'd Love to Hire Them, But...": The Meaning of Race for Employers', in Christopher Jencks and Paul Peterson (eds), *The Urban Underclass*, Washington, DC: The Brookings Institution, pp. 203–34.

Lawrence, Mead (2001), *Beyond Entitlement: The Social Obligations of Citizenship*, New York: Free Press.

Moss, Philip and Chris Tilly (2003), *Stories Employers Tell: Race, Skill and Hiring in America*, New York: Russell Sage Foundation.

Murray, Charles (1994), *Losing Ground: American Social Policy, 1950–1980*, New York: Basic Books.

Pager, Devah (2003), 'The Mark of a Criminal Record', *American Journal of Sociology*, vol. 108, no. 5, pp. 937–75.

—— (2007), *Marked: Race, Crime and Finding Work in an Era of Mass Incarceration*, Chicago: University of Chicago Press.

Pager, Devah and Lincoln Quillian (2005), 'Walking the Talk? What Employers Say versus What They Do', *American Sociological Review*, vol. 7, no. 3, pp. 365–80.

Prime Minister's High Level Committee (2006), *Social Economic and Educational Status of the Muslim Community in India: A Report* (Sachar Committee Report), Delhi: Government of India.

Randall, Collins (1979), *Credential Society: A Historical Sociology of Education and Stratification*, New York: Academic Press.

Sengupta, Somini and Hari Kumar (2006), 'Quotas to Aid India's Poor vs. Push for Meritocracy', *New York Times*, 23 May.

Walker, Andrew (2007), 'India's Economy Nears $1 trillion', BBC News, 6 February, http://news.bbc.co.uk/2/hi/business/ 6334305.stm

Weisskopf, Tom (2006), *Affirmative Action in the United States and India: A Comparative Perspective*, London: Routledge.

Wilson, William Julius (1987), *The Truly Disadvantaged: The Inner City, The Underclass, and Public Policy*, Chicago: University of Chicago Press.

# 3

# Where the Path Leads
## The Role of Caste in Post-university
## Employment Expectations

*Ashwini Deshpande and Katherine S. Newman*

Charges of reverse discrimination are commonplace in all countries with affirmative action. Underlying the issue of reverse discrimination is a popular view that, for instance in the USA, minorities are reaping enormous benefits from affirmative action, while qualified whites are languishing on the unemployment lines. In order to explore the legitimacy of this critique, sociologist Deirdre Royster (2003) developed a longitudinal study, which has inspired the present chapter. Royster's project ferrets out these underlying attitudes and, more importantly, investigates the role that race plays in creating divergent and highly unequal patterns of employment and mobility among they equally qualified blacks and whites.

Royster followed 50 graduates (25 Black and 25 White) from Baltimore's Glendale Vocational High School to examine the school-to-work transition for working class black and white men.[1] She finds that in her carefully matched sample, race continued to be a powerful predictor of wages and employment. The median black man earned only 73 per cent of the earnings of the median white man. Black men were 10 per cent less likely than their white counterparts to be employed at the time of interviews. White men enjoyed an enormous advantage over black men with respect to job quality: 19 out of 25 white men had already held at least one desirable blue-collared job in the first two to three years after graduating, while only eight out of 25 black men had done so.

These findings are particularly sobering in light of the fact that a substantially larger number of black men increased their skill sets and employability by paying for additional training themselves. Black and white men's trajectories began to diverge only two or three years after high school graduation. Despite equal or greater effort to develop marketable skills and work experience, black men were unable to either successfully pursue the trades they had studied in high school or to recover successfully after switching trade preferences, as their white peers seemed to do easily.

Why was this the case? Was it due to racial bias in hiring? Or was it due to unmeasured differences in human capital? Royster argues that the most powerful explanations for the differentials lie in the constitution of social networks that can be mobilized in pursuit of employment. 'Other things being equal—and in this study they are', she points out, 'the stronger one's network, the better one's chances of making stable labor market transitions' (Royster 2003: 176).

In the US, there was a time when families took primary responsibility for assisting non-college bound students with work-entry difficulties, but now that families no longer have access to jobs in the manufacturing sector, schools are increasingly called upon to find ways to assist students in finding and getting work. This should help to level the racial playing field, particularly for students who are graduating from the same trade schools, as the Blacks and Whites in Royster's study have done.

Royster finds the contrast between how schools assist college-bound and work-bound students very stark. Students headed for higher education get abundant information on application procedures, selection criteria, placement rates, prestige ratings, and so forth from their high schools. Students aiming for the labour market are comparatively under-served: there is very little information on training or career options. For this reason, most work-bound students tend to rely on friends and family, rather than schools, for help in finding training and jobs. However, for minority youth, who are more likely than white youth to lack ties to employers, job-trainers, and other employed people in general, schools may provide the only available information about and connections to employers or other post-high school options. Thus, school-based connections could be a potentially equalizing resource between white and black students but, in fact, seem not to be operating in this fashion because they do relatively little for students in either race group.

This leaves the private 'information system' as virtually the only resource for the 'forgotten half'[2] of non-college bound workers. Here, though, at every turn, white men are at an advantage compared to black men. Black men mainly know workers, while white men know bosses as well as workers. White contacts can recommend young men for jobs for which they had little or no training, whereas black men recommend young men only when there was evidence of training or expertise in the field. White men with contacts would be hired for desirable blue-collared jobs without interviews; black men would face screening interviews for all but the most menial jobs, sometimes even for those.

Young white workers are neither permanently ejected from nor unduly stigmatized within networks if they 'act out' or get into trouble. Young black men have to be extra careful not to confirm widely held stereotypes regarding their alleged irresponsibility and unfitness as workers. Young white men get many of their first experiences working in the small businesses of family members or neighbours, where mistakes can be quickly and quietly corrected. Young black men's first jobs may be in white-owned firms where early mistakes confirm racially biased suspicions.

While these major racial differences in early employment outcomes are clear, Royster considers two questions that could be raised about these results: (a) that these findings could indicate progress over an even worse situation—'things are bad but getting better'; and (b) these unequal outcomes may not reflect discrimination but hidden differences in school performance, motivation, and character. Based on detailed and pointed questions to measure the latter, she finds that in this sample, black and white men demonstrated similar academic, character, and motivation/preparedness levels.

Tragically, these are the young men who have done everything society could have asked of them and still they face rampant inequality in life chances, as Royster explains:

These findings are even more troubling when we recall that these are the young people who have done what society suggests they should: they have stayed in school, taken the 'dirty' jobs, gone to school regularly, performed at a satisfactory level, stayed out of police trouble, and impressed school personnel. They have followed the rules, and yet they have been unable to get returns on their educational and behavioral investments comparable to those of their white peers. (Royster 2003: 102)

She terms this result as 'ghetto results without ghetto residence', that is, 'the three black disadvantages—lack of networks, lack of transportation, and the presence of discrimination—operate irrespective of class and residential advantages associated with being a member of the stable working or lower middle class'.

Was the pattern of black disadvantage and white success recognized by the men Royster followed into the labour market? Interestingly, the answer is not only 'No', but a folk theory of white disadvantage developed instead. White men, who were extremely successful compared to their black peers, thought that racial quotas had limited their occupational options, giving their black peers an unfair advantage over them. None of the white students saw themselves as uniquely privileged compared to their black peers, not even those who admitted to having seen black workers put up with harassment on the job.

White men described the job process as meritocratic if they got the job but as biased in favour of blacks if they did not or suspected that they would not get the job. These convictions created disincentives for whites to incorporate blacks into their more effective networks. Why let the 'advantaged' into that tent? The answer is that they did not do so.

## THE INDIAN CONTEXT

This chapter is based on research conducted against a similar backdrop: controversy over quota systems that provide for places in universities and public employment for the historically disenfranchized Dalits. Dalit students who qualify for reservations and their non-Dalit counterparts, who also face extraordinary competition for access to higher education, come together in the proving ground for future employment: the nation's top universities. It cannot be overstated how narrow this bottleneck is. Access to higher education is severely constrained relative to the demand; every place is coveted by hundreds, if not thousands, of applicants.

With so much at stake, claims about special privilege associated with quotas take on a particularly strident tone. Beneficiaries of reservations are often made to feel that they have 'stolen' a place that rightfully belongs to someone more qualified and their peers believe they lack the talent and drive to measure up. The less celebrated aspects of inequality—from differential school quality to the investments well-heeled families can afford in test preparation and tutoring, from the availability of legacy privileges to the upper hand that family resources provides in making donations to secure admissions—are rarely identified as 'unfair' or responsible for special privileges that should be re-examined.

The claim of reverse discrimination often proceeds from the assumption that the playing field that leads to university entrance is level enough or that determining admission on any basis other than pure merit is inimical to modern practice, which should be based on competitive success alone. We have seen these attitudes in play among employers in the previous chapter.

## Research Design

Here we examine the experience of similarly qualified Indian students in some of the nation's most selective institutions of higher education as they move towards the labour market and ask to what extent they expect and then experience a level playing field or one tilted by caste advantage. Accordingly, we identified two groups of comparable university students from different caste backgrounds (in particular, 'reserved category' or Dalit students and the 'general category'[3]) on the eve of their entry into the labour market in order to compare them in terms of job expectations, job search methods, actual placements, and the differential role that social networks (friends and family) play in determining their options in the world of work. The students in question have similar educational credentials, although they come from divergent personal backgrounds.

The students in this study were first interviewed during what they expected would be their last year of university.[4] Two sets of follow-up interviews were conducted subsequently. However, contrary to their prior expectations, several students did not enter the labour market but enrolled for another course and thus, some of what we know about the Dalit experience comes from informants who were still in graduate school.

The present chapter follows all of our respondents—Dalit and non-Dalit alike—for a period of about two years. For those who were in university for the duration, we have learned about their anticipatory experience as they prepare for work. But many respondents, particularly the Dalit students who are from poorer backgrounds, took jobs during their student years and hence already had significant employment experience. Finally, many had already landed full-time positions before graduating and hence had considerable knowledge of the matching process even if they had not been on the job yet.

The baseline questionnaire was administered to an initial sample of 108 students from Delhi University (all in economics), Jawaharlal Nehru University, and Jamia Millia Islamia (in mixed disciplines) in April 2005. Given that Dalit students were a small proportion of the Delhi University sample (owing to a low number of reservation students who met the rigorous minimum entrance standards and the high dropout rates from the economics programme[5]), we added a second cohort of students in April 2006 from Delhi University (again in economics) and from a mix of disciplines at Jawaharlal Nehru University and Jamia Millia Islamia, with matching Dalit and non-Dalit students in each disciplinary 'cell'.

The first follow-up was conducted in November–December 2006, which is roughly a year and a half after the baseline survey for the first part of the sample, and roughly six months after the baseline survey for the second part of the sample. Common to longitudinal studies everywhere, retaining our respondents has been a challenge. While at the time of the baseline survey, all respondents willingly gave their contact information, by the time we pursued them for the first follow-up survey, we found that either their contact information had changed or they were simply unreachable. Moreover, contrary to our initial (and their professed) expectation, not everyone from the initial sample entered the job market. Some failed to graduate and among those who dropped out without the diploma, we were unable to contact any of the reservation students.[6] Some decided to repeat the final year of the Master's programme in order to improve their grades and for this reason did not enter the job market. However, this latter group is contactable and is included in the follow-up survey.

Our sample is primarily drawn from the three national universities: Delhi University (Masters' students in economics), Jawaharlal Nehru University (different disciplines) and Jamia Millia Islamia (different disciplines).[7] These three universities would be considered among the best universities in India by any measure. It would be a reasonable guess that these universities enjoy a 10 per cent acceptance rate. Even more gruelling would be the Indian Institutes of Technology, which are on par with Massachusetts Institute of Technology or Cal Tech in the US. But the institutions from which we have recruited our sample are next in line in the hierarchy of Indian higher education.

| TABLE 3.1: Sample Composition | | | |
|---|---|---|---|
| | Non-reserved | Reserved | Total |
| Jawaharlal Nehru University | 31 | 33 | 64 |
| Jamia Millia Islamia | 9 | 5 | 14 |
| Delhi University | 83 | 9 | 92 |

All the students in our sample completed their undergraduate programmes and we have information about their final exam performance, that is, whether they qualified with a first (60 per cent and above), second (50–59 per cent), or a third (40–49 per cent) division. We consider this data first since it helps us to determine just how closely matched the two groups (reservation and non-reservation students) actually are.

We find significant differences in undergraduate academic background. Fewer Dalit students had first class honours in their undergraduate degrees than non-reservation students (40 per cent versus 46.3 per cent) but this gap was not as large as one might have expected, owing no doubt to the selection pressure induced by minimum scores on the post-secondary entrance exams. For both groups, most had entered their postgraduate training with second-class undergraduate degrees (57.14 per cent of Dalit students, and 53.7 per cent of non-reservation students).

Over half of non-reservation students reported previous job experience, compared to about one-third of Dalit students. Non-reservation students were also more likely to report various computer skills. Most students had computer word-processing skills, but nearly 13 per cent of Dalit students (and only 7 per cent of non-Dalits) lacked that skill. Most students knew how to use Excel spreadsheet, but 27 per cent of Dalit students and 13 per cent of non-reservation students lacked those skills. Non-reservation students were also much more likely to have skills in constructing computer presentations with PowerPoint (79 per cent compared to 55 per cent of Dalit students.)

Since Royster's respondents were in several ways atypical, she believes that her sample may have reflected 'creaming' because the 'sample may reflect those who were most likely to rise to the top or be seen as the cream of the crop, rather than those of average or mixed potential'. This is an advantage in her study since she deliberately sought to compare black and white men with as much potential for success as possible. Our Indian sample is part of the 'creamy layer': it too captures students with a very high potential of success given their educational background. However, the selection is operating at different levels of human capital. The Indian study is looking at the very top of the educational hierarchy, where students are all aiming for the professional labour market.

## PRELIMINARY RESULTS

The analyses include 173 students who were completing postgraduate degrees from three universities in the Delhi area. Over half (53 per cent) were graduating from the MA programme in economics from Delhi University. Most of the remaining students (38 per cent) were completing degrees at Jawaharlal Nehru University. About 35 per cent were women and 65 per cent were men.

Nearly 28 per cent were reserved category students. Reserved category students were disproportionately men: 83 per cent of the reserved category students, compared to 58 per cent of non-reservation students, were men. In terms of religious or communal background, for the sample as a whole, 71 per cent were Hindus and 12.7 per cent were Muslims. The remaining of students were Sikhs, Buddhists, Christians, and Jains.

Reservation students were found in all the religions other than Jainism. All of the Buddhist students, 60 per cent of the Sikhs, 27

per cent of Muslims, and 25 per cent of Hindus and 14 per cent
of Christians were reservation students. These percentages are based
on respondents' self-reporting about their eligibility for reservations.
These percentages diverge from what we would obtain based on
official reservation policy. Reservation applies mainly to Hindu and
Sikh SCs and not to Muslims and Christians, even if they are marked
by caste internally within their faith.[8]

## Diverging Expectations

Long before our sample confronted the labour market, their
expectations of what they would find diverged by reservation/non-
reservation status. These students were in the final months of their
postgraduate studies, and hence, had given considerable thought to
their job prospects. In bivariate comparisons, graduating reservation
students had significantly lower occupational expectations than
their non-reservation counterparts. The average expected monthly
salary for reservation students was Rs 19,510, while non-reservation
students expected to earn about Rs 24,470. The median salary for
the non-reservation students was Rs 22,500 and that for the reserved
category students was Rs 15,000. While the average salary for the
reserved group was lower, the variability (spread) of expected salary
was higher.

We asked each student to describe their ideal job but also to tell
us what job they realistically expected to find. The contrasts between
reservation and non-reservation students in terms of expectations
were sharp. The majority of Dalit students listed jobs in the public
sector: 45 per cent mentioned Administrative Services/Indian Police
Service (IPS), and another 28 per cent stated that they could ideally
seek jobs as teachers or academics or researchers. This reflects the
operation of the affirmative action policy that is applicable only to
public sector enterprises and leaves the private sector completely
untouched.

Non-reservation students were much more likely to report an ideal
job as a business analyst or corporate planner (19 per cent of non-
reservation students compared to 9 per cent of Dalit students) or in
the social or development sector (15 per cent compared to 2 per cent
for Dalit students). Relatively few non-reservation students viewed

the Administrative Services as an ideal job (12 per cent compared to 45 per cent of Dalit students).

The largest area of overlap in terms of ideal job was in teaching, academic, and researcher jobs: many non-reservation students thought that ideal (30 per cent), as did 28 per cent of Dalit students. Also confirming the lower expectations of Dalit students, a small minority of Dalit students (2 per cent) thought of clerical type office jobs as ideal whereas none among the non-Dalit students did.

There was a big disparity, for both categories, between their ideal job and the job they realistically expected to get. This is hardly surprising in view of the enormous glut of well educated but unemployed or underemployed men and women in India. A large number of non-reservation students expected to find work as business analysts and planners (19 per cent), while only 9.2 per cent of Dalits had this expectation. Many non-reservation students also expected to find work as teachers, or academics, or researchers (29.5 per cent), but the proportion of reservation students expecting to find work in those occupations was slightly higher (30.5 per cent).

Surprisingly, even though few Dalit students had listed Planning or Development as their ideal job, only about 2.4 per cent listed this as the most realistic kind of job they thought they would actually find. The expectation among Dalit postgraduates that they would find jobs in the public sector is further confirmed by the proportion who had taken the requisite civil service exams. At the time of the baseline survey, far more reservation students (nearly 67 per cent) had taken the civil service exam than non-reservation students (34 per cent).

## Family Businesses, Family Connections, and Parental Education

The differential ability of reservation and non-reservation students to benefit from family resources—ranging from business as where they might find employment, to social networks that could be activated in the search for employment, to the cultural capital (or 'know how') that will help inform a student of advantageous options—is very pronounced. For example, nearly 18 per cent of non-reservation students said that someone in their family owned a business where the student might be employed compared to only 8.5 per cent of reservation students.

Students were asked whether they expected to rely on family connections in finding a job. About 20 per cent of non-reservation students said they were likely to use family connections for this purpose, compared to about 10 per cent of Dalit students. These two findings parallel Royster's observations about the advantages white men can call on in turning to friends and family members for employment in the small business sector.

Differences in family background (measured by parents' occupations) for the two groups of students are quite stark. The occupational distribution of fathers of the non-reservation students shows that the single largest category (16.5 per cent) is either self-employed or in big business. Thereafter, we find fathers who are managers or in the banking sector or have taken Voluntary Retirement Scheme (VRS) (11.5 per cent each). Ten per cent of the fathers are doctors, engineers, software engineers, or in the information technology (IT) sector. Another 10 per cent are farmers. Smaller proportions (around 5 per cent each) are lawyers or chartered accountants and academics/researchers.

In contrast, the fathers of almost 33 per cent of reservation students are farmers. This is followed by 15 per cent of the fathers who are academics/researchers, and lawyers and chartered accountants (9 per cent each). 8.6 per cent are government servants or members of the civil service. Other than farming, all the other professions either have reservation quotas for public sector jobs or the courses that lead to these occupations (medicine, engineering, law) can be pursued in government institutions via quotas. There is a small proportion, roughly 4 per cent each, in the development sector and manager/banking.

Students were asked if their mother was working outside the home. Fifty-eight per cent of the non-reservation students had non-working mothers compared to 81 per cent of Dalit students. Thus, an overwhelming majority of Dalit students in our sample come from single-income families. The distribution of occupations for mothers who are working is much wider for the non-reservation students as compared to the Dalit students.

Reading this together with the disparities in the parental education level, we can get a sense of how different the family background for the two sets of students is. As the qualitative section shows, family background plays a huge role in the selection process during job interviews.

## Job Search

Both reservation and non-reservation students searched for jobs in similar ways—using university-sponsored placement cells, answering newspaper advertisements, submitting résumés by mail and over the web, turning to family connections and off-campus 'head hunters' or placement firms. However, reservation students were significantly less likely to use campus job fairs or placement cells and were significantly more likely to depend on newspaper ads than their non-reservation counterparts. Again, this illustrates the preference for public sector/ government/university jobs on the part of Dalit students, as a lot of private sector jobs are not advertised and government/public sector organizations cannot recruit without advertising.

## Time to Find a Job

About 47 per cent of the non-reserved students expected to find their jobs in two months. Seventy-five per cent expected to find their job in eight months. Ninety-two per cent expected to find the job within a year. The maximum time quoted was two years. The average expected time was 5.25 months.

The expected time was, on the whole, longer for reservation students than 'general category' students. Forty-five per cent of the reserved students expected to find their ideal jobs in eight months. Eighty-two per cent of this category expected to find their jobs within a year. Ninety-one per cent of the sample expected to find a job within 18 months (as compared to 12 months for the general category). The average time expected was 9.6 months.

### Moving into the Labour Market

These group differences are clearly reflected in the follow-up interviews. We begin with the perceptions and experiences of the Dalit students and then contrast their perspectives on educational opportunity, labour market entry, and the political conflicts surrounding the extension of reservation policy to the private sector with those of their non-reservation counterparts.

## Reservations are Critical

Almost without exception, the Dalits in our sample endorsed the purpose of reservation policy and were convinced that without it, they would have had no chance to obtain a higher degree. 'I am here because of reservations', noted Mukesh, a political science student at Jawaharlal Nehru University.

Because of my background, even though I had the talent, I could not study because of financial problems. We never got a chance to buy books, to get tuition. But we got through because of reservations. I am ahead by a few steps because of reservations. There is nothing wrong with that.

Indeed, for Mukesh, quotas in higher education not only enabled his ascent in the university world, it literally enabled him and his fellow reservation students to 'open their mouths', meaning speak their minds, and 'go to the centre of society', where they could 'meet other people…and get a platform'. The silence imposed by marginality, caste prejudice (enforced by atrocities, especially in rural areas), and poverty is broken by introducing these Dalit students to another world and a different future. They are well aware that without this social policy intervention, they could have remained stuck in a life that would never provide the kind of options they see before them now.

For those aware of the history of the political struggle that resulted in the creation of this quota system, reservation is seen as a noble commitment to equality, struck by the hero of the Dalit social movement, B.R. Ambedkar, the architect of the Indian Constitution. This lineage is sacred to Dalit students, for it represents the first victory in a long and unfinished struggle for human rights and full equality. As Bir Singh, another political science student at Jawaharlal Nehru University explained, that campaign remains as vital as ever as a source of inspiration for the poor and excluded:

Ambedkar…used his education to free the SC/ST and OBC and to…solve their problems…on the basis of equality, liberty and fraternity. He wanted to make them live with self respect and why he was able to do that? Because of education, because of the participation in this society in the form of reservation in every sphere of life.

Education has created an ideal image in the minds of those people who are illiterate...for example where a person (girl or boy) who comes from a rural area [can] enjoy taking reservation in education institutions. He is learning, reading and becoming a very high status profile person. That gives an example which...gives courage and pride to the rest of the illiterate, poor people, who are not getting [an] education, who are suppressed socially and educationally.

These opportunities are critical not only because they promote social mobility, but because reservations literally rescue Dalits from a lifetime of exploitation at the hands of landlords, abusive employers, and neighbours who can turn on them without provocation and remind them forcefully of their subordinate status. Legal guarantees in the form of anti-atrocity regulations mean nothing in the context of weak enforcement.

Karunanidhi, a student of history at Jawaharlal Nehru University, who comes from a rural area near Madurai in Tamil Nadu, is all too familiar with life under the heel. 'I am from a very remote background', he explained. Without reservations, he would have been stuck in a community where his safety was at risk.

In my [native] place...[it] is very brutal, very uncivilized. They can kill anybody for a simple reason...Because of reservations in higher education, I am here. I could not even imagine being here at Jawaharlal Nehru University without reservations....

After my graduation [from undergraduate school], I worked continuously from 6 to 8 hours [in a factory near his home]. If there is work, we have to work, we cannot delay. 'Sir, I am tired I worked so long!' You can't say that If they call you, you have to go and work there whether you are sick or not, whether your father is sick or not....This kind of exploitation is there....I was working in Tiruppur[9] [and the] rules and regulations of the company were on the wall...in English and Tamil. But whatever goes on in the company is just the opposite....There is no clean toilet...no hygienic environment [in the factory] for the workers.

The girls are really exploited by the [hiring] agents and higher positioned people in the factory. If these people asked girls to go to bed with them, they cannot [be] denied. They force the girls, though these people are educated. I think educated people do this kind of exploitation more than others.

Reservations rescued Karunanidhi from a future of this kind.

The policy has always been important to those at the bottom of a social pecking order that was resistant to change, grounded as it was in abiding caste hierarchies and the traditional, pernicious practice of pollution taboos that surrounded the lives of Untouchables, especially in the more remote rural regions of India. Today, however, the importance of reservations—and the fear that their impact may diminish—is heightened by the recognition that the public sector is shrinking. The one sphere where these students could hope to find respectable employment is shedding jobs as liberalization puts pressure on government budgets. Globalization is creating enormous opportunities for the Indian economy, all of which, by and large, fall into the private sector. High growth rates in corporate India have opened opportunities of the kind rarely seen before and it is common knowledge that the big money is to be made there. Increasingly the public sector is seen as a backwater of inefficiency, and students, who can manage it, are flocking to the high technology sector.

Our interview subjects were well aware of this trend and worried by it since reservations do not presently apply to the private sector. Even if they are willing to trade lucrative opportunities (that may or may not be available to them on the grounds of bias or skill) for the accessibility and security of the public sector, this alternative is disappearing. The solution, they argue is to see reservations extended to the private sector, to continue Ambedkar's mission of social justice to the domain where all the action is for the foreseeable future.

Amit, a political science student at Jawaharlal Nehru University, argued that 'both sectors should have reservation'.

Now in India, it is the private sector that is getting bigger. Even in Delhi, just see the size of the public sector, it is very small. So SC/ST, OBC and minorities should all get reservations. If they don't…where will these people adjust?

This view was universally shared by the Dalit students for whom reservations policy is nothing more than a form of social engineering designed to address centuries of oppression and discrimination, extreme inequities in the distribution of educational opportunity, and the formation of a huge class of Indian citizens who are not equipped to compete without this assistance. These are not matters of history. Students cite countless examples from their own experience where they have been interrogated about their caste identities, castigated by prospective employers for their support of reservations, subjected to harassment or disrespect, and denied jobs (as far as they know) solely on account of their caste background.

As long as this injustice persists, they argue, reservations will be needed. The policy levels the playing field at the vital choke points of social mobility. They are not special privileges that unfairly advantage Dalits; they are compensation for historic and contemporary injustice that creates some measure of equality in outcomes. As Bhim, a reservation student studying Korean at Jawaharlal Nehru University, points out, social engineering is necessary to modernize the country, to move it past a traditionalist, antiquated social system ridden with superstitious beliefs that are themselves anti-meritocratic. 'Because of reservations', he notes, 'people of backward classes are developing'.

I think there should be reservation in both private and public sectors. Upper caste people are holding important positions in both sectors. In the public sector, all the positions at the top level are held by upper caste people and they are also filling these positions with their relatives. If we are getting any jobs, we are getting only low level jobs.

Reservation is being misused by some people like one of my classmates, who was from the general category [but] made fake certificates [for himself] of SC/ ST and captured one seat that [was supposed to be] for SC candidates. So there is need of proper implementation of policy. [Still], because of this policy, people are coming from remote areas, they are getting admission, doing their courses and progressing well in their lives.

Of course, these students are aware that their sense of legitimacy is not shared by the dominant classes and castes in India. Reservations policy is condemned for punishing innocent non-reservation students for the damage done in the past, reinforcing caste lines rather than striving for a caste-free society, and exempting Dalits from the rigours of market competition. Critics argue that reservations replace one form of discrimination (against Dalits) with another, equally pernicious form (against non-reserved students or workers).

However, these perspectives are unconvincing from the viewpoint of our reservation interviewees, who argue that the most powerful special privileges actually accrue to high-caste Hindus who can tap into exclusive social networks, bank on the cultural capital their families bequeath to them, or pay the bribes that are demanded by employers for access to jobs. As Rajesh, a student of Korean language and culture at Jawaharlal Nehru University, notes, these forms of advantage are never criticized as unfair:

Some people get admission in medical [school] after giving Rs 25–30 lakh [in bribes]....They don't get admission on the basis of capability. The entry of these people is not ever opposed, but people are against the SC/ST/OBCs who get in on quota. They say that these SC/ST/OBC doctors are [incompetent], leaving their scissors and thread inside the patients' bodies during surgery. But people who [gain] admission through capitation fees, paying huge donations, why are these things [not] said about them?

## Entry into the Labour Market

At the time this study was undertaken, 73 per cent of the reserved students were still enrolled in advanced degree programmes at the three universities from which the sample was taken. However, given the needs they face to support themselves and their families, they are often seasoned in the ways of the labour market even at this juncture. In this section, we examine their experiences to date, for they lay the groundwork—both in terms of expectation formation and actual employment—for the more intense exposure to the competitive matching process to come when they seek positions commensurate with their educational credentials.

Our first observation is that despite their position as students from elite universities seeking employment, they are reminded at every turn that caste matters in the eyes of the hiring managers. For many civil service positions, the lists of candidates to be interviewed are organized by caste and the information is not received in a neutral or respectful fashion. Om Prakash, a sociology student at Jawaharlal Nehru University, applied for a teaching position—one of the 1500 positions advertised that year. 'They had written in the list...in a bracket [next to my name] "SC"'.

Some [interviewers] were asking something of the SC candidates, but some other person was talking like this 'yeah, one knows how much talent they are having and what they can do' [sarcastically, derisively].

Many complained that they would present themselves for job interviews only to discover that they were never given serious consideration, that the selection process had been unfair. Some said that the interview had clearly been a formality as the selection committee members had already made up their minds and hence the questions they were asked were over irrelevant matters having no bearing on the job at issue.

Several of the Dalit respondents explained that because they lack 'push' (pull) it was clear that they had no chance. An influential network of supporters is required to push ahead of the crowd for desirable jobs both in the public or private sector. At times money is the issue. Bribery is reportedly quite widespread. One respondent reports giving Rs 10,000 for a job he did not get and explained that he was unable to get the money back. For most of these students, jobs known to require bribes are simply off limits: they do not have the money and cannot apply. Chandrabhan, a politics student at Jawaharlal Nehru University, applied for a civil service position in a Panchayat (council) in the district headquarters of his home village. He was required to submit the application at the home of the council's headman rather than the official office. But when he tried to get information on the requirements of the post through his father, the headman excoriated his father for thinking that his son, though highly qualified, would be seriously considered:

He told my papa, 'Why is [that boy] going for that job?' Actually, some influential people were going for that job, he told us. You cannot give money; you need to give a lot of money. That was really a shock for me. Someone like me goes for a job, then you get such a response.

Even perfectly legal hiring practices impose barriers on Dalit students from poor backgrounds. For example, travelling to an interview may be prohibitively expensive. Rakesh sat through three examinations for jobs with the national railway company and when called for interviews, could not afford the expense of staying overnight or paying for his food. 'One interview was in Calcutta', he explained, 'another was in Guwahati. I had to go there and stay there and have meals there. For this, I needed money that I was not having, so I could not attend that interview'.

The signals of persistent caste barriers can be subtle as well as direct. Employers recognize the signal of surnames that are caste identified and it is known that names trigger questions during interviews that non-Dalits are never asked. In particular, when private sector employers raise pointed questions about the legitimacy of reservation policy, a policy that presently does not apply to these firms, students are placed on the defensive. They are being asked, in so many words, to defend their own biographies.

Kabir, a reservation student in political science at Jawaharlal Nehru University, went for a job interview in a Delhi hotel in which this topic dominated the conversation:

They asked me...what is the caste system in India? I answered that Indian society is divided by caste and religion. So they asked me...should there be reservations for SC/ST. I answered because SC people are facing problems, they are being discriminated against, their positions is not good, they are backward. Why should there be this difference?...They said they have got reservation for 50 years, why should [this] continue? I said because they want to be equal with others, so that is why reservation should be there for some more years.

They said it is not fair because some SC/ST people are getting privileges. They don't have knowledge, they don't have talent. Taking admissions in good universities/colleges and then coming out [as if they were equivalent to] general category students. I said, madam, they are working hard because they are not in good position economically and socially. But it will take time to be equal to the others.

As reported elsewhere,[10] employers are given to asking questions of all applicants about their 'family background'. For students from non-reservation backgrounds, the questions appear innocuous, and indeed they are regarded by everyone as normal human resources practice. For reservation students, however, the answers they have to give, unless they are willing to lie, point directly to stigma. Their fathers do not have the kinds of occupations that confirm the student's suitability for professional jobs; their families are too large; and most of all, the student is burdened by demands for support from their families (a quality that might be regarded as positive in the US, for it denotes a responsible child, but seems to signal distraction or lack of flexibility in the Indian context).

Nathu Prasad, a politics student at Jawaharlal Nehru University, applied for a job at a national research centre. He expected to be asked 'about my NET [National Eligibility Test] exam or my MA, but there was no need to ask about my background, income source and all these things'. [11]

They asked me about my parents, what they do. So I said they own a small bit of land, they are farmers, but they also do small business. I got the feeling that I was being singled out for these kinds of questions. I later asked some other boys who were there and they said that they had not been asked. The psychological effect of those questions is very negative. Suppose you get selected. Then even after that, you will remain conscious since the person knows about your family background and that person may try to...exploit you.

I don't think that these questions were neutral....I knew the topic that I had to speak on, they knew my qualifications, so if they had asked about that I wouldn't have had any problem. Problem is that by asking other questions, they can find out about our 'low label'.

Nathu Prasad landed the job, but felt awkward that his family background factored into the equation; instead of being taken solely on his own merits, personal information that did not pertain to his qualifications was known by 'company strangers'.

Bidyut, a reserved category political science student at JNU, faced a harsh barrage over his family's circumstances following an equally discomfiting litany of remarks about reservations policy from the director of a research-oriented organization. Everything from his regional origins to his parental occupation was at issue:

Explain where you belong to [I was told]. I said I am from Orissa.[12] So how did you come here to Delhi?....He asked me so many questions about my caste, my family, about my questions. First he asked me, if you are from Orissa, why don't you settle down there....I said that in Orissa, the opportunities are very less, there is no chance [to make it]. I have been in Delhi already for one decade, so I want to join a job here because there are more opportunities. I am very interested in joining a good institute like yours. Then he asked: tell me about your background, what does your father do? I told him I come from a very poor background. My father was a farmer, he died recently. Now my mother is there, my elder brother is there. I am very much responsible for my family, so I want to earn some money.

The director went on to imply that someone from his background should be applying elsewhere, forcing Bidyut on the defensive to make the case for why he should be considered at all. It was made clear that people who come from his family background are not welcome:

You people are struggling for life, so you are not that competent, [he told me]. I answer that is not true....They don't like SC/ST candidates in the private sector.

Dalit students are aware much before their graduation from higher degree courses that these barriers are out there in the labour market. For some, concern runs so high that they decide to conceal the truth in hopes of landing the jobs they want. Arshad, a computer science student at Jamia Millia Islamia, knew that he would face discrimination on this basis and hence reconfigured his biography to look less stereotypically lower caste:

Family background was asked, but I did not tell them the reality, that we are six brothers and sisters. I told them that I have one brother and one sister. They asked me 'What is your father?' I told them he is a teacher. I thought it could have some positive impact because my family background will look like a small family and father is a teacher.

It is a sad irony that in order for reservations policy to work in education and public employment, caste identity must be affixed to qualify. SC status is made clear in official records from high school graduation certificate to university files. If this knowledge was merely part of a bureaucratic record, the story would stop at that. But it becomes part of a moral narrative in which the student's right to the education he has received, his genuine talents, and his fitness for a job are questioned by those who hold negative assumptions on all three counts. In a society where educational opportunity is extremely scarce relative to the demand, in which good jobs are highly coveted since there are too few for all of the qualified people seeking them, the job interview becomes more than a means of matching applicants to positions. It becomes an occasion for political debate that throws Dalit students on the defensive.

## THE OTHER SIDE OF THE FENCE

Royster (2003) chronicles the embittered views of white working class students in the US who also face a competitive labour market in which opportunities have been shrinking, even for skilled blue-collared labour. Lacking much of a grasp of the structural dimensions of this shift, her white interviewees relapse into a politics of blame, focusing on affirmative action and unfair racial preferences for minorities to explain declining opportunities. They certainly saw no particular advantages to being white, either in terms of the social networks they could rely on or in terms of employers' preferences.

Indian students—reserved and non-reserved alike—also face extraordinary competition for spaces in higher education and public/private employment. At the same time, India's unparalleled growth has opened up opportunities for university graduates and the sense throughout our interviews was that students with advanced degrees can look forward to a much better future than might have been true in the past. These truths coincide and help to explain the fractured nature of non-reserved students' opinion on their own opportunity structure, the legitimacy of 'set asides' in higher education and employment, and their views on the best use of available resources for creating equal opportunity. The fractures are best understood as a consequence of deep and pervasive inequality in primary and secondary education (acknowledged by virtually all non-reserved students) and the inherent competition for scarce 'mobility resources', coupled with pronounced advantages in India (and the US) for those at the top of the educational hierarchy.

Those inequalities are powerfully reflected in the overall experience of non-reserved (henceforth 'general' students) in the labour market. These respondents reported far more favourable interviews and selection procedures when job hunting than reserved students, as well as a more positive 'interpretive disposition'. By this we mean that matching procedures that reserved and general students both experience are interpreted by the former as indicative of questionable intent, while experienced as neutral or even positive by general students.

Few general students were asked about their caste or religious background.[13] This was clearly a difference that mattered, but it must be noted that many reserved students were not asked about caste either. Their surnames signal their caste membership in many instances, and questions on family background reveal the rest. When asked about their family background, general students saw the questions as neutral in intent and/or an opportunity for them to shine because their families are more middle class in size and occupational background. They were able to bring to bear on the job interview, fluency in English, confidence in their academic skills, and advanced knowledge of what they would be expected to demonstrate in the way of 'fitness for the firm' than Dalit students, whose cultural capital was weaker.

General students did not see themselves as privileged because of these qualities, even if they recognized that the distribution of these skills was differential. These are merely the talents that firms are looking for, including ease in social situations like interviews. This parallels one of Royster's findings that white men did not see themselves as advantaged, but rather as the neutral case.

## Job Interviews

Bharat, a sociology student at Jawaharlal Nehru University, typified the reaction of general students to their job interview experience. It was an occasion overlaid with tension, because an evaluation is in progress. But on the whole, interviews are a learning experience, not a test of cultural fitness:

> …the interview…teaches you a lot to handle the tension.…Just adjusting to the ambience, the environment of the interview, helps a lot. So many questions are asked and one question is followed by another. You need to keep our mind cool enough in special circumstances.

The only negative experience Bharat could remember from his many rounds of interviews was one where he was 'asked to come at 10 a.m. and the interview began at 1:30 p.m.' This was a 'bitter experience', he noted.

General students experienced a problem that many reserved students interpreted as caste discrimination: the wired interview. For general students, the idea that a job has already been handed over to an inside candidate or someone with social connections superior to their own is a recognized fact. It happens all the time. Preeti, an economics student from the Delhi School of Economics, described the experience in detail:

> I went to another college [for an interview]. There was an internal candidate, so she was given the job and my interview lasted only 2–3 minutes. It was virtually decided that she had to be taken in. [The interview] was a formality for me. I did ask my professor [who was on the interview board] 'You won't ask anything else?' He said, 'Yes, I won't ask anything.' They were not treating me seriously. I

know because just 15 days [before] I faced [an interview at another college] and the interview lasted a complete half hour and [I was] asked lots of questions.

Preeti did not understand this experience as a commentary on her fitness; indeed, she regarded herself as perfectly well qualified, but outmanoeuvred. The wired interview does not lead general students to believe that they will be shut out of upward mobility. If anything, it indicates to them that they too must cultivate their networks. For the Dalit student, a wired interview is one more piece of evidence that they are going to face a very long uphill struggle for mobility because they do not have easy access to the 'inside track'.

The value of cultural capital, of understanding the social skills that need to be on display in an interview cannot be overstated. With so many applicants qualified on the grounds of skills and knowledge, Indian firms are looking for people who 'fit', a matching process noted by American researchers of the labour market as well.[14] For general students, a university education is often a continuation of a lifelong process of cultivation, not unlike what elite students in American ivy league universities experience. They move in to the task of job hunting with a degree of confidence that they have the social skills to function appropriately, to avoid being overly nervous, to project an air of cosmopolitanism that may be the final element that distinguishes them from other students with similar technical credentials.

Abhijit, a general category economics student from the Delhi School of Economics, described his experience with job interviews in tones strikingly different from even the most positive encounters among the Dalit students:

Most of my interviews are very relaxed. No one was assessing my knowledge or anything, but…seeing how well and efficiently I contribute to the company. So, positive feedback purely, in fact, that I had high success rate in terms of clearing interviews that is making me feel good. I was competitive enough to get a job later if I wanted to….

None of my interviews were stressful at all. They were all very friendly for me. For example, when I had my interview with [information firm], he asked me why I want to work in Bombay? That is one of the cities that never sleeps and lots of stuff to do there. So the interview was more in terms of what I like, what I dislike and general chit-chat about what I was looking to do in the future rather than quizzing me about, let's say, what particular topics I had done in a particular [academic] subject or something like that.

None of the Dalit students we interviewed expressed this kind of confidence. Even those who managed to land jobs were apprehensive and stressed by the interviews. They never had the feeling that their interests in the nightlife of the city where a firm was located was a centrepiece of conversation. Instead, they were often interrogated about their command of the academic subjects they had studied, and put on the defensive about the impact of the quota system.

Lacking cultural capital when they arrive in elite universities, Dalit students—especially those from rural backgrounds—are not in a position to improve their cultural exposure beyond what they acquire inside the university itself. This is not minimal. Indeed, coming to a place like Jawaharlal Nehru University from a remote tribal region does indeed create opportunities for exchange and personal growth in a cosmopolitan direction. But if one must work at the same time, it will be hard to take this any farther. Not so for non-reservation students who may have many opportunities to widen their horizons outside of the university during their years as students. Shreekant, a Delhi School of Economics student, commented on the ways in which he had been able to move outside of the university context to broaden himself:

What I expected, I got from my study at Dehli School....Other avenues...like travel, I got enough chances to travel around India or other places through the university. After some time, university education helped me to form a general (overall) understanding and also a social circle. Also helped me to gain general skills....

There are so many ingredients [to being successful]. The most important thing is the peer group. There is a circle of friends/acquaintances in which one gains confidence, learns skills. A person like this will get access easily and he can be identified as a suitable candidate. Now here the background is equally important. So things other than intelligence matter a lot. Most of these ingredients are acquired with money. So [a person's] economic background gives a lot of privileges and it becomes a requirement to access several things. But someone who is less qualified at entry can be trained and learn the requirements of the job.

## The Family Background Test

Virtually all of our study subjects reported being asked about their family backgrounds during employment interviews. Questions about where they come from, what their parents do for a living, the types of jobs their siblings do, and the like were very common. However, non-reservation students can offer biographies that are much closer to the middle class, professional ideal. Hence the questions are rarely interpreted as offensive or prying. And the answers are almost always in line with positive images of family life, as Aditya, a Delhi School of Economics student recounted:

A couple of people asked me about my family background, about what my father does, whether I have any siblings or what my mother does? No one asked me about my religion or caste. I told them that my dad is a government servant, he is working in the Indian Railways and my mom is also in the Bank of [my region]. My sister is a doctor. So that was more courtesy, interested kind of questions that the interviewer broached up. They made me more comfortable rather than judging me on what my parents do or not do. I am sure it did not make any negative kind of influence at all in my case. It might have had positive impact to see in terms of my parents are well educated and my sister is also well educated and everyone is doing well.

While Dalit students often perceive a hidden agenda in family background questions, for non-reservation students the same questions appear to be innocuous or sensible inquiries from a human resources perspective. They are not 'gotcha' questions designed to discredit an applicant who is presenting herself as an educated, highly trained proto-professional.[15] When asked, in our interviews, what these questions were there for, these students invariably had answers that made the whole subject seem completely uncomplicated. For example, Ashok, a general category economics student of the Delhi School of Economics noted:

Yes I was asked about family background. Where do you come from? What is your family business? I tell them I come from UP and my family is in agriculture....

When asked as to what he thought they were trying to get at, he replied:

Maybe they were trying to understand if I will stay on in the organization or leave soon. Because the one major problem that companies face is attrition. So, they do need a bit of an idea....They try and gauge if I will stay or not looking at a variety of factors. The way I told them, it should have been positive information for them. Or at least I felt that way. They must have thought that I will work there.

It is impossible to judge who has the 'right story', on family background from these interviews and it is not clear that they are contradictory either. It is entirely possible that family background questions are used to identify caste or other background information that would be disqualifying in the eyes of employers who are not willing to employ Dalit applicants, or applicants with particularly needy families. It is also quite possible that human resource practice inclines firms to ask questions that help them ascertain the risks of attrition. The questions themselves do not provide a window on what they are used for when the winnowing process begins.

Yet if we couple these findings with the observations from studies of employer interviews (see Jodhka and Newman 2009), there is some reason for concern that family background is used to 'ratify' the claims presented on the surface by a job candidate to be a 'suitable person' for a position, with siblings whose trajectories confirm his or her own 'impression management' (to use Erving Goffman's well-known term). To the extent that this is the case, being able to give a socially acceptable answer about parental occupation or family size will be helpful. The converse could knock an otherwise qualified candidate out.

## Equal Opportunity

Two distinct positions were evident among non-reservation students with respect to quotas aimed at increasing the representation of Dalits, STs, and OBCs in higher education and employment. The first simply rejects the notion that this is appropriate at all, since reservation policy is deemed to be a violation of fairness principles and, therefore, an unfair tipping of the scales in what is meant to be a competition on the basis of merit. A variant of this view sees quotas as perfectly appropriate, but not if given along caste lines. Instead, economic deprivation or social backwardness should be the appropriate test. Here we see lines of convergence with many Dalit students from rural areas who also resent the application of reservation to 'the creamy layer' within their own caste.

The second recognizes the legitimacy and purpose of reservation and seems to be enhanced by the interactive relations between Dalit and high-caste students. The more conservative posture falls in line with Royster's findings among white working class students. The more liberal position emerges from contact and social relations that may be the positive byproduct of desegregation. Indeed, when advocates in the US argue for diversity in higher education, they make the point that mixing students up and insuring that classrooms represent a rainbow of experience will enrich learning and create tolerance. Both outcomes are clear in our sample.

Akhilesh, a sociology general student from Jawaharlal Nehru University, exemplifies the conservative reaction to quotas. 'I am not very happy with the Indian government actually bringing in such reservation', he complained.

I feel that the people who actually need it the most do not get it. There should be a proper identification of who needs it. Since it is absolutely impossible for the Indian government to develop the skill to look for such people, they are giving it to the wrong people. Implementing it means they are actually dividing society. When we are looking for harmony, we are looking towards unity, being in the same country.

I think such barriers should not be allowed because when we are competing, we should compete on the basis of merit. Today one person is getting into IIT [Indian Institute of Technology[16]] with no brains whatsoever, just by virtue of reservations. Whereas certain excellent students are not getting into IIT because general quota is full....

In jobs, also the same thing. Somebody who is an SC...gets the job and somebody like me who is not getting a job because I don't have any caste certificate....It should be equal because we are all living in the same country. If you can really identify the poorest people who have very low annual income... I think then there is some reason to support reservation.

As this quote suggests, Akhilesh objects to reservations on a number of grounds. First and foremost, they are benefiting a generation whose parents have already moved up in the social structure and have been able to give them benefits denied to other, much poorer, and more remote young people. Second, unqualified students are displacing highly qualified students in the race to the top of the educational heap. Many who share this view argue strenuously that the application of reservations will destroy the competitiveness of the Indian economy and drive away foreign investors because of the privileges ensured by reservation. Hence they fuse personal exclusion with a national downfall in the making.

Other critics of reservations argue that the policy may indeed be positive—in the sense that it redresses tremendous inequities—but ends up being a colossal waste because the high dropout rates that SC and ST students suffer from negates their impact. These reserved places could have been taken by non-reservation students who would complete their demanding courses, but instead are taken by people who have almost no chance, by virtue of poor preparation. Kavita, an economics student at Delhi University, was sympathetic in many ways to the cause of reducing inequality, but discouraged by the outcomes on both sides. 'When I was a student', she explained, 'there were about 80 of us in college. Out of these, about 20 were from the quota'.

But by the time we reached the third year, virtually all of the reserved students dropped out, because they could not clear [pass] the courses....Reservation should be given to them only in things that help them gain employment. If the cut-off [on entrance exams] is 90 per cent and you are admitting a person with 35 or 40 per cent in a course like economics, medical, or engineering, you very well know that he/she cannot be. He is not fit to clear the course.

This student went on to explain that forms of social segregation inside the universities did not help matters. 'They are not treated well', she remembered, 'when they go to colleges'.

[SC/ST students] have separate tables to lunch in college [dorms]. They get separate treatment. I don't know whether these people actually gain out of these quotas because there is lots of stress. OK, there have been people who completed their degree, but see in our college, there were hardly any....General category students who were eligible could not get admission and had to go to other colleges or get into worse courses....So this reservation policy is not achieving its objectives at all.

What is the value, she asks, of a policy that produces dropouts and deprives the capable of a place because they lack a quota on their side? This is a view many non-reservation students embrace.

But they are not a monolithic voice. On the other side of the equation are non-reserved students, for whom equality is a high principle and the barriers to achieving it for historically oppressed peoples clear enough. They embrace the purpose of reservation and see in it the possibilities of upward mobility. Among these supporters, there are differences of opinion nonetheless about the effectiveness of reservations for some of the same reasons that critics voice: high dropout rates. The lesson to be learned for these more progressive students, though, is not to abandon reservations, but redouble efforts to address educational inequality at much younger ages. Without a massive commitment to improving primary school education, they argue, we cannot really expect reservations to succeed. If not for reasons of equity, then for reasons of efficiency, differential investment is required.

## CONCLUSION

Following the lead of Royster (2003), this study traces the differential pathways that Dalit and non-Dalit students, from comparable, elite educational backgrounds, traverse in their journey from college to work. As was true in Royster's study, students from these two groups bring very different levels of resources—in the form of family connections, financial security during their university years, obligations to support parental households, and the like—to the starting gate. Hence while the training these two groups receive in the university world, and the credentials they can claim when they finish, are quite comparable, Dalit students lack many advantages that turn out to be crucial, and are subject to scepticism on the part of employers who doubt the legitimacy of reservations (and by extension, the legitimacy of the credentials they present during the job search).

Perhaps as a result, Dalit students from comparable degree programmes as their high-caste counterparts have lower expectations and see themselves as disadvantaged because of their caste and family backgrounds. Because they arrive in college with weaker skills on average, they are 'playing catch up' and often do not succeed in pulling even with more advantaged students, and hence enter the job markets with weaker English language and computing skills.

Dalit support for affirmative action in both higher education and jobs is unanimous and overwhelming, against the backdrop of discriminatory tendencies and their relative handicaps. At the same time, many (though hardly all) join many of their non-reservation counterparts in arguing that either reservations should be more targeted (toward poor and rural Dalits, rather than second or third generation recipients of quota admissions, who are viewed as an internal 'creamy layer') or that reservations should be coupled with generous financial aid. The search for the 'truly disadvantaged' continues in India, with complex political agendas in the mix.[17]

Expectedly, the ideal jobs for the Dalit students are either administrative/civil service or teaching jobs, which are subject to reservation quotas, while high caste students tend to look to the private sector, where wages are quite a bit higher. This may reflect an anticipatory sense of where reservation students will be welcome, or at least find a 'fair shake'. It may also reflect family traditions. In any case, the implications for earnings over the life course are non-trivial. Dalit students who find themselves in public service will undoubtedly see more security, but at much lower wages.

Reservation students experience their employment interviews in a far more negative vein than their non-reserved counterparts. Dalit students often felt that these interviews were pro forma or were put on the defensive because of their caste background, even for private sector jobs, which are not subject to quotas and where caste is not supposed to matter.

Direct questions about caste affiliation are rare for both Dalit and non-Dalit students, but the catch-all question on 'family background' is extensively used by employers to gauge the social and economic status of the applicant. One sees a clear class divide among Dalits, with those from rural backgrounds with relatively less educated parents at a clear disadvantage compared to their urban, second or third generation affirmative action beneficiary, counterparts. Financial constraints are a serious stumbling block for rural Dalits and the good fortune of admission to the university is followed by significant financial burdens both for self-support and for contributions to their natal families' survival.

Non-Dalit students do not see themselves as relatively advantaged. They display a sense of confidence and optimism about the job opportunities that the rapidly growing, globalizing Indian economy is providing to them. In sharp contrast to the Dalit students, their experiences during job interviews, on the whole, are extremely positive, even in cases where they do not get the job. Even though they regarded the question as neutral, their family background places them in a favourable setting during the interview. There are two clear views on quotas among the non-Dalits—one, expectedly, in sharp opposition, but the other, the more progressive view, more cognizant of disparities and discrimination, recognizing the need for reservations but arguing for better focus and outreach.

Our study so far suggests that social and cultural capital (the complex and overlapping categories of caste, family background, network, and contacts) play a huge role in the urban, formal sector labour markets, where hiring practices are less transparent than appear at first sight. While Dalits are severely disadvantaged in this setting, an effective affirmative action programme has the potential to turn things around. In the Indian context, legislative victories, now a little more than 60 years in duration, are not likely to be undone, particularly not in the face of continuing inequalities by caste. The question is whether the remedies will be extended to the fast growing private sector or fade in a numerical sense as the public sector shrinks.

## NOTES

1. Royster uses the case study method (in contrast to the existing studies that rely on survey and archival data) to answer, what she calls, the 'how' and 'why' questions: causal factors in processes or events that develop over time. As Royster points out, the case study approach, which differs from aggregate level surveys and intimate ethnographic methodologies, nevertheless combines aspects of both. This is because it relies on semi-structured interviewing techniques that use some of the same questions with all subjects but allow for considerable unstructured discussion between the interviewer and the respondents.

2. The William T. Grant Foundation issued an influential book in 1998 entitled *The Forgotten Half: Pathways to Success for America's Youth*

*and Young Families* (W.T. Grant Foundation Commission on Work, Family and Citizenship), in which they drew attention to the wholly inadequate educational and training options for non-college bound youth in America.

3. We have used the term non-reserved for symmetry.

4. Our research design consists of administering a baseline questionnaire that respondents completed while they were still students but were very close to graduating. The plan is to track these students with a follow-up questionnaire at periodic intervals that has more focused questions about their job search efforts, interview experiences, and if they have found a job, details about their job, about their job satisfaction, and their overall views about the affirmative action policy.

5. Because the dropout rate of Dalit students is very high, by the time they reach the final semester, it is impossible to match the non-Dalit numbers with the Dalit numbers.

6. Given the difficulties of reaching those who dropped out, it is reasonable to surmise that the data presented in this chapter represents a best case scenario for the Dalit respondents, since they are—on average—likely to be doing better than those we could not contact, who left the university without completing their degrees.

7. We also have two students from the Indira Gandhi National Open University (IGNOU), a distance learning university.

8. In several surveys, Christians and Muslims report themselves as OBCs and/or deserving of reservations. It needs to be noted that this reflects their self-perception about their relative disadvantage and/or discrimination towards their communities rather than the actual reservation policy. In the case of Muslims, it is more complicated because the government OBC list does include some Muslim *jatis*.

9. Tiruppur is a rapidly growing, important garment production/assembly centre in Tamil Nadu.

10. See Surinder S. Jodhka and Katherine S. Newman (2010).

11. Passing the NET (National Eligibility Test), an all-India examination conducted by the University Grants Commission, is a necessary condition to apply for the job of lecturer (assistant professor). For higher level teaching jobs (reader, professor), one is exempt from this examination.

12. One of the poorest states in India.

13. Although caste affiliation can often be identified by the use of occupationally connected surnames, religious background is much more apparent from last names.

14. See Kirshenman and Neckerman (1991).

15. Erving Goffman (1961). Goffman uses the term 'discrediting' information when describing the fault lines in an interactive setting that occur when someone makes a gaff and inadvertently reveals that their claims to a particular identity are false.

16. Indian Institutes of Technology (IITs) are extremely prestigious engineering schools. They were established explicitly with the purpose of providing cutting edge training in engineering and other science programmes. Admission into IITs is highly competitive: the acceptance rate for undergraduate courses is about 1 in 55, with about 300,000 annual entrance test takers for 5500 seats across the seven IITs. For SC/ST students, the cut-off for the entrance exam is lowered by 5 per cent. IITs are not bound to fill the quota: in 2004, 112 out of 279 seats for ST and 11 out of 556 seats for SC were left vacant.

17. Were this to be explored fully, one would have to take seriously the claim that urban Dalits from civil servant families are relatively advantaged over their poor, rural counterparts, but still have a significant disadvantage in competing for managerial and professional jobs compared to their high caste counterparts. The parallel point has been made in the US context. Some have complained that middle and upper class black students are given the benefit of affirmative action, while poor whites are not. Yet the proponents of affirmative action have argued that middle class blacks continue to face racial barriers and are less economically secure than their middle class white counterparts, owing to wealth differences (controlling for income). See esp. Conley (1999).

## References

Conley, Dalton (1999), *Being Black: Living in the Red: Race, Wealth and Social Policy in America*, Berkeley: University of California Press.

Goffman, Erving (1961), *The Presentation of Self in Everyday Life*, New York: Doubleday.

Jodhka, Surinder S. and Katherine S. Newman (2010), 'In the Name of Globalization: Meritocracy, Productivity, and the Hidden Language of Caste', in Sukhadeo Thorat and Katherine S. Newman (eds), *Blocked by Caste: Economic Discrimination in Modern India*, New Delhi: Oxford University Press, pp. 52–87.

Kirshenman, Joleen and Kathryn Neckerman (1991), '"We'd Love to Hire them, But...": The Meaning of Race for Employers', in Christopher Jencks and Paul Peterson (eds), *The Urban Underclass*, Washington DC: The Brookings Institution, pp. 203–34.

Madheswaran, S. and Paul Attewell (2010), 'Wage and Job Discrimination in the Indian Urban Labour Market', in Thorat and Newman (eds), *Blocked by Caste*, pp. 123–47.

Oliver, Melvin and Thomas Shapiro (2006), *Black Wealth/White Wealth: A New Perspective on Inequality*, 2nd edition, New York: Routledge.

Royster, Deirdre (2003), *Race and the Invisible Hand: How White Networks Exclude Black Men from Blue-collar Jobs*, Berkeley: University of California Press.

# 4

# Wage and Job Discrimination in the Indian Urban Labour Market

*S. Madheswaran and Paul Attewell*

Though the occupational placement of caste groups varies across India, a common feature is the sharp contrast in status and income between Scheduled Castes (SC) and Scheduled Tribes (ST) on the one hand, and so-called high castes (HC) on the other. Since Independence, the Indian government has sought to alleviate these inequalities by instituting affirmative action in political representation, higher education, and government and public sector employment. These policies reserve seats in the local and national legislatures for SC and ST applicants, and mandate a certain quota of jobs in the government and public sector for them.

Despite these efforts, the educational level of the SCs continues to lag behind that of the general population, and the overwhelming majority of the SC/ST population is still found in less-skilled and lower-paying jobs. This chapter examines inequalities in employment, occupation, and earnings, between SC/ST and HC Indians, and then statistically decomposes those gaps into separate components, one explainable through differences in factors such as education, and the other representing discrimination in employment and wages.

Many commentators acknowledge the prevalence of caste inequality in rural India, but believe that caste discrimination is much less important in urban India. Others believe that caste discrimination occurs primarily in operative jobs, but not in salaried white-collar positions. This chapter focuses upon inequality in the formal sector in urban India, and pays special attention to caste-related income and employment gaps among highly educated employees.

## SOURCES OF DATA

Data for this study comes from Round 38 (1983), Round 50 (1993–4), and Round 55 (1999–2000) of the all-India household survey conducted by the National Sample Survey Organisation (NSSO) of the Government of India. Our study confines itself to urban regular- or salaried-sector workers aged between 15 and 65 years old. In the first step, we selected sample of workers aged between 15 and 65 years old in the urban areas. In the second step, when we selected sample of regular or salaried sector workers, the age ranges between 21 and 65. For more information on the survey and sample design, see NSSO (1994, 2000). The wage distribution was trimmed by 0.1 per cent at the top and bottom tails. Nominal wages were converted to 1993 prices using an inflation index for wages of urban industrial workers (Consumer Price Index for Industrial Workers, CPIIW).

## THE DECOMPOSITION METHODOLOGY

Three different empirical approaches for studying caste discrimination can be found in prior research. The first of these includes caste as a predictor while predicting earnings from the characteristics of all workers (a single-equation technique). Unfortunately, this approach yields a biased result because it assumes that the wage structure is the same for both non-Scheduled castes (NSC) and SC/ST workers. It thus constrains the values of coefficients of explanatory variables, such as education and experience, to be the same for the SC/ST and the NSC population (Gunderson 1989; Madheswaran 1996).[1]

The second approach employs a 'decomposition technique' to partition the observed wage gap into an 'endowment' component and a 'coefficient' component. The latter is derived as an unexplained residual and is termed the 'discrimination coefficient'. This method was first developed by Blinder (1973) and Oaxaca (1973), and later extended to incorporate selectivity bias (Reimer 1983, 1985) and to overcome the index number problem (Cotton 1988; Neumark 1988; Oaxaca and Ransom 1994).

The third 'expanded approach' incorporates the occupational distribution into the earnings estimation, and was first proposed by Brown and others (1980). One advantage of using this expanded method is that both job discrimination (differential access to certain occupational positions) and wage discrimination (differential earnings within the same job) can be estimated simultaneously.

All three methods mentioned above are used here to estimate the extent of discrimination against lower caste workers in urban India. We have also contributed a new refinement to the expanded decomposition approach by combining Oaxaca and Ransom (1994) and Brown and others (1980) to produce a more detailed decomposition analysis of occupational and wage discrimination. In the following sections, we will lay out the mathematical logic of this decomposition:

### The Blinder–Oaxaca Decomposition Method

Decomposition enables the separation of the wage differential into one part that can be explained by differences in individual characteristics and another part that cannot be explained by differences in individual characteristics. The gross wage differential can be defined as:

$$G = \frac{Y_{nsc} - Y_{sc}}{Y_{sc}} = \frac{Y_{nsc}}{Y_{sc}} - 1 \qquad (4.1)$$

where $Y_{nsc}$ and $Y_{sc}$ represent the wages of HC or NSC individuals and wages of individuals belonging to the lower-caste SC categories, respectively. In the absence of labour market discrimination, the NSC and SC wage differential would reflect pure productivity differences:

$$Q = \frac{Y_{nsc}^{o}}{Y_{sc}^{o}} - 1 \qquad (4.2)$$

where the superscript zero denotes the absence of market discrimination. The market discrimination coefficient ($D$) is then defined as the proportionate difference between $G+1$ and $Q+1$:

$$D = \frac{(Y_{nsc} / Y_{sc}) - (Y_{nsc}^{o} / Y_{sc}^{o})}{(Y_{nsc}^{o} / Y_{sc}^{o})} \qquad (4.3)$$

Equations (4.1)–(4.3) imply the following logarithmic decomposition of the gross earnings differential:

$$\ln (G + 1) = \ln(D + 1) + \ln(Q + 1) \qquad (4.4)$$

This decomposition can be further applied within the framework of semi-logarithmic earnings equations (Mincer 1974) and estimated via Ordinary Least Squares (OLS) such that:

$$\ln \overline{Y}_{nsc} = \Sigma \hat{\beta}_{nsc} \overline{X}_{nsc} + \varepsilon_{nsc} \text{ (NSC wage equation)} \qquad (4.5)$$

$$\ln \overline{Y}_{sc} = \Sigma \hat{\beta}_{sc} \overline{X}_{sc} + \varepsilon_{sc} \text{ (SC wage equation)} \qquad (4.6)$$

where $\ln \overline{Y}$ denotes the geometric mean of earnings, $\overline{X}$ the vector of mean values of the regressors, $\hat{\beta}$ the vector of coefficients, and $\varepsilon$ is the error term with zero mean and constant variance. Within this framework, the gross differential in the logarithmic term is given by

$$\ln(G+1) = \ln(\overline{Y}_{nsc}/\overline{Y}_{sc}) = \ln \overline{Y}_{nsc} - \ln \overline{Y}_{sc} = \Sigma \hat{\beta}_{nsc} \overline{X}_{sc} - \Sigma \hat{\beta}_{sc} \overline{X}_{sc} \qquad (4.7)$$

The Oaxaca Decomposition simply shows that equation (4.7) can be expanded. In other words, the difference in the coefficients of the two earnings functions is taken as *a priori* evidence of discrimination. If, for a given endowment, SC individuals are paid according to the NSC wage structure in the absence of discrimination, then the hypothetical SC earnings function can be given as:

$$\ln \overline{Y}_{sc} = \Sigma \hat{\beta}_{nsc} \overline{X}_{sc} \qquad (4.8)$$

Subtracting equation (4.8) from equation (4.7) we get

$$\ln \overline{Y}_{nsc} - \ln \overline{Y}_{sc} = \Sigma \hat{\beta}_{nsc} (\overline{X}_{nsc} - \overline{X}_{sc}) + \Sigma \overline{X}_{sc} (\hat{\beta}_{nsc} - \hat{\beta}_{sc}) \qquad (4.9)$$

Alternatively, the decomposition can also be done as

$$\ln \overline{Y}_{nsc} - \ln \overline{Y}_{sc} = \Sigma \hat{\beta}_{sc} (\overline{X}_{nsc} - \overline{X}_{sc}) + \Sigma \overline{X}_{nsc} (\hat{\beta}_{nsc} - \hat{\beta}_{sc}) \qquad (4.10)$$

In equations (4.9) and (4.10) above, the first term on the right hand side can be interpreted as education and other endowment differences. The second term in these equations has been regarded in the literature as the discrimination component. Studies use either of these alternative decomposition forms (equation 4.9 or 4.10) based on their assumptions about the wage structure that would prevail in the absence of discrimination. Some authors prefer to take the average of the estimates of the two equations (Greenhalgh 1980). This particular issue is known as 'the index number problem'.

## The Cotton, Neumark, and Oaxaca/ Ransom Decomposition Method

To resolve the index number problem, Cotton (1988) and Neumark (1988) and Oaxaca and Ransom (1994) have proposed an alternative decomposition that extends the wage discrimination component further. They calculate non-discriminatory or competitive wage structures which can be used to estimate overpayment and underpayment. The true non-discriminatory wage would lie somewhere between the NSC and SC wage structure. The Cotton logarithmic wage differential is written as:

$$\ln \overline{Y}_{nsc} - \ln \overline{Y}_{sc} = \Sigma \beta^* (\overline{X}_{nsc} - \overline{X}_{sc}) + \Sigma \overline{X}_{nsc} (\hat{\beta}_{nsc} - \beta^*) + \Sigma \overline{X}_{sc} (\beta^* - \hat{\beta}_{sc}) \quad (4.11)$$

where $\beta^*$ is the reward structure that would have occurred in the absence of discrimination. The first term on the right hand side of equation (4.11) above is skill differences between SC/STs and NSCs, while the second term represents the overpayment relative to NSCs due to favouritism, and the third term the underpayment to SCs due to discrimination. The decomposition specified in equation (4.11) above cannot be made operational without some assumptions about the salary structures for SC and NSC in the absence of discrimination. The theory of discrimination provides some guidance in the choice of the non-discriminatory wage structure. The assumption is operationalized by weighting the NSC and SC wage structures by the respective proportions of NSC and SC in the labour force. Thus, the estimator $\beta^*$ used above is defined as

$$\beta^* = P_{nsc} \hat{\beta}_{sc} + P_{sc} \hat{\beta}_{sc} \quad (4.12)$$

where $P_{nsc}$ and $P_{sc}$ are the sample proportions of NSC and SC/ST populations and $\hat{\beta}_{nsc}$ and $\hat{\beta}_{sc}$ the NSC and SC pay structures, respectively.

Another versatile representation of a non-discriminatory or pooled wage structure is proposed by Neumark (1988) and Oaxaca and Ransom (1994). It can be written as

$$\beta^* = \Omega \hat{\beta}_{nsc} + (I - \Omega) \hat{\beta}_{sc} \qquad (4.13)$$

where $\Omega$ is a weighting matrix. I is the identity matrix. The weighting matrix is specified by

$$\Omega = (X' X)^{-1} (X_{nsc}' X_{nsc})$$

where $X$ is the observation matrix for the pooled sample. $X_{nsc}$ is the observation matrix for the NSC sample. The interpretation of $\Omega$ as weighting matrix is readily seen by noting that:

$$X' X = X'_{nsc} X_{nsc} + X'_{sc} X_{sc} \qquad (4.14)$$

where $X_{sc}$ is the observation matrix of the SC sample, Given $\hat{\beta}_{nsc}$, $\hat{\beta}_{sc}$ and equation (4.13), any assumption about $\beta^*$ reduces to an assumption about $\Omega$.

## An Expanded Decomposition to Estimate Both Wage and Job Discrimination

Both the Oaxaca (1973) and Cotton (1988) and Neumark (1988) methods can be criticized on the grounds that they do not distinguish between wage discrimination and job discrimination.

Brown and others (1980) incorporate a separate model of occupational attainment into their analysis of wage differentials. Banerjee and Knight (1985) used this decomposition by introducing a multinomial logit model that could estimate both wage and occupational discrimination for migrant labourers in India, where the latter is defined as 'unequal pay for workers with same economic characteristics which results from their being employed in different jobs' (Banerjee and Knight 1985: 304). In the following section, we combine elements from Oaxaca and Ransom (1994) and Brown and others (1980) to form a more detailed decomposition analysis of occupational and wage discrimination. We believe that this represents a theoretical advance in terms of examining discrimination as the combined consequence of unequal access to certain jobs and unequal pay within jobs.

We have seen that equation (4.7) was used [following Oaxaca (1973)] to estimate the gross logarithmic wage differential between caste groups. Our concern is with estimating occupational discrimination as well as wage discrimination. The proportion of NSC ($P_{iNsc}$) and the proportion of SC ($P_{isc}$) in each occupation $i$ are included in the decomposition. Equation 4.7 is thus expanded to:

$$\ln(G+1) = \sum [P_{isc} \ln \overline{Y}_{iNsc} - P_{isc} \ln \overline{Y}_{isc}) \qquad (4.16)$$

Using the method in Brown and others (1980), Moll (1992, 1995), and Banerjee and Knight (1985), this can be further decomposed as:

$$\ln(G+1) = \sum_i \ln \overline{Y}_{iNSc} \, (P_{iNsc} - P_{isc}) + \sum_i P_{isc} (\ln \overline{Y}_{iNsc} - \ln \overline{Y}_{isc}) \qquad (4.17)$$

The first term on the right hand side of the equation represents the wage difference attributable to differences in the occupational distribution and the second term is attributable to the difference between wages within occupations. Each of these terms contains an explained and unexplained component. If we define $\hat{P}_{isc}$ as the proportion of SC workers that would be in occupation $i$ if they had the same occupational attainment function as NSC, then decomposing Equation (4.17) further yields:

$$\ln(G+1) = \sum_i \ln \overline{Y}_{iNsc} \, (P_{iNsc} - \hat{P}_{isc}) + \sum_i \ln \overline{Y}_{iNsc} \, (\hat{P}_{isc} - P_{isc})$$
$$+ \sum_i P_{isc} (\ln \overline{Y}_{iNsc} - \ln \overline{Y}_{isc}) \qquad (4.18)$$

where the first term represents the part of the gross wage differential attributable to the difference between the observed NSC occupational distribution and the occupational distribution that SC workers would occupy if they had the NSC's occupational function; the second term is the component of the gross wage differential attributable to occupational differences not explained on the basis of personal characteristics, and may be termed job discrimination; and the third term represents the within-occupation wage differential. The proportions $P_{iNsc}$ and $\hat{P}_{isc}$ are estimated using a multinomial logit model. First we estimate an occupational attainment function for NSC and then we use these estimates to predict the proportion of SC workers that would be in occupation $i$ if they had the same occupational attainment function as NSC. This predicted probability of SC occupation is used in the further decomposition.

The third term in equation (4.18) represents the within-occupation wage differential and is normally decomposed into a wage discrimination and a caste productivity term. However, instead of doing this, the term can be decomposed into an NSC overpayment term, an SC underpayment term, and a within-occupation wage differential explained by productivity characteristics of the two groups. In order to calculate these three terms, the 'pooled' methodology of Oaxaca and Ransom (1994) is used. Equation (4.19) presents the within-occupation gross caste wage differential defined as:

$$\sum_i P_{isc} \ln(G+1) = \sum_i P_{isc} [\ln \overline{Y}_{iNsc} - \ln \overline{Y}_{isc}] \qquad (4.19)$$

The actual proportion of SC workers in each occupational group is dropped for simplicity until the final equation is derived. It will be noted that equation (4.19) is identical to equation (4.7) except for the occupation subscript. Following the methodology of Oaxaca and Ransom (1994), the within-occupation gross wage differential is decomposed into a productivity differential and an unexplained effect that may be attributed to within-occupation wage discrimination. The within-occupation logarithmic productivity differential is defined as $\sum_i \ln (Q+1)$, where 'Q' is the gross unadjusted productivity differential. In order to calculate the logarithmic term, a non-discriminatory or 'competitive' wage structure is required so that:

$$\sum_i \ln(Q+1) = \ln \overrightarrow{Y}_{iNsc}^* - \ln \overrightarrow{Y}_{isc}^* \qquad (4.20)$$

where $\ln \overrightarrow{Y}_{ir}^*$ is the average non-discriminatory wage structure for caste '$r$' in occupation $i$. In order to calculate the pooled wage structure, the NSC and SC logarithmic wage structures are estimated using a earnings function, with the assumption that:

$$\ln \overline{Y}_{ir} = \hat{\beta}_{ir} (\overline{X}_{ir}) \qquad (4.21)$$

where $\tilde{\beta}_r$ and $\bar{X}_r$ are the vector of coefficients and average productivity characteristics of the different caste workers, estimated by OLS. The calculation of the non-discriminatory wage structure depends on the weighting given to the NSC and SC wage structures. We have discussed in equations (4.13) and (4.14) (see Oaxaca and Ransom 1994) about the pooled wage structure. Given the pooled wage structure in equation (4.13), within-occupation logarithmic wage discrimination is calculated by subtracting equation (4.20) from equation (4.19) to give us,

$$\sum_i \ln(D + 1) = (\ln \bar{Y}_{iNsc} - \ln \bar{Y}^*_{iNsc}) + (\ln \bar{Y}^*_{isc} - \ln \bar{Y}_{isc}) \qquad (4.22)$$

The gross wage differential is thus decomposed into a productivity and a discriminatory term, meaning that the final within-occupation gross logarithmic wage differential is equivalent to:

$$\sum_i P_{isc} (\ln (G + 1) = \sum_i P_{isc} [\ln \bar{Y}^*_{iNsc} - \ln \bar{Y}^*_{isc}] + \sum_i P_{isc} [\ln \bar{Y}_{iNsc} - \ln \bar{Y}^*_{iNsc}]$$
$$+ \sum_i P_{isc} [\ln \bar{Y}^*_{isc} - \bar{Y}_{isc}] \qquad (4.23)$$

Substituting equation (4.23) for the third component in equation (4.18) yields the final decomposition of the gross-logarithmic wage differential.

$$\ln(G + 1) = \sum_i \ln \bar{Y}_{iNsc} (P_{iNsc} - \hat{P}_{isc}) + \sum_i \ln \bar{Y}_{iNsc} (\hat{P}_{isc} - P_{isc})$$
$$+ \sum_i P_{isc} [\ln \bar{Y}^*_{iNsc} - \bar{Y}_{Nsc}]$$
$$+ \sum_i P_{isc} [\ln \bar{Y}_{iNsc} - \ln \bar{Y}^*_{iNsc}] + \sum_i P_{isc} [\ln \bar{Y}^*_{isc} - \ln \bar{Y}_{isc}] \qquad (4.24)$$

Hence a multinomial logit non-discriminatory model that can distinguish between within-occupation SC underpayment, within-occupation NSC overpayment, and occupational discrimination can be calculated. Finally, to estimate this model, equations (4.21) and (4.13) are substituted into equation (4.24) to give the final extended decomposition as

$$\ln(G + 1) = \sum_i \bar{\beta}_{iNsc} (\bar{X}_{iNsc}) (P_{iNsc} - \hat{P}_{isc}) \quad \text{(Job explained)}$$

$$+ \sum_i \bar{\beta}_{iNsc} (\bar{X}_{iNsc}) (\hat{P}_{isc} - P_{isc}) \quad \text{(Job discrimination)}$$

$$+ \sum_i P_{isc} [\bar{\beta}_i^* (\bar{X}_{iNsc} - \bar{X}_{isc})] \quad \text{(Wage explained)}$$

$$+ \sum_i P_{isc} [\bar{X}_{iNsc} (\bar{\beta}_{iNsc} - \bar{\beta}_i^*)] \quad \text{(Wage overpayment to NSC)}$$

$$+ \sum_i P_{isc} [\bar{X}_{isc} (\bar{\beta}_i^* - \bar{\beta}_{isc})] \quad \text{(Wage underpayment to SC)} \quad (4.25)$$

The wage overpayment and underpayment together constitute wage discrimination.

## ECONOMETRIC RESULTS

### Mincerian Earnings Function Results

To estimate the earnings differences attributed to discrimination, we estimated an augmented Mincerian earnings function separately for NSC, SC, and OBC in the regular/salaried labour market. The logarithm of the daily wage rate was used as the dependent variable, and age, level of education, gender, marital status, sector, job tenure, union status, occupation, and region were predictors. Generally the results are consistent with Human Capital theory and *a priori* expectations. The Earnings Function results for the year 1999–2000 are given in Table 4.1. Due to space constraints, we have not reported the earnings function for the years 1983 and 1993–4. The descriptive statistics and definition of the variables used in the OLS model is given in the Appendix.[2]

First, we examined the returns to education for NSC and SC workers and the changes in these returns following the economic liberalization of the 1990s. In common with other studies, the marginal wage effects of education are found to be significantly positive and monotonically increasing with education level. Duraisamy (2002) and Dutta (2004) are the only other national studies that compare returns to education in India over time. However, those studies calculated rates of return to education by gender and by sector. To the best of our knowledge, no previous study in India has determined rates of return to education by caste using a nationally representative

TABLE 4.1: Earnings Function: OLS Results—Regular Workers, Urban India

| Variables | 1999–2000 | | | | | |
|---|---|---|---|---|---|---|
| | Other caste | | SC | | OBC | |
| | Coeff. | t-value | Coeff. | t-value | Coeff. | t-value |
| Age | 0.04186 | 14.28 | 0.063607 | 10.86 | 0.050079 | 12.78 |
| agesq | −0.00034 | −9.24 | −0.00062 | −8.32 | −0.00045 | −9.23 |
| Bprim | 0.118523 | 4.46 | 0.125573 | 3.53 | 0.110725 | 3.74 |
| Primary | 0.155207 | 6.48 | 0.095845 | 3.09 | 0.177313 | 6.79 |
| Middle | 0.231942 | 11.06 | 0.225104 | 7.87 | 0.292325 | 12.14 |
| Secondary | 0.457122 | 22.85 | 0.388247 | 13.15 | 0.456787 | 19.28 |
| High school | 0.586235 | 27.78 | 0.564215 | 16.33 | 0.574385 | 21.6 |
| Graduate | 1.217369 | 46.13 | 1.030238 | 11.64 | 1.154985 | 26.52 |
| Graduate other | 0.874313 | 44.76 | 0.723349 | 22.42 | 0.820725 | 32.55 |
| Male | 0.226024 | 19.79 | 0.266195 | 11.22 | 0.375886 | 22.44 |
| Married | 0.108977 | 8.64 | 0.03983 | 1.56 | 0.097785 | 5.54 |
| Public | 0.275494 | 27.34 | 0.309054 | 14.54 | 0.335282 | 21.25 |
| unionmem | 0.216788 | 21.53 | 0.268418 | 12.19 | 0.335363 | 21.64 |
| permanent | 0.278837 | 25.18 | 0.268317 | 11.55 | 0.178827 | 12.05 |
| South | 0.072278 | 6.1 | 0.171682 | 7.27 | 0.091458 | 6.18 |
| West | 0.066188 | 6.59 | 0.065884 | 3.11 | 0.090175 | 4.82 |
| East | −0.04017 | −2.93 | 0.006045 | 0.2 | 0.119431 | 4.17 |
| _cons | 2.667867 | 49.88 | 2.264271 | 22.18 | 2.31265 | 33.37 |
| R-square | 0.514 | | 0.5287 | | 0.5515 | |
| Adj. R² | 0.5136 | | 0.5267 | | 0.5507 | |
| F | 1267.12 | | 287.65 | | 699.94 | |
| N | 20,706 | | 4380 | | 9695 | |

sample. The average rate of return to each education level, $r_j$, can be estimated as follows:

$$\gamma_k = \frac{(\beta_k - \beta_{k-1})}{(S_j - S_{j-1})} \qquad (4.26)$$

where $j$ = primary, middle, secondary, higher secondary, and graduate school; $\beta_j$ is the coefficient in the wage regression models, and $S_j$ the years of schooling at education level $j$. The rate of return to primary education is estimated as follows:

$$\gamma_{Primary} = \frac{\beta_{Prim}}{S_{Prim}} \qquad (4.27)$$

The omitted category for the education dummy variables is that of those workers who are illiterate or have less than two years of any type of formal education. The estimated rates of return to additional years of schooling are reported in Table 4.2.

Table 4.2 suggests that there is an incentive to acquire more education if the individual is in regular wage employment—the returns to acquiring education are all positive. An interesting observation is that the labour market return is the highest for a secondary level of education in 1983 whereas the return to a professional graduate degree is greatest in 1993 and 1999–2000, both for NSC and SC.

TABLE 4.2: Average Private Rate of Return to Education by Caste

(in per cent)

| Educational level | 1983 | | 1993–4 | | 1999–2000 | | |
|---|---|---|---|---|---|---|---|
| | NSC | SC | NSC | SC | NSC | SC | OBC |
| Primary | 4.21 | 4.48 | 3.26 | 1.39 | 3.10 | 1.92 | 3.55 |
| Middle | 5.05 | 6.43 | 3.54 | 3.19 | 2.56 | 4.31 | 3.83 |
| Secondary | 16.95 | 16.28 | 9.86 | 4.77 | 11.26 | 8.16 | 8.22 |
| Higher secondary | NA | NA | 5.21 | 12.92 | 6.46 | 8.80 | 5.88 |
| Graduate professional | 9.61 | 7.47 | 9.67 | 7.23 | 12.62 | 9.32 | 11.61 |
| Graduate general | 8.08 | 5.98 | 7.87 | 4.65 | 9.60 | 5.30 | 8.21 |
| Professional Degree compared to general degree | 12.66 | 10.44 | 12.37 | 11.10 | 17.15 | 15.34 | 16.71 |

Notes: NA: Not Available
     SC: Scheduled Caste
     NSC: Non-Scheduled Caste

When rates of return to education were compared across castes, it was noted that overall, the rate of return to education is considerably lower for SC workers and for OBC than for HC workers. If we look at the 1999–2000 results, the rate of return is usually higher for OBCs than for SC workers. These differential rates of return to education between castes suggest a substantial amount of labour market discrimination.

The premium to skill appears to be increasing over time due to liberalization and this has led to increasing levels of wage inequality in urban India (Kijima 2006). Several other studies have found evidence of increasing educational returns for the more educated during periods of rapid economic change. For instance, Foster and Rosenzweig (1996) found that during the Green Revolution in India, increasing educational returns were concentrated among the more educated. Kingdon (2006) finds in her review on the returns to education in India (mainly computed from specialized surveys in urban areas of a particular state or city) that the rate of return to education, as in Table 4.2, tends to rise with education level. Newell and Reilly (1999) also found in their study on transitional economies during the 1990s that the private rates of return to education rose after a period of labour market reforms. However, we find that there is a markedly lower rate of return to SCs and OBCs compared to other caste workers.

## Decomposition Results

As mentioned in our methodology section, we initially adopt a single equation method. We found that, compared to HC employees, SC workers earned 5.0 per cent less in 1983, 8.4 per cent less in 1993–4, and 8.9 per cent less in 1999–2000. OBCs earned 10.9 per cent less than HC employees in 1999–2000. These coefficients are all statistically significant. A single equation approach assumes that the slope coefficients are the same for all social groups. In order to overcome this limitation, we next estimated an earnings function separately for each social group over the period of time and subjected the earnings equation to decomposition, following the Blinder–Oaxaca approach. The results are reported in Table 4.3.

### TABLE 4.3: Blinder–Oaxaca Decomposition Results

|  |  |  |  | (in per cent) |
| --- | --- | --- | --- | --- |
| Components of decomposition | 1983 | 1993–4 | 1999–2000 | 1999–2000 FC vs. OBC |
| Amount attributable: | 30.9 | 15.2 | –9.7 | –0.5 |
| - due to endowments (E): | 25.1 | 18.8 | 24.4 | 23.8 |
| - due to coefficients (C): | 5.8 | –3.6 | –34.1 | –24.4 |
| Shift coefficient (U): | –1.9 | 11.8 | 40.4 | 35.5 |
| Raw differential (R): {E+C+U}: | 29 | 26.9 | 30.6 | 35 |
| Adjusted differential (D): {C+U}: | 3.9 | 8.2 | 6.2 | 11.2 |
| Endowments as per cent of total (E/R): | 86.55 | 69.6 | 79.0 | 68.1 |
| Discrimination as per cent of total (D/R): | 13.45 | 30.4 | 21.4 | 31.9 |

*Note*: 1. A positive number indicates advantage to high caste; Negative numbers indicate advantage to SC 2. The results from decomposition are presented using Blinder's (1973) original formulation of E, C, U and D. The endowments (E) component of the decomposition is the sum of (the coefficient vector of the regressors of the high-wage group) times (the difference in group means between the high-wage and low-wage groups for the vector of regressors). The coefficients (C) component of the decomposition is the sum of the (group means of the low-wage group for the vector of regressors) times (the difference between the regression coefficients of the high-wage group and the low-wage group). The unexplained portion of the differential (U) is the difference in constants between the high-wage wage and the low-wage group. The portion of the differential due to discrimination is C + U. The raw (or total) differential is E + C + U. The unexplained component is the difference in the shift coefficients (or constants) between the two wage equations. Being inexplicable, this component can be attributed to discrimination. However, Blinder also argued that the explained component of the wage gap also contains a portion that is due to discrimination. To examine this, Blinder decomposed the explained component into: (a) the differences in endowments between the two groups, 'as evaluated by the high-wage group's wage equation'; and (b) 'the difference between how the high-wage equation would value the characteristics of the low-wage group, and how the low-wage equation actually values them'. Blinder called the first part the amount 'attributable to the endowments' and the second part the amount 'attributable to the coefficients', and he argued that the second part should also be viewed as reflecting discrimination: '[this] only exists because the market evaluates differently the identical bundle of traits if possessed by members of different demographic groups, [and] is a reflection of discrimination as much as the shift coefficient is.' Conventionally, the high-wage group's wage structure is regarded as the 'non-discriminatory norm', that is, the reference group. The average endowment differences are now weighted by the high-wage workers' estimated coefficients, and the coefficient differences are weighted by the mean characteristics of the low-wage workers. One can also do the reverse.

Table 4.3 indicates that the endowment component is larger than the discrimination component. Nevertheless, discrimination explains 13.45 per cent (in 1983), 30.4 per cent (in 1993–4), and 20.4 per cent (in 1999–2000) of the lower wages of SC workers as compared to HC in the regular urban labour market. Discrimination causes 31.9 per cent of the lower wages for OBC as compared to HC.

Two points are especially noteworthy. First, the large endowment difference in developing countries such as India implies that pre-market discriminatory practices with respect to education, health, and nutrition are more crucial in explaining wage differentials than labour market discrimination. The endowment difference has decreased over the period from 1983 to 1999–2000. This is consistent with evidence available about the impact of the reservation system in Indian education. Student enrolment, including that of students under the reservation system, has been increasing (Thorat 2005; Weisskopf 2004). However, reservation quotas in employment and educational institutions still fall short of their targets for some levels of education and for some categories of jobs.

Second, in the decomposition, wage discrimination appears to have increased soon after liberalization (1993–4) but it has come down by the year 1999–2000. Nevertheless the raw wage differentials have increased over this period.

We also assessed the relative contribution of each independent variable to the observed wage gap. Table 4.4 shows which part of the wage gap can be attributed to differences in endowments and which part is due to differences in rewards (discrimination) in the earnings function.

If we look at the total difference column, the proxy for experience—the age variable—was favourable to HCs in 1993–4, but the result was quite the reverse in 1999–2000. Note that the large contribution of age during 1999–2000 in favour of SC is more than offset by the constant term, which is in favor of HCs.

The next important variable is the level of education. Secondary/Higher secondary and higher education both favour HCs. Women are in a disadvantaged situation as the male variable is negative and in favour of SCs. The public sector and union membership variables are rather prominent in their effects on the earnings difference.

There is a favourable treatment of SCs in the public sector—SCs gained an earnings advantage of 27.1 per cent in 1993–4 and 9.8 per cent in 1999–2000. The permanent job variable favours high castes. The regional effect on earnings difference is meagre but it favours high caste. Finally there is a large effect of the constant or intercept term that works in favour of high castes; its contribution increases over time.

TABLE 4.4: Relative Contribution of Specific Variables to the Decomposition (in per cent)

| Variables | 1993–4 | | | 1999–2000 | | |
|---|---|---|---|---|---|---|
| | Explained difference | Unexplained difference | Total difference | Explained difference | Unexplained difference | Total difference |
| Age | 0.0 | 10.8 | 10.8 | 3.6 | –126.5 | –122.9 |
| Less than secondary | –7.4 | 14.5 | 7.1 | –8.8 | 2.6 | –6.2 |
| Secondary/ Higher secondary | 20.1 | 11.5 | 31.6 | 14.7 | 4.2 | 19.0 |
| Higher education | 63.6 | 5.9 | 69.5 | 70.3 | 6.5 | 76.8 |
| Male | 1.1 | –46.5 | –45.4 | 1.6 | –10.8 | –9.2 |
| Married | –1.5 | 4.8 | 3.3 | 0.3 | 17.3 | 17.6 |
| Public | –5.9 | –21.2 | –27.1 | –4.9 | –4.9 | –9.8 |
| Union | –4.5 | –0.4 | –4.8 | –2.9 | –8.2 | –11.1 |
| Permanent | 1.9 | 10.4 | 12.3 | 4.9 | 2.3 | 7.2 |
| Region | 3.0 | –3.3 | –0.4 | 1.3 | 5.2 | 6.5 |
| Constant | – | 43.9 | 43.9 | – | 132.0 | 132.0 |
| Subtotal | 69.6 | 30.4 | 100.0 | 79.6 | 20.4 | 100.0 |

Notes: A positive number indicates advantage to high castes
A negative number indicates advantage to SCs

When occupational variables are included in the model, the discrimination coefficient is reduced to 24 per cent from 30 per cent in 1993–4, and to 15 per cent from 20 per cent in 1999–2000. This result implies that discrimination partially operates through occupational segregation, which will be studied in greater detail subsequently.

## Discrimination in the Public and Private Sectors: Decomposition Results

The reservation system that sets aside a certain proportion of jobs for SC/ST applicants operates only within the public sector of the Indian economy. One important issue, therefore, is to look at caste-based wage inequalities separately for the public and private sectors of the urban economy. We estimated separate earnings functions for the public and private sector for each social group, and then decomposed the earnings differentials between HC and SC/ST for each sector. The results are reported in Table 4.5:

TABLE 4.5: Decomposition Results for the Public and Private Sectors

|  |  |  |  | (in per cent) |
| --- | --- | --- | --- | --- |
| Components | 1993–4 |  | 1999–2000 |  |
|  | Public | Private | Public | Private |
| Endowment difference | 82.0 | 69.0 | 86.0 | 70.1 |
| Discrimination | 18.0 | 31.0 | 14.0 | 29.9 |

The decomposition in Table 4.5 reveals that SC/ST workers are discriminated against both in the public sector and the private sector, but that the discrimination effect is much smaller in the public sector. The government policy of protective legislation seems to be partly effective. Over time the discrimination coefficient has decreased slightly in the public sector, whereas the discrimination coefficient has not changed significantly in the private sector. Discrimination still arises in the public sector in part because the reservation quota for lower caste applicants is close to full in the less-skilled class 'C' and 'D' jobs but is far from filled in the higher category 'A' and 'B' jobs, where HCs predominate.

These findings have important implications for the public–private divide and for affirmative action in India. The evidence provided by these decompositions contradicts the argument that there is no discrimination in the private sector. Claims that discrimination does not occur in the Indian urban private sector are based neither on the economic theory of discrimination nor on empirical facts.

## Cotton, Neumark, and Oaxaca/
## Ransom Decomposition Results

We calculated decomposition results using the Cotton (1988), Neumark (1988), and Oaxaca and Ransom (1994) approach. These reveal that the wage difference due to skill is 81.8 per cent using Cotton's method and 85 per cent using a pooled method (Oaxaca/ Ransom). This skill or productivity advantage is estimated as it would have been in the absence of discrimination. The NSC treatment advantage is 5.2 per cent in the Cotton method and 4.1 per cent in the pooled method. This is the difference in wages between what the HC currently receive and what they would receive in the absence of discrimination. The treatment disadvantage component for SC is about 13 per cent in the Cotton method and 11.2 per cent in the pooled method. This is the difference in the current SC wage and the wage they would receive if there was no discrimination. In Table 4.6, in the last two columns of the estimates using the Oaxaca–Blinder method, as expected, the fourth column evaluated at SC means somewhat underestimates the true value of the skill difference, whereas the fifth column evaluated at FC means does the reverse.

TABLE 4.6: Cotton–Neumark–Oaxaca/Ransom Approach— Urban India, 1999–2000

(in per cent)

| Components | Cotton/ Neumark | Oaxaca/ Ransom (pooled method) | Oaxaca-- Blinder (Using SC means as weight) | Oaxaca-- Blinder (Using FC means as weight) |
|---|---|---|---|---|
| Skill Difference (End Diff) | 81.8 (0.010214) | 85.0 (0.01010) | 79.0 (0.01246) | 88.1 (0.01038) |
| Unexplained difference (discrimination) | 18.2 (0.010249) | 15.0 (0.008235) | 21.4 (0.01242) | 11.9 (0.010611 |
| Overpayment to FC | 5.2 | 4.1 | – | – |
| Underpayment to SC | 13.0 | 11.2 | – | – |

*Notes*: 1. Unexplained component = overpayment and underpayment component
2. Figures in parentheses indicate standard errors

This form of the decomposition procedure yields more accurate estimates of the wage differential but it also models the true state of differential treatment by estimating the 'cost' to the group discriminated against as well as the 'benefits' accruing to the favoured group.

Standard errors for each of the three estimates were estimated to determine which of the three was least objectionable. The pooled method has the smallest standard error and should probably be preferred. When this method is used, the discrimination coefficient is somewhat smaller in magnitude (15 per cent), but there is still clear and substantial evidence of discrimination in the labour market against the Scs and STs.

## Combining Wage and Job Discrimination: Expanded Decomposition Results

We analysed occupational attainment within the framework of a multinomial logit model. Using the occupation attainment results, a predicted distribution for SCs, and for NSCs was obtained. The earnings functions by occupation are needed to complete the decomposition based on the full model. Table 4.7 reports a decomposition of the actual earnings difference into its skill difference, an overpayment to FC and an underpayment to SC.

Of the gross wage difference, 24.9 per cent can be explained by education and experience, 18.6 per cent by occupational difference, 20.9 per cent by wage discrimination, and 35.4 per cent by occupational discrimination. Thus, discrimination accounts for a large part of the gross earnings difference, with job discrimination (inequality in access to certain occupations) being considerably more important than wage discrimination (unequal pay within a given occupation, given ones educational and skill levels) in the regular salaried urban labour market. This result is contrary to an earlier study in India by Banerjee and Knight (1985). However, their study focused on migrant workers in Delhi, a small sample compared to our nationwide survey.

To estimate the earnings differences attributed to discrimination, we estimated an augmented Mincerian earnings function separately for NSC and SC/ST in the regular/salaried labour market. The estimated earnings function shows that the rates of return to education

TABLE 4.7: Expanded Decomposition Results — Urban India, 1999–2000

(in per cent)

| Occupation | Job explained | Job discrimination | Wage explained | Wage discrimination | Wage overpayment to FC | Wage underpayment to SC |
|---|---|---|---|---|---|---|
| Professional | −0.06206 | 0.706537 | 0.014075 | 0.00456 | 0.00512 | 0.016564 |
| Administration | −0.00232 | 0.249214 | 0.015555 | 0.00321 | 0.00123 | 0.012567 |
| Clerical | 0.049441 | 0.169439 | 0.014127 | 0.01343 | 0.00033 | 0.00123 |
| Sales | −0.07005 | 0.213229 | 0.002345 | 0.01527 | 0.00434 | 0.017725 |
| Service | −0.11033 | −0.66201 | 0.018874 | 0.01649 | 0.00225 | 0.001123 |
| Production | 0.25565 | −0.56178 | 0.015537 | 0.01474 | 0.00177 | 0.003143 |
| Total | 0.060324 | 0.114629 | 0.080514 | 0.06771 | 0.01504 | 0.052352 |
| (%) to overall raw wage differentials | 18.66 | 35.46 | 24.91 | 20.95 | 4.78 | 16.17 |
| Overall wage differentials between FC and SC | | | 0.323177 | | | |

for SC/ST are considerably lower than for NSC. Our decomposition analysis showed that a major share of the earnings differential between NSC and SC/ST is due to differences in human capital endowments, but that 15 per cent is due to discrimination in the market place. The analyses also revealed that occupational discrimination is more pronounced than wage discrimination. The major policy implications of our findings are as follows.

The size of the education and other endowment differences between SC/ST and HCs indicate the need for continued government policies aimed at education and skill building for the SC. The reservation system has clearly helped in this regard but additional policies should be considered, including additional scholarship support and reduced tuition for poor students.

Our findings have shown that employment discrimination is substantial, especially in the private sector, and that discrimination occurs to a large extent in unequal access to jobs. An equal employment opportunity act would provide legal protection against discrimination in hiring, and a reservation system, with a certain fixed share in certain categories of jobs, would ensure the fair participation of marginalized groups in industrial/tertiary private sector employment. To bring transparency and to monitor the programme requires some administrative mechanism. An Equal Employment Enforcement Office, along the lines of those in the USA and northern Ireland would be desirable.

## NOTES

1. This approach allows only the intercept to vary by caste, but not the slope. In order to overcome this problem, we present earnings functions separately by caste.
2. A longer version of the report that provides the estimates from earlier surveys used for comparing trends over time is available from the authors.

## REFERENCES

Banerjee, B. and J.B. Knight (1985), 'Caste Discrimination in the Indian Labour Market', *Journal of Development Economics*, vol. 17, pp. 277–307.

Blinder, A.S. (1973), 'Wage Discrimination: Reduced Form and Structural Estimates', *Journal of Human Resources*, vol. 8, pp. 436–55.

Brown, R.S., M. Moon, and B.S. Zoloth (1980), 'Incorporating Occupational Attainment in Studies of Male/Female Earnings Differentials', *Journal of Human Resources*, vol. 15, pp. 3–28.

Cotton, C.J. (1988), 'On the Decomposition of Wage Differentials', *Review of Economics and Statistics*, vol. 70, pp. 236–43.

Duraisamy, P. (2002), 'Changes in the Returns to Education in India, 1983–94: By Gender, Age-Cohort and Location', *Economics of Education Review*, vol. 21, no. 6, pp. 609–22.

Dutta, P. V. (2004), 'Structure of Wages in India', PRUS Working Paper No. 25, UK: University of Sussex.

Foster, A.D. and M.R. Rosenzweig (1996), 'Technical Change and Human-Capital Returns and Investments: Evidence from the Green Revolution', *American Economic Review*, vol. 86, no. 4, pp. 931–53.

Greenhalgh, C. (1980), 'Male-Female Differentials in Great Britain: Is Marriage an Equal Opportunity?', *Economic Journal*, vol. 90, pp. 751–75.

Gunderson, M. (1989), 'Male-Female Wage Differentials and Policy Responses', *Journal of Economic Literature*, vol. 27, pp. 46–117.

Hawley, J.D. (2004), 'Changing Returns to Education in Times of Prosperity and Crisis, Thailand 1985–1998', *Economics of Education Review*, vol. 23, no. 3, pp. 273–86.

Kijima, Yoko (2006), 'Why Did Wage Inequality Increase? Evidence from Urban India 1983–89', *Journal of Development Economics*, vol. 81, pp. 91–117.

Kingdon, G.G. (2006), 'Does the Labour Market Explain Lower Female Schooling in India?', *Journal of Development Studies*, vol. 35, no. 1, pp. 39–65.

Labour Bureau, *Indian Labour Statistics*, Labour Bureau, Ministry of Labour, Government of India, various years.

Madheswaran, S. (1996), 'Econometric Analyses of Labour Market for Scientists in India', Unpublished PhD Thesis, University of Madras.

Mincer, J. (1974), *Schooling, Experience and Earnings*, New York: Columbia University Press.

Mohanty, M. (2006), 'Social Inequality, Labour Market Dynamics and Reservations', 2 September, *Economic and Political Weekly*, vol. 41, no. 35, pp. 3777–89.

Moll, P. (1992), 'The Decline of Discrimination Against Coloured People in South Africa, 1970–1980', *Journal of Development Economics*, vol. 37, pp. 289–307.

—— (1995), 'Discrimination is Declining in South Africa, but Inequality is Not', Mimeo, University of Chicago.

National Sample Survey Organisation (2001), *Employment and Unemployment Situation in India, NSS 55th Round, 1999–2000—Part I*, New Delhi, Ministry of Statistics and Programme Implementation, Government of India.

—— (2001b), *Employment and Unemployment among Social Groups India, 1999–2000*, NSS Report No. 469, New Delhi, Ministry of Statistics and Programme Implementation, Government of India.

—— (2001c), *National Sample Survey Organisation, Differences in Level of Consumption among Socio-Economic Groups, 1999–2000*, NSS Report No. 472, New Delhi, Ministry of Statistics and Programme Implementation, Government of India.

—— (2001d), *Literacy and Levels of Education in India, 1999–2000*, NSS Report No. 473, New Delhi, Ministry of Statistics and Programme Implementation, Government of India, 2001.

Neumark, D. (1988), 'Employers Discriminatory Behaviour and the Estimation of Wage Discrimination', *Journal of Human Resources*, vol. 23, pp. 279–95.

Newell, A. and B. Reilly (1999), 'Rates of Return to Educational Qualifications in the Transitional Economies', *Education Economics*, vol. 7, no. 1, pp. 67–84.

Oaxaca, R.L. (1973), 'Male-Female Wage Differentials in Urban Labour Market', *International Economic Review*, vol. 14, pp. 693–709.

Oaxaca, R.L. and M.R. Ransom (1994), 'On Discrimination and the Decomposition of Wage Differentials', *Journal of Econometrics*, vol. 61, pp. 5–21.

Reimer, C.W. (1983), 'Labour Market Discrimination Against Hispanic and Black Men', *Review of Economics and Statistics*, vol. 65, pp. 570–79.

—— (1985), 'A Comparative Analysis of the Wages of Hispanic, Blacks and Non-Hispanic Whites', in G.J. Borjas and M. Tienda (eds), *Hispanics in the U.S. Economy*, New York: Academic Press, pp. 274–90.

Thorat, S.K. (2005), *Reservation Policy for Private Sector: Why and How*, Pune: Sugava Prakashan.

Weisskopf, T.E. (2004), 'The Impact of Reservation on Admissions to Higher Education in India', *Economic and Political Weekly*, vol. 39, no. 39, pp. 4339–49.

## Appendix 4.1: Descriptive Statistics of Main Variables in the Earnings Function

| Variables | Description of the variables | 1999–2000 | | | | | |
| --- | --- | --- | --- | --- | --- | --- | --- |
| | | FC | | OBC | | SC | |
| | | Mean | Std dev. | Mean | Std dev. | Mean | Std dev. |
| lwage | logarithm of daily wage (in Rupees) | 4.952815 | 0.846096 | 4.603097 | 0.866684 | 4.64658 | 0.826999 |
| age | Age in Years | 37.16764 | 11.00094 | 35.99369 | 11.41067 | 36.53055 | 11.18109 |
| agesq | Age square (in Years) | 1502.448 | 846.3519 | 1425.737 | 861.2629 | 1459.47 | 845.4274 |
| Bprim | If the worker has completed below primary education=1; 0 otherwise. | 0.042584 | 0.201922 | 0.06867 | 0.252905 | 0.084835 | 0.278667 |
| Prim | If the worker has completed Primary school=1; 0 otherwise | 0.065295 | 0.247052 | 0.118916 | 0.323706 | 0.134506 | 0.341232 |
| Middle | If the worker has completed Middle school=1; 0 otherwise | 0.13343 | 0.340046 | 0.18798 | 0.390716 | 0.187033 | 0.389981 |
| Secon | If the worker has completed Secondary school=1; 0 otherwise | 0.206962 | 0.405138 | 0.219212 | 0.413733 | 0.161758 | 0.368269 |
| Hsc | If the worker has completed Higher Secondary school=1; 0 otherwise | 0.136175 | 0.342983 | 0.115172 | 0.319246 | 0.094066 | 0.291953 |
| Grad_Prof | If the worker has completed professional degree=1; 0 otherwise | 0.045842 | 0.209147 | 0.023744 | 0.152258 | 0.00989 | 0.098967 |
| Grad_Other | If the worker has completed General degree=1; 0 otherwise | 0.312887 | 0.46368 | 0.162168 | 0.368623 | 0.114945 | 0.318991 |

|  |  | 1999–2000 | | | | | |
| Variables | Description of the variables | FC | | OBC | | SC | |
| --- | --- | --- | --- | --- | --- | --- | --- |
|  |  | Mean | Std dev. | Mean | Std dev. | Mean | Std dev. |
| Male | If the individual sex is male=1; 0 otherwise | 0.835435 | 0.370796 | 0.837833 | 0.368623 | 0.810989 | 0.39156 |
| Married | If the individual is married=1; 0 otherwise | 0.767255 | 0.422591 | 0.72197 | 0.44805 | 0.756264 | 0.429383 |
| Public | If the worker is working in public sector=1; 0 otherwise | 0.384558 | 0.486502 | 0.309754 | 0.462415 | 0.436703 | 0.496032 |
| Unionmem | If the worker is a member in union=1; 0 otherwise | 0.429097 | 0.494959 | 0.381084 | 0.485677 | 0.464835 | 0.498817 |
| Permanent | If the worker is having a permanent job=1; 0 otherwise | 0.72267 | 0.447691 | 0.678325 | 0.467142 | 0.658901 | 0.474131 |
| South | If the individual is working in South=1; 0 otherwise | 0.188207 | 0.390886 | 0.529458 | 0.499156 | 0.22 | 0.414292 |
| West | If the individual is working in West=1; 0 otherwise | 0.341416 | 0.474196 | 0.166108 | 0.372196 | 0.285495 | 0.451699 |
| East | If the individual is working in East=1; 0 otherwise | 0.127798 | 0.333873 | 0.051724 | 0.22148 | 0.101978 | 0.302653 |

# 5

## Caste System and Pattern of Discrimination in Rural Markets

*Sukhadeo Thorat, M. Mahamallik, and Nidhi Sadana*

The economic interpretation of the caste system implies that, in its original form, caste as a system of economic governance (or organization of production and distribution) is governed by certain customary rules and norms, which are unique and distinct. The organizational scheme of the caste system is based on the division of people in social groups (or castes), in which the economic and social rights of each individual caste are predetermined or ascribed by birth and made hereditary. The assignment of economic rights across various castes is, however, unequal and hierarchical. The caste system also provides for a community-based regulatory mechanism to enforce the social and economic organization through the instruments of social ostracism (or social and economic penalties), and reinforces it further with justification and support from philosophical elements in the Hindu religion.

Viewed from this perspective, the caste system's fundamental characteristics of fixed economic rights for each caste, with restrictions on change, implies 'forced exclusion' of the lower castes from certain economic rights (or occupations) that the higher castes (HC) enjoy. Exclusion and discrimination in economic spheres such as occupation and labour employment are, therefore, internal to the system, and a necessary outcome of its governing principles. In the market economy framework, the inter-caste occupational immobility would operate through restrictions on lower-caste persons in various markets such as land, labour, capital, credit, other inputs, and services necessary for any economic activity. Labour, being an integral part of the production process of any economic activity, would obviously constitute a part of market discrimination.

The purpose of this chapter is to empirically study the patterns of economic discrimination—both market and non-market—associated with the institution of caste and untouchability in rural areas, as experienced by low-caste Untouchables.

The analysis of market discrimination is focused on labour markets, markets in factors of production required in farm production, and markets in farm products and other consumer goods. The study is based on a survey of three villages in the states of Orissa, Gujarat, and Maharashtra. While the state of Orissa is located in the eastern part of India, Gujarat is in the north-west, and Maharashtra lies in the south-western part of the country. Three villages from these states were selected to represent characteristics of their respective rural scenarios. In these three villages, all households belonging to low-caste Untouchables and HCs were surveyed. The primary household-level survey was conducted in 2003.

## METHODOLOGY

Systematic empirical studies on caste- and untouchability-based market discrimination in rural area are rare. With the exception of some indirect references to the discrimination experienced by low-caste Untouchables in employment and occupation in some studies conducted by anthropologists and sociologists (Saha *et al.* 2006; Khan 1995; Tripathy 1994; and Venkateswarlu 1990), there is, indeed, a lack of literature on rural market discrimination. This study, therefore, had to first develop the concept of market discrimination with respect to caste and untouchability, and prepare a questionnaire to capture the various forms of discrimination, deeply entrenched in dense social and economic relations. We developed the concept of caste- and untouchability-based market discrimination applicable to the labour, agricultural land, inputs, and product and consumer goods markets. This section discusses the concept of caste- and untouchability-based market discrimination, the database, and the sample design.

## CONCEPT OF LABOUR MARKET AND
## OCCUPATIONAL DISCRIMINATION

Discrimination associated with institutions of caste and untouchability is deeply entrenched in dense social and economic relations.

These relations generally operate through the structures of dominance and power, and through general restrictions faced by low-caste Untouchables in various market and non-market transactions, which in some cases are direct, while in others are indirect and of a subtle nature. Accordingly, the first task is to conceptually define and develop the concept of caste- and untouchability-based market discrimination, and thereafter to capture its dimensions through survey. Since discrimination is embedded in social relations, in addition to quantitative questions, we also collected relevant information through qualitative questions (for a detailed description on this aspect, see Thorat and Mahamallik 2004).

Caste-based labour market discrimination is conceived as (a) the complete exclusion of low-caste persons from employment by the HCs; (b) selective inclusion in hiring, but with unequal treatment, which may be reflected in denial of jobs to low castes in certain economic activities (as they are considered to be polluting and impure and, therefore, Untouchable) and in lower wages (lower than market wages or lower than comparable wages awarded to HC labour); (c) selective inclusion with different terms with respect to hours of work and other working conditions; and (d) inclusion with differential behaviour towards or treatment of low-caste workers in the workplace. Labour market discrimination may also involve forced work for low-caste Untouchables, imposed by traditional caste-related obligations leading to overwork and loss of freedom.

Employment discrimination is measured by disparities in the employment rates of low-caste Untouchables (or Scheduled Castes) hired as casual labour in agricultural and non-agricultural areas for identical work performed by workers with similar manual work skills. Disparities in employment rates of workers doing similar work reflect the hiring preferences of HC employers. Wage discrimination is measured through differences in daily wage rate between HC labourers and low-caste Untouchables for identical work in agricultural and non-agricultural activities. Discrimination in working hours is measured in terms of actual hours put in by low-caste Untouchables compared to HC casual labourers. Untouchability-related discrimination in the workplace is measured by asking the Untouchable labourers direct qualitative questions. .

The exclusion of Untouchables from certain types of jobs owing to notions of pollution and purity is measured by seeking qualitative information from low-caste respondents.

We now discuss the concept of discrimination in other markets. Low-caste Untouchables may also face differential behaviour in various market and non-market transactions other than those in the labour market. Discrimination in these markets refers to complete denial of access and/or selective inclusion with differential treatment in the sale and purchase of factors of production (like agricultural land and other inputs), and denial of opportunities to engage in the sale and purchase of products and consumer goods. Discrimination in this case may be occurring through denial by the HCs of sale inputs and products to low-caste persons, as well as through refusal to buy the same from low-caste sellers.

Discrimination may also take the form of price discrimination. This may be experienced by low-caste Untouchables in the shape of higher prices on purchases, or alternatively, as lower prices received by them for their products and goods as compared to market prices. This may include prices of factor inputs, such as the price of land or rent on land, interest on capital, rent on residential houses, and charges or fees on privately supplied services such as irrigation. Discrimination may also be reflected in differences in the terms and conditions of contracts in market and non-market transactions, which may be unfavourable for low-caste Untouchables. Discrimination may be faced by low-caste Untouchables in differential arrangement in their use of village-level common property resources such as water bodies and common grazing land.

These types of discrimination are measured by asking the low-caste respondents direct questions with respect to (a) restrictions in the sale and purchase of goods (capital and consumer) and services; (b) prices charged and received by low-caste businesspersons; and (c) other terms of contract. These questions relate to restrictions faced by low-caste businesspersons engaged in farm and in non-farm businesses. These may include sale and purchase of agricultural land in the case of land markets, credit availability in the case of the capital market, sale and purchase of various inputs (required in production and business) in the input market, access to implements,

bullocks, and irrigation in the market for essential services, and sale
and purchase of consumer goods in the case of consumer markets.

## DATABASE AND SAMPLE DESIGN

The study is based on the survey of about 664 households from three
villages in the states of Orissa, Gujarat, and Maharashtra. The total
population of the sample villages is 3315. About 2.17 per cent are
Muslims, and the remaining 97.77 per cent come from a Hindu
religious background. All the Muslim families come from the villages
in Maharashtra, where they account for about 5.50 per cent of the
sample population. The total Hindu population of 3,243 is further
classified into four main caste groups, namely Scheduled Castes (low-
caste Untouchables or SC), Scheduled Tribes (ST, Adivasi), Other
Backward Castes (OBC), and HC.

The SCs account for 14.51 per cent of the sample Hindu families,
and OBCs and HCs for about 38.43 per cent and 45.52 per cent,
respectively. The STs account for only 1.54 per cent of the total
sample Hindu families (Table 5.1). Due to the small sample of STs
and Muslims, the analysis is confined to SC, OBC, and HC persons/
households.

TABLE 5.1: Caste-wise Distributions of Sample Hindu Households

|  |  |  |  |  | (in number) |
|---|---|---|---|---|---|
| State | Scheduled Castes | Scheduled Tribes | Other Backward Castes | Higher Castes | Total |
| Gujarat | 44 | 3 | 77 | 70 | 194 |
|  | (22.70) | (1.50) | (39.70) | (36.10) | (100) |
| Orissa | 35 | 4 | 161 | 0 | 200 |
|  | (17.50) | (2.00) | (80.50) | (0) | (100) |
| Maharashtra | 15 | 3 | 11 | 225 | 254 |
|  | (5.60) | (1.10) | (4.10) | (83.30) | (100) |
| All states | 94 | 10 | 249 | 295 | 648 |
|  | (14.51) | (1.54) | (38.43) | (45.52) | (100) |

*Note*: Figures in parentheses indicate percentage of respective value

## CHARACTERISTICS OF SAMPLE VILLAGES

Before undertaking the analysis of discrimination in the labour and other markets, we first describe the social and economic features of the sample households in the three sample villages, as a backdrop to the later analysis. The social and economic characteristics include features related to population, literacy and educational levels, and occupational patterns.

With respect to literacy, the overall literacy rate of the sample population is 63 per cent. Among the four castes, the literacy level is 72 per cent among the HCs, 64 per cent for the SCs, 53 per cent for the OBCs, and 42 per cent for the STs. Thus the literacy level is highest for the HCs, followed by SCs, OBCs, and STs. The level of education in terms of the proportion of those with high school, secondary, graduate, and postgraduate qualifications is high for the HCs as compared to the SCs and OBCs. Thus the quality of human resources of lower-caste persons is relatively low as compared with the HCs.

As mentioned before, the study is based on the complete census of three villages and covers all 664 households and 3315 persons, and, to that extent, it avoids the pitfalls associated with sample data. The number of persons engaged in each of the five occupation groups (see Table 5.2), however, varies across the caste groups. In some cases, responses to a few selective questions are less than the number of original respondents. Therefore, the results on some aspects are based on a small number of respondents, and interpreted with caution. Keeping this in view, the analysis is confined to the prominent occupation groups, namely farm and non-farm casual labour, self-employed farmers, and those engaged in non-farm business. The sample size of regular salaried being small, it has been omitted for discussion. Further, since caste- and untouchability-based discrimination is more acutely faced by the low-caste Untouchables (or SCs), the analysis related to market discrimination is confined to low-caste Untouchables and HCs. The latter include the OBCs and HCs. Thus the analysis is focused on discrimination practised against low-caste Untouchables by the HCs (HCs comprising OBCs and other HCs, that is, all castes other than Untouchables) in market and non-market transactions.

Coming to the occupational pattern, we have classified the
workers into five broad categories for the purpose of analysis—farm
casual labour, non-farm casual labour, salaried worker, self-employed
cultivator, and self-employed businessperson. Tables 5.2 and 5.3
contain the numbers and proportion of workers classified according
to the occupational patterns for the three states.

In all, there are about 791 farm casual labourers and 195 non-
farm casual labourers. These two categories, together, account for 40
per cent of total workers. These are 141 salaried workers, which is
8.3 per cent of total workers. Self-employed cultivators number 409,
and the self-employed engaged in non-farm business are about 160
in number.

Among the SCs, farm casual labourers number about 111 (50.7
per cent of total SC workers), and non-farm casual labourers are 29
(13.2 per cent of total SC workers). Thus 64 per cent of the SC
workers are casual labourers engaged in farm and non-farm activities.
Further, 31 SCs are regular salaried workers (14.2 per cent of the

TABLE 5.2: Occupational Characteristics of Workers in Sample Villages,
2003–4

(in numbers)

| | Farm casual labour | Non-farm casual labour | Salaried person | SEA (cultivator) | SENA (business) | Grand total |
|---|---|---|---|---|---|---|
| Muslim | 9 | 0 | 3 | 11 | 4 | 27 |
| | (33.3) | (0.0) | (11.1) | (40.7) | (14.8) | (100.0) |
| SCs | 111 | 29 | 31 | 30 | 18 | 219 |
| | (50.7) | (13.2) | (14.2) | (13.7) | (8.2) | (100.0) |
| STs | 16 | 3 | 0 | 4 | 5 | 28 |
| | (57.14) | (10.71) | (0.00) | (14.29) | (17.86) | (100.0) |
| OBCs | 484 | 156 | 21 | 114 | 93 | 868 |
| | (55.8) | (18.0) | (2.4) | (13.1) | (10.7) | (100.0) |
| HCs | 171 | 7 | 86 | 250 | 40 | 554 |
| | (30.9) | (1.3) | (15.5) | (45.1) | (7.2) | (100.0) |
| All castes | 791 | 195 | 141 | 409 | 160 | 1696 |
| | (46.6) | (11.5) | (8.3) | (24.1) | (9.4) | (100.0) |

Note: SEA: Self-Employed in Agriculture; SENA: Self-Employed in Non-Agriculture;
Figures in parentheses indicate percentage of respective value

total SC workers). Self-employed SC cultivators number 30 (13.7 per cent) and there are 18 self-employed SCs in non-farm activities (8.2 per cent of total SC workers). These two together account for about 22 per cent of the total workforce among the SC.

Among the OBCs, 484 workers are farm casual labour and another 156 are non-farm casual labour (73 per cent of total OBC workers). The regular salaried workers are 21 in number and account for 2.1 of total OBC workers. The OBC self-employed cultivators number 114 (13.1 per cent of total OBC workers) while self-employed in non-farm activities number 93 (10.7 per cent of total OBC workers). The ST persons in the sample are very few in number, that is 28, of which 16 workers are farm casual labour and three are non-farm casual labour, four are cultivators, and five are self-employed in non-farm activities.

Among the HCs, 171 workers are farm casual labour (30.9 per cent of total HC workers) and seven are non-farm casual labour (1.3 per cent of HC workers). The regular salaried workers are 86 in number and 15.5 per cent in proportion to total HC workers. The self-employed cultivators among the HCs number 250 (45.1 per cent of total HC workers) and self-employed in non-farm activities number 40 (7.2 per cent of HC workers).

To recapitulate, the proportion of farm and non-farm casual labour is maximum for the OBCs, followed by the SCs, and the least among HC workers. On the other hand, the proportion of self-employed workers among the HCs is the highest, followed by OBCs, STs, and SCs in that order.

At the regional level, in the sample village of Gujarat, casual labourers account for 47 per cent of the total workers, about 43 per cent are self-employed, and the rest are engaged in regular salaried and other occupations. At the social group level, SC workers are predominantly engaged as casual labour in agriculture (66.7 per cent), followed by the self-employed (16.7 per cent). A very small proportion of SC workers (6.7 per cent) are engaged as regular salaried workers. OBC workers follow a similar pattern of occupational distribution, with a higher proportion working as casual labour in agricultural activities, followed by self-employment and regular salaried occupations. HC workers work in a higher proportion as self-employed cultivators,

TABLE 5.3: Caste-wise Occupational Distribution of Workers in
Sample Villages, 2003–4

(in per cent)

| | Muslim | SCs | STs | OBCs | HCs | All castes |
|---|---|---|---|---|---|---|
| Non-working member | 62.5 | 58.5 | 70.0 | 54.6 | 66.0 | 60.8 |
| *Casual worker* | | | | | | |
| Non-farm labour | 0.0 | 14.0 | 9.5 | 19.2 | 0.6 | 10.6 |
| Agricultural labour | 29.6 | 39.4 | 42.9 | 31.2 | 25.0 | 30.1 |
| *Self-employed* | | | | | | |
| Cultivator | 40.7 | 15.5 | 19.0 | 20.7 | 49.2 | 31.4 |
| Self-employed in non-farm sector | 14.8 | 9.3 | 23.8 | 16.8 | 7.9 | 12.3 |
| *Regular salaried* | | | | | | |
| Temporary salaried in private sector | 0.0 | 7.8 | 0.0 | 0.9 | 6.1 | 3.9 |
| Permanent salaried in private sector | 0.0 | 4.7 | 0.0 | 1.3 | 1.0 | 1.6 |
| Temporary salaried in co-operative sector | 0.0 | 0.5 | 0.0 | 0.2 | 0.8 | 0.5 |
| Permanent salaried in co-operative sector | 0.0 | 0.5 | 0.0 | 0.0 | 1.4 | 0.6 |
| Temporary salaried in government sector | 3.7 | 0.0 | 0.0 | 0.4 | 1.2 | 0.7 |
| Permanent salaried in government sector | 11.1 | 2.1 | 4.8 | 0.9 | 6.5 | 3.5 |
| *Others* | | | | | | |
| Engaged in household activities | 0.0 | 4.1 | 0.0 | 1.3 | 0.0 | 1.2 |
| Casual labour in both agriculture and non-agriculture sector | 0.0 | 2.1 | 0.0 | 7.2 | 0.0 | 3.4 |
| Pensionary | 0.0 | 0.0 | 0.0 | 0.0 | 0.4 | 0.2 |
| Grand total | 100.0 | 100.0 | 100.0 | 100.0 | 100.0 | 100.0 |

as compared to the SCs and OBCs. In Orissa, 46 per cent of total workers are engaged as casual labour, 36 per cent are self-employed, 6.3 per cent work in regular salaried activities, while 11 per cent are involved in other activities. Workers from the SC and OBC social groups work in a higher proportion as casual labourers, followed by those who are self-employed. On the other hand, in the village of Maharashtra, more than half of the total workers are engaged in self-employed activities, especially in the farm sector. In this village, 30 per cent of the total workers are engaged as casual labourers. This pattern of occupation is observed across social groups as well, with more than 50 per cent of workers engaged in self-employed activities.

## EMPIRICAL RESULTS: PATTERNS OF DISCRIMINATION

### Caste and Labour Market

Labour market discrimination is measured by the difference between low-caste Untouchables and HCs in the number of days employed in an agricultural year. We assumed that the skill required for manual wage labour engaged in agriculture is generally available with low-caste Untouchable as well as HC labourers, and, therefore, the difference in employment rates between the lower-caste and HC manual wage labourers could be attributed to the hiring preferences of HC employers.

Similarly, the differences in the wage rates across all castes for similar manual wage labour could be attributed to wage discrimination practised by high-caste employers. The discrimination in the terms and conditions is reflected in the denial of certain types of jobs, conditions of work, and discriminatory behaviour at the workplace. The time period in all the c ises relates to one agricultural year, that is from July 2003 to June 2004.

Inter-caste differences are fairly clear in access to employment. At an aggregate level, average employment was about 108 days in an agricultural year. Casual labour from the HCs got employment for 154 days, while SC wage labourers were employed for only 100 days. The difference in employment rate between low-caste Untouchable and HC casual farm labourers suggests the discriminatory working of labour markets in favour of HC farm wage labour (see Table 5.4).

Similar differences are clearly visible in the case of non-farm casual wage labour. At an aggregate level, casual labour engaged in rural non-farm activities on an average gets employment for 224 days. The same for the SCs is about 189 days in a year, which is much lower than the 224 days for all, and 290 days for the HC labourer. The gap in the employment rate between the SCs and HCs is, indeed, quite significant.

**TABLE 5.4: Average Days of Employment of Casual Labour in Farm and Non-farm Sectors, 2003–4**

| Economic activities | SC | HC | All |
|---|---|---|---|
| Agricultural activities | 100 | 154 | 108 |
| Non-agricultural activities | 189 | 290 | 224 |

Wage discrimination between lower castes and the HCs is viewed in three different ways—differences in daily wage earnings, intervals in wage payment, and instalment of wage payment. The average daily wage rate is estimated for a whole year, taking *kharif* and *rabi* seasons together for casual farm labour. Table 5.5 clearly depicts that there are differences in wage rates between lower-caste and HC farm casual labour. The overall farm wage rate is about Rs 33 per day. The wage received by the SC farm wage labourer is about Rs 30, which is lower than the wage (Rs 34 per day) received by the HC farm wage labourer.

In the case of non-farm wage labour, the overall wage is about Rs 48 per day. The wage received by the SC non-farm wage labourer is Rs 58, compared with Rs 77 for the HC casual non-farm wage labourer.

**TABLE 5.5: Average Daily Wage Rate in Farm and Non-farm Sectors, 2003–4**

(in rupees)

| | SCs | STs | OBCs | HCs | All |
|---|---|---|---|---|---|
| Farm wages | 30 | 31 | 30 | 34 | 33 |
| Non-farm wages | 58 | 37 | 45 | 77 | 48 |

*Note*: For farm, average wage rates are for both kharif and rabi

## Wage Payment Interval

Besides inter-caste differences in employment rate and daily wage earnings, we have also studied the differences in the wage payment interval between low-caste Untouchables and the HCs. The analysis is done for casual farm labour in the kharif and rabi seasons.

Table 5.6 indicates the percentage of SC and HC farm casual labourers who received wage payment on various days in a week. At the overall level, in the kharif season, 20.5 per cent of our respondents reported that they had received wages on the same day, and 54.9 per cent on the next day. The remaining 24.6 per cent of casual labourers received their wages either after a week or on any day within a week of completing their work. In the case of the HCs, the percentages of farm wage labourers receiving wages on the same day, next day, and after a week are 56 per cent, 38 per cent, and 6 per cent respectively. SC casual farm labourers, however, are found to suffer the most with regard to the payment interval, with nearly 90 per cent of the respondents reporting the receipt of their wage payments a week or more later. Only about 9 per cent reported receiving wages on the same day or the next day, which is much lower as compared to the 94 per cent rate for the HCs. The discriminatory treatment of the SC farm casual labour in wage-payment interval is, thus, quite obvious.

Farm casual labour in the SC community also suffers in the rabi season with respect to wage-payment interval. About 92 per cent and 6 per cent reported to have received wages after a week and on any day within a week respectively. Only 2 per cent received their wages on the same day. As against this, in the case of HC farm labourers, about 55 per cent of the respondents received their wage payment on the same day, and another 41 per cent received their wages on the next day.

Thus the results indicate that SC wage labour suffered discrimination in terms of late payment of wages. The situation with respect to the time interval in wage payment is much less favourable for them as compared to their counterparts from the HCs. This obviously has an impact on their capacity to meet livelihood requirements on a daily basis. Given the meagre capacity of SC wage labour to meet their daily essential needs through own savings, this often compels them to resort to high-cost borrowing from moneylenders and others.

TABLE 5.6: Interval of Wage Payment for Different Work in Farm Activities, Season-wise

| Agricultural season/days employed | SCs | | OBCs | | HCs | | All | |
|---|---|---|---|---|---|---|---|---|
| | No. | Percentage | No. | Percentage | No. | Percentage | No. | Percentage |
| *Kharif* | | | | | | | | |
| Same day | 1 | 1.54 | 54 | 19.01 | 29 | 55.77 | 84 | 20.49 |
| Next day | 5 | 7.69 | 195 | 68.66 | 20 | 38.46 | 225 | 54.88 |
| After a week or more | 49 | 75.38 | 15 | 5.28 | 3 | 5.77 | 71 | 17.32 |
| At any day within a week | 10 | 15.38 | 20 | 7.04 | – | 0 | 30 | 7.32 |
| Total | 65 | 100 | 284 | 100 | 52 | 100 | 410 | 100 |
| *Rabi* | | | | | | | | |
| Same day | 1 | 2.08 | 61 | 63.54 | 25 | 54.35 | 87 | 45.31 |
| Next day | 0 | 0 | 1 | 1.04 | 19 | 41.30 | 20 | 10.42 |
| After a week or more | 44 | 91.67 | 33 | 34.38 | 2 | 4.35 | 81 | 42.19 |
| At any day within a week | 3 | 6.25 | 1 | 1.04 | 0 | 0 | 4 | 2.08 |
| Total | 48 | 100 | 96 | 100 | 46 | 100 | 192 | 100 |

*Note:* The statistics in the table are based on the number of workers who responded. Hence the figures may not match with those of the sample size in Table 5.4

## REASONS FOR LABOUR MARKET DISCRIMINATION

The discussion in the preceding section brings out significant differences between low-caste Untouchable and HC wage labour in labour market outcomes, in terms of employment rate, wage rate, and interval of wage payment. Inter-caste differences in employment rates and wage earnings among casual wage labour with similar manual skills seem to be driven by non-economic factors. Given the limitations of quantitative questions in capturing the reasons for discrimination, which are embedded in dense caste-economic relations, we used qualitative methods and posed some questions relating to working of labour markets to the SC respondents, who face discrimination in employment and wage rate. Hence the analysis relating to causes of discrimination is based on responses from the sample persons belonging to SC wage labour. In order to capture the nature and extent of discrimination faced by farm and non-farm casual labourers, the views of all wage labourers were sought. About 100 wage labourers belonging to the SCs responded to the qualitative questions. Nearly 38 of them mentioned specific reasons. The responses of these 38 persons are given in Table 5.7.

TABLE 5.7: Reasons for Employer Preference for Own Caste and/or HC Persons

| Reasons | Responses | |
|---|---|---|
| | Number | Percentage |
| Caste sympathy | 18 | 47.37 |
| Caste labourers are hard working | 1 | 2.63 |
| Caste labourers are loyal | 17 | 44.74 |
| Unemployment among them is high | 2 | 5.26 |
| Other reasons | – | – |
| Total respondents | 38 | 100 |

Of the total respondents, about one-third reported preference by HC employers for persons of their own caste. In response to the question about the reason for preference for own-caste wage labour by the HCs, about 47 per cent mentioned caste affinity and another 45 per cent reported loyalty of own-caste person. Thus about 92 per cent of SC respondents reported caste preference as a factor in discrimination by the HCs against SC wage labourers in hiring.

Discrimination in hiring was further studied by probing into aspects relating to complete or partial denial of work in some seasons, as well as denial for some specific work. On the question of general denial in hiring, 62 per cent answered in the positive, indicating denial in employment by the HC employer with regard to some areas, which mainly included processing and cutting of some crops. About 7 per cent respondents reported denial in hiring by the HCs in any work; 3 per cent in some season; and about 90 per cent in some specific work. The notion of impurity associated with the status of Untouchable labourers seems to be the factor behind the denial of work in some specific areas of farm operation.

TABLE 5.8: Type of Work Denied in Agricultural and Non-agricultural Activities

| Agricultural | Number of respondents | Per cent | Non-agricultural | Number of respondents | Per cent |
|---|---|---|---|---|---|
| | | | House construction | 3 | 7.14 |
| Processing of crop | 26 | 74.29 | Social ceremony | 27 | 64.29 |
| Cutting of crop | 3 | 8.57 | Work in restaurant | 3 | 7.14 |
| Don't know | 6 | 17.14 | Sales person in grocery shop | NR | NR |
| | | | Any household work | 9 | 21.43 |
| Total | 35 | 100 | Total | 42 | 100 |

This aspect is more obvious in exclusion in hiring of SC labourers in some specific non-farm work (Table 5.8). In the case of non-farm work, it is observed that SC labour faced exclusion in work relating to social ceremonies, house construction, and restaurants. About 64 per cent reported exclusion in work relating to social ceremony; 7 per cent in house construction; 7 per cent in work in restaurants; and about 21 per cent in any household work. Generally, work inside the house of HC persons seems to be confined to HCs only.

We also enquired into the reasons for wage discrimination faced by SC workers. Three out of 10 SC respondents reported lower wages due to their caste background. We have also mentioned the discrimination faced by SC wage labour in the time inteval of wage payment in the earlier section. SC respondents who faced discrimination in the payment of their wages generally attributed the differential treatment to the caste biases of HC employers. SC labourers also reported discrimination through the practice of untouchability in payment (or transfer) of cash. About 22 per cent of SC respondents reported this type of treatment by HC employers due to their social status as 'untouchable', which results in their giving wages either by placing the cash on the ground or dropping it in the hand from a distance to avoid physical contact.

## CASTE AND THE LAND MARKET

The involvement of SCs in the purchase of land for agricultural purposes is very limited. In the entire sample, only five households reported purchase of agricultural land. The land had been purchased from OBCs, their own caste members, and STs. Thus, by and large, land transactions for purchase by SC persons were with landowners belonging to the OBCs, STs, or own caste. HCs did not figure in land transactions with the SCs. Four out of five respondents indicated that they paid more than the market price in the purchase of agricultural land. In other words, SC persons were required to pay higher prices, which indicates price discrimination in the agricultural land market.

The land purchased was reported to be of good quality in four out of five transactions. About 34 persons responded when quizzed about the general difficulties faced by SC persons in the village while purchasing agricultural land (Table 5.9). They reported various kinds of difficulties, which resulted in the purchase of land at long distance from the native village, or away from the catchment areas of irrigation canals, or away from high-caste land, or even purchase of inferior-quality land. Of the total respondents, about 56 per cent reported that the discrimination in the land market came in the

**TABLE 5.9: Problems Faced by the Scheduled Castes in Purchasing Agricultural Land**

| Details of the problem | Number of respondents | Percentage |
|---|---|---|
| SCs are required to purchase land far away from the village | 8 | 23.53 |
| SCs are required to purchase low-quality land | 2 | 5.88 |
| SCs generally get land away from the catchment areas of irrigation facility | 5 | 14.71 |
| SCs generally denied land that is surrounded by land of HCs | 19 | 55.88 |
| Total | 34 | 100 |

form of denial of sale of agricultural land to SC buyers when it involved a common border with a high-caste landowner. About 24 per cent also reported refusal to sell land that was near the village (forcing SCs to buy land a long distance away). Another 15 per cent SC respondents said that they were denied land that was in the catchment area of an irrigation project. Six per cent respondents mentioned that discrimination also figured in the form of refusal by HCs to sell good-quality land, which ultimately forced the SCs into buying inferior quality land.

Instances of sale of agricultural land to the HCs by SCs, or sales transaction by SCs at lower than market prices, were insignificant. However, two households reported that circumstances were created by the HCs under which the SCs were required to sell the land.

There seems to be an instinctive caste preference by the HCs in sale of land to persons of their own caste (Table 5.10). About 64 per cent of the SC respondents reported caste preference as the determining factor in the sale of agriculture land by the HCs, compared to 20 per cent who mentioned price as the only factor in the sale of agricultural land. Another 5 per cent mentioned that at a given market price, the HCs would generally give preference to persons of their own caste. The remaining 10 per cent reported that agricultural land is generally sold by the HCs to anybody, irrespective of caste background and, thus, the sale is governed by the price factor alone.

| TABLE 5.10: Preferences of Higher Castes in the Sale of Agricultural Land | | |
|---|---|---|
| | Number of respondents | Percentage |
| Anybody who gives high price | 11 | 20 |
| Own caste | 35 | 63.64 |
| Anybody who gives high price and own caste | 3 | 5.45 |
| Anybody who gives high price, even Untouchables | 1 | 1.82 |
| Own caste and Untouchables also if ready to give high price | 4 | 7.27 |
| Others, specify | 1 | 1.82 |
| Total | 55 | 100 |

## Homestead Land and Residential Houses

The SC respondents faced various kinds of restrictions in the purchase of land for construction of residential dwellings in predominantly high-caste localities, and in renting property within predominantly high-caste localities. Generally, the HCs do not buy land for construction of houses in a low-caste locality.

Permitting the SCs to buy a house in a high-caste locality, or to rent a house in that locality, or alternatively, for a high-caste person to buy land in a low-caste locality or to rent a house in their locality, means breaking the traditional residential segregation in housing, which is a ubiquitous feature of the caste-wise residential pattern in the rural areas. Thus caste-wise residential segregation in housing is a common pattern that was observed in the sample villages.

About 67 SCs responded to the question regarding the high castes willingness to buy land for house construction in a low-caste locality. Out of 67 respondents, 60 reported that generally the high castes did not buy land for construction of a house in a low-caste locality. Only seven respondents, accounting for 5 per cent of the total, mentioned that the high castes would buy land in a low-caste locality.

A majority (93.3 per cent) of the low-caste Untouchables mentioned that the HCs generally do not buy land for residential purposes in low-caste localities because of caste prejudice. Only 5 per cent mentioned that the price charged by the low castes was the reason for a high-caste person not buying land in a low-caste locality.

During the course of the survey, the low castes were also asked whether they were allowed to buy land to construct houses in a high-caste locality. Out of 67 respondents, about 62 (92 per cent) mentioned that they were generally not allowed to buy land in a high-caste locality. Of the 62 respondents who said that they were not allowed to buy land, about 41 mentioned that the high castes did not like low castes to stay in their locality. About eight of them reported that they themselves were not socially comfortable about staying in a high-caste locality. Thus caste prejudice emerged as the main reason for the low castes not being able to buy land in a high-caste locality for construction of houses. Further, of the 53 respondents who were asked for their opinion on renting a house in a high-caste locality, 39 (73 per cent) mentioned that they would face restrictions in getting house on rent. The unwillingness of the HCs to share housing with Untouchables, thus, prohibits the breaking of the customary patterns of caste-based residential segregation in Indian villages.

## Agricultural Land-rental Market

About 22 SCs had taken agricultural land on lease for the purpose of cultivation. It emerged from the reported evidence that the SCs faced differential treatment either in the form of refusal to rent land by the HCs, or through renting of land on unfavourable terms and conditions. About 33 per cent of the respondents reported that HC landowners had refused to rent land to them. Of those who managed to get some land on lease, about 22 per cent had been offered lease under unfavourable terms and conditions—generally different from those of HC tenants. Thus it appeared from the data that although the land-lease market is fairly open to the SCs, they do face discrimination in terms of selective denial of land on rent and/or unfavourable terms and conditions.

## Agriculture Input Market

The purchase of inputs required in farming is not free of discrimination. Of the total sample households, 30 households (31 per cent) carry out cultivation as their main occupation and participate in the market in purchasing various inputs and services, including hiring of farm implements from HC cultivators. Discrimination in the input market relates to restrictions faced by SC cultivators in the purchase of inputs such as irrigation and agricultural implements, and access to services of high-caste human labour.

Two out of 15 respondents mentioned difficulties faced in the purchase of inputs, including the inability to access the input on time or the requirement to pay more than the prevailing market price. Thus it appeared that access to the input market is fairly open, and the incidence of those who faced caste-related restrictions in the purchase of the inputs is relatively less compared to other markets. Given the small size of the sample, these observations need to be treated with caution.

In the case of access to private irrigation, only two respondents reported difficulties in acquiring water for irrigation from private suppliers, and one of them mentioned higher price for irrigation water. The respondents did not report caste-related restrictions in access to public irrigation.

SC cultivators face some restrictions in the hiring of implements and human and bullock labour from the HCs. Three respondents reported having faced difficulties, which included refusal to provide services of agricultural implements and supply of implements that was not timely. Compared to agricultural implements, caste-related restrictions are more pronounced in the case of hiring of high-caste human labour by SC cultivators. Of the total SC respondents, six (26 per cent) reported HC labour declining to work in the fields of SC farmers. While pointing to the reasons, most of the respondents mentioned that HC wage labourers considered it beneath their dignity to work on the farm of SC cultivators. Thus it seems that SC farmers face restrictions in hiring high-caste labour and, therefore, are required to depend more on wage labour from their own caste.

Similarly, the supply of bullock labour to SC farmers faced caste-related restrictions. Of the total respondents, about six households (20 per cent) were denied the services of bullocks by high-caste households. About 67 per cent of the SC respondents reported that the HCs considered it beneath their dignity to hire out bullocks to 'Untouchable' farmers.

SC households also faced caste-related restrictions on the use of their implements and bullock by high-caste cultivators. About 13 per cent reported that the HCs would not hire implements owned by the SCs. It is important to note that all of them mentioned caste prejudice as a reason for refusal to hire implements and transport equipment owned by SC families.

## MARKET IN SALE AND PURCHASE OF FARM AND NON-FARM GOODS

Discrimination faced by the SCs in the sale and purchase of farm and non-farm consumer goods is measured in terms of refusal by

TABLE 5.11: Discrimination in Sale of Farm Output and Reasons for the Higher Castes Not Buying from Scheduled Caste Sellers

|  | Number of respondents | Percentage |
|---|---|---|
| Place of sale by the SCs |  |  |
| In the village | 4 | 16 |
| Outside the village | 8 | 32 |
| In the regular market | 6 | 24 |
| All the above places | 6 | 24 |
| Other | 1 | 4 |
| Total | 25 | 100 |
| Reasons for not buying from the SCs |  |  |
| SCs charge high price | 0 | 0 |
| SCs sell low-quality products | 4 | 25 |
| SCs are considered to be unclean and polluting | 11 | 68.75 |
| Other | 1 | 6.25 |
| Total | 16 | 100 |
| Distances travelled by the SCs to sell the farm products (in kilometres) |  |  |
| 1–10 | 11 | 52.38 |
| 11–20 | 3 | 14.29 |
| 21–30 | 3 | 14.29 |
| 31–50 | 1 | 4.76 |
| 51–100 | 2 | 9.52 |
| 101–200 | 1 | 4.76 |
| Total | 21 | 100 |

the HCs to buy goods from SC sellers and in not selling goods to them. Of about 25 SC respondents who were engaged in selling of their products, about 16 faced restrictions in selling the goods. The information about the preference of HC buyers was ascertained from the SC respondents. In response to a question about why the HCs do not buy goods from them, about two-thirds of the SC respondents mentioned their impure status as a reason. Low quality of the product was another reason given by HC buyers. This was reported by one-fourth of the SC respondents.

## Sale and Purchase of Vegetables and Milk

Since the notion of the impure status of low-caste Untouchables is an important reason for not buying goods from them, particularly consumer goods, more specific questions were asked about consumer items such as milk and vegetables. Milk and vegetables are important items sold and purchased by all households on a daily basis in rural areas. Given the importance of these goods, and the ways in which they interact with the notion of purity and pollution associated with the Untouchables, we expected instances of discrimination to be

TABLE 5.12: Sources of Vegetable Purchase by High-caste Households and Reasons for Not Purchasing it from Scheduled Castes

| | Number of respondents | Percentage |
|---|---|---|
| Vegetables purchased by HC persons by the caste background of seller | | |
| Anybody | 8 | 33.33 |
| Anybody other than Untouchables | 3 | 12.50 |
| Own caste | 7 | 29.17 |
| Higher caste | 3 | 12.50 |
| Other | 3 | 12.50 |
| Total | 24 | 100 |
| Reasons for not purchasing vegetables from SC sellers | | |
| High price | 3 | 20 |
| Not maintaining cleanliness | 1 | 6.67 |
| Considered polluting | 11 | 73.33 |
| Total | 16 | 100 |

high. To a more specific query about whether the HCs buy vegetables from the Untouchables, about 16 SC respondents indicated that the HCs do not buy vegetables from them, mainly due to the perceived impure status of low-caste Untouchables. Of the total respondents who said that the HCs do not buy vegetables from low-caste sellers, nearly 73 per cent indicated the purity and pollution notion to be the main reason (Table 5.12).

The SC seller faces discrimination while selling milk as well (Table 5.13). About 14 SC respondents indicated that the HCs generally avoided buying milk from the Untouchables. Only 3 per cent indicated that the HC buyer is neutral about the caste of the seller. Of the total respondents who said that the HCs do not buy milk and vegetables from low-caste sellers, nearly 93 per cent indicated that the HCs do so because they consider goods purchased from a low-caste seller to be impure and polluting. Thus the traditional notion of purity and impurity associated with the status of 'Untouchable' persons greatly influences the purchase of

TABLE 5.13: Purchase of Milk by High-caste Households and Reasons for Not Purchasing from Scheduled Castes

| Responses | Number of respondents | Percentage |
|---|---|---|
| Purchase of milk by the HCs | | |
| From anybody | 3 | 13.64 |
| Anybody other than the SCs | 3 | 13.64 |
| Own caste | 7 | 31.82 |
| Higher caste | 6 | 27.27 |
| Other | 3 | 13.64 |
| Total | 22 | 100 |
| Reasons behind not purchasing from the SCs | | |
| High price | 1 | 7.14 |
| Considered polluting | 6 | 42.86 |
| Not maintained cleanliness and notion of pollution and purity | 4 | 28.57 |
| Considered polluting and notion of pollution and purity | 3 | 21.43 |
| Total | 14 | 100 |

consumer goods, such as milk and vegetables, by the high castes from low-caste sellers.

Due to restrictions on the part of high-caste buyers on the purchase of goods sold by SCs, the latter try to use alternative market avenues to sell their products. To a question regarding alternative sales strategies, SC sellers indicated that they focus on buyers from their own caste and also look for sales in outside markets, where their caste identity is hidden. Of the total SC respondents, about 16 persons (17 per cent) indicated that they generally resort to sales in outside markets, which involve travelling for distances ranging from a few kilometres to over 100 kilometres. Another 4 per cent focus on customers from their own caste.

## TRADITIONAL CASTE OCCUPATIONS

There are six occupations that have been identified as traditional caste-related occupations, including barbers, scavengers, tailors, musicians, and sweepers. Out of the 94 households surveyed, 17 reported having traditional occupations. Seven of them reported these occupations as their primary activity.

Looking at three of the services individually—namely barber, washerman, and carpenter—discrimination is evident in various degrees. In the case of barbers, 64 per cent of the respondents mentioned that there are separate barbers for higher- and lower-caste persons. High-caste persons do not avail the services of lower-caste barbers, nor are Untouchables allowed to utilize the services of HC barbers. In the case of washermen, 23 per cent of the respondents reported that there were separate washermen for higher- and lower-caste households. In the case of carpenters, the respondents reported minimal discrimination in the use of their services. Thus discrimination was reported to be high in the case of barbers, less for washermen, and least for carpenters.

## DISCUSSION

The main purpose of this chapter was to develop an understanding of caste- and untouchability-based discrimination experienced by low-caste Untouchables in various market and non-market transactions. The chapter began with the hypothesis that the customary rules and norms that govern the economic organization of the caste system, involve denial of rights to property, education, business, and employment in certain spheres to low-caste Untouchables. In the market framework, this means that the denial of property rights would operate through market transactions such as the labour market, agricultural land market, credit market, input market, and product and consumer goods markets. Although the property regime has changed and the former Untouchables now have equal legal rights to property and employment, the old restrictions still prevail as remnants of the past in modified form, if not in their original form.

With this hypothesis, the chapter studied the pattern of market discriminations experienced by the former Untouchables, based on data from three villages covering 664 households and about 1700 workers engaged in various occupations. Since there is a shortage of studies on this theme, we had to first develop the concept of caste- and untouchability-based market discrimination, and an appropriate questionnaire to capture the various forms of market and non-market discrimination. It needs to be emphasized that the discrimination operates through the network of social relations and, therefore, it often takes forms that are difficult to capture through quantitative questions. We, therefore, supplemented the quantitative questions with qualitative enquiry. The results provided useful insights into the working of markets in the rural area in relation to the former Untouchables. Within the limitations of the data, the results throw light on the nature of the discriminatory working of various markets.

The first point that emerged from the results is a degree of modification and positive change that has occurred in the traditional caste ownership of property and occupation, and in the pattern of employment. Under traditional customary rules, the Untouchables were denied the right to property such as farmland and non-farm business (except some occupations considered to be impure) and, hence, their main occupation was to service the HCs through wage labour. The sample survey indicates that although 64 per cent of SC workers continued with wage labour as the main occupation, about 14 per cent owned some land and practised cultivation as their main occupation, and another 8 per cent were engaged in non-farm production and business. Together, farm and non-farm occupations involving self-employed activities account for about 22 per cent of the total workers. Thus about one-fifth of the former Untouchables are found to be the owners of fixed capital assets. This is a small but important change in property ownership by Untouchables. In view of the fact that the Untouchables were not allowed to own land and undertake farming, or engage in certain businesses, this shift, small as it is, is indicative of the positive outcomes of an egalitarian rule regarding property rights under the present Constitution.

The second important result of the study, however, relates to the continuance of customary restrictions and, hence, discrimination against the low-caste Untouchables in various market and non-market transactions in some form, if not in their original form and character. This mainly includes the employment market in farm and non-farm activities, the market for factors of production (or various inputs and services required in farm production), and the retail markets for sale in consumer and other goods. Discrimination takes various forms at the time of the involvement of the Untouchables in different markets, namely in seeking employment in farm and non-farm operations, in seeking inputs and services necessary for undertaking production, including business, and in the sale and purchase of products and consumer goods. This indicates that although the Untouchables have access to various markets, it is characterized by restrictions and discriminatory behaviour on the part of high-caste persons.

In the case of the labour market, the results indicate that Untouchable casual labourers face discrimination in accessing employment in the farm and non-farm sectors. Their level of yearly employment in both the farm and non-farm sectors, measured by the average number of days employed in a year, turns out to be lower than that of HC casual wage labourers. This happened due to denial of employment to them in some types of work. In the farm sector, operations where they face selective exclusion include harvesting, presumably in the harvesting of fruits and vegetables. In non-farm work, the exclusion of Untouchables is fairly widespread and common in the case of various types of household work.

Similarly, the study also throws up evidence of wage discrimination. The daily wage earnings of the Untouchable labourer in both farm and non-farm work is lower than that of an identical high-caste wage labourer. Wage discrimination is also reflected in the time interval in payment of wages and the manner in which wages are delivered to the Untouchable labourer. Compared to high-caste labourers, the Untouchables receive wage payment after long time intervals. The Untouchable labourers often also face discrimination associated with their so-called impure status, when the employers refuse to give wages in cash in their hands and, instead, either keep the money on the ground or drop it in their hands from a distance to avoid physical touch.

It also emerged from the results that selective denial of employment to Untouchables by HC employers goes hand in hand with a preference to hire workers either of their own caste or of a higher caste. Caste affinity (rather than productivity) appears to be the main reason for preference of own-caste persons. Refusal to hire Untouchables for domestic work in high-caste homes is related to the notions of pollution, namely the belief that physical contact and social interaction with 'Untouchable' persons is polluting.

The results relating to other markets are equally revealing. In the case of the agricultural land market, although sale and purchase is fairly open to everybody, including the SCs and land transactions are governed by market forces, Untouchable buyers confront restrictions of various kinds. Land sales seem to be generally confined to persons of the seller's caste or an HC, and this provides restricted entry for Untouchable buyers. In the event of purchase, the latter face various constraints, which include refusal to sell them land that is adjacent to the farms of high castes, near the village, and/or adjacent to an irrigation project command area. As a consequence, the Untouchables generally end up buying land at a long distance from their native villages, or land that is of inferior quality and away from an irrigation facility.

The agriculture land-lease market seems to be fairly open, although some respondents reported discriminatory treatment in the terms and conditions of lease. Exclusion and discrimination is fairly widespread in the sale and purchase of land for residential construction in localities dominated by high-caste residents. Exclusion of Untouchables is also fairly widespread in the case of renting of a house in a high-caste locality. The HCs also generally do not buy land for construction of a house in a low-caste locality. Residential segregation seems to persist in its traditional form on a fairly wide scale.

The access to the market in various inputs, such as human labour, bullocks, implements, and water for irrigation, seems to be fairly open to the Untouchables. Yet, they face selective restrictions in hiring HC labour and the services of bullocks or implements owned by the HCs. High-caste persons seem to regard it as beneath their dignity to work for wages in the fields of low-caste landowners, or to provide them the services of their bullocks and implements.

Untouchables also face selective restrictions on the sale of consumer goods, particularly vegetables and milk. Accordingly, low-caste sellers must depend on members of their own caste as consumers, and/or sell their products and goods in markets away from their villages, where their identity is not known. This, however, adds to their transportation and labour costs.

These results indicate that although there has been a positive change in the ownership of capital assets and access to employment, traditional caste relations have not altogether disappeared. They continue as remnants of the past and affect the access of low-caste Untouchables to various rural markets for buying of land and inputs necessary for production, as also for the sale of various goods. Discriminatory access has obvious consequences on the ownership of capital assets, employment, and business. The results bring to the fore the linkages between market discrimination and high poverty of the Untouchables. Thus, today if we see persons from the 'Untouchable' community with low ownership of capital assets like agricultural land and business, low ownership of retail business, and low employment and wage earnings, it has close links with the discriminatory access to markets in agricultural land, capital, input and retail consumer goods, and employment. The discrimination-induced/linked deprivation and poverty of the former Untouchables is something that has not yet become the subject of enquiry in theoretical and empirical studies on poverty and deprivation in the discipline of economics. This study has barely opened up the issue of market discrimination in the rural setting, and the consequences for income and poverty of the discriminated groups. However, given the possible wider consequences of market and non-market economic discrimination for economic growth, inequalities, and inter-group conflict, more systematic, theoretical, and empirical research is necessary.

## REFERENCES

Khan, Mumtaz Ali (1995), *Human Rights and the Dalits*, Delhi: Uppal.
Saha, G., H. Mander, Sukhadeo Thorat, Satish Deshpande, and Amita Baviskar (2006), *Untouchability in Rural India*, Delhi: Sage.
Thorat, Sukhadeo (2006), 'On Economic Exclusion and Inclusive Policy', *Little*, vol. VI, nos 4 and 5, pp. 7–17.
—— (2008), 'Labour Maket Discrimantion: Concept, Forms and Remedies in Indian Situation', *Indian Journal of Labour Economics*, vol. 51, no. 1, pp. 31–52.
Thorat, Sukhadeo and M. Mahamallik (2004), 'Labour Market and Occupation Discrimination in Rural Area', Working Paper, Delhi: Indian Institute of Dalit Studies.
Thorat, Sukhadeo and Narendra Kumar (2008), *B.R. Ambedkar: Perspectives on Social Exclusion and Inclusive Policies*, New Delhi: Oxford University Press.
Tripathy, R.B. (1994), *Dalits: A Sub-Human Society*, Delhi: Ashish.
Venkateswarlu, D. (1990), *Harijan: Upper Class Conflict*, Delhi: Discovery.

# Non-market Discrimination
## Health, Education, and Food-related Institutions

# 6

# Inequality in Health Outcomes in India
## The Role of Caste and Religion

*Vani K. Borooah*

The publication of the Black report (Black *et al.* 1980) spawned a number of studies in industrialized countries that examined the social factors underlying health outcomes. The fundamental finding from these studies, particularly with respect to mortality and life expectancy, was the existence of 'a social gradient' in mortality: 'wherever you stand on the social ladder, your chances of an earlier death are higher than it is for your betters' (Epstein 1998). The social gradient in mortality was observed for most of the major causes of death: for example, Marmot (2000) showed that, for every one of 12 diseases, the ratio of deaths (from the disease) to numbers in a Civil Service grade rose steadily as one moved down the hierarchy.

Since, ultimately, it is the individual who falls ill, it is tempting for epidemiologists to focus on the risks inherent in individual behaviour: for example, smoking, diet, and exercise. However, the most important implication of a social gradient to health outcomes is that people's susceptibility to disease depends on more than just their individual behaviour; crucially, it depends on the social environment within which they lead their life (Marmot 2000, 2004). Consequently, the focus on interpersonal differences in risk might be usefully complemented by examining differences in risk between different social environments.

For example, even after controlling for interpersonal differences, mortality risks might differ by occupational class. This might be due to the fact that while low status jobs make fewer mental demands, they cause more psychological distress than high status jobs (Karasek and Marmot 1996; Griffin *et al.* 2002; Marmot 2004) with the result that people in higher-level jobs report significantly less job-related depression than people in lower-level jobs (Birdi *et al.* 1995).

In turn, anxiety and stress are related to disease: the stress hormones that anxiety releases affect the cardiovascular and immune systems, with the result that prolonged exposure to stress is likely to inflict multiple costs on health in the form of, *inter alia*, increased susceptibility to diabetes, high blood pressure, heart attack, and stroke (Marmot 1986; Brunner and Marmot 1999; Wilkinson and Marmot 1986). So, the social gradient in mortality may have a psychosocial basis, relating to the degree of control that individuals have over their lives.[1]

The 'social gradient to health' is essentially a Western construct and there has been very little investigation into whether, in developing countries as well, people's state of health is dependent on their social status. For example, in India, which is the country studied in this chapter, we know from studies of specific geographical areas that health outcomes differ systematically by gender and economic class (Sen *et al.* 2007). In addition, local government spending on public goods, including health-related goods, is, after controlling for a variety of factors, lower in areas with greater caste fragmentation as compared to ethnically more homogenous areas (Sengupta and Sarkar 2007).

Considering India in its entirety, two of its most socially depressed groups—the Adivasis[2] and the Dalits[3]—have some of the worst health outcomes: for example, as Guha (2007) observes, 28.9 per cent of Adivasis and 15.6 per cent of Dalits have no access to doctors or clinics and only 42.2 per cent of Adivasi children and 57.6 per cent of Dalit children have been immunized. Of course, it is possible that the relative poor health outcomes of India's socially backward groups has less to do with their low social status and much more to do with their weak economic position and with their poor living conditions. The purpose of this chapter is precisely to evaluate the relative strengths of economic and social status in determining the health status of persons in India. In other words, even after controlling for non-community factors, did the fact that Indians belonged to different social groups, encapsulating different degrees of social status, exercise a significant influence on the state of their health?

We answer this question using data from the Morbidity and Health Care Survey (M&HC Survey), for the period January–June

2004, conducted over all the states and Union Territories in India, by the Government of India's National Sample Survey Organisation (NSSO).[4] The M&HC Survey covered 73,868 households, encompassing 383,338 individuals. It examined several aspects of morbidity and health care of the respondents, but, from this study's perspective, three of these are of note:

(i)   Particulars of household members who died within the past 365 days.
(ii)  Particulars of economic independence and ailments on the date of survey of persons aged 60 years or more (hereafter, 'elderly' persons).
(iii) Particulars of prenatal and post-natal care for ever married women.

These aspects of morbidity and health care could, *inter alia*, be correlated with the social background of the households to which the respondents belonged. The M&HC Survey offered information about households in terms of the following social groups:

(i)     Adivasis (see fn. 2)
(ii)    Scheduled Tribe (ST) Christians[5]
(iii)   Dalits (see fn. 3)
(iv)    Non-Muslims from the Other Backward Classes (OBC)[6]
(v)     Muslims from the OBC
(vi)    Muslims not from the OBC
(vii)   Forward Caste (FC) Hindus (hereafter, simply 'Hindus')[7]
(viii)  Non-ST Christians
(ix)    Sikhs
(x)     Other religions

This chapter aims primarily to examine whether the following health outcomes varied systematically according to the social group to which people belonged:

(i)   The age of death
(ii)  The self-assessed health status of persons of age 60 years or more
(iii) The likelihood of elderly persons, who were in poor health, taking treatment for their ailments

(iv) The likelihood of women receiving prenatal and post-natal treatment

The purpose was to investigate whether, *after controlling for several non-group factors that might impinge on health outcomes*, people's health outcomes were significantly affected by their social group. The existence of a social group effect—whereby groups higher up the social ladder had better health outcomes than groups further down— would suggest that there was a 'social gradient' to health outcomes in India. Furthermore, there is the possibility that the 'social gradient' existed with respect to some outcomes but not to others. In so doing, the chapter addresses, in the Indian context, an issue which lies at the heart of social epidemiology: estimating the relative strengths of individual and social factors in determining health outcomes.

## DEATHS IN HOUSEHOLDS

The M&HC Survey asked households if any of their members had died in the previous year and, if the answer was in the affirmative, collected information about the deceased and some of the circumstances surrounding the deaths. In total, 1716 deaths were reported: 1634 of these deaths (95 per cent) were from households that had experienced a single death in the past year; 70 deaths (4 per cent) occurred in households that had experienced two deaths; and 12 deaths (1 per cent) occurred in households that had experienced three deaths.

Of these 1716 deaths, 9.1 per cent were Adivasis, 17.6 per cent were Dalits, 12 per cent were Muslims, and 21.3 were Hindus (Table 6.1).

By contrast, Adivasis, Dalits, and Hindus comprised 7.9, 16.9, and 23.6 per cent, respectively, of the total of the 383,288, persons in the M&HC–NSS sample. Thus, in respect of Adivasis and Dalits, there was a difference between their proportionate presence in the number of deaths and their proportionate presence in the sample.[8]

A more marked difference between the groups was in terms of the mean and median ages at death: as Table 6.1 shows, the mean age of death was 43.3 years for Adivasis, 41.6 years for Dalits, 43.4 years for OBC Muslims, and 43.8 years for non-OBC Muslims; by contrast,

**TABLE 6.1: Deaths in India by Social Groups**

| | NSS persons by social group | NSS persons by social group (%) | Deaths by social group (%) (Total: 1716) | Mean age of death by social group | Median age of death by social group |
|---|---|---|---|---|---|
| Adivasi | 30,158 | 7.9 | 9.2 | 43.3 | 45 |
| Christian (ST) | 15,160 | 4.0 | 3.8 | 49.4 | 55 |
| Dalits | 64,942 | 16.9 | 17.6 | 41.6 | 45 |
| OBC (non-Muslim) | 125,508 | 32.8 | 33.4 | 48.4 | 55 |
| OBC (Muslim) | 18,591 | 4.9 | 4.8 | 43.4 | 51 |
| Hindu (FC) | 90,371 | 23.6 | 21.3 | 54.2 | 60 |
| Muslim (non-OBC) | 29,785 | 7.8 | 7.2 | 43.8 | 50 |
| Christian (non-ST) | 3428 | 0.9 | 1.1 | 57.6 | 60 |
| Sikh | 3268 | 0.9 | 1.2 | 57.5 | 65 |
| Other religions | 2077 | 0.5 | 0.5 | 64.6 | 70 |
| Total | 383,288 | 100 | 100 | 47.7 | 54 |

*Source*: NSS 60th Round, Health File

the mean age at death was 57.5 for Sikhs and non-ST Christians, 54.2 years for Hindus, 49.4 years for ST Christians, and 48.4 years for the non-Muslim OBCs.

Table 6.2 shows whether the deceased received medical attention before death. The group least likely to receive medical attention before death were Adivasis and ST Christians: only 59 per cent of Adivasi deaths and 53 per cent of ST Christian deaths received medical attention in contrast to 76 per cent of Dalit deaths and 73 per cent of Muslim deaths. Although, in terms of the overall sample, there was little difference between the proportions of men and women receiving medical attention before death (69 per cent men, 71 per cent women) there were marked gender differences between some of the social groups: Muslim deaths were more likely to receive medical attention if they were women (80 per cent as compared to 70 per cent for Non-OBC Muslims) while Dalit deaths were more likely to receive medical attention if they were men (80 per cent as against 71 per cent for women).

TABLE 6.2: Medical Attention Received Before Death by Gender and Social Groups

| | Total deaths | Medical attention received before death as % of total deaths | Total male deaths | Medical attention received before death as % of total male deaths | Total female deaths | Medical attention received before death as % of total female deaths |
|---|---|---|---|---|---|---|
| Adivasi | 157 | 59 | 85 | 52 | 72 | 67 |
| Christian (ST) | 64 | 53 | 28 | 57 | 36 | 50 |
| Dalits | 302 | 76 | 166 | 80 | 136 | 71 |
| OBC (non-Muslim) | 573 | 69 | 338 | 66 | 235 | 74 |
| OBC (Muslim) | 82 | 73 | 46 | 70 | 36 | 78 |
| Hindu (FC) | 366 | 71 | 215 | 72 | 151 | 70 |
| Muslim (non-OBC) | 123 | 74 | 73 | 70 | 50 | 80 |
| Christian (non-ST) | 18 | 67 | 13 | 62 | 5 | 80 |
| Sikh | 21 | 81 | 14 | 86 | 7 | 71 |
| Other religions | 8 | 75 | 7 | 71 | 1 | 100 |
| Total | 1714 | 70 | 985 | 69 | 729 | 71 |

*Source*: NSS 60th Round, Health File

Table 6.3 presents the estimates from regressing the 'age at death' on a number of explanatory variables.[9] The first column shows the regression estimates obtained from all deaths in the sample; the second and third columns show the regression estimates obtained from all deaths in, respectively, the 'forward' and 'backward' states (and Union Territories) of India.[10] The mean ages at death in the forward and backward states were, respectively, 52.4 and 43.7 years—a difference of 8.7 years. After imposing all the controls shown in Table 6.3, the difference between forward and backward states in their averages at death was reduced to 7.4 years (Table 6.3, column 1).

The second variable in the regression was gender: Table 6.3 shows that, after controlling for other variables, there was no significant

TABLE 6.3: Regression Estimates of the Age at Death Equation, by
'Forward' and 'Backward' States

| | All deaths | Deaths in forward states | Deaths in backward states |
|---|---|---|---|
| Forward state | 7.4*** | – | – |
| | (4.80) | – | – |
| Female | –1.2 | –1.9 | –0.5 |
| | (0.83) | (0.94) | (0.25) |
| Labourer | –4.3** | –5.7** | –2.7 |
| | (2.49) | (2.30) | (1.15) |
| Rural | 4.9** | 2.2 | 7.8*** |
| | (2.51) | (0.83) | (2.63) |
| Structure | –2.9 | –0.7 | –3.7 |
| | (1.43) | (0.19) | (1.50) |
| Latrine | 1.5 | 2.5 | 0.5 |
| | (0.71) | (0.94) | (0.14) |
| Drain | 0.1 | –3.2 | 4.2 |
| | (0.06) | (1.10) | (1.25) |
| Water source | 1.9 | –2.5 | 6.2** |
| | (1.15) | (1.13) | (2.46) |
| Water treated | –2.2 | –2.9 | –2.3 |
| | (1.01) | (1.06) | (0.65) |
| Water treatment | 11.8*** | 10.9*** | 12.6*** |
| | (4.25) | (3.12) | (2.79) |
| Cooking fuel | 5.0** | 4.6 | 6.2* |
| | (2.17) | (1.55) | (1.75) |
| Total monthly household expenditure | 0.0004* | 0.0004 | 0.0005 |
| | (1.67) | (1.00) | (1.31) |
| Adivasis | –4.9* | –2.9 | –6.7* |
| | (1.71) | (0.59) | (1.78) |
| Christian (ST) | –3.9 | 0.0 | –6.5 |
| | (0.94) | (.) | (1.39) |
| Dalits | –7.1*** | –2.1 | –11.5*** |
| | (3.00) | (0.64) | (3.32) |
| OBC (non-Muslim) | –2.5 | –1.8 | –3.0 |
| | (1.29) | (0.69) | (1.04) |

*(Contd)*

*(Table 6.3 contd)*

|  | All deaths | Deaths in forward states | Deaths in backward states |
|---|---|---|---|
| OBC (Muslim) | –8.6** | –5.3 | –11.9** |
|  | (2.50) | (1.07) | (2.46) |
| Muslim (non-OBC) | –6.1** | –6.8* | –6.1 |
|  | (2.03) | (1.66) | (1.41) |
| Constant | 43.7*** | 53.6*** | 41.3*** |
|  | (13.05) | (10.67) | (8.82) |
| Observations | 1624 | 696 | 928 |
| R-squared | 0.08 | 0.06 | 0.07 |

*Notes:*
(i) Absolute value of *t*-statistics in parentheses
(ii) * significant at 10 per cent; ** significant at 5 per cent; *** significant at 1 per cent
(iii) 'Forward states': Andhra Pradesh, Chandigarh, Dadra and Nagar Haveli, Daman and Diu, Delhi, Goa, Gujarat, Haryana, Himachal Pradesh, Karnataka, Kerala, Maharashtra, Punjab, Tamil Nadu, and West Bengal. The remaining states and Union Territories were classified as 'backward'
(iv) Structure=1 if housing type was *pucca*, or semi-*pucca*, or 'serviceable' *kutcha* (i.e. good); 0 otherwise
(v) Latrine=1 if the latrines were flushing toilets or emptied into a sceptic tank; 0 otherwise
(vi) Drain=1 if drains were underground or were covered *pucca*; 0, otherwise
(vii) Water source=1 if the source of drinking water was from a tap; 0 otherwise
(viii) Water treated=1 if drinking water treated; 0 otherwise
(ix) Water treated=1 if the nature of treatment was boiling, filtering, or ultra-violet/resin/reverse osmosis; 0 otherwise
(x) Cooking fuel=1 if the cooking fuel was gas, *gobar* gas, kerosene, or electricity; 0 otherwise

difference between the average ages of the male and female deceased.[11] The next variable was whether the household type in which the deceased lived was a 'labourer' household:[12] Table 6.3 shows that, after imposing all controls, the average age at death was 4.3 years lower for labourer, compared to non-labourer, households. Since the sample differences between non-labourer and labourer households in the ages of their deceased was 6.9 years, imposing the controls reduced this difference but without eliminating it. Table 6.3 also shows that the average age at death was significantly different between labourer and non-labourer households in the forward states but not in the backward states. The average age of the deceased was significantly higher, by 4.9 years, in rural, compared to urban areas and, in the backward states, the rural–urban difference in average age at death was 7.8 years; however, in the forward states, there was no significant difference between rural and urban areas in the average age at death.

After these four controls—state type, gender, household type, and rural–urban sectors—the next set of controls related to the conditions in which the deceased lived.

(i)   The first component of this was the *type of housing structure* in which the deceased lived: this variable ('structure') was assigned the value 1 if the type was *pucca*, or semi-*pucca*, or 'serviceable' *kutcha* (that is, good); and 0 otherwise.

(ii)  The second component of living conditions related to the *quality of the latrines* used by the deceased: the variable 'latrine' was assigned the value 1 if the latrines were flushing toilets or emptied into a sceptic tank; and 0 otherwise.

(iii) The third component of living conditions related to the *quality of the drains*: the variable 'drain' was assigned the value 1 if the drains associated with the deceased's home were underground or were covered *pucca*; and 0 otherwise.

(iv)  The fourth component of living conditions related to the *quality of the source of drinking water* used by the deceased: the variable 'water source' was assigned the value 1 if the source of drinking water was from a tap; and 0 otherwise.

(v)   The fifth component of living conditions related to whether the drinking water used by the deceased was *treated*: the variable 'water treated' was assigned the value 1 if the drinking water was treated; and 0 otherwise.

(vi)  If the drinking water in the deceased's household was treated, the sixth component of living conditions related to the *nature of the treatment* of the drinking water: the variable 'water treatment' was assigned the value 1 if the nature of treatment was boiling, filtering, or ultra-violet/resin/reverse osmosis; and 0 otherwise.

(vii) The seventh, and last, component of living conditions related to the *nature of the cooking fuel* used by the deceased's household:

the variable 'cooking fuel' was assigned the value 1 if the cooking fuel was gas, *gobar* gas, kerosene, or electricity; and 0 otherwise.

Table 6.3 shows that, of these seven living conditions controls, it was only the nature of treatment of drinking water and the type of cooking fuel used that had a significant effect on the age of the deceased. The average age of deceased persons whose drinking water was boiled or treated through chemical means was, over India in its entirety, 11.8 years higher than that of those whose drinking water was either not treated or treated through 'other means'; for 'forward' and 'backward' states, this difference was, respectively, 10.9 and 12.6 years. Similarly, the average age of deceased persons whose households used gas (including gobar gas), kerosene, or electricity as their cooking fuel was five years higher than that of those whose households used 'other' fuels.[13]

After controlling for the living conditions of the deceased, the next set of controls related to the economic position of the deceased's households. This was measured by a household's consumer expenditure in the past 30 days. Table 6.3 shows that an increase of Rs 1,000 in monthly household expenditure would raise the average age of death by approximately 0.4 years though, it must be added that, after the other controls had been imposed, the significance of the relation between monthly expenditure and the mean age of death was very weak.

Table 6.3 shows that, *even after imposing all the above controls*, the average age of the deceased was significantly affected by the social group to which they belonged. Compared to the average age at death of Hindus (the control group), the average age at death of: Adivasis was 4.9 years lower for India in its entirety and 6.7 years lower for the backward states; Dalits was 7.1 years lower for India in its entirety and 11.5 years lower for the backward states; OBC Muslims was 8.6 years lower for India in its entirety and 11.9 years lower for the backward states; and non-OBC Muslims was 6.1 years lower for India in its entirety and 6.8 years lower for the forward states. By contrast, there was no significant difference in the ages of deceased persons between Hindus and the (non-Muslim) OBCs.

## THE HEALTH OF ELDERLY PERSONS

Table 6.4 shows the perceptions of persons, aged 60 years or more ('elderly persons'), about their state of health: excellent/very good; good/fair; poor. While 25 per cent of the entire sample of 33,155 elderly persons described themselves as being in poor health, this description was offered by 28 per cent of Dalits and 31 per cent of Muslims (OBC and non-OBC). By contrast, only 16 per cent of ST Christians and 20 per cent of Adivasis regarded themselves as being in poor health.

TABLE 6.4: Own Perception of State of Health of Persons 60 Years and Above, by Social Groups (in per cent)

| | Excellent/Very good health | Good/Fair health | Poor health | Total |
|---|---|---|---|---|
| Adivasis | 143 | 1525 | 428 | 2096 |
| | (6.8) | (72.8) | (20.4) | (100.00) |
| Christian (ST) | 76 | 534 | 115 | 725 |
| | (10.5) | (73.7) | (15.9) | (100.00) |
| Dalits | 220 | 3440 | 1423 | 5083 |
| | (4.3) | (67.7) | (28.0) | (100.00) |
| OBC (non-Muslim) | 529 | 7848 | 2746 | 11,123 |
| | (4.8) | (70.6) | (24.7) | (100.00) |
| OBC (Muslim) | 73 | 819 | 409 | 1301 |
| | (5.6) | (63.0) | (31.4) | (100.00) |
| Hindus (FC) | 629 | 6867 | 2179 | 9675 |
| | (6.5) | (71.0) | (22.5) | (100.00) |
| Muslims (non-OBC) | 73 | 1315 | 628 | 2016 |
| | (3.6) | (65.2) | (31.2) | (100.00) |
| Christians (non-ST) | 29 | 328 | 143 | 500 |
| | (5.8) | (65.6) | (28.6) | (100.00) |
| Sikhs | 32 | 295 | 78 | 405 |
| | (7.9) | (72.8) | (19.3) | (100.00) |
| Other religions | 23 | 158 | 50 | 231 |
| | (10.0) | (68.4) | (21.6) | (100.00) |
| Total | 1827 | 23,129 | 8199 | 33,155 |
| | (5.5) | (69.8) | (24.7) | (100.00) |

Table 6.5 shows the *marginal probabilities* obtained from estimating an ordered logit model in which the dependent variable took the value 1, 2, or 3 depending on whether a person described his/her state of health as excellent/very good; good/fair; poor. The marginal probability associated with a variable is the change in the probability of an outcome, following a change in the value of a variable. For each variable, these probabilities sum to zero across the three outcomes (that is, the three states of health) and for discrete variables—all the explanatory variables used, except *age*— the marginal probabilities refer to changes in the probability of the outcomes, consequent on a move from the default category for that variable to the category in question.[14] For ease of exposition, the subsequent discussion focuses, in the main, on the marginal probability of regarding oneself to be in poor health (hereafter, simply, 'the probability of poor health').

According to Table 6.5: (i) moving from a backward state to a forward state would reduce the probability of poor health by 1.1 points; and (ii) being female would increase the probability of poor health by 4.3 points. The effect of age on the probability of poor health depends not only upon the increase in age but, because of the presence of the non-linear term $age^2$, also upon the age itself. So, for an additional year in age from $N$ years, $age^2$ would increase by $(N+1)^2 - N^2 = 2N+1$. Therefore, if $N = 60$, the probability of poor health would increase by $5.2 - 121 \times 0.03 = 1.57$ points for an additional year; if $N = 75$, the probability of poor health would increase by $5.2 - 151 \times 0.03 = 0.67$ points for an additional year. In other words, the probability of poor health would increase with age, but at a diminishing rate, and, after a certain age ($N = 87$), would not change with increasing years.

Table 6.5 suggests that people's perception of the state of their health was significantly affected by their level of education. Compared to an illiterate person (the default level), the probability of poor health was: 1.6 points lower for a person educated up to primary schooling ('low education'); 4.2 points lower for a person educated above primary and up to secondary level; and 7.4 points lower for a person educated up to higher secondary or more.

TABLE 6.5: Marginal Probabilities from the Ordered Logit Model of Own Perception of State of Health: Persons 60 Years and Above

|  | Poor health | Good/Fair health | Excellent/Very good health |
|---|---|---|---|
| Forward State | −0.011** | 0.008** | 0.003** |
|  | (2.33) | (2.32) | (2.33) |
| Age | 0.052*** | −0.039*** | −0.013*** |
|  | (11.95) | (11.80) | (11.75) |
| Age squared | −0.0003*** | 0.0002*** | 0.0001*** |
|  | (8.95) | (8.88) | (8.88) |
| Female | 0.043*** | −0.032*** | −0.011*** |
|  | (9.22) | (9.17) | (9.09) |
| Low education | −0.016*** | 0.012*** | 0.004*** |
|  | (2.82) | (2.86) | (2.71) |
| Medium education | −0.042*** | 0.030*** | 0.012*** |
|  | (5.76) | (6.11) | (4.98) |
| High education | −0.074*** | 0.048*** | 0.025*** |
|  | (8.24) | (10.06) | (6.00) |
| Rural | −0.009 | 0.007 | 0.002 |
|  | (1.44) | (1.46) | (1.46) |
| Structure | −0.032*** | 0.025*** | 0.007*** |
|  | (4.38) | (4.26) | (4.79) |
| Latrine | −0.010 | 0.008 | 0.003 |
|  | (1.59) | (1.59) | (1.57) |
| Drain | −0.002 | 0.001 | 0.0004 |
|  | (0.26) | (0.26) | (0.26) |
| Water source | −0.031*** | 0.023*** | 0.008*** |
|  | (6.20) | (6.22) | (6.06) |
| Water treated | −0.043*** | 0.032*** | 0.012*** |
|  | (5.88) | (6.81) | (6.12) |
| Water treatment | 0.054*** | −0.042*** | −0.012*** |
|  | (5.88) | (5.67) | (6.65) |
| Cooking fuel | −0.034*** | 0.025*** | 0.009*** |
|  | (5.12) | (5.20) | (4.85) |
| Lowest quartile of monthly expenditure | 0.044*** | −0.034*** | −0.010*** |
|  | (6.20) | (6.03) | (6.73) |

*(Contd)*

*(Table 6.5 contd)*

| | *Poor health* | *Good/Fair health* | *Excellent/Very good health* |
|---|---|---|---|
| Second quartile of monthly expenditure | 0.037*** | −0.029*** | −0.008*** |
| | (4.77) | (4.63) | (5.25) |
| Third quartile of monthly expenditure | 0.022*** | −0.017*** | −0.005*** |
| | (3.58) | (3.53) | (3.73) |
| Adivasis | −0.050*** | 0.035*** | 0.015*** |
| | (5.81) | (6.41) | (4.74) |
| Christian (ST) | −0.083*** | 0.052*** | 0.031*** |
| | (7.07) | (9.79) | (4.75) |
| Dalits | 0.026** | −0.020*** | −0.006*** |
| | (3.37) | (3.30) | (3.60) |
| OBC (non-Muslim) | 0.001 | −0.001 | −0.0004 |
| | (0.29) | (0.29) | (0.29) |
| OBC (Muslim) | 0.055*** | −0.043*** | −0.011*** |
| | (4.19) | (4.01) | (5.29) |
| Muslim (non-OBC) | 0.081*** | −0.065*** | −0.016*** |
| | (7.23) | (6.84) | (9.16) |
| Christian (non-tribal) | 0.035* | −0.027* | −0.008** |
| | (1.79) | (1.74) | (2.05) |
| Sikh | −0.026 | 0.018* | 0.007 |
| | (1.59) | (1.66) | (1.43) |
| Other religions | −0.021 | 0.015 | 0.006 |
| | (0.82) | (0.85) | (0.75) |
| Observations | 33,130 | 33,130 | 33,130 |

*Notes*: See notes to Table 6.3
Low education: literate without schooling, below primary, primary;
Medium education: middle or secondary school;
High education: higher secondary or more

Living conditions exerted a significant effect on the probability of poor health: good housing conditions ('structure') reduced this probability by 3.2 points; a good source of drinking water ('water source') reduced it by 3.1 points while treating drinking water and, furthermore, treating it 'properly' reduced it by, respectively, 4.3 and 5.4 points; lastly, using a 'clean' fuel for cooking lowered the probability of poor health by 3.4 points. In total, therefore, good living conditions were capable of reducing the probability of poor health by nearly 20 points.

Over and above these factors, the economic position of a household also had a significant effect on the probability of poor health: compared to elderly persons from households whose monthly expenditure was in the top quartile (the control group), elderly persons from households whose monthly expenditure was in the lowest, second, and third quartile were more likely to be in poor health by, respectively, 4.4, 3.7, and 2.2 points.

Lastly, even after controlling for all the above factors, Table 6.5 shows that the social groups to which people belonged had a significant effect on their probabilities of poor health: compared to Hindus (the control group), Adivasis and ST Christians were less likely to be in poor health by, respectively, 5.0 and 8.3 points; on the other hand, Dalits, OBC Muslims, and non-OBC Muslims were more likely to be in poor health by, respectively, 2.6, 5.5, and 8.1 points.

Table 6.6 records the primary ailments of elderly persons who regarded their state of health as 'poor'. For example, of the 258 such persons who happened to be Adivasis, 5 per cent primarily suffered from gastro-intestinal problems (GASTR), 9 per cent from cardiovascular disease (CARD), 11 per cent from respiratory problems (RESP); 12 per cent from disorders of the joints (JOINT); 2 per cent from diseases of the kidney or urinary system (KIDNY); 4 per cent from neurological disorders (NEURO); 10 per cent from eye disorders (EYES); 2 per cent from diabetes (DIABT); 4 per cent from fever-related illness (FEVER); 24 per cent from disabilities (DISAB); 2 per cent from accidents/injuries/burns (ACC); 1 per cent from cancer (CANC); and 14 per cent from other ailments (OTHER).

The distribution of the incidence of cardiovascular disease (including hypertension) between the social groups is interesting: 33 per cent of non-ST Christians and 19 per cent of Hindus, Sikhs, and persons from other religions—aged 60 or more and in poor health—suffered from cardiovascular diseases; by contrast, this ailment affected only 4 per cent of ST Christians, 9 per cent of Adivasis and Dalits,

TABLE 6.6: Ailments of Persons 60 Years and Above Who Regarded their State of Health as 'Poor', by Social Groups

| Social groups ailments | Adivasi | ST Christian | Dalit | OBC non-Muslim | OBC Muslim | Hindu FC | Muslim non-OBC | Christian, non-ST | Sikh | Others | Total |
|---|---|---|---|---|---|---|---|---|---|---|---|
| GASTR | 13 | 13 | 48 | 96 | 14 | 91 | 55 | 4 | 1 | 0 | 335 |
|  | (5.04) | (16.25) | (5.13) | (5.43) | (4.70) | (5.77) | (12.39) | (3.45) | (1.85) | (0.00) | (6.02) |
| CARD | 23 | 3 | 85 | 223 | 49 | 298 | 71 | 38 | 10 | 7 | 807 |
|  | (8.91) | (3.75) | (9.09) | (12.62) | (16.44) | (18.88) | (15.99) | (32.76) | (18.52) | (18.92) | (14.50) |
| RESP | 28 | 10 | 130 | 233 | 46 | 187 | 60 | 7 | 8 | 2 | 711 |
|  | (10.85) | (12.50) | (13.90) | (13.19) | (15.44) | (11.85) | (13.51) | (6.03) | (14.81) | (5.41) | (12.77) |
| JOINT | 32 | 8 | 117 | 248 | 25 | 186 | 49 | 22 | 10 | 5 | 702 |
|  | (12.40) | (10.00) | (12.51) | (14.04) | (8.39) | (11.79) | (11.04) | (18.97) | (18.52) | (13.51) | (12.61) |
| KIDNY | 5 | 0 | 20 | 30 | 3 | 44 | 6 | 2 | 3 | 1 | 114 |
|  | (1.94) | (0.00) | (2.14) | (1.70) | (1.01) | (2.79) | (1.35) | (1.72) | (5.56) | (2.70) | (2.05) |
| NEURO | 10 | 2 | 43 | 71 | 16 | 86 | 23 | 3 | 1 | 2 | 257 |
|  | (3.88) | (2.50) | (4.60) | (4.02) | (5.37) | (5.45) | (5.18) | (2.59) | (1.85) | (5.41) | (4.62) |
| EYES | 26 | 3 | 121 | 154 | 22 | 103 | 41 | 11 | 1 | 3 | 485 |
|  | (10.08) | (3.75) | (12.94) | (8.72) | (7.38) | (6.53) | (9.23) | (9.48) | (1.85) | (8.11) | (8.71) |
| DIABT | 4 | 2 | 13 | 65 | 13 | 101 | 19 | 9 | 2 | 3 | 231 |
|  | (1.55) | (2.50) | (1.39) | (3.68) | (4.36) | (6.40) | (4.28) | (7.76) | (3.70) | (8.11) | (4.15) |
| FEVER | 10 | 6 | 35 | 53 | 6 | 27 | 12 | 1 | 1 | 0 | 151 |
|  | (3.88) | (7.50) | (3.74) | (3.00) | (2.01) | (1.71) | (2.70) | (0.86) | (1.85) | (0.00) | (2.71) |

| Social groups ailments | Adivasi ST, Christian | Dalit | OBC non-Muslim | OBC Muslim | Hindu FC | Muslim non-OBC | Christian, non-ST | Sikh | Others | Total |
|---|---|---|---|---|---|---|---|---|---|---|
| DISAB | 63 | 26 | 153 | 282 | 53 | 183 | 41 | 6 | 8 | 7 | 822 |
|  | (24.42) | (32.50) | (16.36) | (15.96) | (17.79) | (11.60) | (9.23) | (5.17) | (14.81) | (18.92) | (14.77) |
| ACC | 4 | 0 | 18 | 40 | 7 | 46 | 5 | 0 | 2 | 0 | 122 |
|  | (1.55) | (0.00) | (1.93) | (2.26) | (2.35) | (2.92) | (1.13) | (0.00) | (3.70) | (0.00) | (2.19) |
| CANC | 3 | 1 | 17 | 33 | 4 | 31 | 4 | 3 | 0 | 1 | 97 |
|  | (1.16) | (1.25) | (1.82) | (1.87) | (1.34) | (1.96) | (0.90) | (2.59) | (0.00) | (2.70) | (1.74) |
| OTHER | 37 | 6 | 135 | 239 | 40 | 195 | 58 | 10 | 7 | 6 | 733 |
|  | (14.34) | (7.50) | (14.44) | (13.53) | (13.42) | (12.36) | (13.06) | (8.62) | (12.96) | (16.22) | (13.17) |
| TOTAL | 258 | 80 | 935 | 1767 | 298 | 1578 | 444 | 116 | 54 | 37 | 5567 |
|  | (100) | (100) | (100) | (100) | (100) | (100) | (100) | (100) | (100) | (100) | (100) |

*Source*: NSS 60th Round, Health File

*Notes*: Figures in parentheses denote percentages

Definition of Ailments:

GASTR: Gastro-intestinal problems, CARD: Cardiovascular disease, RESP: Respiratory problems;,JOINT: Disorders of the joints, KIDNY: Diseases of the kidney or urinary system, NEURO: Neurological disorders, EYES; Eye disorders, DIABT: Diabetes; FEVER, Fever-related illness, DISAB: Disabilities, ACC: Accidents/injuries/burns, CANC: Cancer, OTHER: Other ailments

12 per cent of non-Muslim OBCs, and 16 per cent of Muslims. Similarly, compared to the 6 per cent of Hindus who were diabetic, only 2 per cent of Adivasis and 1 per cent of Dalits had diabetes. On the other hand, 33 per cent of ST Christians, 24 per cent of Adivasis, 16 per cent of Dalits, and 18 per cent of OBC Muslims—compared to only 12 per cent of Hindus—suffered from disabilities.[15]

TABLE 6.7: Proportion of Persons 60 Years, and Who Regarded their State of Health as 'Poor', Taking Treatment for Reported Ailment, by Social Groups

|  | Not taking treatment | Taking treatment | Total |
|---|---|---|---|
| Adivasis | 98 | 157 | 255 |
|  | (38.43) | (61.57) | (100.00) |
| Christian (ST) | 33 | 42 | 75 |
|  | (44.00) | (56.00) | (100.00) |
| Dalits | 302 | 626 | 928 |
|  | (32.54) | (67.46) | (100.00) |
| OBC (non-Muslim) | 470 | 1273 | 1743 |
|  | (26.97) | (73.03) | (100.00) |
| OBC (Muslim) | 62 | 233 | 295 |
|  | (21.02) | (78.98) | (100.00) |
| Hindus (FC) | 239 | 1326 | 1565 |
|  | (15.27) | (84.73) | (100.00) |
| Muslims (non-OBC) | 118 | 319 | 437 |
|  | (27.00) | (73.00) | (100.00) |
| Christians (non-ST) | 13 | 102 | 115 |
|  | (11.30) | (88.70) | (100.00) |
| Sikhs | 10 | 44 | 54 |
|  | (18.52) | (81.48) | (100.00) |
| Other religions | 4 | 32 | 36 |
|  | (11.11) | (88.89) | (100.00) |
| Total | 1349 | 4154 | 5503 |
|  | (24.51) | (75.49) | (100.00) |

Source: NSS 60th Round, Health File
Note: Figures in parentheses denote percentages

Table 6.7 shows the proportion of elderly persons, who were in poor health, from the different social groups who were not taking any treatment for their ailments: 38 per cent of Adivasis, 44 per cent of ST Christians, and 33 per cent of Dalits were not taking any treatment for their ailments in contrast to 15 per cent of Hindus, 11 per cent of non-ST Christians, and 18 per cent of Sikhs. In order to determine the probabilities of the different person's taking/not taking treatment for their ailments, we estimated a logit model over the

**TABLE 6.8: Marginal Probabilities from the Logit Model of Treatment Received for Ailments: Persons, 60 Years and Above, Who Regarded their State of Health as 'Poor'**

| | *Marginal probability of receiving treatment for reported ailment* |
|---|---|
| Forward state | 0.110*** |
| | (9.28) |
| Female | 0.013 |
| | (1.01) |
| Low education | 0.066*** |
| | (4.67) |
| Medium education | 0.108*** |
| | (5.82) |
| High education | 0.094*** |
| | (3.11) |
| Living son(s) | 0.083*** |
| | (2.85) |
| Living daughter(s) | −0.21 |
| | (0.98) |
| Rural | −0.016 |
| | (1.22) |
| Economically independent | 0.049*** |
| | (3.23) |
| Economically partially dependent | 0.035** |
| | (2.08) |
| Living alone | 0.004 |
| | (0.15) |

*(Contd)*

*(Table 6.8 contd)*

| | Marginal probability of receiving treatment for reported ailment |
|---|---|
| Living with spouse | 0.051*** |
| | (3.93) |
| Confined to bed | 0.055*** |
| | (2.92) |
| Confined to home | −0.009 |
| | (0.69) |
| Lowest quartile of monthly expenditure | −0.161*** |
| | (7.84) |
| Second quartile of monthly expenditure | −0.115*** |
| | (5.19) |
| Third quartile of monthly expenditure | −0.046*** |
| | (2.64) |
| Adivasis | −0.106*** |
| | (3.15) |
| Christian (ST) | −0.225*** |
| | (3.59) |
| Dalits | −0.090*** |
| | (4.20) |
| OBC (non-Muslim) | −0.057*** |
| | (3.34) |
| OBC (Muslim) | −0.007 |
| | (0.24) |
| Muslim (non-OBC) | −0.077** |
| | (2.82) |
| Christian (non-tribal) | 0.017 |
| | (0.34) |
| Sikh | −0.059 |
| | (0.97) |
| Other religions | 0.068 |
| Pseudo-R-squared | 0.0793 |
| Observations | 5484 |

*Notes*: Dependent variable = 1 if treatment received for reported ailment, =0, if not received

Absolute value of z values in parentheses

* significant at 10 per cent; ** significant at 5 per cent; *** significant at 1 per cent

sample of 5484 elderly persons, who were in poor health, in which the dependent variable took the value 1 if the person was taking treatment and 0 if he/she was not.

The marginal probabilities from this model are shown in Table 6.8. Compared to living in a 'backward' state, living in a 'forward' state significantly increased the probability of taking treatment by 11.0 points. However, there was no significant difference between women and men, or between persons in the rural and urban sectors, in their probabilities of taking treatment. Having a living daughter had no significant effect on the probability of taking treatment though having a living son raised it by 8.3 points!

The level of education of a person, and the economic position of his/her household, had a significant effect on the probability of taking treatment. Compared to an illiterate person (the default level), the probability of taking treatment was: 6.6 points higher for a person educated up to primary schooling ('low education'); 10.8 points higher for a person educated above primary and up to secondary level; and 9.4 points higher for a person educated up to higher secondary or more. Compared to persons from households whose monthly expenditure was in the top quartile (the control group), persons from households whose monthly expenditure was in the lowest, second, and third quartile were less likely to take treatment by, respectively, 16.1, 11.5, and 4.6 points.

Another set of factors affecting the probability of people taking treatment was comprised of their degree of economic independence, living arrangements, and degree of mobility. Compared to a person who was totally dependent (the default case), the probability of taking treatment was 4.9 points higher for someone who was completely independent and 3.5 points higher for someone who was only partially dependent. Compared to living with a spouse, people living without a spouse—whether living alone or with others—were less likely, by 5.1 points, to take treatment. Compared to persons who were totally mobile or else with mobility restricted to the home, people who were confined to bed were more likely, by 5.5 points, to take treatment.

However, even after controlling for all the above factors, Table 6.8 shows that the social groups to which people belonged had a

significant effect on their probabilities of taking treatment: compared
to Hindus (the control group), Adivasis, ST Christians, and Dalits
were *less* likely to take treatment by, respectively, 10.6, 22.5, and 9.0
points; and non-OBC Muslims and non-Muslim OBCs were less
likely to take treatment by, respectively, 7.7 and 5.7 points.

Table 6.9 assesses the predictive performance of the logit model
of taking treatment. A person was predicted as taking (not taking)
treatment if the predicted probability from the logit model, of his
taking treatment, was greater (less) than half. Table 6.9 shows that
of the 5238 persons predicted to be taking treatment, 4027 were
actually taking treatment—a predictive accuracy of 77 per cent;
however, only 131 of the 246 predicted to be not taking treatment,
were actually not taking treatment—a predictive accuracy of 53 per
cent. Overall, therefore, 4158 persons out of 5484 were correctly
classified—a predictive accuracy of 76 per cent.

TABLE 6.9: Predictive Performance of the Logit Model of the
Probability of Taking Treatment for Ailment

|  | Taking treatment (M) | Not taking treatment (−M) | Total |
|---|---|---|---|
| Predicted as taking treatment (+) | 4027 | 1211 | 5238 P(M\|+) = 76.9% |
| Predicted as not taking treatment (−) | 115 | 131 | 246 P(−M\|−)=53.3% |
| Total | 4142 P(+\|M) = 90.2% | 1342 P(−\|−M)=2.8% | 5484 Correctly classified = 75.8% |

*Note*: Persons, 60 years and above, who regarded their state of health as 'poor'

## PRENATAL AND POST-NATAL CARE

The M&HC–NSS provided information, by social group, on the
prenatal and post-natal care received by ever married women below
50 years of age. Table 6.10 shows that, compared to 15 per cent of
Hindu women who did not receive prenatal care, such care was not
received by: 31 per cent of Adivasis, 38 per cent of ST Christians,
26 per cent of Dalits, 33 per cent of OBC Muslims, and 26 per

cent of non-OBC Muslims. Similarly, compared to 27 per cent of Hindu women who did not receive post-natal care, such care was not received by: 44 per cent of Adivasis and ST Christians, 37 per cent of Dalits, 36 per cent of OBC Muslims, and 34 per cent of non-OBC Muslims. In order to determine the probabilities of women receiving prenatal and post-natal care, we estimated a logit model in which the dependent variable took the value 1 if the woman received the relevant care and 0 if she did not. The marginal probabilities from this model are shown in Table 6.11.

TABLE 6.10: Proportion of Ever Married Women Who did Not Receive Pre- and Post-natal Care

|  | Prenatal care | Post-natal care |
| --- | --- | --- |
| Adivasi | 30.5 | 43.7 |
| Christian (ST) | 37.9 | 44.1 |
| Dalits | 26.2 | 36.5 |
| OBC (non-Muslim) | 22.7 | 31.3 |
| OBC (Muslim) | 32.7 | 36.4 |
| Hindu (FC) | 14.7 | 26.7 |
| Muslim (non-OBC) | 26.1 | 34.5 |
| Christian (non-ST) | 1.5 | 10.4 |
| Sikh | 18.3 | 31.8 |
| Other religions | 14.3 | 41.0 |
| Total | 23.5 | 33.2 |

Source: NSS 60th Round, Health File

Compared to living in a 'backward' state, living in a 'forward' state significantly increased the probability of prenatal care by 15.3 points but it did not have a significant effect on the probability of post-natal care. However, compared to urban women, the probability of rural women receiving prenatal and post-natal care was significantly lower by, respectively, 2.8 and 4.7 points.

The level of education of women had a significant effect on the probability of their receiving both prenatal and post-natal care. Compared to an illiterate person (the default level), the probabilities of receiving prenatal and post-natal care were, respectively: 9.0 and 4.0 points higher for a person educated up to primary schooling

TABLE 6.11: Marginal Probabilities from the Logit Model of Pre- and Post-natal Care

| | Prenatal care | Post-natal care |
|---|---|---|
| Forward state | 0.153*** | 0.019 |
| | (17.8) | (1.53) |
| Age | −0.002*** | −0.001 |
| | (3.56) | (0.59) |
| Low education | 0.090*** | 0.040** |
| | (10.5) | (2.73) |
| Medium education | 0.140*** | 0.110*** |
| | (16.0) | (7.64) |
| High education | 0.157*** | 0.140*** |
| | (16.9) | (7.81) |
| Rural | −0.028** | −0.047*** |
| | (2.85) | (3.55) |
| Labourer | −0.011 | −0.020 |
| | (0.64) | (0.85) |
| Lowest quartile of monthly expenditure | −0.033** | −0.010 |
| | (2.33) | (0.52) |
| Second quartile of monthly expenditure | −0.045*** | −0.013 |
| | (3.33) | (0.73) |
| Third quartile of monthly expenditure | −0.020* | −0.017 |
| | (1.81) | (1.14) |
| Adivasis | −0.025 | −0.082*** |
| | (1.38) | (3.14) |
| Christian (ST) | −0.115*** | −0.123*** |
| | (4.19) | (3.09) |
| Dalits | −0.019 | −0.030 |
| | (1.25) | (1.51) |
| OBC (non-Muslim) | −0.003 | 0.004 |
| | (0.21) | (0.25) |
| OBC (Muslim) | −0.088*** | −0.041 |
| | (3.62) | (1.40) |
| Muslim (non-OBC) | −0.043** | −0.029 |
| | (2.16) | (1.15) |
| Christian (non-tribal) | 0.163*** | 0.173 |
| | (4.46) | (2.78) |
| Sikh | −0.110* | 0.005 |
| | (1.86) | (0.09) |
| Other religions | 0.039 | −0.163* |
| | (0.67) | (1.96) |
| Pseudo-R-squared | 0.113 | 0.028 |
| Observations | 9696 | 6874 |

('low education'); 14.0 and 11.0 points higher for a person educated above primary and up to secondary level; and 15.7 and 14.0 points higher for a person educated up to higher secondary or more. The economic position of the women's households exercised a significant positive influence on their probability of receiving prenatal care but not on their probability of receiving post-natal care: compared to women from households whose monthly expenditure was in the top quartile (the control group), women from households whose monthly expenditure was in the lowest, second, and third quartile were less likely to take treatment by, respectively, 3.3, 4.5, and 2.0 points.

However, even after controlling for all the above factors, Table 6.11 shows that the social groups to which women belonged had a significant effect on their probabilities of receiving prenatal care: compared to Hindus (the control group), ST Christians, OBC Muslims, and non-OBC Muslims were less likely to receive prenatal care by, respectively, 11.5, 8.8, and 4.3 points and non-ST Christians were more likely to receive prenatal care by 16.3 points. By contrast, after controlling for all the above factors, the effects of social group on the probability of receiving post-natal care were much more muted: the only significant social group effects were that, compared to Hindus, ST Christians were less likely (by 12.3 points), and non-ST Christians were more likely (by 17.3 points), to receive post-natal care.

This chapter investigated whether there was a social gradient to health in India with respect to four health outcomes: the age at death; the self-assessed health status of elderly persons; the likelihood of elderly persons, who were in poor health, taking treatment for their ailments; and the likelihood of receiving pre-natal and post-natal care. The evidence suggested that living in a forward state (compared to living in a backward state) and belonging to a relatively affluent household significantly improved all four health outcomes. In addition, the age at death and the self-assessed health status of elderly persons was significantly affected by their household living conditions.

The level of education of persons exercised a significant influence on the likelihood of their receiving treatment or care. *Ceteris paribus*, the likelihood of elderly people, who were in poor health, taking treatment increased with their level of education; similarly, compared to poorly educated women, better educated women were more likely to receive prenatal and postnatal care.

However, even after controlling for these 'group independent' factors, the social group to which people in India belonged had a significant effect on their health outcomes. Compared to (forward caste) Hindus, the average age at death in India—after imposing all the controls—was 4.9 years lower for Adivasis, 7.1 years lower for Dalits, and 6.1 years lower for Muslims. Similarly, compared to elderly Hindus, elderly Dalits, OBC Muslims, and non-OBC Muslims were—after imposing all the controls—*more* likely to be in poor health by, respectively, 2.6, 5.5, and 8.1 points. Again compared to elderly Hindus in poor health, Adivasis, ST, Christians, and Dalits were—after imposing all the controls—less likely to take treatment by, respectively, 10.6, 22.5, and 9.0 points and non-OBC Muslims and the non-Muslim OBCs were less likely to take treatment by, respectively, 7.7 and 5.7 points. Finally, compared to Hindus, ST Christians, OBC Muslims, and non-OBC Muslims were after imposing all the controls-less likely to receive prenatal care by, respectively 11.5, 8.8, and 4.3 points.

There can be little doubt, therefore, that, on the basis of data from the M&HC sample, the sample analysed in this paper offered *prima facie* evidence of a social group bias to health outcomes in India. However, it is important to note that there are several deficiencies inherent in this study. First, there are important health-related attributes of individuals (smoking, diet, taking exercise, the nature of work) that are not—and, indeed, given the limitations of the data, cannot—be taken account of. All these factors are included in the package of factors termed 'unobservable'. If these unobservable factors were randomly distributed among the population this, in itself, would not pose a problem. However, there is evidence that there may be a group bias with respect to at least some of these factors. For example, if hard physical work is more inimical to health than more sedentary jobs, then of males aged 25–44 years, 42 per cent of Adivasi and 47 per cent of Dalits, compared to only 10 per cent of Hindus, worked as casual labourers (Borooah *et al.* 2007).

There is a natural distinction between inequality and inequity in the analysis of health outcomes. Inequality reflects the totality of differences between persons, regardless of the source of these differences and, in particular, regardless of whether or not these sources stem from actions within a person's control. Inequity reflects that part of inequality that is generated by factors outside a person's control. In a fundamental sense, therefore, while inequality may not be seen as 'unfair', inequity is properly regarded as being unfair. The point about group membership is that while it may not be the primary factor behind health inequality, it is the main cause of health inequity. This chapter's central message, conditional on the caveats noted earlier, is that being an Adivasi, Dalit, or Muslim in India seriously impaired, using the language of Sen (1993), the capabilities of persons to function in society. This is because, as this study has shown, for people at the bottom of the social ladder in India, the risk of suffering premature death, poor health, and a lack of treatment and care is substantially higher than it is for the better-off people.

## NOTES

1. Psychologists distinguish between stress caused by a high demand on one's capacities—for example, tight deadlines—and stress engendered by a low sense of control over one's life.

2. There are about 85 million Indians classified as belonging to the 'STs'; of these, Adivasis (meaning 'original inhabitants') refer to the 70 million who live in the heart of India, in a relatively contiguous hill and forest belt extending across the states of Gujarat, Rajasthan, Maharashtra, Madhya Pradesh, Chhattisgarh, Jharkhand, Andhra Pradesh, Orissa, Bihar, and West Bengal (Guha 2007).

3. Dalits, who number about 18 million, refer to those who belong India's 'Scheduled Castes' and may be broadly identified with the 'Untouchable' castes, i.e. those with whom physical contact—most usually taken to be the acceptance of food or water—is regarded by FC Hindus as ritually polluting or unclean.

4. For background on the NSSO, see Tendulkar (2007).

5. As Guha (2007) notes, ST Christians have been exposed to modern education in English and have a much greater chance of being absorbed

in the modern economy. They also live mainly in the hills of north-east India, which are some of the remotest and less accessible parts of the country.

6. These are persons who, while not belonging to the ST/SC, nevertheless belong to economic and socially backward groups.

7. FC Hindus denote Hindus who are not included in the OBC/Dalit/ST categories. However, since the designation of groups in the OBC category is a state responsibility a particular (caste) group may be included in the OBC category in one state (i.e., be excluded from FC Hindus) but be excluded from the OBC category in another state (i.e., be included in FC Hindus).

8. Of the 1716 deceased, 58 per cent were men. For all the groups the majority of deaths were male except for ST Christians, where 55 per cent of the 65 deaths in this group were female.

9. Excluding the 27 deaths which occurred during pregnancy.

10. 'Forward states': Andhra Pradesh, Chandigarh, Dadra and Nagar Haveli, Daman and Diu, Delhi, Goa, Gujarat, Haryana, Himachal Pradesh, Karnataka, Kerala, Maharashtra, Pondicherry, Punjab, Tamil Nadu, and West Bengal. The remaining states and Union Territories were classed as 'backward' states.

11. The sample averages for age at death were 48.4 and 46.2 years for male and female deaths, respectively.

12. Agricultural or other labour for rural households and casual labour for urban households.

13. For backward states, this difference was significant only at 10 per cent and for forward states it was not even significant at this level.

14. In an ordered logit model, the signs of the coefficient estimates associated with a variable do not predict the directions of change in the probabilities of the outcomes and these probabilities have to be separately calculated.

15. Locomotor; visual (including blindness, excluding cataract); speech; hearing.

## References

Birdi, K., P. Warr and A. Oswald (1995), 'Age Differences in Three Components of Employee Well-Being', *Applied Psychology*, vol. 44, pp. 345–73.

Black, Douglas, Jerry Morris, Cyril Smith and Peter Townsend (1980), *Inequalities in Health: A Report of a Research Working Group*, London: Department of Health and Social Security.

Borooah, V.K., A. Dubey and S. Iyer (2007), 'The Effectiveness of Jobs Reservation: Caste, Religion, and Economic Status in India', *Development and Change*, vol. 38, no. 3, pp. 423–55.

Brunner, E. and M. Marmot (1999), 'Social Organisation, Stress and Health', in M. Marmot and R. Wilkinson (eds), *The Social Determinants of Health*, New York: Oxford University Press, pp. 17–43.

Epstein, H. (1998), 'Life and Death on the Social Ladder', *The New York Review of Books*, vol. 45, pp. 26–30.

Griffin, J.M., R. Fuhrer, S.A. Stansfeld, and M. Marmot (2002), 'The Importance of Low Control at Work and Home on Depression and Anxiety: Do These Effects Vary by Gender and Social Class?', *Social Science and Medicine*, vol. 54, pp. 783–98.

Guha, R. (2007), 'Adivasis, Naxalities, and Indian Democracy', *Economic and Political Weekly*, vol. 42, pp. 3305–12.

Karasek, R. and M. Michael (1996), 'Refining Social Class: Psychosocial Job Factors', paper presented at The Fourth International Congress of Behavioral Medicine, Washington, DC.

Marmot, M. (1986), 'Does Stress Cause Heart Attacks', *Postgraduate Medical Journal*, vol. 62, pp. 683–6.

——— (2000), 'Multilevel Approaches to Understanding Social Determinants', in L. Berkman and I. Kawachi (eds), *Social Epidemiology*, New York: Oxford University Press, pp. 349–67.

——— (2004), *Status Syndrome: How Our Position on the Social Gradient Affects Longevity and Health*, London: Bloomsbury Publishing.

Sen, A.K. (1993), 'Capability and Well-Being', in M. Nussbaum and A.K. Sen (ed.), *The Quality of Life*, Oxford: Clarendon Press, pp. 30–53.

Sen, G., A. Iyer, and A. George (2007), 'Systematic Hierarchies and Systemic Failures: Gender and Health Inequalities in Koppal District', *Economic and Political Weekly*, vol. 42, pp. 682–90.

Sengupta, J. and D. Sarkar (2007), 'Discrimination in Ethnically Fragmented Localities', *Economic and Political Weekly*, vol. 42, pp. 3313–22.

Tendulkar, Suresh D. (2007), 'National Sample Surveys' in Kaushik Basu (ed.), *The Oxford Companion to Economics in India*, New Delhi: Oxford University Press, pp. 367–70.

Wilkinson, Richard G. and Michael Marmot (1998), *Social Determinants of Health: The Solid Facts*, Copenhagen: World Health Organisation.

# 7

# Caste and Patterns of Discrimination in Rural Public Health Care Services

*Sanghmitra S. Acharya*

Poverty has been recognized as an important determinant of access to public health care services (Carstairs 1955; Zurbrigg 1984). Most low-caste people being poor, their low access to public health care services is generally attributed to their poor background. The National Family Health Surveys (IIPS and ORC Macro 1995, 2000, 2006) observed much lower level of utilization by the Scheduled Castes (SC) as compared to others (Ram *et al.* 1998; Acharya 2002; Kulkarni and Baraik 2003; Srinivasan and Mohanty 2004; Srinivasan and Srinivasan 2005). Studies have observed a close link between low utilization of health services by the SCs and their high poverty and illiteracy level (Thorat and Sabharwal 2006). However, very few studies direct the causality towards their social status as low-caste Untouchable as a factor in the low use of public health services in rural areas in the country. Studies on access to health services have generally ignored the role of caste- and untouchability-related discrimination and exclusion in the meagre access by low-caste Untouchables to public health services. The lack of studies on this aspect has constrained the capacity of the government to develop measures to overcome the obstacle created by caste discrimination in the delivery of public health services.

The main purpose of this chapter is to identify the forms and nature of caste- and untouchability-related discrimination as a factor in low access of the SCs to public health services in rural areas. In order to undertake this exercise, the concept of discrimination in relation to health care services; and the methods to measure discrimination in accessing public health care services by the Dalits in rural areas were also developed. This essay aims to derive an insight into the forms and nature of discrimination experienced by the Dalit children in accessing the health services provided by the primary health centres and private sector providers in the rural areas. The purpose is to identify the forms and spheres of discrimination, including the type of service providers.

## Concept, Methodology, and Database

The methodology adopted in the present chapter addresses three interrelated issues—the definition of the concept of discrimination in access to health care as well as provision of services, the methods of measuring the discrimination, and the database for the study.

Before the discussion on the issue of social exclusion in the health care delivery system is initiated, it is quite imperative to look into the concept of social exclusion and discrimination as it evolved in the social science literature in general and caste-based discrimination in particular. In the relevant literature, the concept of social exclusion is defined as the denial of equal access to opportunities imposed by certain groups of society upon others. Thus, social exclusion has group focus; it is embedded in social relations (the processes through which individuals or groups are wholly or partially excluded from full participation in the society in which they live); and the denial to equal rights brings deprivation to the excluded groups.

Extending this concept to the institutions of caste system and untouchability, it becomes obvious that social exclusion is embedded in the Hindu social order, insofar as social relations in the caste system are based on unequal and hierarchical (graded) entitlement to civil, education, economic, and cultural rights. The predetermined and fixed nature of rights under the caste system involve 'forced exclusion' of the lower castes from having equal rights in multiple spheres by the higher castes (HC). The unequal access to economic and social rights implies that every caste, except those at the top of the caste hierarchy, suffers from unequal division of rights. The former Untouchables (or SCs, or Dalits), who are placed at the bottom of the caste hierarchy, have suffered the most. Due to the notion of untouchability, the low-caste Untouchables also suffer from physical and social segregation. Untouchability, thus, adds an additional dimension to the physical, social, and economic exclusion of this social group. The notion of pollution and purity associated with Untouchables, as will be discussed later, has particular implication in health care service, insofar as delivery of health services involve close interpersonal interaction and physical proximity and touch.

The application of the concept of caste and untouchability based social exclusion, to the health sector is explicit by the different types of health care providers: the public sector, the private sector, and non-profit organizations. The government health care system in rural areas entails providing services to all without any discrimination. However, despite the provision of equal access to all, it is likely that the low-caste Untouchables will suffer from unequal access to the health care services supplied by various providers, including the public health institutions in rural areas. The concept of social exclusion—the way it is defined in the literature—would imply that a low-caste person may face either complete exclusion from access to some health services, or may have access but with differential treatment in the delivery of some services. While the former may be termed as complete exclusion, the latter may be called unfavourable inclusion (Sen 2000).

Complete exclusion of the Untouchables (or Dalit) from access to health care services may occur in some cases. In most of the situations, however, they may have access, but this access may come with differential treatment and behaviour in various spheres and various forms on the part of the service providers. The discrimination through differential treatment and behaviour may take a number of forms.

Discrimination in access to health care may occur at the health care centre due to neglect by the providers—doctors and the supporting staff—and at home during the visit by the health worker. Discrimination is likely to be practised during diagnosis and counselling, dispensing of medicine, or laboratory tests, and even while waiting in the health centre and in paying the user fee. Discrimination during diagnosis may take the form of time spent in asking about the problem, or may be manifest in touching the user during diagnosis. Discrimination during dispensing the medicine may be practised in the way the medicine is given to the user—kept on the palm, or on the window sill/floor—or when someone else is asked to give the medicine to the Untouchable customer to avoid physical touch.

The Untouchables may face discrimination in waiting and payment of user fee, reflected in the duration of waiting, space for waiting, waiting till the other dominant castes have been provided care, and attitude of the paramedics while waiting. Discrimination during payment of user fee, if any, will reflect in the actual amount being paid, time spent for waiting to pay, space for waiting, and a separate queue for payment.

Discrimination at home during the visit by the health worker may occur while entering the house, touching the user, sitting, drinking/eating in the user's house, and giving medicine and information regarding health camps/programmes to them. It may also take the form of selective dissemination of information regarding health camps and programmes, and exclusion of Dalits in accessing certain type of services where touch is involved (such as vaccination). Thus, discrimination can be practised by different providers in various spheres and it may take different forms.

The forms of caste- and untouchability-based discrimination likely to be experienced in different spheres by low-caste Untouchables can be identified along with their consequences, with a set of indicators. A typology of discrimination is developed to identify the spheres in which different forms of discrimination may occur. The focus is on spheres and forms of discrimination.

The spheres of discrimination broadly include visit to/by the provider for diagnosis and counselling, dispensing of medicine, conduct of pathological tests, and referrals. The forms include duration of interaction, touch, speaking gently or otherwise, use of derogatory words or phrase, and long waiting time.

Among the formal providers are included primary health centres and primary health sub-centres, and private individuals/clinics; and among the non-formal providers are traditional healers. The latter are those who do not have formal training in health care service; they are considered to have inherited the practices from their forefathers. The persons engaged in formal health care service include the doctor, lab technician, pharmacist, and grassroots-level health workers such as auxiliary nurse midwife (ANM)/village health worker (VHW)/lady health visitor (LHV), and *anganwadi* worker (AWW).

## SAMPLE DESIGN AND DATABASE

The study is confined to the former Untouchables (or those designated as Dalit or SC) who suffered from discrimination—against which the government has developed legal safeguards and equal-opportunity policies. The study is also confined to the rural area where more than two-third of the Dalits live. The analysis is based on the survey of 12 villages in the two states of Gujarat and Rajasthan. Ahmedabad in Gujarat and Barmer in Rajasthan were the two districts selected for the study. The villages were selected from Dholka *taluka* in Ahmedabad district and Barmer *tehsil* in Barmer district. Two primary health centres in villages, two villages with sub-centres, and two without a sub-centre were selected from each state.

Two hundred Dalit and 65 non-Dalit children were interviewed from the 12 selected villages. In case of those aged below 12 years, their mothers were interviewed. About 6–10 in-depth interviews were held in each village. The respondents were mothers, children, Panchayat Raj Institution (PRI) members, non-government organization (NGO)/government organization (GO) members/self-help group (SHG) workers, AWWs; ANMs, and health workers. At least two group discussions and 1–2 consultative meetings were also held in each of the villages.

## METHODS OF MEASURING DISCRIMINATION

The methods for measurement of discrimination involved selection of the indicators to capture discrimination in spheres, forms, and personnel who may practise discrimination. These indicators were used to derive the nature of discrimination experienced in a given sphere and form by any provider. They were also ranked to understand the perception of Dalits and non-Dalits regarding discrimination and used for construction of a composite index. A narrative analysis of the consultative meetings was also done.

### Selection of Indicators

For the present chapter, 15 variables of discrimination in different spheres, forms, and providers were selected. The recall period was one year prior to the field work.[1] The variables included visit to the doctor (diagnostic), conduct of the pathological test, counselling, dispensing of medicine, seeking referral (spheres); duration of interaction with the care provider, touch (without offending), tone of speaking, usage of demeaning words/phrases, and having to wait till the dominant caste persons are attended to by the care providers such as doctor, lab technician, pharmacist, ANM, and health worker (Table 7.1).

TABLE 7.1: Selected Variables for Discrimination by Sphere, Form, and Provider

| Sphere | Form | Provider |
|---|---|---|
| Visit to/by provider (diagnostic) | Duration of interaction with the care provider | Doctor |
| Counselling | Touch (without offending) | Lab technician |
| Dispensing of medicine | Manner of speaking (gently or otherwise) | Pharmacist |
| Pathological test | Use of demeaning words/ phrases | ANM/ VHW/ LHV |
| Seeking referral | Wait to give chance to the dominant caste person(s) | AWW |

Note: ANM: Auxiliary Nurse Midwife; VHW: Voluntary Health Worker; LHV: Lady Health Visitor

Prevalence of discrimination in different spheres and forms by providers was measured by simple percentages, calculated on the basis of total number of times that Dalit children were exposed to an event—for instance, dispensing of medicine—and experienced any form of discrimination. Ranking of the selected variables was used to understand the perception of Dalit children about the discriminating health care providers and the treatment desired from them.

## Index of Discrimination

Respondents who reported having experienced some discrimination (in form and sphere, and by provider) at least five times during one year prior to the survey were given a score of 5; those who reported having experienced discrimination at least 3–4 times were given a score of 2.5; and those who reported discrimination less than three times were given a score of 1. The scores for each respondent were computed using these weights assigned to them on the basis of the number of times they experienced discrimination. The scores accrued by the respondents ranged from 5 to 25. The average score for each respondent was computed for 'sphere', 'form', and 'provider' separately. The sum of scores on all variables was divided by 5 (total number of variables used in 'sphere' to derive the average score). Similarly, scores were obtained for 'form' and 'provider'. Then, an average of the three values was derived to get the index of discrimination.

The index was computed for sphere, form, and provider separately. They were used to compute a composite index of discrimination. Thus,

Index of discrimination:

(ID) = {(Index of sphere discrimination) + (Index of form discrimination) + (Index of provider discrimination)}/3

$$\text{Or} \qquad \Sigma (IDs + IDf + IDp)/3 \qquad\qquad (7.1)$$

Index of sphere discrimination:

$$(IDs) = ([Ss1 + Ss2 + Ss3 + Ss4 + Ss5])/5$$

$$\text{Or} \qquad \Sigma\, Ss/5 \qquad\qquad (7.2)$$

Index of form discrimination:

$$(IDf) = ([Fs1 + Fs2 + Fs3 + Fs4 + Fs5])/5$$

$$\text{Or} \qquad \Sigma\, Fs/5 \qquad\qquad (7.3)$$

Index of provider discrimination:

$$(IDp) = ([Ps1 + Ps2 + Ps3 + Ps4 + Ps5])/5$$

$$\text{Or} \qquad \Sigma\, Ps/5 \qquad\qquad (7.4)$$

where

Ssi, $i$ = 1, 2, 3, 4, 5 is the score of a respondent on variable $i$ of sphere of discrimination; Fsi, $i$ = 1, 2, 3, 4, 5 is the score of a respondent on variable $i$ of form of discrimination; and Psi, $i$ = 1, 2, 3, 4, 5 is the score of a respondent on variable $i$ of discrimination by provider.

The weighted average for all the variables was the score for the respondent. These scores were used to assess which form of discrimination was more prevalent in which sphere, and practised by which personnel (Table 7.2).

| TABLE 7.2: Scores and Weightage for Degree of Discrimination | | |
|---|---|---|
| Score categories | Degree of discrimination | Weights for scores |
| <2 | Low | Less than 2 times: 1 |
| 2–4 | Medium | 2–4 times: 2.5 |
| 4> | High | More than 4 times: 5 |

Information gathered from the consultative meetings and discussions were used for narrative analyses, largely to reflect on the causes of discrimination from the viewpoints of the dominant community members as well as the Dalit children and their mothers.

## Results

Empirical results of data from the field have been processed and analysed using three methods—ranking, composite index, and narrative analysis. In the following section, the prevalence of discrimination has been measured using simple percentages and ranking of the experience of discrimination in terms of different forms, spheres, and providers. Subsequently, the discussion turns to discrimination differentials between public and private sector providers in different spheres, and perception of Dalit children about the providers who discriminate, and desired treatment from them. The level of discrimination in different study villages has been discussed in the next section using the composite index. The third section deals with causes of discrimination as perceived by non-Dalits and Dalits.

## PREVALENCE OF DISCRIMINATION

### Spheres of Discrimination

As regards the spheres of discrimination, factors that were taken into account included visit to/by provider, dispensing of medicine, counselling, conduct of pathological test, and seeking referral for further care. Most children experienced caste-based discrimination in dispensing of medicine (91 per cent), followed by the conduct of pathological test (87 per cent). Of the 1298 times that the 200 Dalit children were given any medicine, they experienced discrimination on 1181 occasions. Nearly 9 out of 10 times, Dalit children experienced discrimination while receiving medicine or during a pathological test. While seeking referral, about 63 per cent times Dalit children were discriminated. Also, nearly 6 in every 10 times Dalit children were discriminated during diagnosis and while seeking referral.

## Forms of Discrimination

Forms of discrimination, in terms of complete or partial exclusion and inclusion, with differential treatment were examined through: duration of interaction with the care providers; whether the user was being touched (sympathetically) and spoken gently to, or referred to by the provider without using demeaning words; and whether the Dalit child was made to wait for longer duration than due while accessing care. It was observed that the most discrimination was experienced by Dalit children in the form of 'touch'—94 out of 100 times—when they accessed health care services. The duration of time spent by the provider with Dalit children was the next most discriminating form. Dalit children were not given as much time by the providers compared to other children; in about 81 per cent of the total time that all Dalit children used a health facility. Use of derogatory words and waiting at the place of care provisioning were the forms where less discrimination was experienced, as compared to duration of interaction and touch. Seven out of 10 times, children were discriminated by doctors, lab technicians, and registered medical practitioners (RMPs) in the form of touch. Discrimination through touch was more vigorously practised by pharmacists, ANMs, and AWWs. They did not touch the Dalit children in almost all the times they interacted with the children (Table 7.4).

As regards the place of discrimination, most discrimination occurs while providing and receiving care at home. Providers either do not enter the house, or enter up to a certain limit only. Comparatively lesser discrimination is evident at the care centre. There are no separate places for waiting, but Dalit users feel inhibited about sharing the same space as the dominant caste. There is no evidence of difference in time spent. There is some evidence, though, of use of less respectful words—for instance, 'They are dirty, so falling ill is natural.' Dispensing of medicine is done directly by hand through a piece of paper, and not in small packets conventionally used for putting the medicines (tablets)—'They can digest even stone, so...' Using the water pot is subtly discouraged—'Do not touch, it will break.'

## Discrimination by Providers

As regards discrimination by providers, grassroots-level workers like ANMs and AWWs were more discriminating than the higher-order providers such as doctors and lab technicians. Of the total number of times that Dalit children accessed health care services, more than 93 per cent times they experienced discrimination by ANMs and AWWs; and about 59 per cent times, they experienced any form of discrimination by doctors and lab technicians. Pharmacists discriminated the most while giving medicine, and the least in making the Dalit children wait for their turn. Lab technicians seem to be the most discriminating in terms of making them wait (91 per cent times) and the least in the conduct of pathological tests (71 per cent times). While most other providers discriminate mostly when it comes to touching the Dalit child, due to the nature of the work that lab technicians do, 'touching' becomes inevitable. They need to position a Dalit child's body part for an x-ray, or a blood test, for instance, as much as they need to do for the others. So, this form of discrimination is 'less' practised by them. As regards the ANMs, for more than half of the total visits that they made to the Dalit households, it was after they had visited the others. Almost all the times that they visited Dalit households, they had not entered the house and had taken great care to not touch their children, and spent less time than what they usually would have spent with non-Dalit children. Almost always (98 per cent times), the AWWs served the food last to the Dalit children. The traditional healers and RMPs appear to be less discriminating than other providers (Table 7.3).

TABLE 7.3: Nature of Discrimination Experienced by Dalit Children in Health Care Access—by Sphere, Form, and Provider

| Nature of discrimination | Total response | Positive response | Children experiencing discrimination (in percentage) |
|---|---|---|---|
| **Sphere:** | | | |
| During diagnosis or visit to the doctor | 1045 | 596 | 57 |
| During counselling | 1167 | 864 | 74 |
| During dispensing of medicine | 1298 | 1181 | 91 |
| During conduct of pathological test | 708 | 616 | 87 |
| While seeking referral | 652 | 411 | 63 |
| **Form by providers (doctors):** | | | |
| Less time given by doctor | 943 | 594 | 63 |
| Doctors do not touch | 1041 | 718 | 69 |
| Doctors do not speak gently | 904 | 253 | 28 |
| Users have to wait | 979 | 235 | 24 |
| **Form by providers (lab technicians and pharmacists):** | | | |
| LTs do not touch during pathological test | 1041 | 720 | 71 |
| LTs do not speak gently | 704 | 612 | 87 |
| LTs make them wait | 519 | 473 | 91 |
| Pharmacists do not touch while dispensing medicine | 931 | 903 | 97 |
| Pharmacists do not speak gently | 530 | 408 | 77 |
| Pharmacists make them wait | 698 | 579 | 83 |
| **Form by providers (grassroots-level workers):** | | | |
| ANMs do not enter the house | 567 | 533 | 94 |
| ANMs spend less time | 531 | 488 | 92 |
| ANMs do not speak gently | 208 | 144 | 69 |
| ANMs visit them last | 142 | 78 | 55 |
| ANMs do not touch them while dispensing medicine | 339 | 780 | 93 |
| AWWs do not touch them | 1931 | 1680 | 87 |
| AWWs make them sit separately | 1703 | 1465 | 86 |
| AWWs do not speak gently | 839 | 604 | 72 |
| AWWs serve them food last | 1902 | 1864 | 98 |
| **Form by providers (traditional healers):** | | | |
| THs do not touch | 593 | 332 | 56 |
| THs do not speak gently | 936 | 665 | 71 |
| THs make them wait | 431 | 220 | 51 |
| THs make them sit separately | 321 | 67 | 21 |

| Nature of discrimination | Total response | Positive response | Children experiencing discrimination (in percentage) |
|---|---|---|---|
| Form by providers (registered medical practitioners): | | | |
| RMPs spend less time during interaction | 104 | 69 | 64 |
| RMPs do not touch | 987 | 679 | 71 |
| RMPs do not speak gently | 213 | 113 | 53 |
| RMPs make them wait | 297 | 86 | 29 |
| Total Dalit children | 200 | – | – |

*Note*: LT: Lab Technician; ANM: Auxiliary Nurse Midwife; AWW: Anganwadi Worker; TH: Traditional Healer; RMP: Registered Medical Practitioner

## DEGREE OF PREVALENCE OF CASTE-BASED DISCRIMINATION

Discrimination is least prevalent in interaction with doctors and in waiting time for them. Traditional healers (THs) make the Dalit children sit separately, while registered medical practitioners make them wait before attending to them. In all, though, less than 30 per cent of the time the Dalit children had to face discrimination during such interactions with doctors, traditional healers, and RMPs. Discrimination is a little more pronounced in visit to or by the doctor; waiting for, and being touched by, the THs; ANMs visiting them last; and the way RMPs speak to them. Prevalence of discrimination in these spheres and forms, practised by some providers, ranges between 50 per cent and 60 per cent. Most Dalit children face discrimination 60–70 per cent of the times while seeking referral, in time given and being touched by the doctors, in time given by the RMPs, and in verbal interactions with the ANMs. The spheres and forms in which 70–80 per cent discrimination prevails are counselling, lab technicians not touching during conduct of pathological test, and verbal interaction with pharmacists, AWWs, and traditional healers. Conduct of pathological test and interaction with the lab technicians, waiting time before the pharmacists attend to them, and AWWs refraining from touching them and making them sit separately are spheres and forms where 80–90 per cent discrimination is prevalent. The spheres and forms with highest prevalence of discrimination, at more than 90 per cent, are dispensing of medicine, and not being touched by the pharmacists and the ANMs while dispensing the medicine; waiting

## TABLE 7.4: Caste-based Discrimination Experienced by Dalit Children while Accessing Health Care— by Degree of Prevalence

| 20–30% | 50–60% | 60–70% | 70–80% | 80–90% | 90%+ |
|---|---|---|---|---|---|
| Doctors do not speak gently | During diagnosis or visit to the doctor | While seeking referral | During counselling | During conduct of pathological tests | During dispensing of medicine |
| THs make them sit separately | ANMs visit them last | Less time given by doctor | LTs do not touch during pathological test | LTs do not speak gently | LTs make them wait |
| RMPs make them wait | THs do not touch | Doctors do not touch | Pharmacists do not speak gently | Pharmacists make them wait | Pharmacists do not touch them while dispensing the medicine |
| Users have to wait for doctors | THs make them wait | ANMs do not speak gently | AWWs do not speak gently | AWWs do not touch them | ANMs do not enter the house |
| | RMPs do not speak gently | RMPs spend less time during interaction | THs do not speak gently | AWWs make them sit separately | ANMs spend less time |
| | | | RMPs do not touch | | ANMs do not touch them while dispensing medicine |
| | | | | | AWWs serve them food last |

*Note*: LT: Laboratory Technician; TH: Traditional Healer; RMP: Registered Medical Practitioner; ANM: Auxiliary Nurse Midwife; AWW: Anganwadi Worker for lab technicians; ANMs not entering the house and spending less time; and AWWs serving them food last. While doctors, THs, and RMPs are the providers who practise least discrimination in some spheres and forms (20–30 per cent), lab technicians, pharmacists, ANMs, and AWWs are the providers who practise it most (90 per cent) (Table 7.4).

During diagnosis, doctors are sometimes less probing regarding the health problem, and adopt unsympathetic attitude and rude behaviour towards the Dalit children. The pharmacist, while dispensing of medicine, often keep it on the window sill, without explaining the doses properly. The lab technician does not touch the Dalit children during the conduct of a test, and often tests are not conducted properly; the patient is told that the 'time for test is over', and demeaning words are used as well. While applying medicine, or putting the bandage on to a Dalit user, nurses show lack of any concern or sympathy. They do not explain to the Dalits how to take care of the wound/dressing. The ANM/LHV/VHW often do not visit the Dalit quarters for counselling or dispensing of medicine, or for dissemination of information regarding a health programme or camp, except in the case of target-based programmes like immunization, particularly polio.

Having seen the nature and prevalence of discrimination in different spheres and forms, it is worthwhile to examine which providers in public and private sector health care are more discriminating than the others.

## DISCRIMINATION DIFFERENTIALS IN PUBLIC AND PRIVATE SECTOR PROVIDERS

A comparison between the proportion of children who have experienced discrimination in the hands of public and private sector providers suggests that the latter are less discriminating (Table 7.5). All the private sector providers other than those in the lowest end of the providers' hierarchy (Anganwadi workers) have fewer number of children who have faced discrimination as compared to the public sector providers in the similar levels of providers' hierarchy (other than traditional healers). This is why the private sector providers may be considered less discriminating than their counterpart in the public sector. In both the sectors, grassroots-level providers are more discriminating as compared to the higher-order providers. Traditional healers in the private sector and AWWs in the public sector have discriminated in one form or another against 38 and 82 children respectively. Lab technicians and pharmacists in the private sector are less discriminating than their counterparts in the public sector. The most discriminating providers in the public sector are the ANMs, who were found to have discriminated against 54 children. In comparison, the most discriminating in the private sector are the RMPs, who have discriminated against 44 children. The most discriminating sphere in both the sectors is dispensing of

**TABLE 7.5: Discrimination by Public and Private Sector Providers in Different Spheres**

| Sphere | Public sector providers who discriminate | | | | | |
|---|---|---|---|---|---|---|
| | Doctor | LT | Pharmacist | ANM/HW | AWW | Total |
| Diagnostic | 10 | – | – | 10 | 10 | 30 |
| Counselling | 14 | – | – | 16 | 14 | 44 |
| Dispensing of medicine | – | – | 44 | 22 | 14 | 80 |
| Pathological test | – | 34 | – | – | – | 34 |
| Seeking referral | 6 | – | – | 4 | – | 10 |
| Total | 30 | 34 | 44 | 52 | 38 | 200 |

| Sphere | Private sector providers who discriminate | | | | | |
|---|---|---|---|---|---|---|
| | Doctor | LT | Pharmacist | RMP | TH | Total |
| Diagnostic | 02 | – | – | 08 | 30 | 40 |
| Counselling | 02 | 02 | 04 | 06 | 14 | 28 |
| Dispensing of medicine | 10 | – | 32 | 20 | 36 | 98 |
| Pathological test | 00 | 20 | – | 06 | – | 26 |
| Seeking referral | 02 | 02 | – | 04 | 02 | 10 |
| Total Dalit children | 16 | 24 | 36 | 44 | 82 | 200 |

*Note*: Actual number of respondents reporting at least one experience of discrimination (which they perceive as most discriminating)
LT: Lab Technician; ANM: Auxiliary Nurse Midwife; HW: Health Worker; RMP: Registered Medical Practitioner

medicine. The public sector, however, is less discriminating (80) than the private (98). Most children have experienced discrimination in this sphere in the hands of the traditional healer. Traditional healers are, most of the time, local people from within the village and, thus, prefer to adhere to the norms of discriminatory practices against Dalit children. In the perception of the children, the ANMs and the traditional healers are seen as most discriminating, and the doctors as least (Table 7.6).

TABLE 7.6: Perception of Dalit Children about Discriminating Health Care Providers in Public and Private Sectors

| Discriminating health care personnel: Public and private sector | | |
|---|---|---|
| Provider | Rank | |
| Public sector | Gujarat (100) | Rajasthan (100) |
| Doctor/specialist | 5 (96) | 5 (98) |
| Lab technician | 3 (89) | 3 (91) |
| Pharmacist | 2 (73) | 2 (83) |
| ANM | 4 (64) | 4 (71) |
| AWW | 1 (51) | 1 (62) |
| Private sector | | |
| Traditional healer | 1 (73) | 1 (82) |
| RMP | 3 (61) | 3 (75) |
| ISM practitioner | 2 (52) | 2 (65) |
| Allopathic doctor | 4 (40) | 4 (51) |

(Based on individual interviews)
Note: Figures in parentheses denote the number of respondents who gave a specific response
ANM: Auxiliary Nurse Midwife; RMP: Registered Medical Practitioner; ISM: Indian Systems of Medicine; AWW: Anganwadi Worker

The treatment the Dalit children desire from the providers is reflective of the fact that they value self-esteem and can articulate their rightful wish to be treated with dignity. Dalit children in both the states desired that the providers speak to them gently, without using derogatory and demeaning words. Time spent with the provider was ranked fifth in both states as the desired form of behaviour. Being touched gently, without being offended, appeared low in the ranking among the children in both states, largely because they may not be visualizing it as an important element in care giving (Table 7.7).

| Forms | Rank | |
| --- | --- | --- |
| | Gujarat | Rajasthan |
| Time spent | 5 | 5 |
| Touch gently (without offending) | 4 | 6 |
| Speak gently | 1 | 1 |
| Use of respectful words | 2 | 2 |
| Consider as equals | 3 | 3 |
| Prioritize severity of illness | 6 | 4 |

TABLE 7.7: Desired Treatments from the Providers

*Note*: '1' denotes that the highest number of respondents ranked a specific indicator as most desired treatment expected undesirable for living condition as perceived by others

## VARIATION IN NATURE OF DISCRIMINATION IN THE TWO STATES

Having examined the differentials in the experience of discrimination among Dalit children by sphere, form, and providers, both in the public and private sectors, we now examine the levels at which the study villages get placed. In the following section, a composite index has been used to examine this.

The experience of discrimination among Dalit children, when disaggregated at state level, reflect that children in Rajasthan experienced more discrimination in spheres such as interaction with the provider during diagnosis, visit to the doctor, counselling, dispensing of medicine, conduct of pathological tests, and seeking of referral. On the other hand, Dalit children in Gujarat experienced more discrimination in interaction with the doctor by way of duration of time spent with them, being forced or obliged to let the dominant caste user see the provider before them, and not being touched or spoken gently to by the providers. Thus, while Gujarat seems to be experiencing discrimination in spheres, in Rajasthan it was higher in the form of discrimination.

## REASONS FOR DISCRIMINATION: PERCEPTION OF DOMINANT CASTE

After having brought selective evidence on the nature of discrimination faced by the Dalit children in seeking the health services, we now look in to the reasons for discrimination. The discriminatory behaviour is based on particular notions harboured by the HC persons with respect to the social status of low-caste Untouchables. The views of about 67 HC persons were sought.

The HC persons held a certain stereotypical notion regarding the lifestyle, living conditions, personal hygiene, and cleanliness of the Dalits. These notions are used not only as identifiers, but also as justification to discriminate against them. Responses from about 67 HC persons were obtained. Table 7.8 presents the responses of HC persons about their notion of low-caste individuals. A set of responses reflecting perception and prejudices of HC about the living conditions of Dalit children were ranked. The living conditions that received the maximum responses was given rank—followed by the rest in descending order.

TABLE 7.8: Perception of Dominant Castes about Dalit Children Based on Living Conditions

| Indicators* | Rank | |
| --- | --- | --- |
| | Gujarat | Rajasthan |
| Dirty house | 7 | 7 |
| Presence of flies | 6 | 5 |
| Eat stale/unclean food/meat | 5 | 6 |
| Children have running nose (which they keep licking) | 1 | 4 |
| Children often half/ill-clad or naked | 4 | 1 |
| Children play in dirty lanes | 3 | 2 |
| Domestic animals live with persons | 2 | 3 |

Table 7.8 indicates that improper hygienic condition in which the Dalit children live and the way they organize themselves mark the understanding of the HC about the Dalit children. Both in Rajasthan and Gujarat, the HC tend to attribute the discriminatory

TABLE 7.9: How Others Perceive Dalits

| Issue | Experience | Expression | Solution/expected change |
| --- | --- | --- | --- |
| Sanitation and drainage | Mostly poor drainage in the Dalit quarters | Overflowing drains, clogged with filth, litter on the sides of the lanes and outside the house<br><br>Often, the drains are not constructed or they are broken<br><br>More evident in Gujarat as compared to Rajasthan | Local self-governing bodies should take the initiative<br><br>People should participate in keeping their surroundings clean<br><br>Non-Dalits should not consider Dalit quarters as their trash-dumping ground<br><br>Improve environmental education among all children |
| Personal hygiene | Depends on availability of water. Often clean; sometimes, some smell is present | Dirty and smelling Children unclean and smelling<br><br>'Children often have running nose that they lick'—a non-Dalit woman, Undkha, Barmer | Inculcate cleanliness<br><br>Remove bias against Dalits |
| Physical hygiene | Depends on the cleaners who clean the lanes<br><br>Domestic water collects in a ditch in front of the house, and channellized to the fields | Houses are dirty; there are flies<br><br>Often, the lanes are dirty too<br><br>Domestic water sometimes overflows from the ditch, and lanes become dirty<br><br>They live with the animals<br><br>Engage in rearing of pigs | Proper outlet for waste water into the fields to be put in place |

| Issue | Experience | Expression | Solution/expected change |
|---|---|---|---|
| Children's perspective | 'Mothers clean us.' 'We oil our hair and comb.' 'We even tuck our shirts in the pants...how can we be dirty?' | Dishevelled hair, smell, wears dirty and crumpled clothes, often are half-clad or naked, especially the smaller children. They often cry<br><br>Play in dirty lanes and with dirty animals | 'We should play together, eat together, study together...we... sit together in the classroom...', school children in Ranoda, Gujarat |

*Note*: Based on consultative meetings with mothers and children

behaviour to unhygenic conditions such as: Dalit children remain with 'running nose', are ill-clad or naked, play in the dirty streets, and stay in a place where animals are also housed. Consumption of meat or stale or unclean food and 'dirty house' were also used as identifiers and reasons for discrimination, though by fewer people in both the states.

This perception of HC persons about the living conditions of Dalits is reflective of their biases and prejudice about the social situation of Dalit children. The pitiable situation of Dalit children does not evoke sympathy and concern for help; on the contrary, it generates feelings of contempt and disregard towards them.

There are obvious consequences of discriminatory access by public and private providers on the use of health services by Dalit children. Complete exclusion and/or access with differential treatment may reduce the use of health services, and result in poor health and high mortality of the Dalit children. The evidences from the field data suggests that high-caste service providers particularly the lower level workers' attitudes towards the low-caste users is still governed by customary notions of their social status and notion of purity, and pollution. This results in denial of equal treatment to Dalit children in rendering the health services. It emerged from the discussion with the Dalits respondents, that providers avoid visit to Dalit quarters by giving reasons which include preference for a central location to enable access for everyone, and contending that Dalit quarters are inwards into the village. The location of primary or sub-primary health centre in high-caste locality reduces the social access to health services to the Dalits children.

Thus it is apparent that the government needs to recognize these social constraints faced by the Dalit children in accessing the public health services and develop necessary safeguards and codes so that Dalit children are enabled to enjoy equal access to these services. This also indicates the need for specific policy and set of measures to prevent discriminatory practices in the delivery of heath care services both by public and private sector providers. The present policy does not include safeguards against caste- and untouchability-based discrimination, and also lacks the use of positive practices to promote humanly and non-discriminatory relations in the provision of health care services.

## NOTE

1. The questions pertaining to discrimination in different spheres, in different forms, and by different providers were chosen to compute this index. Responses of the mothers for children below 12 years and of children above 12 years of age were included. There were 50 respondents from the four primary health centre (PHC) circles (that is, a PHC village, a sub-centre village in the same PHC circle, and a non sub-centre village from the same PHC circle)—Koth and Amaliyara in Gujarat, and Ranigaon Khurd and Sanawada in Rajasthan. Thus, there were 200 respondents in all.

## REFERENCES

Acharya, Sanghmitra (2002). 'Health Care Utilisation in Rural North India—A Case of Nirpura, District Meerut', Study undertaken as part of the Monitoring Health Sector Project, Centre of Social Medicine and Community Health and European Union Project. Unpublished Report, Centre of Social Medicine and Community Health, School of Social Sciences, Jawaharlal Nehru University, New Delhi.

Carstairs, G.M. (1955), 'Medicine and Faith in Rural Rajasthan', in B.D. Paul (ed.), *Health, Culture and Community*, New York: Russell Sage Foundation.

IIPS and ORC Macro (1995), *National Family Health Survey (NFHS-1), 1992–93: India*, Mumbai: International Institute for Population Sciences (IIPS).

IIPS and ORC Macro (2000), *National Family Health Survey (NFHS-2), 1997–98: India*, Mumbai: International Institute for Population Sciences (IIPS).

—— (2006), *National Family Health Survey (NFHS-3), 2004–5: India*, Mumbai: International Institute for Population Sciences (IIPS).

Kulkarni, P.M. and V.K. Baraik (2003), 'Utilisation of Health Care Services by Scheduled Castes in India', Working Paper No. 39, Indian Institute of Dalit Studies, New Delhi.

Ram, F., K.B. Pathak and K.I. Annamma (1998), 'Utilisation of Health Care Services by the Underprivileged Section of Population in India—Results from NFHS', *Demography India*, vol. 30, no. 2, pp. 29–38.

Sen, Amartya (2000), *Development as Freedom*, New Delhi: Oxford University Press.

Srinivasan, K. and S.K. Mohanty (2004), 'Health Care Utilisation by Source and Levels of Deprivation in Major States of India: Findings from NFHS-2', *Demography India*, vol. 33, no. 2, pp. 107–26.

Srinivasan, K. and P. Srinivasan (2005), 'Caste Affiliation and Poverty among Major Religious Groups in Four States in India: An Empirical Analysis using NFHS-2 Data', *Demography India*, vol. 34, no. 1, pp. 17–39.

Thorat, S. (2002), 'Oppression and Denial: Dalit Discrimination in the 1990s', *Economic and Political Weekly*, vol. 37, no. 6, February, pp. 9–15.

Thorat, S. and Nidhi Sadana Sabharwal (2006), *Rural Non-farm Employment of the Scheduled Castes: A Comparative Study*, Working Paper Series, vol. 1, no. 5, Indian Institute of Dalit Studies, New Delhi.

Zurbrigg, S. (1984), *Rakku's Story: Structure of Ill-health and Sources of Change*, Madras. (George Joseph on behalf of Centre of Social Action, 899, Ramdev Gardens, Bangalore.)

# 8

# Segmented Schooling[*]
## Inequalities in Primary Education

*Sonalde Desai, Cecily Darden Adams, and Amaresh Dubey*

India is a predominantly Hindu nation with substantial religious diversity. According to the 2001 census, Muslims form about 13 per cent of the nation with other religious minorities such as Christians, Sikhs, and Jains forming another 3 per cent. However, the remaining population is also highly differentiated. About 8 per cent of the population identifies itself as being Adivasi (the original inhabitants of the land) or tribal, located outside the Hindu caste system. Another 16 per cent of the population is considered Dalit, belonging to the lowest castes that were considered impure by high-caste Hindus. Adivasis and Dalits are officially listed in a schedule appended to the Indian constitution and called Scheduled Tribe (ST) and Scheduled Caste (SC), respectively.

While a variety of affirmative action programmes are in place to bridge educational, occupational, and income disparities between the Dalits (SC), Adivasis (ST), and general populations, substantial educational disparities persist. Table 8.1, based on our past research (Desai and Kulkarni 2008), shows that the Dalits and Adivasis as well as Muslims tend to lag behind Hindus and other religious groups. We have also found that a great deal of this inequality emerges of the primary school level, with children from

* The results reported in this chapter are based primarily on India Human Development Survey (IHDS), 2005. This survey was jointly organized by researchers at University of Maryland and the National Council of Applied Economic Research (NCAER). The data collection was funded by grants from the National Institutes of Health to University of Maryland. Part of the sample represents a resurvey of households initially conducted in the course of IHDS 1993–4 conducted by NCAER.

TABLE 8.1: Educational Attainment and Transition Probabilities at
Various Educational Levels
(Survey Year 1999–2000, NSS 55th Round)

| | Educational attainment | Transition probability** |
|---|---|---|
| *Upper Caste Hindu and Other Religion* | | |
| Illiterate and below primary | 30.40 | |
| Primary | 17.45 | 0.70 |
| Middle | 23.88 | 0.82 |
| Secondary | 22.82 | 0.66 |
| College | 5.45 | 0.34 |
| | 100.00 | |
| *Dalit* | | |
| Illiterate and below primary | 50.45 | |
| Primary | 17.88 | 0.50 |
| Middle | 18.49 | 0.71 |
| Secondary | 11.61 | 0.52 |
| College | 1.57 | 0.22 |
| | 100.00 | |
| *Adivasi* | | |
| Illiterate and below primary | 57.29 | |
| Primary | 15.08 | 0.43 |
| Middle | 16.58 | 0.72 |
| Secondary | 9.57 | 0.52 |
| College | 1.48 | 0.25 |
| | 100.00 | |
| *Muslim* | | |
| Illiterate and below primary | 48.05 | |
| Primary | 17.95 | 0.52 |
| Middle | 19.53 | 0.71 |
| Secondary | 12.56 | 0.52 |
| College | 1.91 | 0.25 |
| | 100.00 | |

*Notes*: * Only people who completed the previous level and are of appropriate age
are included in calculating transition probabilities
** Transition refers to the probability of enrolment in the next level after completing
the preceding level, e.g., the transition probability of 0.70 for the middle level is the
probability of enrolment in the middle for those who have successfully completed
primary level

the marginalized groups dropping out before completing primary school. In fact, if these children manage to complete primary school, their likelihood of completing middle school is much closer to that of the other groups (Desai and Kulkarni 2008). This suggests that primary school is an important site for the creation of educational inequality.

## SOURCES OF EDUCATIONAL INEQUALITIES

Racial and ethnic educational inequalities around the world have received considerable research attention, with different lines of research emphasizing different factors. Research on developing countries has tended to focus on two sets of factors: (a) lack of access to schools: since marginalized communities often live in distant locations they may lack access to schools within a reasonable commuting distance; and (b) family factors including poverty, lack of parental motivation, or labour demands on children (for a review of this literature, see Shavit and Blossfeld 1993). This has led to a strong policy emphasis on building schools and motivating parents to get children into schools. But in a rush to get children into schools, the functioning of schools themselves has received little attention.

Research on industrial societies has tended to go beyond access and family factors to look at the role of the schools and communities in facilitating or inhibiting learning outcomes. In the United States, research has sought to clarify the individual, family, and school compositional causes of racial, ethnic, and class educational inequality. At the individual level, poor academic performance, retention, lack of teacher support and guidance, disliking school or teachers, and taking on adult responsibilities such as work and childcare have been found to contribute to lower achievement and dropping out of school (Barro 1987; Croninger and Lee 2001; Jimerson 1999; Rumberger 1995). Parental educational attainment, parental involvement, household income, and household wealth have informed family contributions to educational attainment (Rumberger 1987, 1995; Hauser *et al.* 2000) Analyses of school and neighbourhood composition have found that urban/city and socio-economic composition of the school significantly predict academic achievement (Rumberger and Palardy

2005; Okpala *et al.* 2001). Specifically, Rumberger, and Palardy (2005) found that the socio-economic composition of the school has as much effect on educational attainment as the individual socio-economic status of the student, regardless of race, social class, or prior academic achievement, although high teacher expectations and positive academic climate eliminate the school-level effect of socio-economic composition. Disaggregate data often find that the effect of these factors varies across racial, ethnic, and socio-economic measures (Rumberger 1995). Thus, the American literature suggests that an interaction of individual and environmental factors contribute to educational attainment at the intersection with race, ethnicity, and socio-economic status.

While qualitative literature in developing countries has also highlighted the role of schools and teachers in creating educational inequalities, much of this evidence tends to be anecdotal. For India, qualitative research paints a stark picture of the indignities suffered by Dalit and Adivasi children. There are reported instances of Dalit children suffering from discrimination by teachers and other students. Eighty per cent of the Dalit students at a college in Aurangabad said that they were made to sit outside the classroom in primary school. In another study, a Dalit school teacher recalled, 'We were asked to sit separately. Our copy or slates were not touched by the teachers' (The Probe Team 1999). Dalit homes are located outside of the main village and consequently farther from schools. It was observed in a village in Tamil Nadu that 'None of the SCs were even allowed to walk through the residential areas of the dominant castes or through the village's main street running through the residential areas of the dominant castes. They had to walk a long way along the periphery of the village to reach their huts' (Nambissan and Sedwal 2002). Teacher behaviour often tends to humiliate Dalit students. Upper caste teachers have low expectations of Dalit pupils and consider them as 'dull' and 'uneducable' (The Probe Team 1999).

Adivasis, in addition to suffering from the same low expectations, face a different set of issues. They often live in hilly regions or forests that are relatively inaccessible. Demographically, tribal habitations are small and sparsely populated and hence, lack many infrastructure facilities, including schools and roads. Even when schools are within walking distance for pupils, during monsoons it is not unusual for the roads to become impassable and for the teachers, who often live in larger towns, to surreptitiously close the school. These factors are particularly constraining for tribal children who live in isolated communities. Language poses another major challenge for tribal education. Tribals normally speak local dialects rather than the main state language. Consequently, tribal students feel further alienated when the teachers are not well trained to communicate in the tribal dialects (Sujatha 2002).

Muslim students suffer from similar disadvantages. Many Muslims would like to see education take place in Urdu, their mother tongue, but few schools accommodate this. Children often face harassment and ridicule and rising religious tensions lead to children's alienation from the school. Some Muslim students get primary education at the madrasa, the religious school, which makes mainstreaming for secondary schooling often difficult.

Poor quality of schooling and teacher discrimination seems to play an important role in school dropout. A survey of 226 never-enrolled children found that 32 per cent of the boys and 23 per cent of the girls were never enrolled because the child was not interested. Among 106 dropouts in the same survey, it was observed that 35 per cent of the boys and 16 per cent of the girls dropped out because the child did not wish to continue (The Probe Team 1999).

We expect that a less than congenial environment and learning difficulties may play an important role in a child's lack of interest in schooling. Thus, children's achievements are both important as measurements of the quality of education and markers of dropout potential.

## CONCEPTUAL FRAMEWORK AND RESEARCH QUESTIONS

Much of the literature has focused on access to schooling, with the debate ranging between what is more important—supply of schools or parental demand for education manifested in school enrolment. This would imply that once schools are available to all children and parents can be persuaded to send children to school, there is little reason to expect inequalities in school outcomes between children of various social and ethnic groups.

We argue that above and beyond school enrolment, children's educational outcomes are a function of school interactions with children from privileged sections of society faring better than children from marginalized communities. Poor learning outcomes lead to higher dropout rates among these children.

In order to examine this avenue of educational inequalities, we focus on reading and arithmetic attainment of children aged 8–11 years from different strata of Indian society. Specifically we address the following questions:

1. Do reading and arithmetic skill levels for children differ by caste, ethnicity, and religion?
2. Does this relationship persist after we control for school attendance, as measured by current enrolment level and grade completed?
3. How much of this inequality can be attributed to parental socio-economic factors?

## DATA

In 2004–5, the University of Maryland and National Council of Applied Economic Research designed and fielded a survey of 41,550 households. This survey, India Human Development Survey 2005 (IHDS), contained questions about health, education, employment, income, and gender empowerment. The survey was conducted all over India—in 25 states and Union Territories—and included urban as well rural areas.

A major innovation of this survey was to conduct short assessments of reading, writing, and arithmetic skills for children aged 8–11 years. Conducting educational assessment in developing countries—particularly India—is difficult for a variety of reasons: children's ability varies tremendously and an instrument must capture children at both ends of the distribution; tests must be translated in many different languages with similar difficulty levels; the instrument must be simple and intuitive so that interviewers can administer it easily and it would not frighten children who are not used to standardized tests. Luckily, we were able to work with Pratham, a voluntary organization that has worked in the field of elementary education for many years. They have developed simple assessment tools to measure the effectiveness of their training programmes. These tools have been pretested on more than 250,000 children. Working in collaboration with Pratham, we were able to develop simple tests to measure whether a child is not able to read at all, or is able to read letters, words, sentences, paragraphs, or stories. Simple addition, subtraction, multiplication, and division problems were also developed. Children were asked to write simple sentences and were considered able to write if they could write a simple sentence such as 'I like blue colour' with zero or one mistakes.

Interviewers were trained extensively by Pratham volunteers using specially developed films so that they could differentiate between a child's shyness and inability to read. They were also taught how to develop a rapport with children. Tests were developed in a variety of Indian languages as well as English and children were asked to take the test in whichever language they were most comfortable.

As a result, we have access to a survey that contains unique child assessment data as well as a wealth of household socio-economic information. Children are classified according to their ability to read in one of the five categories: (a) cannot read at all; (b) can read letters but not form words; (c) can put letters together to read words but not read whole sentences; (d) can read a short paragraph for 2–3 sentences but not fluent enough to read a whole page; (e) can read a one page short story.

Children's mathematical skills are classified in four categories: (a) cannot read numbers above 10; (b) can read numbers between 10 and 99 but not able to do more complex number manipulation; (c) can subtract a two-digit number from another; (d) can divide a number between 100 and 999 by another number between 1 and 9. Note that we focus on two-digit numbers to avoid calculations on fingertips and to get a better estimate of true understanding of subtraction and division. Also, given the Indian system of expecting children to memorize multiplication tables from 1 to 20, we chose to test children on division rather than multiplication skills.

The primary independent variable of interest is social group, defined using a combination of caste, ethnicity, and religion. Higher-caste groups, 20 per cent of the sample, form the omitted category. The rest of the sample is divided between: Dalits, the lowest caste or the SCs (23 per cent), Adivasi or the ST (7 per cent), Other Backward Classes (OBC)—castes located between Dalits and high-caste Hindus—(36 per cent), Muslim (13 per cent), and other religious groups, including Christians, Jains, and Sikhs (2 per cent). These are mutually exclusive categories.

In addition to the social group of the respondent, we included several other independent variables in our models (summary statistics of these variables are reported in Table 8.2). The learning tests were administered to children aged 8–11 years old. The average age was nine and a half years, with 25 per cent of the sample aged 8 years, 22 per cent aged 9 years, 34 per cent aged 10 years, and 19 per cent of the sample being 11-year-olds. Forty seven per cent of the

| TABLE 8.2: Summary Descriptives | | | | |
|---|---|---|---|---|
| Variable | Mean | Standard deviation | Minimum | Maximum |
| Reading learning test score | 2.55 | 1.35 | 0 | 4 |
| Math learn test score | 1.53 | 1.03 | 0 | 3 |
| Age | 9.47 | 1.07 | 8 | 11 |
| Gender (male=0, female=1) | 0.47 | 0.50 | 0 | 1 |
| Other forward castes | 0.19 | 0.40 | 0 | 1 |
| OBC | 0.36 | 0.48 | 0 | 1 |
| SC/Dalit | 0.23 | 0.42 | 0 | 1 |
| ST/Adivasi | 0.07 | 0.25 | 0 | 1 |
| Muslim | 0.13 | 0.34 | 0 | 1 |
| Christian, Sikh, Jain | 0.02 | 0.13 | 0 | 1 |
| Standard completed (0–5+) | 2.95 | 1.46 | 0 | 5 |
| Currently enrolled (not enrolled=0, Enrolled=1) | 0.89 | 0.32 | 0 | 1 |
| Residence (rural=0, urban=1) | 0.25 | 0.43 | 0 | 1 |
| Assets quintile | 2.87 | 1.35 | 1 | 5 |
| Highest standard completed, adults in household | 6.55 | 1.55 | 0 | 15 |
| Literate adult in household | 0.98 | 0.45 | 0 | 1 |
| Observations 12,302 | | | | |

*Source*: Special tabulations by the authors using unit record level IHDS 2005 survey data

sample was female. Educational standard completion is measured from no standards completed (0) to five or more standards (5+). The respondents averaged completion of the third standard, with 5 per cent completing no standards, 13 per cent one, 20 per cent two, 23 per cent three, 20 per cent four, and 18 per cent completing five standards. Current enrolment is a self-reported measure of the child's current enrolment status. Eighty-nine per cent of the children tested were currently enrolled in school.

Several household level variables were also included in the analysis. Twenty-five per cent of the children resided in households in urban areas, with the remainder living in rural locations. Household assets were measured on a scale of 30 household consumer goods and housing assets, and reported in quintiles for the survey sample. The highest standard completed by an adult in the household was also measured. The average standard completed was seventh, or less than the completion of middle school. Eighteen per cent of the households in the sample reported not having a literate adult in the household.

Each model also included controls for the state of residence, measured by a series of dummy variables.

## RESULTS

Since this is possibly the first all India survey of reading and mathematical achievement using a household rather than school sample, descriptive results are of interest in themselves.

Tables 8.3 and 8.4 show reading and mathematical ability levels for children 8–11 years by grade completed and current enrolment status. As might be expected, currently enrolled students score higher on both outcomes than those currently not in school and skill level improves with grades completed. However, even among children who have completed three or more grades, reading skills remain low. Among kids with completed education of three or more grades, about four per cent cannot recognize any letters, about 9 per cent can recognize letters but cannot combine them to form words, and a further 16 per cent can read words but cannot put them together to read a paragraph of 2–3 simple sentences.

Mathematical skills show a worse distribution. Among children who have completed 3rd or higher grade, 11 per cent cannot read

TABLE 8.3: Reading Ability by Enrolment Status and Highest Standard
Completed for 8–11-year-olds

| Standard completed | Not Enrolled | | | | |
|---|---|---|---|---|---|
| | Does not read | Letter | Word | Paragraph | Story |
| 0 | 72.11 | 11.58 | 12.55 | 2.19 | 1.58 |
| 1 | 31.1 | 15.33 | 31.21 | 13.3 | 9.06 |
| 2 | 15.67 | 16.67 | 22.4 | 21.05 | 24.22 |
| 3 | 8.05 | 12.04 | 16.43 | 36.4 | 27.08 |
| 4 | 4.05 | 5.2 | 18.27 | 30.75 | 41.73 |
| 5 | 7.36 | 5.61 | 9.61 | 22.02 | 55.4 |
| Total | 19.07 | 10.81 | 17.98 | 23.44 | 28.71 |
| Standard completed | Currently Enrolled | | | | |
| | Does not read | Letter | Word | Paragraph | Story |
| 0 | 37.99 | 29.41 | 22.68 | 5.55 | 4.38 |
| 1 | 19.93 | 24.79 | 31.62 | 11.25 | 12.42 |
| 2 | 10.96 | 17.57 | 27.58 | 22.19 | 21.7 |
| 3 | 5.85 | 12.7 | 22.44 | 25.49 | 33.51 |
| 4 | 3.16 | 8.68 | 15.28 | 26.04 | 46.85 |
| 5 | 3.56 | 5.96 | 10.76 | 22.42 | 57.31 |
| Total | 9.2 | 13.94 | 21.05 | 21.6 | 34.21 |

Source: Special tabulations by the authors using unit record level IHDS 2005 survey data

numbers between 10 and 99, and 28 per cent can read numbers but cannot subtract two-digit numbers.

Tables 8.5 and 8.6, Tables 8.7 and 8.8 show the basic distribution of these skills for urban and rural children and children of various social groups separately. Not surprisingly, reading and mathematical skills are higher for urban than for rural children. Social group differences are also clearly evident in these descriptive statistics. Even among children at the same grade level, children from upper castes and religious groups like Christian, Sikh, and Jains do far better in their educational attainment than the four other groups—OBC or the middle castes, Dalits, Adivasis, and Muslims.

**TABLE 8.4:** Mathematics Ability by Enrolment Status and Highest Standard Completed for 8–11-year-olds

| | Not Enrolled | | | |
|---|---|---|---|---|
| Standard completed | Does not read numbers >10 | Number | Subtraction | Division |
| 0 | 78.42 | 18.44 | 2.57 | 0.58 |
| 1 | 43.35 | 40.17 | 12.73 | 3.75 |
| 2 | 30.02 | 39.26 | 17.12 | 13.6 |
| 3 | 18.57 | 29.96 | 29.77 | 21.7 |
| 4 | 9.62 | 29.89 | 30.06 | 30.43 |
| 5 | 10.87 | 18.71 | 30.17 | 40.25 |
| Total | 27.89 | 29.69 | 22.24 | 20.18 |
| | Currently Enrolled | | | |
| Standard completed | Does not read numbers >10 | Number | Subtraction | Division |
| 0 | 51.01 | 41.28 | 5.78 | 1.93 |
| 1 | 31.02 | 45.34 | 17.1 | 6.54 |
| 2 | 22.88 | 39.13 | 25.81 | 12.18 |
| 3 | 13.06 | 35.76 | 31.58 | 19.6 |
| 4 | 7.89 | 27.7 | 29.79 | 34.61 |
| 5 | 7.08 | 20.14 | 30.49 | 42.3 |
| Total | 16.94 | 33.38 | 26.81 | 22.88 |

*Source:* Special tabulations by the authors using unit record level IHDS 2005 survey data

**TABLE 8.5:** Reading Ability by Residence and Standard Completed for 8–11-year-olds

| | Rural | | | | |
|---|---|---|---|---|---|
| Standard completed | Does not read | Letter | Word | Paragraph | Story |
| 0 | 50.02 | 24.13 | 18.8 | 4.36 | 2.68 |
| 1 | 23 | 24.43 | 32.82 | 9.58 | 10.17 |
| 2 | 12.98 | 18.28 | 28.4 | 20.64 | 19.7 |
| 3 | 7.08 | 14.27 | 22.67 | 26 | 29.98 |
| 4 | 3.64 | 9.13 | 16.92 | 26.82 | 43.48 |
| 5 | 4.59 | 6.53 | 12.04 | 22.21 | 54.62 |
| Total | 11.87 | 14.68 | 21.98 | 20.92 | 30.56 |

| | | *Urban* | | | |
|---|---|---|---|---|---|
| *Standard completed* | *Does not read* | *Letter* | *Word* | *Paragraph* | *Story* |
| 0 | 32.49 | 27.54 | 25.73 | 6.09 | 8.15 |
| 1 | 12.39 | 22.09 | 26.57 | 18.93 | 20.02 |
| 2 | 6.61 | 14.83 | 22.53 | 26.69 | 29.34 |
| 3 | 3.15 | 7.81 | 19.33 | 28.45 | 41.26 |
| 4 | 2.19 | 5.74 | 11.95 | 26 | 54.12 |
| 5 | 2.11 | 4.43 | 7.17 | 22.83 | 63.46 |
| Total | 5.49 | 10.24 | 16.78 | 24.55 | 42.95 |

*Source*: Special tabulations by the authors using unit record level IHDS 2005 survey data

TABLE 8.6: Reading Ability by Social Background for 8–11-year-olds

| | | *All* | | | |
|---|---|---|---|---|---|
| *Standard completed* | *Does not read* | *Letter* | *Word* | *Paragraph* | *Story* |
| Other Forward Castes | 4.37 | 8.49 | 15.46 | 25.1 | 46.57 |
| OBC | 10.53 | 12.92 | 20.09 | 21.52 | 34.95 |
| SC/Dalit | 12.64 | 17.26 | 23.02 | 19.78 | 27.29 |
| ST/Adivasi | 13.15 | 15.32 | 26.25 | 23.16 | 22.12 |
| Muslim | 14 | 16.75 | 24.26 | 20.75 | 24.24 |
| Christian, Sikh, Jain | 2.36 | 5.16 | 13.24 | 20.76 | 58.48 |
| Total | 10.31 | 13.59 | 20.71 | 21.81 | 33.6 |
| | | *Rural* | | | |
| *Standard completed* | *Does not read* | *Letter* | *Word* | *Paragraph* | *Story* |
| Other Forward Castes | 5.35 | 9.73 | 17.34 | 24.85 | 42.73 |
| OBC | 12.13 | 13.95 | 21.02 | 20.62 | 32.28 |
| SC/Dalit | 14.2 | 18.05 | 24.14 | 18.2 | 25.4 |
| ST/Adivasi | 13.7 | 15.63 | 26.42 | 22.72 | 21.53 |
| Muslim | 15.7 | 17.92 | 25.11 | 20.78 | 20.5 |
| Christian, Sikh, Jain | 1.74 | 3.58 | 15.12 | 20.55 | 59.01 |
| Total | 11.87 | 14.68 | 21.98 | 20.92 | 30.56 |

*(Contd)*

*(Table 8.6 contd)*

### Urban

| Standard completed | Does not read | Letter | Word | Paragraph | Story |
|---|---|---|---|---|---|
| Other Forward Castes | 2.54 | 6.18 | 11.96 | 25.56 | 53.76 |
| OBC | 4.42 | 9 | 16.51 | 24.94 | 45.14 |
| SC/Dalit | 6.18 | 13.96 | 18.41 | 26.33 | 35.11 |
| ST/Adivasi | 7.92 | 12.4 | 24.59 | 27.36 | 27.73 |
| Muslim | 10.84 | 14.56 | 22.67 | 20.7 | 31.23 |
| Christian, Sikh, Jain | 3.55 | 8.23 | 9.61 | 21.15 | 57.47 |
| Total | 5.49 | 10.24 | 16.78 | 24.55 | 42.95 |

*Source*: Special tabulations by the authors using unit record level IHDS 2005 survey data

TABLE 8.7: **Arithmetic Ability by Residence and Standard Completed for 8–11-year-olds**

### Rural

| Standard completed | Does not read numbers >10 | Number | Subtraction | Division |
|---|---|---|---|---|
| 0 | 60.99 | 34 | 3.94 | 1.07 |
| 1 | 34.86 | 45 | 14.34 | 5.8 |
| 2 | 26.29 | 40.12 | 22.52 | 11.07 |
| 3 | 15.78 | 38.56 | 28.57 | 17.09 |
| 4 | 8.6 | 31.45 | 28.41 | 31.54 |
| 5 | 8.72 | 22.52 | 29.67 | 39.1 |
| Total | 20.54 | 35.27 | 24.12 | 20.08 |

### Urban

| Standard completed | Does not read numbers >10 | Number | Subtraction | Division |
|---|---|---|---|---|
| 0 | 45.09 | 41.35 | 9.61 | 3.95 |
| 1 | 20.9 | 44.44 | 26.36 | 8.31 |
| 2 | 15.11 | 35.97 | 32.47 | 16.45 |
| 3 | 7.33 | 25.15 | 39.69 | 27.83 |
| 4 | 6.67 | 17.98 | 33.89 | 41.46 |
| 5 | 4.12 | 13.72 | 32.46 | 49.7 |
| Total | 10.87 | 25.89 | 32.99 | 30.25 |

*Source*: Special tabulations by the authors using unit record level IHDS 2005 survey data

TABLE 8.8: Arithmetic Ability by Social Background for
8–11-year-olds

### All

| Standard completed | Does not read numbers >10 | Number | Subtraction | Division |
|---|---|---|---|---|
| Other Forward Castes | 8.97 | 26.79 | 27.35 | 36.89 |
| OBC | 17.9 | 32.42 | 26.85 | 22.83 |
| SC/Dalit | 22.6 | 36.76 | 24.66 | 15.99 |
| ST/Adivasi | 26.78 | 36.82 | 23.77 | 12.63 |
| Muslim | 22.3 | 36.89 | 24.78 | 16.03 |
| Christian, Sikh, Jain | 3.72 | 18.38 | 45.28 | 32.62 |
| Total | 18.17 | 32.96 | 26.3 | 22.58 |

### Rural

| Standard completed | Does not read numbers >10 | Number | Subtraction | Division |
|---|---|---|---|---|
| Other Forward Castes | 11.02 | 32.06 | 23.22 | 33.71 |
| OBC | 20.25 | 34.34 | 25 | 20.4 |
| SC/Dalit | 24.68 | 37.67 | 23.17 | 14.48 |
| ST/Adivasi | 27.98 | 37.87 | 22.29 | 11.86 |
| Muslim | 23.76 | 38.3 | 23.01 | 14.93 |
| Christian, Sikh, Jain | 2.65 | 18.31 | 44.7 | 34.34 |
| Total | 20.54 | 35.26 | 24.12 | 20.08 |

### Urban

| Standard completed | Does not read numbers >10 | Number | Subtraction | Division |
|---|---|---|---|---|
| Other Forward Castes | 5.14 | 16.97 | 35.05 | 42.84 |
| OBC | 8.93 | 25.09 | 33.89 | 32.08 |
| SC/Dalit | 13.94 | 32.99 | 30.82 | 22.25 |
| ST/Adivasi | 15.42 | 26.86 | 37.77 | 19.94 |
| Muslim | 19.56 | 34.26 | 28.08 | 18.09 |
| Christian, Sikh, Jain | 5.78 | 18.53 | 46.39 | 29.31 |
| Total | 10.87 | 25.89 | 32.99 | 30.25 |

*Source*: Special tabulations by the authors using unit record level IHDS 2005 survey data

While these descriptive statistics are of interest, they do not control for such factors as urban/rural residence, state of residence, and age and gender of the child. Hence, we next turn to multivariate analyses. Since our outcome variables are ordinal, they are modelled using ordinal logit regression, which takes the following form:

$$\gamma_i^* = \chi_i \beta + \varepsilon_i \qquad (8.1)$$

$$\gamma_i = m \text{ if } \tau_{m-1} \leq \gamma_i^* < \tau_m \text{ for } m = 1, 2, 3, 4, 5 \qquad (8.2)$$

Ordinal logit models are particularly suited to phenomena that contain measurement errors. In this case, our interviewers were specifically trained to distinguish between students at varying levels of reading and mathematical ability but nonetheless, the same student may well be classified by one interviewer as being able to read letters and not words and by another interviewer as being able to put the letters together in words. So the outcome variable is better classified as a propensity to read rather than a specific skill level. Observed reading levels are tied to this latent variable by the measurement model underlying the ordinal logit regression with cut off points $\tau$:

$\gamma_i = 1$ (does not read)        if $\tau_0 = -\infty \leq \gamma_i^* < \tau_1$

$\gamma_i = 2$ (letter)        if $\tau_1 \leq \gamma_i^* < \tau_2$

$\gamma_i = 3$ (word)        if $\tau_2 \leq \gamma_i^* < \tau_3$

$\gamma_i = 4$ (paragraph)        if $\tau_3 \leq \gamma_i^* < \tau_4$

$\gamma_i = 5$ (story)        if $\tau_4 \leq \gamma_i^* < \tau_5 = \infty$     (8.3)

*Note*: $\gamma_i$ is the skill level categorization such as word, paragraph, or story level; $\gamma_i^*$ is the unmeasured propensity to read and $\tau$ reflects the cut off points for categorization.

Tables 8.9 and 8.10 show the effect of covariates of interest on reading and arithmetic skill levels of children in our sample using from these ordinal logit models. Each model contains dummy variables for state of residence. In order to simplify the discussion, these coefficients are not included in the discussion.

TABLE 8.9: Reading Ability Ordinal Logistic Regression, Odds Ratios

| | Model (1) | Model (2) | Model (3) | Model (4) | Model (5) |
|---|---|---|---|---|---|
| Age | 1.494** | 1.046 | 1.057* | 1.100** | 1.129** |
| | (0.033) | (0.027) | (0.027) | (0.029) | (0.030) |
| Gender | 0.848** | 0.842** | 0.837** | 0.835** | 0.824** |
| | (0.04) | (0.04) | (0.04) | (0.04) | (0.04) |
| OBC | 0.561** | 0.623** | 0.671** | 0.819** | 0.87 |
| | (0.038) | (0.043) | (0.046) | (0.058) | (0.062) |
| SC/Dalit | 0.362** | 0.397** | 0.426** | 0.581** | 0.629** |
| | (0.027) | (0.03) | (0.032) | (0.047) | (0.052) |
| ST/Adivasi | 0.319** | 0.379** | 0.436** | 0.699** | 0.785* |
| | (0.029) | (0.034) | (0.04) | (0.068) | (0.077) |
| Muslim | 0.385** | 0.473** | 0.456** | 0.556** | 0.643** |
| | (0.031) | (0.039) | (0.038) | (0.047) | (0.056) |
| Christian, Sikh, Jain | 0.937 | 1.081 | 1.072 | 1.055 | 1.099 |
| | (0.146) | (0.171) | (0.173) | (0.17) | (0.177) |
| Standard completed | | 1.816** | 1.818** | 1.745** | 1.697** |
| | | (0.04) | (0.04) | (0.039) | (0.038) |
| Currently enrolled | | 1.345** | 1.366** | 1.382** | 1.307** |
| | | (0.123) | (0.125) | (0.125) | (0.119) |
| Urban residence | | | 1.834** | 1.160** | 1.162* |
| | | | (0.085) | (0.065) | (0.066) |
| Assets quintile | | | | 1.466** | 1.303** |
| | | | | (0.036) | (0.035) |
| Highest standard completed by adult in household | | | | | 1.059** |
| | | | | | (0.007) |
| Literate adult in household | | | | | 4.051** |
| | | | | | (0.825) |
| Observations | 12,271 | 12,271 | 12,271 | 12,271 | 12,271 |

Source: Special tabulations by the authors using unit record level IHDS 2005 survey data

Notes: # Highest standard of the adult in the household, Robust standard errors in parentheses; * Significant at 5 per cent; ** Significant at 1 per cent

Model 1 of Table 8.9 shows the impact of basic demographic variables and social group on the reading skills of children aged 8–11. The results show that children's skill level improves as they get older. Females have lower reading levels than males—a finding that contrasts with most of the US literature where girls have slightly higher reading scores than boys. The impact of social stratification on reading level is very large for this model. OBCs are about half as likely to attain any given reading level as upper castes, Dalits are slightly more than one-third as likely (0.36 times as likely) and Adivasis are only 0.32 times as likely.

Model 2 controls for current enrolment and completed education. As can be expected, the differences between different social groups diminish, suggesting that at least some of the achievement differences are mediated through school enrolment and grade promotion between various groups. But surprisingly, this dampens inter-group differences at only a modest level. Muslims are 0.39 times as likely as upper caste Hindus to attain a given reading level in Model 1; after controlling for current enrolment and grade completed, Muslim children are only about 0.47 times as likely to attain a reading level as upper caste Hindu children.

Models 3 and 4 add two basic socio-economic factors, viz. urban residence and household economic status measured by the household ownership of consumer durables and housing assets. These two factors, particularly the household assests variable, dampen the relationship between social group and reading achievement substantially. But even so, Dalits are only about 0.58 times as likely to achieve a given reading level as upper caste Hindus. Similar differences persist for other social groups.

The two variables controlling for adult education in Model 5 further reduce this relationship, although surprisingly this reduction is not very large. The number of years of completed education for the most educated adult in the household, and a dummy variable for literate adult in the household, shows that higher level of household education helps diminish the negative impact of caste, ethnicity, and religion on children's reading achievements. However, even after all these controls are added, OBC children are 0.87 times as likely as upper caste children to attain higher reading scores, comparable

TABLE 8.10: Mathematics Ability Ordinal Logistic Regression, Odds Ratios

| | Model (1) | Model (2) | Model (3) | Model (4) | Model (5) |
|---|---|---|---|---|---|
| Age | 1.496** | 1.056* | 1.070* | 1.118** | 1.144** |
| | (0.033) | (0.028) | (0.029) | (0.031) | (0.031) |
| Gender | 0.736** | 0.718** | 0.709** | 0.703** | 0.690** |
| | (0.035) | (0.036) | (0.035) | (0.035) | (0.035) |
| OBC | 0.506** | 0.553** | 0.610** | 0.760** | 0.815* |
| | (0.035) | (0.039) | (0.043) | (0.055) | (0.061) |
| SC/Dalit | 0.308** | 0.327** | 0.358** | 0.505** | 0.555** |
| | (0.023) | (0.026) | (0.029) | (0.043) | (0.048) |
| ST/Adivasi | 0.272** | 0.314** | 0.374** | 0.631** | 0.716** |
| | (0.026) | (0.03) | (0.036) | (0.064) | (0.075) |
| Muslim | 0.328** | 0.393** | 0.375** | 0.470** | 0.549** |
| | (0.029) | (0.036) | (0.035) | (0.044) | (0.053) |
| Christian, Sikh, Jain | 0.856 | 0.962 | 0.959 | 0.966 | 1.004 |
| | (0.107) | (0.121) | (0.126) | (0.13) | (0.135) |
| Standard completed | | 1.781** | 1.787** | 1.718** | 1.680** |
| | | (0.04) | (0.041) | (0.039) | (0.039) |
| Currently enrolled | | 1.298** | 1.321** | 1.325** | 1.284** |
| | | (0.114) | (0.118) | (0.116) | (0.111) |
| Urban residence | | | 2.076** | 1.234** | 1.234** |
| | | | (0.097) | (0.071) | (0.072) |
| Assets quintile | | | | 1.550** | 1.361** |
| | | | | (0.04) | (0.039) |
| Highest standard completed by adult in household | | | | | 1.067** |
| | | | | | (0.007) |
| Literate adult in household | | | | | 2.997** |
| | | | | | (6.07) |
| Observations | 12,271 | 12,271 | 12,271 | 12,271 | 12,271 |

*Source*: Special tabulations by the authors using unit record level IHDS 2005 survey data

*Notes*: # Highest standard of the adult in the household, Robust standard errors in parentheses; * Significant at 5 per cent; ** Significant at 1 per cent

proportions for Dalits, Adivasi, and Muslims are 0.63, 0.79, and 0.64, respectively. There is a decline in social group differences in reading skills as we progressively control for more background factors. But it is important to note that even with these controls the negative effect of caste, ethnicity, and religion persists.

We note that many of the variables that are included in our final model, Model 5, are themselves affected by caste, ethnicity, and religion. Educational attainment in parental generation is also a function of social stratification. Additionally, the same school factors that result in lower skill attainment for children may also affect their progression from one grade to another. So, controlling for these factors underestimates the impact of caste, ethnicity, and religion on children's skill attainment. But even so, substantial differences between children from different social backgrounds are obvious in the result we present.

Results for arithmetic skills in Table 8.10 are similar, although the differences between different social groups are even wider. It is important to note that ordinal logit models assume that the slope coefficients are identical across different levels of outcome variables. This proportional odds assumption can be tested using the Wald test. While an omnibus likelihood ratio test for our model rejects the assumption that all coefficients, particularly the coefficients for state dummies, are identical across different levels of outcome variables, the Wald test for specific coefficients associated with social groups, confirms for at least these variables of interest, the odds ratios are more or less similar across different levels of reading and arithmetic skills.

## SELECTIVITY IN TEST ADMINISTRATION

Interpretation of results presented in this paper are somewhat complicated by the fact that we were able to administer these tests to only 12,302 of the 17,069 eligible children. A variety of reasons underlie our ability to test only 72 per cent of the eligible children. The primary goal of this survey was to complete the household interview. While the interviewers were asked to make all possible effort to visit the households when children were present or to revisit the household, in some cases children were working or at school and could not be reached. In other cases, children were too shy to be interviewed and refused. Our interviewers were well trained to develop rapport with children, but were also told to respect children's reluctance to be tested and not pressure them.

Table 8.11 provides some background characteristics for the children who were tested and those who were not tested. This table suggests that the children who were not tested are somewhat more likely to have characteristics that are associated with lower test scores. Girls, those who are not currently enrolled, Dalit, Adivasi, and Muslim children are less likely to have been tested than others. Thus, if a child's refusal is likely to be associated with fear of obtaining a lower

TABLE 8.11: Learning Test Completion by Enrolment Status and Age for 8–11-year-olds

| | | Reading | | | Mathematics | |
|---|---|---|---|---|---|---|
| | All | Currently enrolled | Not enrolled | All | Currently enrolled | Not enrolled |
| Gender | | | | | | |
| Female | 71.0 | 77.3 | 18.7 | 70.8 | 77.0 | 18.7 |
| Male | 73.3 | 78.0 | 17.1 | 73.0 | 77.8 | 17.1 |
| Age | | | | | | |
| 8 | 72.6 | 79.1 | 11.2 | 72.4 | 78.9 | 11.2 |
| 9 | 73.0 | 77.9 | 17.9 | 72.9 | 77.8 | 17.9 |
| 10 | 73.9 | 79.2 | 20.6 | 73.7 | 79.1 | 20.6 |
| 11 | 68.1 | 73.1 | 22.3 | 67.5 | 72.6 | 22.3 |
| Social group | | | | | | |
| Forward Caste | 77.2 | 78.4 | 22.9 | 76.9 | 78.0 | 22.9 |
| OBC | 73.0 | 78.1 | 19.3 | 72.7 | 77.8 | 19.3 |
| SC/Dalit | 72.9 | 78.9 | 19.8 | 72.8 | 78.8 | 19.8 |
| ST/Adivasi | 67.1 | 76.8 | 16.1 | 66.9 | 76.5 | 16.1 |
| Muslim | 65.8 | 75.3 | 14.3 | 65.7 | 75.1 | 14.3 |
| Christian, Sikh, Jain | 68.2 | 68.9 | 29.8 | 68.1 | 68.8 | 29.8 |
| Total | 77.2 | 78.4 | 22.9 | 76.9 | 78.0 | 22.9 |

*Source*: Special tabulations by the authors using unit record level IHDS 2005 survey data

test score, then our results actually underestimate the skill differences between different social groups.

## DISCUSSION

The results presented in this chapter document substantial differences in reading and arithmetic skills between children from different caste, ethnic, and religious backgrounds in India. These differences persist even after controlling for current school enrolment, grade completion, and parental socio-economic status.

This suggests that the differences in educational attainment between people of different social strata are not simply due to difference in enrolment rates nor are they solely due to parental lack of education and resources. Even when children from disadvantaged groups attend school, they fail to learn as much as their peers. Qualitative research and anecdotal evidence provides a variety of explanations for these findings. Teachers typically come from higher castes and have very low expectations of children from marginalized groups. They are also more predisposed to seeing the behaviour of these children as being problematic than that of higher caste children. In our survey, we also asked children if the teacher treats them nicely. We found that children were extremely reluctant to say that the teacher did not treat them nicely but even so, while 76 per cent of the upper caste children responded that their teacher treated them nicely, only 66 per cent of the Dalit and 65 per cent of the Muslim children felt that way.

Parental inability to negotiate the school system may be another mechanism through which social differences operate. In another paper using data from the same survey (Vanneman *et al.* 2006), we find that upper caste households have substantially greater social networks than lower caste households. With increased social contacts within formal systems, individuals are increasingly more likely to be able to negotiate these systems and become their children's advocates when children experience difficulties in school. Thus, teachers' discriminatory behaviour, combined with parental lack of social capital, increases the likelihood that the school experiences of marginalized children are far more negative than those of upper caste children, resulting in lower levels of academic skill acquisition.

Our results also point to a need to better understand the diversity across different marginalized groups. Much of the disadvantage of OBCs seems to be associated with lower income and lower parental education. But once we control for these factors, the OBC disadvantage is smaller and not statistically significant in acquisition of reading skills. Adivasis have the lowest performance in both reading and arithmetic skills but a substantial part of their disadvantage is associated with lack of enrolment and lower parental socio-economic resources. In the final models, controlling for all these factors, Dalits and Muslims appear to be the most disadvantaged groups.

These findings have important policy implications. Much of the current discourse has focused on the importance of constructing schools or encouraging parents to send their children to school. Very little attention has been directed towards what happens in schools. Our results suggest that even holding school enrolment and grade attainment constant, children from disadvantaged backgrounds are likely to attain lower levels of reading and arithmetic skills. Since low performance at primary levels is likely to result in lower academic performance at subsequent levels, improving school quality and reducing discrimination may be the next challenge facing Indian educational policy.

## REFERENCES

Barro, Stephen M. (1987), *Who Drops Out of School and Why? Findings From High School and Beyond*, NCES87397, Washington, DC: National Center for Education Statistics.

Croninger, Robert G. and Valerie E. Lee (2001), 'Social Capital and Dropping Out of High School: Benefits to At-Risk Students of Teachers' Support and Guidance', *Teachers College Record*, vol. 103, no. 4, pp. 548–81.

Desai, Sonalde and Veena Kulkarni (2008), 'Changing Educational Inequalities in India in the Context of Affirmative Action', *Demography*, vol. 45, no. 2, pp. 245–70.

Hauser, Robert M. and David L. Featherman (1976), 'Equality of Schooling: Trends and Prospects', *Sociology of Education*, vol. 49, no. 2, pp. 99–120.

Hauser, Robert M., Solon J. Simmons, and Devah I. Pager (2000), *High School Dropout, Race-Ethnicity, and Social Background from the 1970s to the 1990s*, New York, NY: Russell Sage Foundation.

Jimerson, Shane R. (1999), 'On the Failure of Failure: Examining the Association Between Early Grade Retention and Education and Employment Outcomes During Late Adolescence', *Journal of School Psychology*, vol. 37, no. 3, pp. 243–72.

Nambissan, Geetha B. and Mona Sedwal (2002), 'Education for All: The Situation of Dalit Children in India', in R. Govinda (ed.), *India Education Report*, New Delhi: Oxford University Press.

Okpala, Comfort O., Amon O. Okpala, and Frederick E. Smith (2001), 'Parental Involvement, Instructional Expenditures, Family Socioeconomic Attributes, and Student Achievement', *The Journal of Educational Research*, vol. 95, no. 2, pp. 110–15.

Rumberger, Russell W. (1987), 'High School Dropouts: A Review of Issues and Evidence', *Review of Educational Research*, vol. 57, no. 2, pp. 101–12.

—— (1995), 'Dropping Out of Middle School: A Multilevel Analysis of Students and Schools', *American Educational Research Journal*, vol. 32, no. 3, pp. 583–625.

Rumberger, Russell W. and Gregory J. Palardy (2005), 'Does Segregation Still Matter? The Impact of Student Composition on Academic Achievement', *Teachers College Record*, vol. 107, no. 9, pp. 1999–2045.

Shavit, Yossi and Hans-Peter Blossfeld (1993), *Changing Educational Attainment in Thirteen Countries*, Boulder, Colorado: Westview Press.

Sujatha, K. (2002), 'Education Among Scheduled Tribes', in R. Govinda (ed.), *India Education Report*, New Delhi: Oxford University Press, pp. 74–86.

The Probe Team (1999), *Public Report on Basic Education in India*, New Delhi: Oxford University Press.

Vanneman, Reeve, James Noon, Sonalde Desai, Mitali Sen, and Abusaleh Shariff (2006), 'Social Capital in India: Caste, Tribe and Religious Variation in Social Networks', Paper presented at the Population Association of America Meetings, Los Angeles.

# 9

# Exclusion and Discrimination in Schools[*]
## Experiences of Dalit Children

*Geetha B. Nambissan*

The position of Dalit communities as 'Untouchables' in the caste structure was the most important factor that historically led to their exclusion from knowledge and education in traditional Hindu society. Though schools were legally opened to these communities in the mid-nineteenth century, attempts by Dalits to avail education were met with considerable caste opposition (Nambissan 1996). At the time of India's independence in 1947, Dalits (officially Scheduled Castes) had significantly lower literacy and school enrolment rates as compared to the rest of the population. In the post independence decades, Constitutional provisions, policy thrusts in education, as well as parental aspirations for the education of their children brought an increasing proportion of Dalit children into schools. However at the close of the last century it was found that barely 48 per cent of Dalit children had completed even primary schooling (IIPS 2000). Even today, the vast majority of Dalit children 'dropout' from school well before they complete eight years of education.

To what extent do the oppressive and unjust hierarchies of the caste system continue to 'lock' Dalit children out of full participation in education and in what ways does this happen within schools? This

* This chapter is based on a study sponsored by the Indian Institute of Dalit Studies, New Delhi and UNICEF, New Delhi. I thank Sukhadeo Thorat for encouraging me to carry out this research and Annie Namala for her constant support. I am indebted to the project team—Madhumita Pal, Prashant K. Kain, Sanjay Kumar, Keerti, Pravin, and Gobind Pal. I thank Nidhi Gulati for her valuable comments while helping edit this chapter.

is an issue that has surprisingly been neglected by education policy, pedagogic discourse, as well as research. There are a few studies that have broadly pointed to the role of caste in education, for instance in discriminatory teacher attitudes, denigration of Dalit students, assigning them menial tasks in school, as well as caste based peer relations (Balagopalan and Subrahmanian 2003; Nambissan 2006). However there is little research that identifies spheres and processes of exclusion and discriminatory practices in school and how they influence Dalit children's experiences of education.

This chapter is based on an exploratory study of the experiences of Dalit children in schools. The objective of the study was to identify spheres of exclusion, discrimination, and opportunity in education and practices and processes in which they manifest in school and thereby deny or enable Dalit children full access to cultural and symbolic resources and social relations, including dignity and social respect within these institutions. Bringing in the standpoint of Dalit children, this chapter will focus on their experiences in relation to (a) access to school including facilities and resources, (b) participation in different spheres of school life—curricular and co-curricular, and (c) social relations with teachers and peers.

The study is located in Rajasthan, considered a feudal state with relatively still rigid caste hierarchies especially in rural areas. Rajasthan is one of the educationally backward states in India where as many 22 per cent of children remained out of school in 2004–5. Scheduled Castes (SC) comprise around 18 per cent of the population of Rajasthan. Only 71.5 per cent of SC children in the state were attending schools. This was below the national average school attendance rate of 78.3 per cent for SC children. Urban school attendance rates for SC children in Rajasthan are lower (64.6 per cent) than that in rural areas (73.5 per cent).[1]

A village in the Phagi tehsil of Jaipur district as well as a poor settlement—a '*Tila*'—within the state capital of Jaipur were chosen as the two sites of the study to understand the rural and urban context of educational exclusion.[2] An initial survey of 234 Dalit households (129 urban and 105 rural households from the Village and Tila, respectively) was conducted. Children (64) from a range of Dalit sub-castes, at different stages of education and in both government and private schools from the two locations (34 from the Tila and 30 from the Village) were purposively selected in order to map, through their experiences, spheres of exclusion, discrimination (and opportunity) in school, and the forms in which they manifest. An attempt was made to explore whether Dalit respondents experienced/perceived unequal or differential treatment *vis-à-vis* their non-Dalit peers in school.

## THE CONTEXT: TILA AND VILLAGE

The Tila or urban settlement chosen for the study is one of seven such settlements within a geographical stretch on the outskirts of Jaipur. The Dalit sub-castes in the Tila include the *Bairwa, Raigar, Khatik, Dhobi,* and *Balmiki,* all of who are officially categorized as SCs in Rajasthan. The settlements are generally referred to as *basti*s or low income shanties. A residential locality across the road from the basti has middle and lower middle class families belonging to non Dalit, Sindhis, Punjabis, and castes that come presently under the category of Other Backward Classes (OBC).

The Village is 60 kilometres from Jaipur and has a significant presence of *Jat*s and *Gujar*s (OBCs), *Rajput*s, and a few *Brahmin* and *Bania* families (locally acknowledged as 'higher'/dominant castes).[3] The Bairwa, Raigar, and Balai are the main Dalit sub-castes in the Village and the nearby habitations. As compared to the Tila, the proportion of Balmiki families is negligible in the Village. A number of *Bhagaria* families live at one end of the Village.

The Dalit families are economically poor and are at the lowest rung of the social hierarchy in both the Tila and the Village. This is far more pronounced in the Village where they live in separate habitations and segregated spaces, and 'untouchability' is practised in different spheres of daily life. Common water sources, public spaces for worship such as the temple, and even tea shops continue to be sites for discriminatory practices, though this varies in different contexts. Hierarchies are relatively less rigid in the Tila, partly because of the exigencies of urban life, but pervade interpersonal relations. Balmikis continue to practise their traditional occupation of sweeping in 'modern' spaces in government and private sector offices as well as in homes in the neighbourhood.

## Schools and Facilities

Enrolment rates among children in the surveyed households decline from 74 per cent among children aged 5–13 years to 35 per cent in the age group 14–18 years in Tila households. Children who have never been enrolled in school still comprise a significant proportion (17 per cent) of the primary school-going age group (5–10 years). In comparison in the Village, only 68 per cent of children in the 5–10 year age group are enrolled in school. Among SC households, the enrolment of children among Balmikis, drops from a low of 34 per cent in the 5–10 year cohort to an abysmal 20 per cent in the 14–18 year age group. Among Bhagarias, hardly any child goes to school. Gender differences are sharp. Among Balmikis for instance, the percentage enrolment of girls barely reaches double figures.

Children, in the Tila and especially the Village, access mainly government schools. Some children go to private schools that are largely 'unrecognized' and unregulated. A social divide is quite visible in the government schools that cater to the basti as well as the Tila— between children who come from the *colony* (referred to as 'colony children') lower/middle socio-economic status but 'higher' caste as compared to the Dalits from the basti (referred to as 'basti children'); and the 'higher', including the dominant OBC, castes as compared to the Dalits in the village schools.[4] Teachers in the schools mainly belong to the non-Dalit castes.[5]

A striking feature of the journey through schools is the significant 'shifting' between schools that takes place for an individual Dalit student. This can result in a sense of unease, for instance in making new friends and establishing rapport with the teachers, especially for children from socially discriminated groups.

On changing schools frequently, one has to sit behind, and in a new school you feel scared also. It takes time to know the teacher and make friends.... Problem is there in making new friends. Adjustment with them takes a long time. It also takes a long time to know the teacher. Till then we can't ask from them (the teacher/peers) (Bairwa boy, Tila).[6]

Government schools are characterized by poor quality infra-structure, less than adequate number of teachers, and lack of resources. There were a number of schools where toilets were either not available or in very poor condition or dirty and all children were constrained by this. No respondent reported that they were denied the use of toilets or other school facilities. Water, however, was a sphere where group identities came into play, especially in the village.

## Access to Water

Piped water through taps, water tank, and hand pump ('boring') are the main sources of drinking water for children in schools (see Table 9.1). No respondent reported being denied direct access to water. However, some did say that as recently as around three to five years ago, when the only available drinking water in school was that which was stored in tanks and in pots and jars, Dalits were not permitted to take water directly by themselves. At the time, they were forced to drink water from the hand pump situated at a little distance away from the school.

When we were in class IX, then all the students kept one *matka* (earthen pot). Then Jat boys said that 'we will give you water, to drink water you will not touch the pot…'. Now when we drink water from the hand pump, then Jat boys drink after washing the hand pump (Balai boy, Village).

In primary school, Jat boys did not allow us to touch the water jug. If we happened to touch it then they used to clean it with sand. We were not allowed to drink water from the pot. Jats used to forbid us. Teachers did not forbid them (to do this) but scolded only us. We used to drink water from the hand pump a little far away from school. Just since the last 2–3 years we have started drinking water from the school hand pump (Bairwa boy, Village).

An integral part of school culture (particularly in the Village) is practices around the drinking of water. Some (5/30) of the Dalit respondents from the Village said that they make way/stand at a distance when general caste children come to drink water and that 'we do not drink water together'. What appears more common is the practice of washing of the mouth of the hand pump/tap by general castes after Dalit students drank water (Table 9.1). This is a practice indulged in by general castes *vis-à-vis* Dalits at the village hand pump to deliberately communicate to the latter their 'polluted' and 'inferior' status. What is significant is that the same discriminatory practice has been re-contextualized within the domain of the school.

When I go to drink water, the boys of Jats and upper castes tell me to move aside a little. 'First let us drink water. You drink afterwards'. They say 'you are "Bhangi" (pejorative term for Balmiki), stand off'. They wash the tap after I drink and tell me that 'if you drink first then we will have to wash the tap'. So I drink last of all. At that time, it comes to my mind that I must beat them.... I sometimes tell the teachers but they also do not pay attention and fob me off, saying that 'no one will do this again' (Balmiki boy, Village).

After we drink water, they scrub the tap with sand. Once I said 'does it (water) become better on scrubbing?' They did not reply (Balmiki boy, Village).

Dalit students are deeply resentful of this practice as of the fact that they are often forced to make way for their classmates. A few Balmiki respondents mentioned that when they complained to the teacher, the latter tended to ignore or gloss over the matter. One way in which Dalits have begun to contest these practices and make a symbolic statement is by washing the tap after Jat and Rajput children have had water!

| TABLE 9.1: Provision of and Social Access to Water in Schools—Tila and Village | | |
|---|---|---|
| Provision of/ Access to water | Tila* | Village* |
| A. Provision | | |
| • Tap | 17 | 4 |
| • Tank | 14 | 5 |
| • Hand pump | 1 | 18 |
| • Cooler/fridge** | 9 | 2 |
| • Earthen pot (matka)** | 11 | 19 |
| B. Access | | |
| • All can take water | 18 | 20 |
| • General castes/colony boys take first | 6 | 5 |
| C. Practices around water | | |
| • Tap washed before drinking | | |
| • By general castes | – | 11 |
| • By Dalits | – | 2 |
| • Habit/hygiene | 2 | 1 |
| • General castes pour water for Dalits | 1 | 4*** |

Notes: * Figures refer to number of respondents who reported the above practices access. Categories have been evolved from responses and tabulated accordingly
** For teachers only *** Two respondents mentioned this as having happened a few years earlier

In the Tila schools, the preponderance of numbers (colony boys as against those from the basti), gender (girls stepping aside for boys), and difference in physical size (bigger as against smaller children) were seen to give some children the 'privilege' to drink water first. Washing of the mouth of the tap was reported in a few instances in relation to hygiene and habit (which Dalit children also followed). There were suggestions that caste status may have been a consideration occasionally.

When we drank water then we wash the tap a little. Because this has become a habit (Balmiki boy, Tila).

When any basti child remains filthy (and uses the tap), because of being lower caste, upper caste boys, colony boys wash the tap before drinking water. They overawe you, saying 'first we will drink water' (Bairwa boy, Tila).

What emerges from the experiences of respondents is that with the provision of 'running water' through taps and hand pumps the blatant denial of access to water for Dalits in school is less widespread today than some years earlier. However, where water is stored in pots, jugs, and even tanks, caste-based discrimination (Dalit children not being allowed to touch the jug/glass of water) continues to be practised in some schools often with the indulgence of teachers.

## Participation in the Classroom

While there has been some research on teacher attitudes, and peer interaction in relation to the more marginal groups, there has been no attempt to explore how children participate in the transaction of the curriculum.[7]

## Segregation in Class

A fairly large number of respondents (25/64) said that they were free to sit where they pleased. However, only one respondent in the Tila, and three in the Village, actually reported to having sat in the front row in their class. The actual seating arrangements tend to be influenced largely by teacher expectations and preferences ('intelligent'/*hoshiar* students in the front rows and those considered 'weak'/*kamzor* behind), peer group dynamics (in relation to caste/social dominance), and 'locational' identity (basti as against colony). Individual inclinations had a relatively smaller role to play.

Dalit children were well aware of teacher's notions about hoshiar front benchers—who could 'memorize the lesson' and 'answer the teacher's questions'. Most of them found it difficult to do either. While it was rare for the teacher to ask them to sit in the front row, respondents often strategized to sit behind for 'fear that madam/sir may scold and insult us in front of all because we do not know'. In the Village, children usually sat with those who came from their own caste group. In the Tila schools, the intersection between class and caste is probably reflected in comments such as 'we actually sit with people like us'. In the Village, the social location of the general castes, preponderance of numbers in class and brute strength facilitated their dominance over space in the classroom. The colony children often had their way in the Tila schools. Dalit children are hence usually relegated to the back benches in the class. One of the respondents, a Bhagaria boy who had left school, mentioned that his Jat classmates would not permit them to sit on the mat (*durrie*).

We sit with people who are like us—friends. Colony girls sat with colony girls and basti girls sat with girls of the basti. Colony people used to sit in the front and basti girls behind....The girls themselves used to sit there. If the teacher asks any basti girl to sit in front, then firstly she herself does not sit there...the colony girls will not let them sit there (Bairwa girl, Tila).

In class, we sit in three lines. I-girls, II-intelligent ones, III-weak ones. I used to sit in the third line (Balmiki boy, Tila).

Jat children sat on the durrie (mat). We could not sit on it. One day I sat on the durrie and they snatched it from me. The other children started laughing. I also wanted to sit on the durrie. There were other children also who could not sit on the durriea (Bhagaria boy, Village).

One of the respondents referred to the abhorrent practice of making Balmikis sit in the corner of the class in his school some years earlier. He went on to insightfully observe that this segregation had detrimental consequences for Balmiki students' interest in their studies.

When I was in class V–VI, then 'Harijans' were made to sit in the corner. Then they don't feel like studying. Therefore they don't come to study. The children of general caste and OBC look down upon them. If there was a 'Harijan' boy then he used to sit behind (Balai boy, Village).

We ourselves sat where we wanted to. Seats changed also. But I sat alone. Other children used to sit nearby but separately (Balmiki girl, Tila).

## 'Silencing'

When asked, the majority of respondents (56/64) said they were largely silent in class when it came to curriculum transaction (see Table 9.2). Only 26/64 said they had asked their teachers for explanations when they did not understand what was being taught. Of these, as many as 14/26 said they could do so only with some teachers, often just one teacher. The reasons respondents gave for not asking questions/clarifications of their teachers were: being 'scared that teachers would scold, beat or insult us' and 'peers will make fun of us for what we do not know'. Some said they were shy and hesitant to speak and they 'prefer to wait for another child to ask the teacher for clarifications', 'ask a friend instead', or else they just 'leave out that portion of the lesson', if need be.

The messages that teachers often conveyed in their interactions with children—that they lack ability, are not intelligent, or do not deserve to study—tended to increase the latter's uneasiness in the class. Though respondents said that some teachers (usually this was a specific teacher) do try to make them comfortable this appeared to be the quality of the individual teacher rather than institutionalized in the culture of the school or based on a pedagogy of how children learn.

'Learner' categories have become part of the 'common sense' constructed within schools. These influence not only seating arrangements but confer identities such as 'intelligent' and 'weak' on children. Teachers are generally inclined to focus attention on the former to the neglect of the latter group of children. This leads to inadequate and unequal pedagogic attention to children of marginal groups, in this study, Dalits.

Giving assignments or 'homework' to be completed by students after school is a regular practice in most schools. The regularity of teachers correcting/reviewing homework ranged from every second or third day to a week, or, at times, never at all. While all children receive homework, the support available within the home to complete

### TABLE 9.2: Participation in Class—Tila and Village

| Respondents in class | Tila N=34 | Village N=30 |
|---|---|---|
| A. Had asked questions and explanations | 15 | 11 |
| • only from specific teachers | 6 | 8 |
| B. Were mainly silent | 29 | 27 |
| • scared to ask questions | 19 | 20 |
| C. Reasons for being silent | The teacher:<br>• Scolds us if we ask<br>• May beat us if we do not know<br>• May start asking us questions<br>• Says why don't you pay attention when I am teaching<br><br>Others:<br>• I am shy/hesitant<br>• I ask friend to ask and then explain<br>• I am not comfortable<br>• Classmates may tease | The teacher:<br>• Scolds us if we ask<br>• Says come later<br>• May make fun if wrong<br>• Will not explain so that we can understand<br>• Makes you hold your ears<br>• She/ he does not know the answer<br><br>Others:<br>• I may be insulted because I do not know<br>• What is explained cannot be understood. |

such tasks is uneven. Dalit students suffer in comparison to others as they come from homes where parents are usually non-literate or poorly schooled and hence are unable to provide the necessary academic inputs. They are usually penalized, and often beaten when they fail to comply with what teachers expect of them. This has been referred to in earlier studies (Jha and Jhingran 2005; Anitha 2000; Nambissan 1996).

Respondents varied in their perception of whether teachers discriminated in meting out punishments to children. A number of respondents, especially from the Tila, said that when homework was incomplete 'all were beaten equally', or 'those who are beaten more are those who did not do it daily'. Only a few of them suggested that colony children were beaten or scolded less than those from the basti.[8] Many more of the Village respondents felt that teachers were less harsh towards some children. Reasons given for differential treatment were intelligence ('clever ones are scolded less'), gender ('girls are beaten less whatever their caste'), and caste ('teachers used to beat children of their caste less'). For the majority of Dalit children, homework remains an onerous task and many in desperation take resort to the 'pass book' (guide book), which is used as a major support for 'learning' (memorizing lessons).

## Official Curriculum

It is also pertinent to understand whether SCs, their communities as well as leaders and heroes, find representation in curriculum transaction or 'legitimate school knowledge'?[9] For instance, respondents were asked whether the life and work of Ambedkar was discussed in school. Most respondents said that they had not hitherto given much thought to the issue of whether SCs or their own communities were absent or present in 'official school knowledge'. However, when urged to look back, some of them felt that it is rare for the text lesson to highlight, or the teacher to draw attention to, SCs, their lives, or leaders. Reflecting on this, a few went on to say that if they were taught about a leader, such as Ambedkar, and if his life and achievements were discussed in class, it could inspire Dalit students as well as raise their self image.

## The 'Co-curricular'

The participation of children in 'co-curricular' activities is important for developing their personalities and confidence, strengthening peer relations, and building secular identities in school. Research on Dalit and marginal groups often ignores this important sphere of school life. Respondents were asked whether they participated in games and school celebrations during the two national festivals, Independence Day (15 August) and Republic Day (26 January). In order to understand whether such opportunities were available in school and to all children equally, they were asked whether their classmates participated in them as well as reasons for their (Dalit) non participation.

Of the 64 Dalit respondents, only 18 had participated in games in school and 20 in functions organized on 26 January and 15 August the previous year. The numbers were larger in the Tila (16/34 participated in games and 13/34 in functions) than in the Village (2/30 and 7/30 participated in games and functions respectively). On the other hand, as many as 25 respondents in the Tila and 20 in the Village said that their classmates participated in games, and a similar number reported that this was so for celebrations during the two national festivals the previous year (see Table 9.3).

TABLE 9.3: Participation in Games and Functions—Tila and Village

| Stage | Respondents | | Tila | | | | Village | | | |
|---|---|---|---|---|---|---|---|---|---|---|
| | Tila | Village | Games | | Functions | | Games | | Function | |
| | | | Resp | CM | Resp | CM | Resp | CM | Resp | CM |
| Elementary | 12 | 14 | 4(1) | 8(2) | 3(1) | 5(2) | 0(2) | 8(2) | 4(2) | 10(3) |
| Secondary | 22 | 16 | 12(1) | 17(2) | 10 | 19(1) | 2(3) | 12(4) | 3(4) | 11(4) |
| Total | 34 | 30 | 16(2) | 25(4) | 13(1) | 24(3) | 2(5) | 20(6) | 7(6) | 21(7) |
| Balmiki | 13 | 3 | 3 | 10 | 3 | 9 | 0(1) | 2(1) | 0(1) | 2(1) |

Note: Respondents were asked to give their experiences in the last class they attended. Those who discontinued school also recalled experiences in the last class attended

Resp: Respondents; CM: classmates. Respondents were asked to recall if they/their classmates participated. Non responses are given in parentheses

The number of respondents who did not participate in functions was significantly larger in the Village as compared to the Tila. Reasons offered by respondents for non participation included feeling shy and scared, not considered 'good' enough by teachers, and apprehensions that they would be laughed at or insulted in front of classmates and the 'villagers' (local guests) if they did not perform well. The tendency of the teacher to include members of his caste rather than Dalits was also suggested by comments such as 'The one who prepared children (for programmes) was a Brahmin teacher. They used to take us less and used to take Jat boys more.' Children also acknowledged that 'prior knowledge of dancing' was a factor that influenced who would be chosen for a performance. This 'cultural capital' was more likely to be with children belonging to families of the general castes as compared to the Dalits.

From the beginning, I have not spoken in front of anyone. So I used to feel scared, there is hesitation. Only one classmate (Jat community) always remains ahead in speaking and playing (Balmiki boy, Village).

I never participated in any thing. Teacher selects the 'good' children of our class before hand, those who listen to what she says and do good work. We do good work but even then she does not write our name (Raigar boy, Tila).

I do wish that I also should participate as other children....But no one takes me. Sir never even asks me and I also have never told Sir...because they take children of Brahmans, Jats only. I am of 'low caste' so they don't take me. There is fear in my heart that there will be a mistake. Then all the villagers will make fun of me. I do wish to participate but have not till today (Bairwa boy, Village).

Where group performances were concerned it was important to be 'included'. Both in Tila as well as in the Village, children reported being excluded by their peers in such activities.

Colony girls never included us. Where possible I used to take part alone as there was no one to take part with me. Even the only friend I had from the colony, Ritu used to take part with the colony girls and not with me (Raigar girl, Tila).

Among Dalit children, Balmikis were likely to be most 'left out' of co-curricular activities and school functions. Not only do they tend to be 'hesitant' given the manner in which caste relations pervade the school, teachers also fail to 'choose' them. In addition, their peers, including those among the SC, may also exclude them. One of the Balmiki girls from the Tila recalled an instance where a group of girls who were to perform for a function refused to include her, saying:

'It is full (the group); there is no place for you. We will not take you.' Then I felt very bad. I also wanted to participate in the song. The other girls did not take me (Balmiki girl, Tila).

Where games were concerned, some of the reasons for non participation cited were that there was no equipment for games in school and when available it was given to the students from the higher classes (grades). It was mentioned that the conflict between the older Dalit and Jat boys was played out often in the games field.

Some respondents preferred to avoid situations involving violence and squabbling and stated this as the reason for not participating in games.

## GENDER, CASTE, AND EDUCATION: INTERSECTIONS

Caste and gender identities intersect to make the schooling of Dalit girls relatively more at risk than that of boys. The survey of households indicates that rates of enrolment in the primary school-going age group are lower among Dalit girls (68 per cent in the Tila and 60 per cent in the Village) as compared to boys (80 per cent and 75 per cent, respectively). Within the family, the time and space made available for girls to go to school and to be able to devote time to their education is relatively more constrained as compared to boys. In addition, girls find that social relations, especially within the Tila, are extremely circumscribed and the boundaries between home (*ghar)* and outside (*bahar*) are clearly drawn.

While this may be partly true for girls in the colony as well, social and community norms as well as the environment within the Tila constrain parents from sending their daughters outside the home. Girl respondents said that the school gave them a greater sense of freedom in comparison to the Tila and was the only space where they could meet their friends. This is also reflected in the nostalgic memories that linger about school regardless of the fact that facilities are inadequate and beating often commonplace.

The strength of larger numbers of their own gender becomes important for girls' education. Girl respondents said that it is easier for them to obtain parental and extended family approval to go to school and carry on to higher levels of education if they have the company of other girls. Parents are also able to resist community pressures that continue to favour marriage for girls at a young age and fears of their 'getting spoilt in school'. Girls find that in a group they are better able to protect themselves from harassment from boys and to ignore comments that are directed at them as they walk to school—a regular experience especially for Tila girls. Intra-caste social distance, that is maintained to different degrees, within Dalit communities poses serious problems especially for Balmiki girls. One of the girls specifically mentioned that she had no friend within the

Tila and also that she was not part of any group of girls and hence had to walk to school mainly on her own.

The present study was unfortunately not able to adequately dwell on the experiences of Dalit girls in school though we know that gender discrimination, sexual harassment, and abuse of girl students is a reality that is little acknowledged or addressed. Given the relative powerlessness of Dalit girls because of caste and gender identity, this is an area that requires urgent research.

## RESPONSIBILITIES AND TASKS

An important responsibility assigned to one or two students in a class is that of 'monitor'. The monitor is usually expected 'to manage' the class in the teacher's absence and he/she is also given charge (along with others) of odd jobs linked to the academic and other work of teachers such as bringing the register, chalks, and teaching aids. In addition, children are also involved in making/serving tea and water, sweeping the classroom and school grounds, and serving of the mid-day meal.

### The Monitor

All respondents reported the presence of monitors in schools that they attended. Most schools in the village had two monitors (first and second). Students belonging to the OBC/general castes were more likely to be appointed monitors in class as compared to the Dalits. As many as 25 of the 30 respondents from the Village said that the monitors in their classes were always non-Dalits. Where there were monitors belonging to the Dalits, these were usually one of two monitors, in some cases the second or junior monitor.

Respondents, especially from the Village, felt that caste status mattered in the selection of monitors. Many teachers were reported to appoint monitors from among students belonging to their own caste. Some teachers followed the practice of voting of monitors but a respondent reported that 'they would not make SC students stand' as contenders before their peers. Further, Dalits were smaller in number than Jats/OBCs, and hence, at a disadvantage where voting was concerned. Caste dynamics and social dominance of general castes made it difficult for Dalit monitors to maintain order in class. A respondent said that if made monitor, 'higher caste students would not listen to me and would make trouble for me and have me removed'. The possible discriminatory division of labour among monitors is reflected in the quote below where a respondent mentions that the teacher made the second/Dalit monitor do the more menial tasks as compared to the first monitor (a Jat). Or again where a Balmiki boy was appointed 'safai (cleanliness) monitor' and made to sweep the classroom.

> Two monitors were made, one from Jat and one from Bairwa. The teachers make Rajesh (Bairwa) sweep the office, wash the cups, lock the office, keep the mats inside. They make Sriram (general caste) bring tea, water…(Bairwa boy, Village).

> Teachers did not make a 'low caste' a monitor….If they make me, then Jat boys would not listen to me (Bairwa boy, Village).

> Once in Class V, I was selected as the Safai Monitor (Balmiki boy, Tila).

## Other Tasks

Children in many schools are involved in the sweeping of classrooms, a task that teachers say is shared by all students. However, while a fairly larger number of respondents (28/50) said that in their school all students (Dalits and general caste) were involved in sweeping the classroom, and a smaller number (8/50) said that only SC students were involved in such tasks, *there was not a single instance reported of a school where only general caste/OBC students were involved in such work* (see Table 9.4). Even where children were supposed to sweep in turns, it was often the case that boys from the general/dominant castes would refuse to do so and pass on this task to Dalit students.

Caste lines were more sharply defined in serving water and tea to teachers who, with few exceptions, were non-Dalits. As many as 34 of the respondents said that except for a few schools, (more so in the Tila), only 'higher caste' students served water to the teacher. It was clearly stated by some that only students from Jat/OBC/Rajput castes could serve teachers. This was a responsibility much sought after as it enhanced status amongst ones' peers. Dalit students were involved in a slightly larger number of schools in the serving of tea to their teachers (in the Village, this was mainly to SC teachers). In the Tila schools, especially in the primary classes where SC children

| Site/Social group | Sweeping classroom | Serving water | Serving tea |
|---|---|---|---|
| **TABLE 9.4: Distribution of Tasks and Responsibilities\*** | | | |
| **in Government Schools\*\*** | | | |
| *Tila* | | | |
| • Only SC | 2 | [1] | – |
| • Only GC | – | 11 | 11 |
| • SC and GC | 13 | 3 | 3 |
| • Others (peon etc.) | 7 | 3 | 6 |
| • No response | 1 | 2 | 3 |
| • All | 23 | 23 | 23 |
| *Village* | | | |
| • Only SC | 6 | [5] | [5] |
| • Only GC | – | 23 | 19 |
| • SC and GC | 15 | 1 | 4 |
| • Others (peon etc.) | 6 | 3 | 4 |
| • No response | – | – | – |
| • All | 27 | 27 | 27 |
| *Tila and Village* | | | |
| • Only SC | 8 | [6] | [5] |
| • Only GC | – | 34 | 30 |
| • SC and GC | 28 | 7 | 7 |
| • Others (peon etc.) | 13 | 7 | 10 |
| • No response | 1 | 2 | 3 |
| • All | 50 | 50 | 50 |

*Notes*: SC refers to Dalits; GC—general castes
\* Gives number of respondents who reported this
\*\* Pertain only to government schools in which enrolled
[ ] Only served Dalit teachers

comprise a relatively large proportion of students, teachers tend to differentiate between the 'cleaner' and 'most polluted' among Dalit castes. Thus, though Dalit respondents did serve non-Dalit teachers in some schools in the Tila, they were unlikely to be from the Balmiki caste.

In school all do cleaning daily by turn....We bring water for the teacher. Only 'Harijan' (Balmiki) children are not asked to serve/bring water for the teacher... (Group discussion, Dalit students, Tila).

When asked if she would make tea for the teacher, Rani the Balmiki girl from the Tila broke down saying 'I will make but will she drink from my hand?' (Balmiki girl, Tila).

The inclusion of rituals linked to the Hindu religion in the daily routine of the school and the division of responsibilities to carry them out is another domain of school life that is yet to receive attention.[10] The morning assembly in most schools includes a prayer that is led by a student (*prarthana bulvana*). In the Tila, some of the respondents did mention that they began the prayer, but in most government schools in the Village, it was the general caste child who led the singing of prayers. In one of the Village schools, a statue of the Hindu goddess Saraswati had been installed, and children were involved in performing minor rituals such as lighting the incense stick while the teacher performed the 'puja' (worship). There was no question of Dalit children being asked to light the incense stick or participate in these rituals in any manner, a visible acknowledgement of their traditionally 'low' ritual status, which causes them great anguish.

In our school, Ramesh Maheshwari lights agarbatti (incense stick) in the temple. We do not light it. We are not allowed to light it. And we do not even ask. I wish to light the agarbatti (Group discussion, Dalit students, Village).

What is clear from the observations in schools and children's own comments, is that these practices, built into the daily school routine, lead to and reinforce caste-based boundaries that get drawn in the process of the construction of the 'sacred' and, thereby, the 'polluted' within the institution.

## Sharing/Serving Food in School

As discussed, caste hierarchies come sharply into play where serving of water (and food) to teachers is concerned. What is the experience of Dalits in relation to regular school programmes that involve sharing and serving of food among peers?

The officially sponsored Mid-day Meal (MDM)[11] is now a part of the daily routine of government primary schools to address the nutritional needs of poor children. It also provides space to bring principles of equality and non-discrimination within schools and strengthen peer relations. Mid-day meals are provided to all schools in the city of Jaipur by a non-governmental organization (NGO). In the Village, local women are engaged to cook meals. The schools visited during the study had engaged only cooks belonging to Jat/OBC and none of them were Dalits. General caste cooks did not permit Dalit children to enter the kitchen while it was possible for other caste children to do so, making it easier for the latter to ask for and receive an extra helping. Children are involved in the serving of the MDM, though Dalit children are not involved in this task in the Village. In Tila schools, older Dalit children are being involved in serving the meal. However, only children belonging to the 'cleaner castes' among Dalits appear to participate in carrying out such tasks. The Balmiki student is never asked to serve the meal nor wash the teacher's plate after she has eaten.

Jats served and sat separately from us. We sat with our friends. Each one washed their plates and the Jat boys washed the teacher's plate. Lower castes are not asked to serve. There is a Jat lady cook (Group discussion, Dalit students, Village).

We used to stay outside the kitchen and Jat boys used to enter into the kitchen and used to take more food. When we asked for a second serving they (cooks) did not give us, but gave to Jat boys. To us, however, they used to say, 'this much is enough for you' (Group discussion, Dalit students, Village).

I have never been asked to wash the teacher's plate. If I serve no one will eat (Balmiki girl, Tila).

School ceremonies, rituals, and functions are another domain where students participate in preparing, serving, and eating food. Respondents in the Village reported not being allowed to serve guests during the annual celebrations of national festivals. The school leaving functions, organized by class X/XI students to bid farewell to those who are in class XII (their final year in school), is another celebration marred by casteist practices. These are functions where students are expected to contribute financially as well as assist in preparing food and serving their seniors. From respondents in the Village we learn that while they contribute financially as do other students, they are not allowed to prepare and serve food. They find this discriminatory and extremely hurtful. On the other hand, the positive experience of a respondent at a programme where boys of all caste groups were brought together to interact with each other highlights the importance of providing such opportunities in school.

Teachers did not let us offer drink or water to guests on 15th August/26th January. They used to say that '10–15 boys should stand up and serve drinking water. But children of "lower caste" do not stand'. So we did not…stand. We were asked to make a separate line… (Group discussion, Village).

For the farewell party to XII class, they take money from us, the same amount as from all, but they do not even allow us to touch the food. It is kept away from us. On 15 August we are not allowed to serve food 'with our hands'….They say. that 'you are Bairwa, you are "lower caste"', 'we won't eat from your hands…'. (Bairwa boy, Village).

We 50–60 boys had gone there (for a programme organized by an NGO). The boys of all the castes were there. So we ate food together, there was no '*chuachut*' (untouchability). I made good friends among them. If it had been like this (always) then it would be better (Bairwa boy, Village).

## PEER RELATIONS

The foregoing discussion highlights the manner in which caste relations pervade school processes and suggests that they are likely to vitiate social interaction among children as well. Peer relations are a neglected sphere of school life but one that is extremely critical for academic and interpersonal relations and their interface. Relationships and networks among children in school are seen as crucial for academic and emotional support systems. The extent to which one is included or excluded from such relationships hence is important for one's identity and well being in school.

Dalit students appear to largely interact with members of their own sub-caste and nearly as often with those of another SC. The number of respondents who said they interacted with members of another Dalit caste was smaller in the Village (15/30) as compared to the Tila (30/34), possibly reflecting the sharper intra-Dalit hierarchies in the rural as compared to urban settlement (see Table 9.5). On the other hand, only around half the Dalit respondents (33/64) said that they interacted with general caste children. Except in a few cases, such interaction was infrequent and usually with a classmate or two. In a few cases, older youth made a mention of roaming around in multi-caste groups.

A relatively small number of respondents (24/64) said that they invited their general caste friends to their homes. A smaller number (12/64) said that these friends had actually visited and a negligible few (5/64) said that non-Dalit classmates had had a cup of water/tea in their (Dalit) homes. Only one respondent reported that a friend from a general caste actually ate a meal in the former's home. The main reasons cited for a larger number of Dalits not inviting their general caste friends home was that 'they will not come home even if we invite them', 'we are of "low caste" so their parents will not allow them', 'they will not eat and drink what we offer, so what is the point of inviting them', and so on. None of the Balmikis covered in the study with the exception of one in the Tila reported that a friend came home and had a cup of tea (Table 9.5).

Despite the fears and apprehensions voiced, a fairly large number of respondents (32/64) in both the Tila and even the Village said they would like to have general caste friends. Among the reasons cited were that general caste friends can help them with school work,

**TABLE 9.5: Peer Relations—Tila and Village**

| Respondents Dalit and (Balmiki)** | Tila* 34(14) | Village* 30(3) | All* 64(17) |
|---|---|---|---|
| 1) Who play/talk with peers in school from: | | | |
| • own caste | 29(9) | 25(2) | 53(10) |
| • other SC/ST | 30(13) | 15(2) | 44(15) |
| • GC | 19(7) | 15(1) | 33(18) |
| 2. Have 'good' GC friends | 19(7) | 14(0) | 33(7) |
| • have called them home | 15(5) | 9(0) | 24(5) |
| • have been visited by friends | 7(3) | 5(0) | 12(3)* |
| • they have taken food/water in our homes | 4(1) | 1(0) | 5(1) |
| 3. Have visited homes of GC friends | 18(8) | 14(0) | 32(8) |
| • felt hesitant/ uncomfortable doing so | 17(7) | 10(–) | 27(7) |
| • did not enter/went from outside | 3(2) | NA | 3(2) |
| • were offered food/water | 10(6) | 8(–) | 18(6) |
| • were offered but did not eat/drink | 5(3) | 2(–) | 7(3) |
| 4. Making friends from GC | | | |
| • like to make such friends | 16(6) | 16(2) | 32(8) |
| • do not want to make such friends | 7(3) | 11(0) | 18(3) |
| • want friends—caste unimportant | 1(1) | – | 1(1) |

*Notes*: GC: general castes
* The number of respondents who gave such responses has been tabulated
** *Balmiki* respondents' answers are given separately in parentheses

lend them 'pass' books that they often cannot afford, and support them in their studies in other ways. Some respondents in the Village mentioned that being friends with Jat and Brahmins can help prevent others from discriminating against them. Of course, the caveat also expressed was that such friendships were possible only if the non-Dalits in question did not discriminate against them. In some cases, this was happening, as reported by the following respondent:

We share refreshment, namkeen, tea with the friends (general caste). When any boy objects and says why you are eating with this Bairwa, then they (the friends) used to tell them that you 'expel' (remove) caste. (Bairwa boy, Tila)

Some respondents were, however, clear they did not want 'higher caste' friends and said that 'we are shown by them as low and degraded', 'they will never eat and drink with us', and 'their parents discriminate', while others felt that 'one can be comfortable only with "one's" own caste group'.

## Peers and Academic Support

Few Dalits who enter class I actually reach class X, as reflected in the relatively high proportion of dropout from school.[12] From those who spoke about failure it emerged that the inability to understand lessons and to be able to seek clarifications from the teacher were important reasons for not being able to perform well in school and pass examinations. When asked, Dalit respondents reported that as many as 64 of the 82 of their classmates whom they named as the 'top three performers' came from the 'non-Dalit' castes. However, it is noteworthy that the remaining 18 were Dalits and included four respondents (three of whom were Balmikis) who said they stood first in their class.

To what extent are Dalits able to ask for academic support from their classmates? It is significant that a fairly large number of the respondents did ask for help from classmates who were considered to 'perform well'. Not all classmates gave of their time and what they knew. In the Village for instance, of the 40 odd children named as good performers there were only around 16 from whom Dalit respondents received help. Of these, 13 belonged to the non-Dalit castes (three were Dalits). Some children said they 'felt shy' to ask a classmate of the opposite gender and that 'they (Jats) will not explain'. In a couple of instances, casteist abuse was mentioned as a deterrent to seeking help from peers.

I ask less from Lata Jain because she is of Banias. So she does 'chuachut'. She does not even touch my books or tell me the answers to questions. She says that you are of 'lower caste....Do not come to me' (Balmiki boy, Village).

Because they (general caste students, rank 1 and 2) do not even tell us. So we also do not ask them (Bairwa boy, Village).

As mentioned earlier, Balmikis bear the brunt of caste discrimination and this is likely not only to constrain school friendships but also the peer support they are able to receive for their studies. Intra-caste hierarchies though less marked are also likely to compound the unease and discomfort that some Dalits experience within the classroom. Balmiki/Bhagaria children who are the minorities among Dalit castes in school find classrooms extremely lonely, with detrimental consequences for their interest and motivation in studies. This is evocatively described by the Balmiki and Bhagaria respondents below.

Because of caste, studies were affected. Children never used to tell me. They used to avoid our questions....'Upper caste' boys did not tell. I did not dare to ask from them (Balmiki boy, Village).

I do feel that why there is less of our caste....they do not make me play with them. Say that you are Harijan, we won't make you play. I feel angry that if today there had been more of our caste then I would have also played with them. In school, teachers call me Munna Balmiki. And Jat boys say that '"ai bhangi" boy! We won't make you eat.' So I come home in the interval (school break) and return after the break (Balmiki boy, Village).

No one sat near me. I sat right at the back of the class and alone (Bhagaria boy, Village).

Did Dalit students wish to help their classmates? A large number of respondents in the Tila (22/34) and the Village (18/30) replied in the affirmative. Respondents (mostly in higher secondary school) said they felt 'good', 'happy' if someone, especially from the general castes, came to them to learn something. It made them feel important and 'clever', and that 'we know something'. Saying that some of their classmates 'refused to tell even when they knew', respondents made it a point to say 'what ever we know we will tell anyone who asks us' and 'will not do *bhed bhav* (discriminate)'. Most of such interaction remained confined to the school and non-Dalits rarely came to their homes, as seen earlier. However, occasionally, consulting on studies provided an opportunity for this as well. For the Balmiki respondent, for whom other Dalit castes are also 'higher' in the social hierarchy, it is a matter of satisfaction even when Dalit classmates seek their help.

I feel happy. When somebody comes to ask me, then I tell them sincerely. I do not discriminate with anyone in answering any question. What ever I know I tell them nicely (Balai boy, Village).

Yes, I feel good when I help. Other children come to take help but in school. They don't come to my house but on the pretext of studying, they have come. My family also likes it when Jats' children come to ask....

I, Kumar Harijan stood first in class. So I do not seek help, rather others ask me for help. I feel nice that they ask for my help (Balmiki boy, Tila).

### IDENTIFYING AND NAMING: 'OUR CASTE IS WRITTEN ON OUR FOREHEADS'[13]

Integral to the process of socialization is the learning of ones jati/caste identity—children learn who they are, whom they should interact with, and other social practices that are informed by hierarchical caste relations. From early childhood, a boy/girl is identified as the son/daughter of his/her parent, who again is known largely by his caste name and epithets for it. School practices institutionalize and reinforce these identities at the very time of admission as the common practice is to add the sub-caste to a child's name. Teachers, the majority of whom are from non-Dalit castes, carry to schools the beliefs and practices that they follow in their villages where interaction with 'lower castes' is based on the identity of the group to which they belong rather than the attributes of individuals. A regular practice in school is that of teachers calling children by their 'caste name', or 'son of a caste'. Peers often did likewise, making the Dalit student 'lose my confidence' and 'feel myself low'. Respondents clearly articulated that naming by caste caused them tension and distress. Teachers and school administrators seem to give it little thought.

Teachers used to call me less by my own name. They used to say, '*O Balai ke chorai* (son of Balai) come here'....used to tell another child, that, 'the newly admitted Balai ka chora, go and call him' (Balai boy, Village).

At start of the session, teachers used to say, '...stand and tell your name, father's name, where you come from....' They also ask your community, 'whom you are of', and then we tell our caste. When they ask about our caste...I feel sad...why do they ask about caste? Because..., other children come to know of our caste...then they will call us 'Chamar' and they will do bhedbhav (discriminate). Therefore, we feel angry with the teacher, but we tell the caste.... On knowing our caste, children's behaviour 'shrinks'. They keep a distance. They won't eat drink with us, won't tell us questions, and won't give books on our asking. So we feel a little bad (Bairwa boy, Village).

Scholarships for Dalit children are seen as enabling incentives provided by the state to facilitate their education. Discussions around scholarships largely centre round their meagre value, lack of adequate coverage, delay in receiving funds, and malpractices. Though scholarships are usually delayed, and the amounts received are relatively small, many respondents use these funds to tide over part of the incidental school expenses. What appears significant and little commented upon is the manner in which scholarships tend to reinforce stigmatizing of Dalit identity as 'lower castes'. Ironically, to claim incentives under affirmative action programmes and facilitate inclusion, those who have suffered from disadvantage must publicly proclaim identities that are still the target of discriminatory practices. They are often required to do so in the school assembly and before their classmates, ostensibly to 'facilitate' their identification as SC students and thereafter to receive fellowships and other incentives. A few respondents brushed aside this 'name calling' and appeared to be able to take on adverse comments from general caste peers. However, the majority said they suffered considerable anguish as their identities are brought into public 'gaze' again and yet again, and they are constantly at the receiving end of disparaging barbs from peers, office staff, as well as teachers.

I have not received the scholarship; we used to get it before the annual examination. Teacher used to announce in class that SC/ST children can take their scholarship. Jat boys tease us that you are of low caste, you get scholarship, we do not. It comes to my mind that I also should stop taking scholarship because children tease us saying 'we are "upper caste" so we do not get it' (Balai boy, Village).

...teacher used to call out our whole name (including caste). So all used to understand 'in their mind' that he is of 'low caste', that is why he is getting a scholarship (Bairwa boy, Village).

## TEACHERS: INTERACTION AND SUPPORT

An important concern for Dalit respondents was how teachers taught and interacted with them. It is not surprising that the experience of abuse, especially physical abuse, prevalent in all schools is one of the major factors for dislike of a teacher. Respondents were also unhappy when teachers 'did not teach well'. 'Teaching well' meant explaining to them, repeating more than once for their benefit, and not wasting time in class. Whether a teacher discriminated against them was an important factor in their construction of 'a good teacher'. In contrast to a few who were 'good natured' and treated them 'with love', there were many who 'differentiated on the basis of caste', which included 'not asking us to serve them water', 'insulting us', and 'making us sit at the back of the class'. Respondents were quick to identify and describe a teacher whom they considered 'fair'—one who asked questions from everyone, did not insult them in front of their classmates, and who did not discriminate or practice untouchability. A 'fair' teacher was seen to punish only when it related to studies and pardon if mistakes were made.

What kind of support did Dalit respondents receive from their teachers? Of the 64 respondents, 31 (only eight from the Village) said that they had received support that appeared to be of a very minimal kind from non-SC teachers during their schooling. For instance, some respondents said that their teacher had given them a book (usually the 'pass' book), notes for the examination, 'question bank', and so on. A few teachers gave moral/emotional support, such as encouraging respondents to study and get ahead in life, appreciating their efforts, and so on.

A smaller number of Tila respondents (6/34) seem to have been taught by SC teachers as compared to the Village (23/30). Most of the Village respondents who were taught by Dalit teachers found them supportive and those who did not have Dalit teachers were keen to be taught by them. The overwhelming reasons given were that these teachers were 'different from others'—they spoke 'nicely' to them, scolded/beat them 'less', and understood them 'more'. They emphasized that the Dalit teacher took more time to explain to them, listened to their questions, did not beat them as much, and if he did, was fair about it. Most importantly, respondents said that SC teachers did not practise 'untouchability', and by making them serve water, raised their 'self respect'. These factors were highlighted as respondents were using their experiences with 'non-Dalit teachers' as their frame of reference.[14]

The implication of the above discussion is not that only SC teachers should teach Dalit students but that their educational concerns should be understood in a nuanced manner. For instance, it is because social relations that govern the relationship of Dalits with SC teachers are less hierarchical as compared to 'higher caste' teachers that some respondents find learning to be relatively more comfortable with the former.

## EXCLUSION, INCLUSION, AND EDUCATION: SOME REFLECTIONS

A review of education policy and programmes for Dalit children would have us believe that the major impediments to their education are inadequate access to schools, poverty, and apathetic attitudes of parents. Hence, increasing the number of schools within easy physical access, provision of incentives, and mobilizing of local communities have been and continue to be major thrusts of education policy for the SCs in India. Caste-based discrimination in education has never seen a mention in policy documents.[15] However, the foregoing discussion based on an exploratory study in two sites in the state of Rajasthan points to a number of spheres where Dalit children, despite being 'included' in schools, continue to experience exclusion and discrimination within these institutions. The study also suggests that there are institutional spaces within schools that provide opportunities for equitable inclusion.

One of the most important spheres within the school where exclusionary practices continue to flourish are those that are concerned with water and food, which have been traditionally potent sites of caste-based discrimination. Where 'running water' is not available in schools through taps (and hand pumps) and drinking water is 'stored' in earthen pots and jars or served in glasses, Dalit children are likely to continue to face caste prejudice reflected in discriminatory practices such as not being allowed to take water themselves. Though respondents in the study said they were not denied access to drinking water this could partly be attributed to the fact that the hand pump and piped water were now available in their schools. What is, however, pronounced especially in the Village (and hence likely in many rural areas of the state) are practices such as the washing of taps after Dalits drink water and forcing them to give right of way to general caste students. Water sources in schools are hence spheres where practices that communicate 'polluted' status to Dalits outside school are being recontextualized within it.

Programmes, functions, and ceremonies where food is cooked, served, and eaten are also sites where Dalit students experience unfair treatment and are denied equal participation because of their caste identity. The study indicates that Dalit respondents became targets of discriminatory treatment where food was served/eaten together (the MDM), where it was cooked and served to seniors (farewell functions) or where it had to be distributed to guests from the village. Balmiki students were likely to be most vulnerable to such practices. Though the intensity of such discriminatory processes is likely to vary in different school contexts, this domain of school life requires serious attention. Given that the school provides probably the only space where children from different castes can eat together, as well as the symbolic significance of cooking/sharing food in a society where caste hierarchies are still rampant, it is pertinent that conscious efforts be made to encourage such sharing in an equitable manner.

The manner in which identities of caste (and class) constrain peer interaction and friendships as revealed in the study, is particularly deleterious for Dalit children as it circumscribes not only interpersonal relations but also possibilities for them to seek resources and support both for curricular and co-curricular activities. In the present study, children across castes/classes in the Tila, Village, and colony come into contact with each other and interact in however constrained a fashion only in school. Also important is that children can support each other academically and for Dalit children, the majority of whom come from non-schooled homes, such friendships can provide invaluable support.

The agency of the teacher and school administrator in addressing and confronting discriminatory practices is critical. However, the study shows that teachers, the majority of whom belong to the general castes, largely ignore such practices by non-Dalit children, even when attention is drawn to them. Of greater concern are the many different ways in which teachers themselves tend to engage in caste-based discrimination in school. This is most strikingly seen in the division of responsibilities among children within the school. The study reveals that tasks considered to be menial and 'polluting' (such as sweeping) are more likely to be assigned to Dalit as compared to general caste children while those concerned with serving of water and food to teachers (with its caste-based implications) are assigned mainly to those belonging to general castes.

There are also classroom processes that tend to deny Dalits fair participation in curriculum transaction and give them a voice in classroom discourse. The study highlights the labelling by teachers of Dalit children as 'weak', giving them inadequate pedagogic attention, and the failure to give them the confidence to ask questions and clarifications in class. Quite contrary to the teachers' possible view of them as not interested in their studies, Dalit children want to ask questions but are afraid to, feel they will be punished, not be listened to, insulted, and discriminated against.

Dalit children are often excluded from co-curricular activities. Teachers are partly complicit in the poor participation of Dalit children in cultural programmes and functions as they fail to 'choose' them and often do not encourage them to take part in these activities. These activities provide children opportunities to nurture their self-confidence and also to build co-operative relations and secular identities. This sphere also offers children, especially from Dalit and other socially discriminated communities, opportunities for status enhancement and secular identities in school, and they must be encouraged to participate.

The singing of prayers in daily assembly and performing of worship leads to the construction of 'sacred spaces' within the school where Dalits are likely to be excluded because of their perceived 'low' ritual status, as seen in the study. Embedded in the daily rhythm of school life are processes of naming of students by caste. This causes considerable distress to Dalit children as their identities are 'stigmatized' and repeatedly brought into public 'gaze' at the time of admissions to a new school, when a new teacher comes to class, to claim incentives, and so on. The politics of 'naming' in school is hence an issue that needs to be addressed. The tendency to largely view SC as homogenous groups has resulted in inadequate attention to intra-caste inequalities among Dalits. The study points to the heavy burden of caste identity and brunt of discriminatory practices that Balmiki students have to shoulder. This is likely to constrain friendships and resource support that they receive relative to other Dalit children.

What emerges from the study are diverse spheres of school life where social relations and pedagogic processes fail to ensure full participation of Dalit children, and they are in fact subject to discriminatory and unequal treatment in relation to their peers. While on the one hand these experiences are detrimental to children's self-esteem and self-worth, on the other hand they are likely to have serious implications for their interest and motivation in studies. It is not surprising that the majority of Dalit children who enter and are formally 'included' in schools often fail/perform poorly and discontinue their studies. However, there are a significant few who despite odds are able to complete their education and, in fact, perform well. This evokes a sense of pride in them and brings recognition among peers and teachers. The fact that Dalit respondents wish to give of their knowledge sincerely and treat all classmates equally, something they usually do not experience, speaks for a level of sensitivity and maturity that must be acknowledged and appreciated. What has also emerged in the study is the agency of Dalit youth, who do try to contest and attempt to resist discrimination by their peers and teachers.

Teachers and school administrators have a responsibility in building a culture within schools that encourages participation of children from hitherto educationally deprived and socially discriminated groups and an environment that values their dignity and provides social respect. When teachers fail to confront, ignore, and actually indulge in unequal treatment of Dalit children, they give legitimacy to sites of exclusion and reinforce discriminatory practices within schools. Though the study did see individual teachers (more so among SC) who are supportive of Dalit students, there is a need for systemic attention and institutionalized response. For instance, a critical rethinking of teacher education is necessary if teachers are to engage with and confront their deep-seated beliefs on caste (and gender), and if a pedagogy sensitivity to issues of caste and other social inequalities as well as the academic needs of children from marginal groups is to be developed. In other words, the professional training of teachers must aim to equip them with a pedagogy that addresses issues of deprivation, discrimination, and social justice.

There is among Dalit communities today growing demand for education and aspirations for social mobility. While the socio-historical experience of disadvantage these communities have experienced due to caste discrimination must be kept in mind, the manner in which caste identity continues to impinge on their education must be squarely addressed. Education for marginal groups is increasingly vulnerable to policy shifts, pressures, and interests that are leading to the breakdown of the public system of education. A growing number of private schools are dotting the educational landscape with claims of 'better quality education' and the promise of occupational opportunities that all marginal groups increasingly aspire to achieve. What these changes mean for education for Dalit groups particularly in the context of exclusion, equitable inclusion, and future life chances in a globalizing world requires serious research and policy attention.

## NOTES

1. These figures relate to the 5–14 year age group and are taken from the National Sample Survey 61st Round Report.
2. The two sites have been named 'Village' and 'Tila' to ensure confidentiality especially of the schools/teachers that could otherwise be identifiable. Names of persons mentioned have been changed to protect their identities.
3. Brahmins, Rajputs, and OBCs are locally referred to as 'higher' and socially dominant castes, '*unchhi jati*', and the Dalits as 'lower'/'*neechi jati*'. As these terms are discriminatory and reinforce popular attitudes and perceptions of unjust hierarchies, the terms 'general caste' for

non-Dalits and Dalit/SC for Scheduled Castes are used here. The term *Harijan* which is locally used for the Balmiki sub-caste traditionally associated with the task of scavenging/sweeping has been rejected by Dalits. We desist from unfair naming, other than to make a specific point or where these terms are used directly in quotes by respondents.

4. An increasing proportion of children in urban government schools belong to the educationally hitherto most deprived communities who are coming into these institutions even as middle and lower middle classes/castes are abandoning them in favour of private schools.

5. The proportion of SC teachers in schools is relatively small. According to the NCERT (1998), the percentage of SC among school teachers in Rajasthan was only around 12 per cent. In urban areas, this was even smaller—5 per cent at the primary stage and barely 2 per cent at the secondary stage of schooling.

6. The sub-caste, gender, and location (Tila/Village) of the Dalit respondent is given.

7. It must be kept in mind that the dominant pedagogy is primarily one of chalk, talk, and making children copy from textbooks or the blackboard, or reading aloud.

8. Reprimands, scolding, and beating are also quite common for coming late to school. Most Tila respondents felt that punishment for coming late was meted out equally to all children who were not punctual and in that sense there was no differential treatment. However, it is also true that it was the basti children who mainly came late to school and hence received more than their share of verbal abuse and also physical punishment. What is important is that punishment for late coming often results in the further cutting down of the learning time of already late children, by extending their time out of class.

9. Bernstein's (1971) reference to power relations that influence selection of 'valid knowledge' represented in the curriculum as well as to the strength of 'boundaries' between what may/may not be taught is pertinent.

10. There were a number of spheres of discrimination that were revealed only in the course of research as respondents cited experiences that disturbed them, such as being excluded from leading the singing of prayers and rituals associated with worship in school. These are areas to be explored to see how widespread these practices are.

11. A directive from the Supreme Court of India presently directs government schools to serve cooked meals to all children in

government-run primary schools; this is popularly known as the Mid-day Meal programme.

12. Though there is very little data specifically on this phenomenon, NCERT (1998) does provide information on 'repeaters' in school. The data reveal that while 'repeaters' for Rajasthan state as a whole in classes IX–X in 1993 was around 11 per cent, that for SC communities was as high as 15 per cent. For classes XI–XII the figures are around 8 per cent for all students and 13 per cent for SC.

13. Statement of a Dalit teacher in one of the Village schools.

14. It is not surprising that there were some respondents (7 in the Tila) who were clearly not in favour of Dalit teachers as in their experience these teachers tended to ignore them or were indifferent to them, did not specially reach out to them, or as one respondent mentioned, beat them severely.

15. See *National Policy on Education 1986/1992* (Ministry of Human Resource Development, 1986; 1992).

## REFERENCES

Anitha, B.K. (2000), *Village, Caste and Education*, Jaipur: Rawat.

Balagopalan, S. and R. Subrahmanian (2003), 'Dalit and Adivasi Children in Schools: Some Preliminary Research Findings', *IDS Bulletin*, Brighton: Institute of Development Studies, vol. 34, no. 1, pp. 55–62.

Bernstein, Basil (1971), 'On the Classification and Framing of Knowledge', in M.F.D. Young (ed.), *Knowledge and Control: New Directions for the Sociology of Education*, London: Collier-Macmillan, pp. 47–52.

International Institute for Population Sciences (IIPS) (2000), *National Family Health Survey (NFHS-2) 1998–99*, Mumbai: IIPS.

Jha, J. and D. Jhingran (2005), *Elementary Education for the Poorest and Other Deprived Groups*, Delhi: Manohar.

Ministry of Human Resources Development (1986), *National Policy on Education 1986*, New Delhi: Government of India.

—— (1992), *National Policy on Education 1992; Programme of Action 1992*, New Delhi: Government of India.

Nambissan, G.B. (1996), 'Equity in Education? Schooling of Dalit Children in India', *Economic and Political Weekly*, vol. 31, nos 16 and 17, pp. 1011–24.

—— (2006), 'Terms of Inclusion: Dalits and the Right to Education', in Ravi Kumar (ed.), *The Crisis of Elementary Education in India*, New Delhi: Sage Publications, pp. 225–65.

National Council of Educational Research and Training (1998), *Sixth All India Education Survey, National Tables*, vols III and VI, New Delhi: NCERT.

National Sample Survey Organisation (2006), *National Sample Survey, 61st Round Report 516. Employment and Unemployment Situation among Social Groups in India 2004–5*, New Delhi: Department of Statistics, Government of India.

# 10

# Food Security Schemes and Caste Discrimination

*Sukhadeo Thorat and Joel Lee*

Conceived as means to complement and fill gaps in the existing Right to Food research,[1] the purpose of undertaking this chapter was to obtain a ground-level view of how, where, and to what degree caste discrimination and untouchability operate in the government-run Mid-day Meal Scheme (MDMS) and Public Distribution System (PDS) programmes as they are implemented in villages across India. In doing so, the chapter attempts to address the broader question of how caste functions as a barrier to the universal attainment of the Right to Food.

The findings of the Indian Institute of Dalit Studies (IIDS) survey conducted in April–June 2004, in 531 villages across five states, exposed patterns of caste discrimination that afflict, if not overwhelm, the Indian government-run MDMS and PDS programmes. In addition to examining the treatment of Dalits in these government programmes, the survey attempted to measure various indicators of Dalits' access to and participatory empowerment in the MDMS and PDS. Through an analysis of the resultant data, it discerned potential avenues for improvement. This survey data is the basis of the present essay.[2]

## THE MID-DAY MEAL SCHEME

In November 2001, in response to a Public Interest Litigation filed by the People's Union of Civil Liberties, Rajasthan, the Supreme Court of India ordered all state governments to implement the central government's lagging 1995 National Programme of Nutritional Support to Primary Education, providing free cooked meals to all children in government primary schools, within six months. In states where it had been implemented, this programme was popularly known as the MDMS. Of the states considered in this study, Rajasthan, Andhra Pradesh, and Tamil Nadu had implemented the MDMS. Uttar Pradesh and Bihar were among those who had not implemented the MDMS in 2004, when the survey was conducted. Instead, they continued with a programme originally intended as a temporary, intermediate step leading to the cooked mid-day meals, that is monthly provision of a fixed quantity of dry grain to government school children. For the following discussion, then, Uttar Pradesh and Bihar data will refer to this pre-MDMS dry grain distribution system, and, it will consider, apart from this data the fully implemented MDMS in Rajasthan, Andhra Pradesh, and Tamil Nadu.

In order to assay caste discrimination and exclusion in the MDMS, the survey considered the following three factors: Dalit children's access to meals, Dalits' participatory empowerment/ownership of the MDMS, and the treatment of Dalits in the MDMS. In gauging Dalit access to the MDMS, three measurable indicators were applied to the scheme's actual material presence in the village: the existence of a functioning MDMS, its physical setting, and its location in terms of caste geography. First, is there a functioning and implemented MDMS in the village? Second, is the MDMS held in a physical setting accessible to Dalit children, for instance in the school building as opposed to a Dalit-exclusive temple? Third, is the physical setting of the MDMS situated in the village's dominant caste locality, in a Dalit colony, or in some third area?

Two measurable indicators were used to evaluate Dalits' participatory empowerment/ownership of the MDMS. First, in what percentage of all MDMS programmes were the cooks Dalit? Second, in what percentage of all MDMS programmes were the organizers (a decision-making role: those ultimately responsible for ensuring the smooth functioning of the MDMS—usually teachers, but sometimes *sarpanche*s or PDS dealers) Dalit? Finally, in order to measure treatment of Dalits in the MDMS, the following indicators were considered. Do dominant castes oppose the hiring of Dalit cooks? Do Dalit and dominant caste children sit and eat together in the MDMS, or is some form of segregation practised?

# Findings

Access to the MDMS is first and foremost contingent on the implementation of the scheme by state governments. The governments of Rajasthan, Andhra Pradesh, and Tamil Nadu had taken the initial step towards facilitating access, by implementing the MDMS. Out of 306 villages surveyed in these three states, 301 villages, or 98.4 per cent, had a functioning MDMS in the government school in their village. A functioning MDMS, however, does not always assure access. In six respondent villages in Andhra Pradesh and Tamil Nadu, Dalit children were completely barred from the MDMS by dominant caste communities on account of either caste discrimination generally or 'untouchability' specifically. While these six villages constitute only 2 per cent of the 306 villages surveyed, the living practice of outright exclusion anywhere has profound implications for the Right to Food and Dalits' access to that Right.

Uttar Pradesh (UP) and Bihar, on the other hand, where one-third of India's Dalits live (NCERT 1997), denied Dalit and other poor children access to their legislated entitlements from the very beginning, by simply refusing to implement the shared, cooked MDMS. In the distribution of dry grains to government school children that continues to substitute for the MDMS in Bihar and UP, regularized corruption and caste-based discriminatory distribution were widely reported and in some cases outright exclusion of Dalit children from distribution was reported. Epitomizing the former phenomenon, in Sonadi village in Ghazipur District, UP, respondents reported that the dominant caste teacher arbitrarily withholds the monthly rice allotment from some Scheduled Caste (SC) children, while giving it to other SC children and all of the dominant caste children. When the Dalit community approached the dominant caste PDS dealer to lodge a complaint, the dealer responded that the grain is 'not for your children anyway'. Thus the discriminatory behaviour by the high caste is acting as a restriction in seeking access to the MDMS scheme in UP and Bihar.

A second critical factor affecting Dalits' access to the MDMS was the physical setting of the programme. Ninety-three per cent of respondent villages in Rajasthan, Andhra Pradesh, and Tamil Nadu hold the MDMS in the school building itself, as is appropriate.

Requiring immediate relocation, however, were two villages in Tamil Nadu in which the MDMS was held in Hindu temples, spaces from which Dalits are excluded. In UP, the pre-MDMS distribution of dry grain to government school children was conducted in the school building itself in only 57 per cent of respondent villages, while in another 37 per cent of villages it was conducted in 'another place', unacceptably often the home or shop of a PDS dealer.

If the physical setting of the MDMS is important, the locality in which that space is situated is equally, if not more, significant. Rajasthan and Tamil Nadu had very low percentages of villages in which the MDMS was held in Dalit localities (12 per cent in Rajasthan and 19 per cent in Tamil Nadu), whereas villages in more than double that percentage in both states held the MDMS in dominant caste localities. In notable contrast, 46 per cent of respondent villages in Andhra Pradesh held the MDMS in Dalit localities, which goes a long way toward assuring Dalits' access and should help erode dominant caste prejudices against entering Dalit localities.

In UP, the distribution of dry grain to government school children took place in dominant caste localities in 85 per cent of respondent villages, while in less than 10 per cent of villages the distribution was conducted in Dalit localities.

In Uttar Pradesh, Rajasthan, and Tamil Nadu, then, the vast majority of Dalit children must enter an area of heightened vulnerability, tension, and threat in order to avail the MDMS or its dry grain equivalent. Access for Dalit children is, thus, conditional and hostage to the fluctuating state of caste relations in the village or region. Incidents like those at Kamalaputhur village and others documented in the IIDS study demonstrate how Dalit children's access to the MDMS, already tenuous because it is held in dominant caste localities, is then cut off when dominant castes feel the need to demonstratively reassert their hegemony.

In measuring Dalits' participatory empowerment in and ownership of the MDMS, the IIDS survey data unearths interesting patterns both in terms of national trends and interstate variations. In hiring practices, Rajasthan was consistently the least likely to employ Dalits, with 8 per cent of respondent villages having a Dalit cook and not a single respondent village having a Dalit MDMS organizer.

**Table 10.1: Caste Background of Cooks and Organizers**

(in per cent)

| Caste of MDMS cooks organizers (Percentage of respondent villages) | Rajasthan | | Andhra Pradesh | | Tamil Nadu | | 3-state average | |
|---|---|---|---|---|---|---|---|---|
| | Cooks | Organizers | Cooks | Organizers | Cooks | Organizers | Cooks | Organizers |
| Only SC | 8 | 0 | 49 | 45 | 31 | 27 | 29 | 24 |
| Only ST | 4 | 14 | 1 | 2 | 0 | 0 | 2 | 5 |
| Only dominant caste | 88 | 86 | 47 | 51 | 65 | 73 | 67 | 70 |
| Various castes* | 0 | 0 | 3 | 2 | 4 | 0 | 2 | 1 |
| Total | 100 | 100 | 100 | 100 | 100 | 100 | 100 | 100 |

*Note:* * More than one cook/organizer, from any combination of SC, ST, and dominant castes

Tamil Nadu hired proportionally more Dalits, while still keeping
them firmly in the minority, with 31 per cent of respondent villages
having Dalit cooks and 27 per cent having Dalit organizers. Andhra
Pradesh leads the three states in indicators of Dalit empowerment
and ownership of the MDMS, with 49 per cent and 45 per cent of
respondent villages having Dalits as cooks and organizers, respectively
(Table 10.1).

Before properly addressing the particularly volatile issue of Dalit
cooks, let us complete our brief review of data regarding Dalit
participatory empowerment. In UP, measurable indicators point
to an extremely low level of Dalit participatory empowerment and
ownership of the pre-MDMS dry grain distribution system. In
94 per cent of respondent villages, the distribution organizer was
dominant caste; SC and Scheduled Tribe (ST) organizers were found
in a combined 6 per cent of respondent villages.

In terms of treatment of Dalits in the MDMS, the findings of
the IIDS study indicated that caste discrimination in one form or
another did in fact plague a significant percentage of MDMS across
the country. Fifty-two per cent of respondents from Rajasthan, 24
per cent from Andhra Pradesh, and 36 per cent from Tamil Nadu
(giving a three-state national average of 37 per cent) reported that
there was a problem of caste discrimination in the MDMS in their
village (Table 10.2).

| TABLE 10.2: Caste Discrimination | | |
|---|---|---|
| | | (percentage) |
| *States* | *Yes* | *No* |
| Rajasthan | 52 | 48 |
| Andhra Pradesh | 24 | 76 |
| Tamil Nadu | 44 | 66 |
| Average | 37 | 63 |

Taking a closer look, what are some of the manifestations of
discrimination that arose? Of the 79 respondent villages that
specified the character of caste discrimination in the MDMS in
their schools, the largest portion, that is 48.3 per cent reported the
problem of dominant caste opposition to Dalit cooks. The second

most common issue, at 31 per cent, was segregated seating. A more intensified practice of segregation, in which Dalits and dominant caste children are served separate meals altogether, was reported by 9.2 per cent of respondent villages. Another 9.2 per cent villages reported that teachers discriminated among students by giving inferior or insufficient food to Dalit children and 2.3 per cent of respondents identified other problems (Table 10.3).

| TABLE 10.3: Types of Discrimination | |
|---|---|
| *Types* | *Percentage* |
| Separate seating | 31 |
| Separate meal | 9.2 |
| When cook is SC, high caste refused to eat | 48.3 |
| Inferior or insufficient food | 9.2 |
| Others | 2.3 |

## Opposition to Dalit Cooks

'Opposition to Dalit cooks' is actually a blanket term describing several different patterns of specific acts of caste discrimination and exclusion observed in the IIDS study. The patterns can be grouped into five, which can be placed at different points during the process of MDMS institution and continuance. First, when local administrators are putting the MDMS into place, dominant caste community members intervene to block the hiring of Dalit cooks, favouring dominant caste cooks instead. Where a Dalit cook has been hired, dominant caste parents then begin sending their children to school with lunches packed at home or require their children to come home for lunch, in any case forbidding their children to eat food prepared by the Dalit cook. In the third stage, dominant caste parents or community members pressurize the local administration to dismiss the Dalit cook, on any pretext, and hire a dominant caste cook instead. Where this is ineffective or sometimes without the intervening step, the dominant caste parents campaign to shut down the MDMS in the village school altogether. Finally, some dominant caste parents react to the hiring of a Dalit cook by withdrawing their children from the school and sometimes admitting them in a different school where the cook is not a Dalit.

Some examples may help illustrate the above patterns. The first is adequately exemplified by Komara village in West Godavari district, Andhra Pradesh. There, dominant caste women organized in the state government's Development of Women and Children in Rural Areas (DWACRA) scheme successfully mobilized community and administrative support to prohibit a qualified Dalit women's DWACRA group from obtaining employment as cooks in the village MDMS.[3]

Bhunabhay village in Ajmer district, Rajasthan illustrates two of the trends identified above. In Bhunabhay, when the MDMS began in July 2002, Sunita Bhil, a ST widow, was hired to prepare food. Dominant caste parents who considered Sunita polluted on account of her caste ordered their children not to eat the MDMS food at their school, effectively launching a proxy hunger strike through their children. Alongside this, the dominant caste parents met with and pressured the dominant caste headmaster of the school to dismiss Sunita Bhil from employment. Ultimately, the headmaster consented, expelled Sunita Bhil, and hired a dominant caste woman to cook in her place.

Typifying the fourth trend, the MDMS of a government school in Ranga Reddy district, Andhra Pradesh, lasted exactly ten days before the dominant caste community, incensed that Dalit cooks had been hired, shut down the school.[4]

Behind all these trends of dominant caste behaviour is the classic Hindu understanding of purity and pollution, according to which food prepared by a Dalit—that is an 'Untouchable'—is considered 'polluted' by virtue of its contact with the intrinsically polluted Dalit. On another level, dominant caste opposition to Dalit cooks also represents a power struggle over livelihood rights. In the manner of social boycotts, concerted dominant caste opposition to Dalit cooks functions to break Dalit economic aspirations, that is Dalit entry into new livelihood domains such as government employment as MDMS cooks at the village level. The rural dominant caste establishment, which traditionally enjoys the economic dependence of the Dalit community, perceives Dalit entries into new economic spheres as threatening and, therefore, responds with a backlash.

## Segregation and Opposition to Shared Meals

Several variations on the theme of segregation surfaced in the IIDS survey data. Thirty-one per cent of the villages specified the form of caste discrimination in their MDMS and identified separate seating as the primary problem. In these instances, Dalit children are required to sit apart from the dominant caste children—sometimes simply apart within the same space or, at other times, outside the school building while the dominant caste children sit inside; on the floor or on dirt when dominant caste children sit on mats; or on a lower level than their dominant caste peers.

Dalit children and dominant caste children were required to eat separate meals altogether in 9.8 per cent of the villages. This was most often the case where there were two MDMS cooks for the same school—one Dalit and one dominant caste. The practice of separate meals usually implies segregated drinking water arrangements as well.

Another 9.8 per cent reported more subtle forms of discrimination. In these villages, dominant caste teachers practised caste favouritism in serving the MDMS meals, treating the dominant caste children preferentially and reserving the smaller or less desirable portions for Dalit children.

Interestingly, segregated seating is not always an institution from the beginning of the MDMS. In Enathi village in Sivagangai district of Tamil Nadu, for instance, in 2001, the dominant caste community instituted segregated seating in the MDMS in a primary school where Dalit and dominant caste children had previously been sitting and eating together. In Enathi, following a dispute between a dominant caste woman and a Dalit woman over the latter's right to draw water from a public well, the dominant caste woman's community attacked the Dalit colony, causing the Dalit woman and her husband to be hospitalized. When the Dalit community approached the police and local administration for justice, Enathi's dominant caste community organized a rigorous social boycott of Dalits, physically enforced by barricading the Dalit colony. It was in this context, as part of the social boycott, that segregation was launched in the previously shared MDMS.

Similar incidents reported in the IIDS survey suggest a trend in which caste conflict unrelated to the MDMS flares up in a village, often as a result of Dalit assertion of rights and as part of the effort to re-establish caste hegemony; the dominant caste community inaugurates new forms of segregation (in the MDMS, for instance), and asserts new practices of untouchability. In one village in Tamil Nadu, respondents to the IIDS survey stated that the dominant caste government school teacher 'solved' the caste tensions in their village by introducing segregated seating. While it is common in popular discourse to describe the phenomenon of caste discrimination as 'remaining', 'still continuing', and 'lingering', such language does not accurately characterize the ground realities. Like all social phenomena, caste and caste discrimination continually adapt to new circumstances, finding new resources and new media of expression, rather than ceasing suddenly when confronted with 'education', 'modernity', or 'progress'. Discourses aimed at eradicating caste discrimination, if they are to be effective, must take into account the dynamism of caste phenomena, erroneously portrayed by the dismissive language of inevitable social progress.

## Implications

One argument against hiring Dalit cooks is that where the society is not prepared to accept a shared meal cooked by a Dalit, it will 'create tension', schools will be paralysed and (dominant caste) children's attendance will drop, thus defeating the purpose of the MDMS. This argument has been made with reference to Rajasthan, formulated as follows: 'In a socially conservative environment like Rajasthan's, where people are not ready for Dalit cooks, hiring them now will cause more harm than good.' Significantly, however, opposition to Dalit cooks is the most frequently reported problem, not only in Rajasthan, but in Andhra Pradesh as well (and is a close second to segregated seating in Tamil Nadu). In other words, Andhra Pradesh's success in hiring a significant proportion of Dalit cooks is *not* due to lack of opposition, but is rather a matter of political will (generated by sustained pressure from people's movements). The fact that Andhra Pradesh's relatively progressive hiring practices have not been accompanied by a corresponding crisis of dropping school attendance or paralysis of the school system suggests that the above argument against hiring Dalit cooks, speculative in nature anyway, is in fact spurious.

If we closely examine the interstate variations for responses to 'is there caste discrimination in the MDMS in your village?' it can hardly escape notice that this configuration is a nearly exact inverse of the interstate variation for percentage of villages with Dalit cooks, percentage of villages with Dalit organizers, and percentage of villages in which the MDMS was held in a Dalit locality. That is to say, Andhra Pradesh, which has the highest percentage of Dalit cooks, Dalit organizers, and MDMSs held in Dalit localities, simultaneously, has the lowest percentage of reported caste discrimination in the MDMS. Rajasthan, which has the lowest percentage of Dalit cooks, organizers, and MDMSs held in Dalit colonies, simultaneously, has the highest rate of reported caste discrimination, and Tamil Nadu stands about midway between Rajasthan and Andhra Pradesh in each of these variables (compare Table 10.2).

While direct causality cannot be proven, quantitative and qualitative evidence from the field suggests that the above variables have a significantly influential relationship with the degree of reported discrimination in each state. Considering each variable alone, for instance, the rates of reported discrimination were consistently lower when Dalit organizers were in charge of the MDMS, when Dalit cooks were cooking for the MDMS, and when the MDMS was held in a Dalit colony, than when dominant caste organizers were in charge of the MDMS, dominant caste cooks were cooking for the MDMS, and the MDMS was held in dominant caste localities. Subjective comments from researchers and respondents also affirmed that these trends were interlinked.

What, then, sets Andhra Pradesh apart? A quick glance at the annual reports of the National Commission for Scheduled Castes and Scheduled Tribes (NCSCST) or the annual reports of human rights organizations such as Sakshi—Human Rights Watch, Andhra Pradesh will disabuse any reader of the notion that Andhra Pradesh's relatively positive picture in the IIDS survey data can be linked to lower levels of casteism in the society generally.

Instead, as the patterns in the data suggest, the higher percentages of Dalit cooks and organizers and higher percentage of villages in which the MDMS was held in Dalit localities appeared to be responsible for Andhra's relatively low incidence of reported caste discrimination in the MDMS. But how is it that Andhra Pradesh has these higher levels of Dalit participatory empowerment and MDMSs held in Dalit colonies? One primary reason seems to be that the Andhra Pradesh government conducts the MDMS through local women's organizations (DWACRA groups). As an alternative to implementing the scheme only through the usual channels of entrenched government machinery, having a joint set-up between the government and local social organizations appears to have an invigorating effect on all actors involved. Given the opportunity to take up leadership roles and local level government employment, mothers of government school children take an increased interest in and engagement with the school and the MDMS and begin to demand access and extract accountability from the government machinery.

Sustained mass action by mobilized people's movements in Andhra Pradesh should be credited with creating the political atmosphere in which the state government has been forced to engage and cooperate with local non-governmental organizations (NGOs) in implementing its schemes. While DWACRA groups are government sponsored, they are clearly influenced by the models provided by social movements. Just as people's participation has a proven record of decreasing corruption by government officials, so likewise it seems that people's participation, particularly Dalit women's participation, is beginning to reduce levels of exclusion and caste discrimination in government schemes.

It would be incorrect to suggest that the DWACRA group model alone is sufficient to eradicate the problems of the MDMS or that Andhra Pradesh has 'arrived' in terms of enabling Dalits' Right to Food through the MDMS. There is still a 24 per cent rate of reported caste discrimination in the MDMS in Andhra Pradesh, meaning that Dalit children in one out of four schools face segregated seating, opposition to their community's cooks, and segregated meals altogether or other forms of discriminatory treatment. Dominant caste DWACRA groups, too, have a record of practising caste discrimination and there remain three cases of brazen exclusion of Dalit children from the MDMS for Andhra Pradesh's government to eradicate before it can make any meaningful claims about the success of its policies.

A study of Andhra Pradesh's MDMS provides not an ideal model, but a work in progress, with mixed success, from which some directional ideas can be taken. What policies/approaches seem to be working there, that can be applied in other states? One policy is to locate more schools and MDMS centres in Dalit colonies. Another is to promote Dalit participatory empowerment and ownership of the MDMS through hiring and promoting larger proportions of Dalit cooks and Dalit organizers. This can be catalysed partly by implementing the MDMS through or with the collaboration of people's movements and local organizations such as Dalit women's Self-Help Groups (SHGs), which will also help increase accountability in the programme.

## THE PUBLIC DISTRIBUTION SYSTEM

The Indian government's Targeted Public Distribution System (TPDS), or, often, simply PDS, is reputed to be the largest system of controlled food distribution in the world. In it, government stocks of essential food commodities, notably rice, wheat, sugar, and oil, are distributed through the Food Corporation of India (FCI) to needy areas, where people of Below Poverty Line (BPL) status can purchase the goods at subsidized, below-market prices fixed by the government. At the local level, stocks are provided through government-recognized 'Fair Price Shops' or PDS shops, run by local, government-recognized PDS dealers.

As with the MDMS, access, participatory empowerment/ownership, and treatment are the factors according to which the IIDS survey evaluated caste discrimination and exclusion in the PDS. Two measurable indicators were employed to gauge Dalit access to PDS: existence and number of functioning PDS shops in the village, and location in terms of caste geography. First, are there PDS shops operating in the village, and second, are these shops placed in dominant caste localities, Dalit quarters, or elsewhere?

Dalits' participatory empowerment and ownership of the PDS was measured by the percentage, out of all PDS shops in respondent villages, of PDS shops owned by Dalits.

Finally, treatment of Dalits at the PDS shops was measured by quantifying respondents' responses to questions about various reported forms of caste discrimination in the context of PDS distribution, namely discrimination in price and quantity, caste favouritism by PDS dealers, and the practice of 'untouchability' by PDS dealers.

## Findings

In terms of access, it is to the credit of the PDS that throughout the country, PDS shops are largely up and running. As a national average, 87 per cent of respondent villages in the IIDS study reported having at least one functioning PDS shop in their village: 73 per cent of respondents had exactly one PDS shop in their village, while 14 per cent had more than one PDS shop per village. Thirteen per cent of respondent villages, however, had no PDS shop in their village, and must travel outside to avail themselves of their legislated entitlements of subsidized goods.

Most of the villages without PDS shops were in UP and Bihar. Taking a look at interstate variations; UP shows itself to be the most recalcitrant in assuring PDS accessibility, with 39 per cent of respondent villages lacking PDS shops and only 7 per cent having more than one shop. Bihar followed, with 16 per cent of villages lacking a PDS shop and only 10 per cent having more than one shop. Rajasthan and Tamil Nadu scored about equally—and adequately— while access appears most assured in Andhra Pradesh, where 44 per cent of respondent villages had more than one shop, 53 per cent had exactly one shop, and only 3 per cent have no shop.

A second factor conditioning Dalit access to the benefits of the PDS was the location in which the PDS shops were physically situated. In Rajasthan, PDS shops were located in dominant caste localities in 91 per cent of respondent villages, while not a single village had a shop in a Dalit colony, and 9 per cent had shops located elsewhere. In UP, shops were located in dominant caste localities in 82 per cent of villages, with 16 per cent in Dalit colonies, and 2 per cent elsewhere. In Bihar, dominant caste colonies hosted the shops in 76 per cent of villages and the other 24 per cent were located in Dalit colonies. In Tamil Nadu, dominant caste localities had the shops in 53 per cent of the villages, Dalit colonies in 16 per cent (same as UP), and 31 per cent were elsewhere. Andhra Pradesh had the highest proportion of PDS shops in Dalit colonies at 30 per cent and the lowest proportion in dominant caste colonies at 48 per cent, with 22 per cent elsewhere. As a national average, then, 17 per cent of villages had PDS shops in Dalit colonies, while 70 per cent (more than four times the former) had PDS shops located in dominant caste localities and 13 per cent of villages had PDS shops located elsewhere.

In terms of participatory empowerment, the preponderance of dominant caste PDS dealers and the paucity of Dalit dealers in the IIDS survey data were equally striking. Here again, Andhra Pradesh stood out as the only state in which Dalits had attained a significant degree of participatory empowerment, at 32 per cent, with another 7 per cent ST ownership of PDS shops, and 61 per cent dominant caste ownership. In an interesting departure from earlier patterns, however, in PDS shop ownership, it was Tamil Nadu that boasted the most complete dominant caste hegemony (91 per cent) and the lowest level of Dalit empowerment (9 per cent), followed by UP (90 per cent and 10 per cent respectively), Rajasthan (85 per cent and 15 per cent respectively), and Bihar (78 per cent and 22 per cent respectively). The national average came to 81 per cent dominant caste ownership of PDS shops and 19 per cent combined SC and ST ownership (Table 10.4).

TABLE 10.4: Caste of PDS Dealer (in per cent)

| State | SC | ST | Higher caste |
|---|---|---|---|
| Rajasthan | 15 | – | 85 |
| Uttar Pradesh | 10 | – | 90 |
| Bihar | 22 | – | 78 |
| Andhra Pradesh | 32 | 7 | 61 |
| Tamil Nadu | 9 | – | 91 |
| Average | 17.6 | 1.4 | 81 |

In terms of treatment of Dalits in the PDS, various forms of discriminatory practices in varying degrees of currency were reported. As a national average, 40 per cent of respondent villages reported that Dalits received, for the same price, lesser quantities than the dominant castes received from PDS shopkeepers (Table 10.5). In ascending order of reported discrimination, 16 per cent of respondent villages in Rajasthan reported discrimination in quantity, followed by 29 per cent in Tamil Nadu, 30 per cent in Andhra Pradesh, 56 per cent in Uttar Pradesh, and 70 per cent in Bihar.

| Table 10.5: Discrimination in PDS (Average) | |
|---|---|
| Type | Percentage |
| In quality | 40 |
| In prices | 28 |
| Favour to own caste by dealer | 48 |
| Dealer practised untouchability | 26 |

Less common, but still a problem, was the practice by some PDS dealers of charging Dalit customers extra for the same quantity that dominant castes purchased at lower costs. The national average of villages reporting this practice was 28 per cent.

At a national average of 48 per cent, the most commonly reported form of caste discrimination in the PDS was caste-based favouritism by PDS dealers towards their own community. Respondents described this phenomenon taking numerous forms. In some places, PDS dealers serviced their own caste community members or all dominant castes throughout the week, while only serving Dalit communities on arbitrarily designated 'Dalit days', falling once or twice in a week. Preferential order in service, meaning that Dalits were kept waiting and served last while PDS dealers' caste fellows or other dominant caste members were served immediately, was widely reported. Describing the way in which caste-based favouritism works in the PDS in their village, respondents in Tarka village of Ghazipur district, UP, related an incident in which members of the Dalit community were in severe need of sugar and other goods from the PDS, but the dominant caste PDS dealer flatly refused, saying that his stock had run out. The same day, members of the PDS dealer's own caste had a wedding, for which they received 'quintal after quintal' of sugar and other supposedly absent goods from the PDS shop.

In Andhra Pradesh, 17 per cent of respondent villages reported a problem of the PDS dealer practising caste-based favouritism in the distribution of goods. In Tamil Nadu, 41 per cent; in Rajasthan, 42 per cent; in UP, 54 per cent; and in Bihar, a remarkable 86 per cent of villages contended regularly with this manner of casteist treatment from their PDS dealers.

Outlawed in 1950 with the ratification of the Indian Constitution, the dominant caste practice of 'untouchability' towards Dalits continues unabated in the twenty-first century, not only as a social neurosis, but also as an unofficial policy of various government actors, notably the PDS dealers. A national average of 26 per cent of PDS dealers, according to the IIDS survey respondents, practised untouchability in the distribution of government goods to Dalits. One classic untouchability practice is the dominant caste dropping of goods (water, food, and money) from above into cupped Dalit hands below, so as to avoid the possibility of 'polluting' contact between the 'upper' and 'lower' castes. This remains in evidence, but other untouchability practices, such as dominant caste dealers hanging purdah before dealing with Musaher Dalits in Bihar, also emerges in the survey data.

In the IIDS study, none of the small sample of respondent villages in Rajasthan reported 'untouchability' practices in their local PDS shops, though such practices in Rajasthan have been documented elsewhere. In Andhra Pradesh, 11 per cent of respondent villages reported 'untouchability' practices; in Tamil Nadu, 25 per cent; in UP, 35 per cent; and in Bihar, most disturbingly, 59 per cent.

## Implications

The PDS is arguably the strongest available tool with which the poor and marginalized populations in India can at present actualize their Right to Food. Whether it is operated well or poorly can—indeed, does—make the difference between sustenance and preventable starvation for SC and ST communities in certain areas. While the intent of the PDS is to bring food from where it is most plentiful to where it is most needed and to deliver it into the hands of those who need it the most, there are problems with the system's practical implementation, such that the food often ends up in hands other than of those who need it the most.

So long as the intended beneficiaries of the PDS are kept out of the decision-making and implementation processes, indications suggest that the discrimination would continue to flourish. On the other hand, where Dalit participation in PDS implementation through ownership of PDS shops is increased and where greater proportions of PDS shops are accessibly located in Dalit localities, levels of reported caste discrimination are lower. As with the MDMS, so also with the PDS, Andhra Pradesh emerges from the data as having relatively low levels of reported caste discrimination in comparison to most other states. Qualitative data also suggest that increased degree of participation by Dalits in PDS implementation has helped increase accountability in the government machinery in Andhra Pradesh. While 11 per cent of continuing 'untouchability' in PDS goods distribution still demands vigorous action by the state, the higher percentage of PDS shops located in Dalit colonies in Andhra Pradesh seems to have decreased the scope for dominant caste dealers to practise 'untouchability'. Empowerment through participation and ownership, as well as empowerment through sensitive relocation into Dalit areas, emerge from the data as potentialities currently being realized in Andhra Pradesh that can also be realized in other states.

Notably, as a national average, Dalit communities in 75 per cent of respondent villages said that SC/STs should have their own separate shops from those owned by the dominant castes. Relocating PDS shops in Dalit colonies and building Dalit ownership of the PDS is, thus, not only an idea that data trends suggest as successful in decreasing levels of discrimination, but is also a demand of the Dalit community.

One argument against such approaches is that they are not integrative solutions. They seem to ring with a distrustful and separatist tone. This is true. But the empowerment of the oppressed group on its own terms is a necessary stage in the process. Integration on the oppressor group's terms is never equal integration, but continued exploitation.

The survey data present us with some positive trends. First, 87 per cent of all respondent villages had at least one functioning PDS shop and 98.4 per cent of respondent villages in Rajasthan, Andhra Pradesh, and Tamil Nadu had a functioning MDMS. These are remarkable achievements of the government and without establishing this first crucial step toward actualizing the Right to Food, further talks of access would indeed be remote. Moreover, 63 per cent of respondents reported that caste discrimination does not afflict the MDMS in their villages and while acknowledging extremely wide variation from state to state; the national averages of respondents who reported discrimination in quantity and price in the PDS, as well as caste favouritism and 'untouchability' practised by PDS dealers, were each less than 50 per cent. In many places, then, these government food-related programmes were living up to their legal and constitutional obligations.

However, the problem of dominant castes sabotaging the progressive potential of the MDMS and the PDS, through discriminatory practices and exclusion toward Dalits, remains massive. In terms of scale, caste discrimination afflicts more than one out of three PDS shops and more than one out of three government schools serving MDMS (national averages of 35.5 per cent and 37 per cent, respectively). In terms of geographical spread, it is unquestionably a nation-wide problem—from 24 per cent in Andhra Pradesh to 52 per cent in Rajasthan, to the vast majority in UP and Bihar: respondent villages from every state reported problems of caste discrimination and exclusion in the MDMS or its dry grain equivalent. Likewise with the PDS, no state is free of patterns of discrimination, from 17 per cent in Andhra Pradesh to 86 per cent in Bihar, for instance every state reported a substantial percentage of dominant caste PDS dealers practising caste-based discrimination in the distribution of PDS goods, as for instance preferential order of service by caste or hierarchically segregated timings for dominant caste and Dalit customers.

While the problem is nation-wide, its degree varies considerably from state to state and this variation, considered in the light of a parallel variation in other indicators, points to possible solutions. Where higher percentages of MDMS cooks and organizers are Dalits and where a higher percentage of the MDMS programmes is held in Dalit colonies, lower incidences of caste discrimination in the MDMS were reported. In Andhra Pradesh, where indicators of Dalit participatory empowerment and access were relatively high (49 per cent of respondent villages had Dalit cooks, 45 per cent had Dalit organizers, and 46 per cent were held in Dalit localities), reported caste discrimination in MDMS stood at 24 per cent. In

Tamil Nadu, where the same empowerment and access indicators were lower (31 per cent, 27 per cent, and 19 per cent, respectively), reported discrimination stood at 36 per cent. In Rajasthan, where indicators were alarmingly low (8 per cent Dalit cooks, 0 per cent Dalit organizers, and 12 per cent held in Dalit colonies), reported discrimination was extremely high at 52 per cent.

Simply put, it appears that increased Dalit access (in terms of village caste geography) and participatory empowerment (in terms of employment and decision-making power in the government programmes) correspond with decreased incidence of exclusion and caste discrimination. A similar pattern emerges in the PDS data, where higher proportions of Dalit PDS dealers and PDS shops held in Dalit colonies corresponded with lower proportions of reported discrimination and 'untouchability' practices. Here again, Andhra Pradesh surfaces as higher than the other states in access and participatory empowerment/ownership indicators and lower in incidence of discrimination. While the Andhra Pradesh government still has a formidable problem of caste discrimination to deal with, its relative success *vis-à-vis* the other surveyed states appears to lie in its engagement with locally based women's groups, NGOs, and people's movements in the practical implementation of the government programmes. Implementation of the MDMS through DWACRA groups, as opposed to the usual government machinery for instance, increases the scope for Dalit women to make empowered, effective, and participatory interventions to ensure their children's equal access to the Right to Food and the Right to Education, as well as their own Right to Employment (as MDMS cooks, organizers, or teachers).

Other states might well pursue and refine this model. In addition to relocating or newly locating MDMS centres and PDS shops in Dalit colonies or other accessible caste-neutral localities, state governments can begin tackling the exclusion/discrimination problem by seeking partnerships with Dalit women's groups and other NGOs to jointly implement and monitor the programmes. Where Dalit participatory empowerment is fostered, dominant caste communities will not be able to chase away Dalit students, like second-year student Kalpana from Kamalaputhur, from the MDMS, nor force them to sit separately or otherwise terrorize them on account of their caste backgrounds. In that case, the Right to Food might become a reality for Dalits, too.

## NOTES

1.   The idea to conduct the survey was conceived in April 2003 at a meeting between activists of the National Campaign on Dalit Human Rights (NCDHR) and researchers of the IIDS, on the one hand, and Right to Food activists at the Human Rights Law Collective, on the other.
2.   The identities of people have been altered for the chapter.
3.   This was an outcome of a discussion during the interview.
4.   This example comes not from the IIDS survey, but from media reports in the Telugu daily *Vaartha*, Ranga Reddy district pullout, 4 January 2003.

## REFERENCES

Aravind, H.M. (2003), 'Parents "Caste" Aside Govt. Mid-day Meal', New Delhi: *The Times of India*, 4 July.

Chakrabarty, G. and P.K. Ghosh (2000), *Human Development Profile of Scheduled Castes and Tribes in Rural India: A Bench Mark Survey*, New Delhi: National Council of Applied Economic Research.

Dreze, Jean and Aparajita Goyal (2003), *The Future of Mid-day Meals*, Delhi: Centre for Equity Studies.

National Commission for Scheduled Castes and Scheduled Tribes, *Sixth Report, 1999–2000 and 2000–2001*, Delhi: Government of India.

National Council for Educational Research and Training (NCERT) (1997), *Sixth All-India Educational Survey*, New Delhi: MHRD, Government of India.

Sainath, P. (2001), 'Hero by Name and Deed', *The Hindu*, Madras, 21 January.

Sakshi Human Rights Watch (2003), *Dalit Human Rights Monitor 2000– 2003*, Andhra Pradesh. Secunderabad: Sakshi Human Rights Watch.

Sreenivas, Janyala (2003), 'These Kids Told: You are Dalit, Go Eat Elsewhere', *The Indian Express*, New Delhi: 16 December.

Thorat, Sukhadeo (2001), 'Caste and Untouchability Based Economic and Market Discrimination: Theory, Concept and Consequences', *Artha Vijnana*, vol. 153, nos 1–2, pp. 123–46.

# DISCRIMINATION-INDUCED INEQUALITIES

## CAPITAL ASSETS AND POVERTY

# 11

# Caste and Ownership of Private Enterprises
## Consequences of Denial of Property Rights

*Sukhadeo Thorat, Debolina Kundu, and Nidhi Sadana*

One of the important features of the caste system relating to property rights is restrictions on owning business or undertaking production activity for low-caste Untouchables. Except those economic activities that are considered impure and polluting (like those relating to leather and sanitary products), the former Untouchables were not entitled to undertake business and/or production activities, or own property. This also included restrictions on the ownership of agricultural land for production purposes (Olivelle 2005; Ambedkar 1987). The new legal framework of rights under the Indian Constitution removes the customary restrictions on the ownership of property and business by the Untouchables. The government has also initiated policy measures to improve access and ownership of private enterprise for the Untouchables, to correct the disparities created by the historical denial of these rights (Planning Commission 2008). However, notwithstanding these efforts, the consequences of the past denial still continue. The impact of denial of property rights is seen even today in the lack of ownership of private enterprise by the Untouchables in India.

This chapter examines the access of low-caste Untouchables to private enterprise—and captures the disparities between them and the higher castes (HC) against this background. The study is based on the data provided by the Fourth Economic Census pertaining to the year 2005. Private enterprise constituted about 95 per cent of the total enterprises in the country in 2005. As per the 1998 Economic Census, about 39.61 million enterprises were owned by the private sector out of a total of 41.82 million enterprises in the country.

## Database and Methodology

As mentioned above, the main objective of this chapter is to analyse the relative situation of the Scheduled Castes (SC) in comparison to the Other Backward Castes (OBC) and the HCs with respect to ownership of private enterprise in India for the latest census year, 2005. The Economic Census for 1998 and 2005 provides data on the ownership of private enterprise by castes, which include SCs, Scheduled Tribes (ST), OBCs, and HCs (HC defined as residual category net of SC, ST, and OBC). Besides differences in ownership of private enterprise at the aggregate level, the chapter also examines the differences between SCs and HCs by ownership of different type of enterprises, occupation categories, and employment.

## Ownership of Private Enterprise

In India, about 95 per cent of the enterprises were owned by the private sector in 2005. Table 11.1 provides the share of each of the social groups in total private enterprise. The table also provides the share of the four groups in the total population of the country for 2004–5, based on the 61st National Sample Survey (NSS)—which is the same year as that of the 2005 Economic Census. The SCs, STs, OBCs, and HCs respectively account for about 10 per cent, 21 per cent, 43 per cent, and 25 per cent of the total population located in the rural areas in the country. The share of each of these social groups is disproportionate to their population share. The ownership of private enterprise is unevenly distributed among the social groups. In 2005, the SCs, STs, OBCs, and HCs accounted for about 10 per cent, 4.6 per cent, 40 per cent, and 45 per cent of the total rural private enterprise in the country respectively (Figure 11.1). While the share of the SCs and STs is much lower than their share in the country's population, the share of the HCs is much above their population share. In the case of the OBCs, their share in private enterprise is fairly close to their share in population. Between 1998 and 2005, there has been a marginal decline in the share of the STs, with the difference going to the HCs. The share of the SCs and OBCs remained the same.

A similar pattern is observed in urban areas as well. In 2005, the share of the SCs in private enterprise was much lower than their share in the total population. While their share in the country's

TABLE 11.1: Percentage Distribution of Private Enterprises Across Social Groups, 1998 and 2005, All-India (in per cent)

| | Rural India | | | | |
| --- | --- | --- | --- | --- | --- |
| | ST | SC | OBC | HC | All |
| Total private enterprises, 1998 | 5.84 | 10.22 | 40.77 | 43.16 | 100 |
| Total private enterprises, 2005 | 4.6 | 10.00 | 40.57 | 44.83 | 100 |
| Population (Census 2001) | 10.42 | 17.91 | – | 71.67* | 100 |
| Population (NSS 61st Round, 2004–5) | 10.2 | 21.3 | 42.9 | 25.5 | 100 |
| | Urban India | | | | |
| Total private enterprises, 1998 | 2.42 | 6.07 | 30.49 | 61 | 100 |
| Total private enterprises, 2005 | 2.13 | 6.97 | 34.19 | 56.71 | 100 |
| Population (Census 2001) | 2.44 | 11.75 | – | 85.81* | 100 |
| Population (NSS 61st Round, 2004–5) | 3 | 15 | 36 | 45.90 | 100 |

Source: Based on the Fourth Economic Census, 1998 and 2005
Note: * Includes OBC population

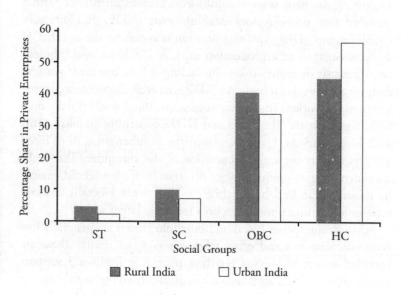

FIGURE 11.1: Ownership of Private Enterprises Across Social Groups: Rural/Urban India, 2005

population is about 21 per cent, they account for only 6 per cent of the country's private enterprise, which is almost three-and-a-half times less than their share in the urban population. In the case of the HCs, the share was much above their population share— the percentage share in enterprise being 57 per cent as against a population share of 45 per cent. In the case of the OBCs and STs, the share in enterprise was fairly close to the population share and, hence, in their case the disparities were relatively less. Between 1998 and 2005, there was some increase in the percentage share of the OBCs, which was mainly at the cost of the HCs.

## Ownership by Type of Enterprise and Ownership by Major Activity

The Economic Census classified private enterprises into own account enterprises (OAE) and establishments. An OAE is one that is normally run by a household without hiring any worker on a fairly regular basis. An enterprise employing at least one hired worker on a fairly regular basis is an establishment. Establishments are further classified into non-directory establishments (NDE) and directory establishments (DE). This classification is based on the number of workers engaged in a production unit. A DE is an establishment employing six or more workers (including at least one hired worker) daily on a fairly regular basis. An NDE is an establishment employing less than six workers (including at least one hired worker) daily on a fairly regular basis. Thus DEs and NDEs constitute establishments with hired workers. Understandably, the number/strength of hired workers reflects the scale of operation of the enterprise. The OAEs are generally petty production activities run by the household, mainly by means of family labour, while establishments generally indicate economic ventures undertaken on a relatively larger scale.

Further, enterprises based on household labour are generally low economic ventures and often taken up as a last resort. These are regarded as residual-sector activities providing livelihood support similar to traditional agricultural activities carried out at subsistence level. A lot of informalization and casualization takes place in the form of self-employment. The DEs, on the other hand, are better economic ventures with higher capital–output ratio, electricity consumption, use of institutional capital, capital per worker, and so on.

The Economic Census of 2005 does not provide data separately for NDEs and DEs. It gives the total of both, that is all enterprises working with hired workers.

At the overall level in rural India in 2005, household-based enterprises constituted the highest proportion at 71 per cent of total enterprises. Thus the OAEs accounted for the bulk of private enterprise in rural areas, and the remaining 29 per cent was shared by enterprises that were operated with hired workers (Table 11.2).

TABLE 11.2: Percentage Distribution of Private Enterprises within Social Groups by Type of Enterprise: 1998 and 2005

| Percentage distribution within social groups (rural) | ST | SC | OBC | HC | All |
|---|---|---|---|---|---|
| OAEs to total private enterprises, 1998 | 90.53 | 90 | 84.57 | 82.06 | 84.4 |
| OAEs to total private enterprises, 2005 | 80.86 | 81.40 | 77.56 | 61.55 | 70.93 |
| NDEs, 1998 | 8.21 | 8.65 | 13.22 | 14.73 | 13.1 |
| DEs, 1998 | 1.24 | 1.33 | 2.2 | 3.19 | 2.5 |
| Total hired, 1998 | 9.45 | 9.98 | 15.42 | 17.92 | 15.6 |
| Total hired, 2005 | 19.14 | 18.59 | 22.44 | 38.45 | 29.07 |
| Total | 100 | 100 | 100 | 100 | 100 |
| Percentage distribution within social groups (urban): | | | | | |
| OAEs to total private enterprises, 1998 | 70.87 | 75.95 | 68.04 | 59.78 | 63.6 |
| OAEs to total private enterprises, 2005 | 61.64 | 67.17 | 60.02 | 48.80 | 54.19 |
| NDEs, 1998 | 23.93 | 20.13 | 27.55 | 32.33 | 29.9 |
| DEs, 1998 | 5.19 | 3.9 | 4.4 | 7.87 | 6.5 |
| Total hired, 1998 | 29.12 | 24.03 | 31.95 | 40.2 | 36.4 |
| Total hired, 2005 | 38.36 | 32.83 | 39.96 | 51.2 | 45.81 |
| Total | 100 | 100 | 100 | 100 | 100 |

Source: Based on the Fourth Economic Census, 1998 and 2005

Between 1998 and 2005, there was a significant change in the composition of OAEs and establishments in rural areas. There is a significant decline in the share of OAEs and a shift towards establishments with hired workers. The share of establishments increased from 15.56 per cent in 1998 to 29 per cent in 2005, indicating a 14 per cent increase in the share of establishments.

In 2005, among social groups in rural areas, the SC and ST households operate a relatively higher proportion of household-based enterprises as compared to the all-India average. The share in the case of both groups is about 80 per cent each, which is higher than the all-India average of 71 per cent as well as the share of the OBCs (77 per cent) and HCs (61 per cent). Thus the ownership of household enterprises by the OBCs and HCs was lower than for the SCs and STs. However, the opposite is true in the case of NDEs and DEs. The SCs and STs own less of these two categories of enterprise as compared to the OBCs and HCs. This is clear from Table 11.2, which indicates that the SCs owned a relatively lower share of NDEs and DEs, and the figure goes up as we move from SCs and STs to OBCs and HCs. Put together, the SCs own about 32 per cent of hired worker enterprises, compared to 51 per cent for HCs.

The same pattern is observed in urban India as well. In 2005, the SCs owned a relatively higher proportion of OAEs—and the share falls as we move from the SCs and STs to OBCs and HCs. For instance, 67 per cent of the total enterprises owned by the SCs were OAEs, as compared to 61 per cent for the STs, 60 per cent for the OBCs, and 49 per cent for others. The percentage shares of owning hired worker-based enterprises were 33 per cent for the SCs, 38 per cent for the STs, 40 per cent for the OBCs, and 51 per cent for the HCs.

Between 1998 and 2005, there has been some decline in the share of OAEs for all social groups, and a corresponding increase in the share of enterprises based on wage labour.

The results clearly reveal a higher share for the HCs in the ownership of private enterprises in both rural and urban areas. The concentration among the HCs, particularly in enterprises with hired worker, is quite clear from their share in total enterprises in the rural and urban areas during 1998 and 2005. In 1998, in rural areas, the share of ownership of the SCs and STs is lowest in the case of hired worker-based enterprises. The STs, SCs, OBCs, and HCs respectively account for about 2.93 per cent, 5.5 per cent, 36.11 per cent, and

TABLE 11.3: Percentage Distribution of Private Enterprises Across Social Groups by Type of Enterprise, 1998 and 2005

| Percentage distribution across social groups (rural) | ST | SC | OBC | HC | All |
|---|---|---|---|---|---|
| OAEs to total PE, 1998 | 6.26 | 10.9* | 40.85 | 41.97 | 100 |
| OAEs to total PE, 2005 | 5.24 | 11.48 | 44.37 | 38.91 | 100 |
| NDEs, 1998 | 3.65 | 6.73 | 41.1 | 48.49 | 100 |
| DEs, 1998 | 2.93 | 5.5 | 36.11 | 55.43 | 100 |
| Total hired, 2005 | 3.02 | 6.39 | 31.30 | 40.71 | 100 |
| Population (Census 2001) | 10.42 | 17.91 | – | 71.67* | 100 |
| Percentage distribution across social groups (urban) | | | | | |
| OAEs to total PEs, 1998 | 2.7 | 7.26 | 32.65 | 57.38 | 100 |
| OAEs to total PEs, 2005 | 2.43 | 8.64 | 37.86 | 51.07 | 100 |
| NDEs | 1.93 | 4.08 | 28.07 | 65.9 | 100 |
| DEs | 1.93 | 3.64 | 20.63 | 73.78 | 100 |
| Total hired, 2005 | 1.79 | 5.00 | 29.84 | 63.37 | 100 |
| Population (Census 2001) | 2.44 | 11.75 | – | 85.81 | 100 |

Source: Based on the Fourth Economic Census, 1998 and 2005

55.43 per cent of the total DEs in the country. Further, the share of SCs and STs owning DEs is much lower (5.5 per cent and 2.93 per cent respectively) than their share in the country's population, which is 17.91 per cent and 10.42 per cent respectively. On the other hand, the share of the OBCs and HCs owning DEs (92 per cent) is much above their population share (71.7 per cent). For 2005, separate figures for DEs and NDEs by social groups are available. However, both taken together also indicate the concentration of establishments with hired worker among the OBCs and HCs, particularly among the latter.

A similar pattern is observed in urban areas as well. In 1998, the share of the SCs in DEs is much lower than their share in the total population. While their share in the country's population is about 12 per cent, they account for only 3.6 per cent of the DEs. The OBCs and HCs together account for almost 94.4 per cent of the total DEs in the country. This reflects higher inequality in business ownership carried out at a higher scale of operation.

TABLE 11.4: Percentage Distribution of Private Enterprises by Workers, 1998

| Percentage distribution across social groups (rural) | ST | SC | OBC | HC | All |
|---|---|---|---|---|---|
| Total workers in PEs | 5.47 | 8.82 | 38.82 | 46.87 | 100 |
| Hired workers | 2.67 | 4.68 | 33.96 | 58.66 | 100 |
| Perennial | 4.75 | 10.01 | 41.35 | 43.87 | 100 |
| Percentage distribution across social group (urban) | | | | | |
| Total workers in PEs | 2.34 | 4.96 | 25.52 | 67.16 | 100 |
| Hired workers | 1.81 | 3.39 | 20.49 | 74.29 | 100 |
| Perennial | 2.34 | 5.96 | 30.27 | 61.41 | 100 |

*Note*: PE: private enterprises
*Source*: Based on the Fourth Economic Census, 1998 and 2005

## OWNERSHIP PATTERN BY EMPLOYMENT

In the earlier section, we have analysed the ownership pattern by social group in terms of number of enterprises. The Economic Census also provides data on employment of workers, total workers, and hired and perennial workers for 1998 (the data on employment by social groups for 2005 is not yet released). We look at the distribution of workers across social groups in rural and urban areas. In rural India, private enterprises owned by the HCs employed about 47 per cent of the total workers in all enterprises, and another 39 per cent were employed in enterprises owned by the OBCs. Put together, enterprises owned by the HCs and OBCs employed about 86 per cent of the total workers in private sector enterprises located in rural areas. The remaining 14 per cent were engaged in enterprises owned by the SCs and STs. Enterprises owned by the SCs accounted for about 9 per cent of the total workers.

Workers classified into hired and perennial categories follow a similar pattern. In the case of hired workers, the HCs account for about 58.55 per cent of the total hired workers, and the OBCs comes next with 34 per cent. The rest 7 per cent are accounted for by SC- and ST-owned private enterprises. The same pattern is observed for perennial workers, the HCs accounting for about 44 per cent, followed by 42 per cent for the OBCs, 10 per cent for the SCs, and only 4.75

per cent for the STs. It may be noted that the HCs and OBCs account for nearly the same proportion of hired workers in rural areas.

Urban India follows a pattern that is similar to that of rural India. In urban India also, the HCs employ 67 per cent, followed by the OBCs at 25.50 per cent. The SCs and STs account for 5 per cent and 2.3 per cent respectively. With respect to hired and perennial workers, the HCs employ the majority of both categories in the enterprises owned by them, again followed by the OBCs (Table 11.4). The others employed about three-fourths of the total workers in urban areas, which may be attributed to the higher scale of operation in enterprises in urban industrial locations. The OBCs account for about 20 per cent of the total hired workers. SC- and ST-owned enterprises claim a very small share of hired labourers as their enterprises are mainly OAEs, and much less NDEs and DEs. The SCs and STs account for a small proportion of hired workers. The same pattern is observed in the case of perennial workers. As a matter of fact, the concentration of employment in enterprises owned by the HCs indicates the dependence of workers, particularly the low-caste ones, on the HC and OBC enterprise owner.

## OWNERSHIP OF PRIVATE ENTERPRISES BY MAJOR ACTIVITY

Private enterprises operate both in agricultural and non-agricultural activities. Agricultural activities include livestock production and agricultural services, with hunting, trapping, and game propagation, forestry, logging, and fishing being part.[1] 'Importantly, enterprises engaged in activities pertaining to agricultural production and plantations are not covered under the Economic Census.'[2] Enterprises engaged in all activities other than agricultural activities are termed as non-agricultural enterprises. These activities include mining and quarrying; manufacturing; activities related to electricity, gas, and water; construction and wholesale trade; retail trade; hotel and restaurant; transport; storage and warehousing; communication; finance and insurance; and community services. Understandably, a higher share of entrepreneurship in the sectors of manufacturing; construction and wholesale trade; hotel and restaurant; transport; storage and warehousing; communication; and finance and insurance shows the diversification of the economy away from agriculture.

Table 11.5 shows the share of 17 major activities in the total enterprises for four social groups in rural areas. These include activities associated with agricultural and non-agricultural enterprises. At the overall level, retail trade with 35 per cent, agriculture with 22 per cent, and manufacturing with 20 per cent account for the major segments

TABLE 11.5: Share of Major Activities in the Total of Non-agricultural and Agricultural Enterprises by Social Groups in Rural Areas, 2005

(in per cent)

| Major activity group | Total | Social group of owner | | | |
|---|---|---|---|---|---|
| | | SC | ST | OBC | HC |
| Agriculture | 22.36 | 22.79 | 31.42 | 25.30 | 18.67 |
| Mining and quarrying | 0.24 | 0.32 | 0.46 | 0.25 | 0.19 |
| Manufacturing | 20.20 | 25.11 | 25.39 | 23.97 | 15.17 |
| Electricity, gas, and water supply | 0.17 | 0.04 | 0.03 | 0.06 | 0.30 |
| Construction | 0.67 | 1.12 | 0.82 | 0.70 | 0.52 |
| Sale, paint, and repair of motor vehicles and motorcycles | 0.93 | 0.65 | 0.48 | 1.02 | 0.96 |
| Wholesale trade | 1.44 | 1.27 | 0.85 | 1.29 | 1.68 |
| Retail trade | 30.50 | 32.48 | 29.26 | 31.14 | 29.61 |
| Hotels and restaurants | 3.12 | 2.18 | 2.94 | 3.66 | 2.85 |
| Transport, storage | 3.34 | 5.73 | 3.10 | 2.70 | 3.41 |
| Post and telecommunications | 1.20 | 0.74 | 0.47 | 1.00 | 1.56 |
| Financial intermediation | 0.50 | 0.12 | 0.11 | 0.23 | 0.87 |
| Real estate, renting, and business services | 1.59 | 1.37 | 1.02 | 1.61 | 1.67 |
| Public administration and defence; compulsory social security | 1.53 | 0.18 | 0.28 | 0.18 | 3.17 |
| Education | 4.21 | 0.75 | 0.82 | 0.72 | 8.50 |
| Health and social work | 1.68 | 0.84 | 0.50 | 0.91 | 2.68 |
| Other community, social, and personal service activities | 6.33 | 4.31 | 2.04 | 5.25 | 8.19 |
| Other (unspecified) activities | 0.004 | 0.003 | 0.004 | 0.003 | 0.006 |
| Agriculture and non-agriculture combined | 100.00 | 100.00 | 100.00 | 100.00 | 100.00 |

Sources: Estimated from Fifth Economic Census, 2005

of private enterprise in rural India. These three activities put together account for about 77 per cent of the total entrepreneurial activities. Other community, social, and personal service activities, with 6.33 per cent, and education, with 4.22 per cent, come next.

Retail trade, manufacturing, and agriculture also occupy a prominent position for all social groups, although their percentage share varies among the four social groups in rural areas. In the case of retail trade, which is the most preferred activity by all groups, there is not much variation across the four social groups—the percentage share is close to the all-India average. In the case of activities relating to agriculture, while the share of the SCs, STs, and OBCs is more or less similar, the share of agriculture for the HCs is lower. The same is the pattern for manufacturing activity. Thus the share of the HCs is relatively low in the case of agriculture and manufacturing, as compared to SCs, STs, and OBCs. However, the HCs enjoy a relatively greater share in activities associated with education, other community, social, and personal service activities, and health and social work. The difference between the SCs and HCs in the case of these activities is particularly pronounced. For instance, in the case of the HCs, education activity accounts for about 8.50 per cent of the total, as against 0.75 per cent for the SCs, STs, and OBCs.

Table 11.6 gives the share of social groups in rural areas in each of these activities. It brings out some inter-social group differences. The SC share in activities relating to construction, transport and storage, mining and quarrying, retail trade, and agriculture is fairly close to their population share. This is particularly so with respect to their share in construction and transport and storage. However, in the case of education, health and social work, and other community, social, and personal service activities, the share is much less. The HCs enjoy a much higher share in these activities. For instance, almost 90 per cent of education activity is accounted for by the HCs, compared to only 1.78 per cent and 0.79 per cent for the SCs and STs respectively. It is about 7 per cent for the OBCs.

We now look at the urban situation. Table 11.7 provides the share of each social group in 17 activity groups. At the overall level, like in rural areas, retail trade with 44 per cent and manufacturing with 20 per cent account for a major segment of private enterprise in urban

TABLE 11.6: Major Activity of Non-agricultural and Agricultural
Enterprises Across Social Groups in Rural Areas, 2005

(in per cent)

| Major activity group | Social group of owner | | | | |
|---|---|---|---|---|---|
| | SC | ST | OBC | HC | All |
| Agriculture | 10.20 | 6.46 | 45.90 | 37.44 | 100.00 |
| Mining and quarrying | 13.49 | 8.87 | 42.57 | 35.08 | 100.00 |
| Manufacturing | 12.43 | 5.78 | 48.12 | 33.67 | 100.00 |
| Electricity, gas, and water supply | 2.38 | 0.88 | 14.90 | 81.85 | 100.00 |
| Construction | 16.73 | 5.62 | 42.60 | 35.04 | 100.00 |
| Sale, paint, and repair of motor vehicles and motorcycles | 7.02 | 2.37 | 44.59 | 46.02 | 100.00 |
| Wholesale trade | 8.81 | 2.71 | 36.31 | 52.17 | 100.00 |
| Retail trade | 10.65 | 4.41 | 41.42 | 43.52 | 100.00 |
| Hotels and restaurants | 6.99 | 4.34 | 47.63 | 41.04 | 100.00 |
| Transport and storage | 17.14 | 4.26 | 32.80 | 45.79 | 100.00 |
| Post and telecommunications | 6.20 | 1.81 | 33.83 | 58.16 | 100.00 |
| Financial intermediation | 2.39 | 1.03 | 18.90 | 77.67 | 100.00 |
| Real estate, renting, and business services | 8.66 | 2.96 | 41.13 | 47.25 | 100.00 |
| Public administration and defence; compulsory social security | 1.17 | 0.84 | 4.91 | 93.08 | 100.00 |
| Education | 1.78 | 0.90 | 6.90 | 90.43 | 100.00 |
| Health and social work | 5.00 | 1.37 | 21.94 | 71.69 | 100.00 |
| Other community, social, and personal service activities | 6.81 | 1.48 | 33.70 | 58.01 | 100.00 |
| Other (unspecified) activities | 6.12 | 3.96 | 31.56 | 58.36 | 100.00 |
| Agriculture and non-agriculture combined | 10 | 4.60 | 40.57 | 44.84 | 100.00 |

Source: Estimated from Fifth Economic Census, 2005

areas. These two activities put together alone account for about 64 per cent of the total entrepreneurial activities. The other community, social, and personal service activities, with 6.20 per cent, and hotels and restaurants, and transport and storage, with 4 per cent each, come next.

TABLE 11.7: Share of Major Activity Group of Non-agricultural and
Agricultural Enterprises by Social Groups in Urban Areas, 2005

. (in per cent)

| Major activity group | Total | Social group of owner | | | |
|---|---|---|---|---|---|
| | | SC | ST | OBC | HC |
| Agriculture | 2.28 | 2.72 | 4.42 | 3.43 | 1.45 |
| Mining and quarrying | 0.15 | 0.19 | 0.22 | 0.18 | 0.12 |
| Manufacturing | 19.42 | 20.03 | 17.36 | 23.98 | 16.67 |
| Electricity, gas, and water supply | 0.14 | 0.07 | 0.09 | 0.09 | 0.18 |
| Construction | 0.92 | 1.70 | 1.52 | 0.95 | 0.78 |
| Sale, paint, and repair of motor vehicles and motorcycles | 2.94 | 2.04 | 2.44 | 3.02 | 3.02 |
| Wholesale trade | 2.97 | 2.09 | 2.40 | 2.46 | 3.41 |
| Retail trade | 43.98 | 44.09 | 44.66 | 42.59 | 44.78 |
| Hotels and restaurants | 4.27 | 3.93 | 5.18 | 4.70 | 4.02 |
| Transport and storage | 4.05 | 7.78 | 6.81 | 3.46 | 3.84 |
| Post and telecommunications | 2.40 | 1.97 | 2.23 | 2.17 | 2.60 |
| Financial intermediation | 1.00 | 0.34 | 0.53 | 0.62 | 1.33 |
| Real estate, renting, and business services | 3.74 | 2.85 | 2.91 | 3.17 | 4.23 |
| Public administration and defence; compulsory social security | 1.13 | 0.17 | 0.39 | 0.22 | 1.82 |
| Education | 2.24 | 1.02 | 1.34 | 1.12 | 3.11 |
| Health and social work | 2.17 | 1.11 | 1.38 | 1.48 | 2.74 |
| Other community, social, and personal service activities | 6.20 | 7.91 | 6.11 | 6.36 | 5.91 |
| Other (unspecified) activities | 0.00 | 0.00 | 0.00 | 0.00 | 0.00 |
| Agriculture and non-agriculture combined | 100.00 | 100.00 | 100.00 | 100.00 | 100.00 |

Source: Estimated from Fifth Economic Census, 2005

Retail trade and manufacturing are also the major activities for all social groups. In the case of retail trade, the share of each of the social groups was quite close to the all-India average of 40 per cent. In the case of the second-most important activity, namely manufacturing, the share varies across social groups. The share for the HCs was lower as compared to the SCs and OBCs. Similarly, in the case of education, and health and social work, the share was also greater among the HCs as compared to the SCs and other social groups. For instance, while the share of education activity for the HCs was about 3 per cent, it was about 1 per cent in the case of other social groups.

Table 11.8 also provides the share of each social group in 17 major activities in urban areas. It indicates that the share of the SCs and STs in

TABLE 11.8: Major Activity of Non-agricultural and Agricultural Enterprises Across Social Groups in Urban Areas, 2005

(in per cent)

| Major activity group | Social group of owner | | | | |
| --- | --- | --- | --- | --- | --- |
| | SC | ST | OBC | HC | All |
| Agriculture | 8.34 | 4.14 | 51.48 | 36.04 | 100.00 |
| Mining and quarrying | 8.76 | 3.15 | 41.35 | 46.74 | 100.00 |
| Manufacturing | 7.19 | 1.91 | 42.22 | 48.68 | 100.00 |
| Electricity, gas, and water supply | 3.50 | 1.41 | 22.18 | 72.91 | 100.00 |
| Construction | 12.95 | 3.54 | 35.32 | 48.19 | 100.00 |
| Sale, paint, and repair of motor vehicles and motorcycles | 4.85 | 1.77 | 35.13 | 58.25 | 100.00 |
| Wholesale trade | 4.89 | 1.72 | 28.29 | 65.09 | 100.00 |
| Retail trade | 6.99 | 2.17 | 33.11 | 57.73 | 100.00 |
| Hotels and restaurants | 6.41 | 2.59 | 37.64 | 53.36 | 100.00 |
| Transport and storage | 13.41 | 3.59 | 29.24 | 53.77 | 100.00 |
| Post and telecommunications | 5.72 | 1.98 | 30.94 | 61.36 | 100.00 |
| Financial intermediation | 2.35 | 1.12 | 21.25 | 75.27 | 100.00 |
| Real estate, renting, and business services | 5.31 | 1.66 | 28.95 | 64.09 | 100.00 |
| Public administration and defence; compulsory social security | 1.02 | 0.74 | 6.55 | 91.69 | 100.00 |
| Education | 3.17 | 1.27 | 17.04 | 78.52 | 100.00 |
| Health and social work | 3.58 | 1.36 | 23.38 | 71.68 | 100.00 |
| Other community, social, and personal service activities | 8.89 | 2.10 | 35.05 | 53.97 | 100.00 |
| Other (unspecified) activities | 7.19 | 2.14 | 37.31 | 53.36 | 100.00 |
| Agriculture and non-agriculture combined | 6.97 | 2.13 | 34.19 | 56.70 | 100.00 |

Source: Estimated from Fifth Economic Census, 2005

two prominent activities, namely retail trade and manufacturing, was much lower (than their share in their population) as compared to that of the OBCs and HCs. The share of the HCs was particularly high in the case of public administration, defence, compulsory social security, education, and financial intermediation. In fact, in the case of financial intermediation, the share of the HCs in total activity was above 91 per cent. In two other activities, it was more than 75 per cent.

This chapter examined the pattern of ownership of private enterprise by caste, which includes the SCs, STs, OBCs, and HCs, for 1998 and 2005 in rural and urban areas. The study observed significant inter-caste disparities in the ownership of private enterprise in rural and urban areas. While the share of the SCs and STs was much lower than their share in the county's population, the share of the HCs was much above their population share in the rural areas. In the case of the OBCs, their share in private enterprise was fairly close to their share in population. Thus the OBCs and HCs had better access to private enterprise in rural areas. A similar pattern is observed in the urban areas as well. The share of the SCs in private enterprise is much lower than their share in total population. While their share in the country's population is about 21 per cent, they account for only 6 per cent of the country's private enterprise, which is three-and-a-half times less than their share in the urban population. The HC share was much above their population share. In the case of the OBCs and STs, like in rural areas, their shares in enterprise were fairly close to population share, and hence, disparities were relatively less in their case. The concentration of ownership of private enterprises among the HCs was reflected in employment as well. The bulk of the employment total and of hired workers were concentrated in private enterprises owned by the HCs, followed by the OBCs. The quite meagre ownership of private enterprises by the SCs reflects the negative consequences of the historical denial of property rights to low-caste Untouchables.

It also emerged from the results that most of the private enterprises owned by the SCs and STs were OAEs operated with family labour at the household level. Their share in enterprises with hired labour, namely NDEs and DEs, was relatively less as compared to the OBCs and HCs. The share of SC and ST enterprise was also less in some types of enterprises, which include retail trade, hotel and restaurants, manufacturing, and particularly education and health and social services. The latter are mainly concentrated among the HCs.

These results clearly revealed the negative consequences of the historical denial of property rights (that is right to undertake production and business except for some occupations that are considered as impure and polluting) to the SCs, and was evident in their meagre ownership of private enterprise and business in rural and urban areas. The government had recognized the problem of lack of ownership of capital among the SCs and developed policies to enhance their access to enterprises and business (Planning Commission 2008). As these results revealed, there is still a lot to be done to ensure equitable access to private enterprise and business for the SCs. It seems obvious that in order to improve the ownership of capital in terms of enterprise and business, a definite policy is necessary to ensure not only availability of capital, but also provision of basic infrastructure in terms of land, power, credit, and market support. Some kind of affirmative-action policy is necessary to promote ownership of enterprise and business among the SCs in rural and urban areas. In this respect, the experience of countries such as Malaysia and South Africa, which are faced with similar problems with respect to their Malaya and Black population, may be used for Dalit economic empowerment through the promotion of enterprises and businesses (Balshaw and Goldberg 2005).

## NOTES

1. Corresponding to Divisions 02, 03, 04, 05, and 06 of Section 1 of National Industrial Classification (NIC)–1987.
2. Divisions 00 and 01 of Section 1 of NIC–1987.

## REFERENCES

Ambedkar, B.R. (1987), 'Essential Features of Hindu Social Order', in Vasant Moon (ed.), *Dr. Babasaheb Ambedkar: Writings and Speeches*, vol. 5, Education Department, Government of Maharashtra.

Balshaw, Tony and Jonathan Goldberg (2005), *Cracking Broad-based Black Economic Empowerment, Code and Scorecard Unpacked*, Cape Town: Human and Rousseau.

Ministry of Statistics and Programme Implementation (1998), *Fourth Economic Census*, Government of India.

Ministry of Statistics and Programme Implementation (2005), *Fifth Economic Census*, Government of India.

Olivelle, Patrick (2005), *Manus Code of Law, A Critical Edition and Translation of the Manava-Dharmastra*, New Delhi: Oxford University Press.

Planning Commission, Government of India (2008), *Eleventh Five Year Plan (2007–2012)*, vol. II, Social Sector, New Delhi: Oxford University Press.

Thorat, Sukhadeo (1999), 'Social Security in Unorganised Sector: How Secure are the Discriminated Groups?', *Indian Journal of Labour Economics*, special issue, vol. 48, no. 4, pp. 15–49.

Thorat, Sukhadeo and Narendra Kumar (2008), *B.R. Ambedkar: Perspectives on Social Exclusion and Inclusive Policies*, New Delhi: Oxford University Press.

# 12

## Minority Status and Labour Market Outcomes[*]
### Does India Have Minority Enclaves?

*Maitreyi Bordia Das*

This chapter examines how minority status—which, more than a numerical construct, is a social construct—plays out in labour market outcomes. It builds on a conceptualization of the labour market not merely as a market in the economic sense but as a site where cultural and social relations play out (see Das 2005, 2006; Das and Desai 2003). It assumes that social, historical, and cultural factors play a major role in the functioning of the market. Based on data from the 61st Round of the National Sample Survey (NSS) this chapter addresses employment outcomes for two sets of minorities in India—Dalits and Muslims. The first is a caste minority and the second a religious minority and, despite differences, they are similar in many respects.

The central question this chapter asks is: do minority groups build 'enclave labour markets' if they have the requisite wherewithal? The idea of 'ethnic enclaves' or 'ethnic labour markets' was first developed in the US context by Alejandro Portes and his colleagues (Wilson and Portes 1980; Portes and Jensen 1989; 1992; Wilson and Martin 1982) who maintain that ethnic minorities who enter the US labour market are discriminated against because they are unfamiliar with the language and culture and are obviously distinct from the mainstream. But they do not necessarily enter at a disadvantage if they have the human capital. If they do, they build 'ethnic enclaves' of

[*] The findings and interpretations are those of the author and should not be attributed to the World Bank or any of its member countries or affiliated institutions.

self-employment and do well in these ventures. This chapter applies this conceptual model to the Indian context by testing it for two minorities—each historically discriminated against in different ways. Unfortunately, lack of earnings data does not allow us to directly test whether self-employment has higher rewards than regular salaried work and, therefore, whether these ventures are successful.

## ETHNIC ENCLAVES AND INDIAN LABOUR MARKET

The role of ethnicity in labour market outcomes has long engaged the attention of sociologists interested in social inequality. In hypothesizing about how minority status could affect employment allocation, as noted earlier we use the work of Portes and others (Wilson and Portes 1980; Portes and Jensen 1989, 1992; Wilson and Martin 1982) and their idea of 'ethnic labour markets'. Some of their arguments can be applied more readily in the Indian context than others, which therefore, need adaptation. The main thrust of the argument made by Portes, Wilson, and their colleagues is that immigrants who enter the US labour market are discriminated against. They may also face restrictions on work due to their immigrant status. Often they live in geographical concentrations or ghettos. However, Portes and others disagree with the conventional notion that all immigrants enter the labour market at the bottom end and, with assimilation, work their way up. On the contrary, they argue, when immigrants have the necessary human capital, they build their own 'ethnic enclaves'—self-employed ventures which are a part of an 'ethnic labour market'. The role of ethnicity in labour markets has been empirically tested in other places as well (Semyonov 1988 for Israel; Evans 1989 for Australia; Clark and Drinkwater 1999 for the UK), and the ethnic enclave idea has held up in a variety of cultural and geographical settings.

Portes and others argue that 'ethnic enclaves' in fact provide positive rewards to their members and 'ethnic entrepreneurship' is an 'unorthodox, but important avenue for social mobility of ethnic minorities...(and can) suggest alternative policies for those still mired in poverty' (Portes and Jensen 1992: 418). Thus immigrant entrepreneurs actually produce the characteristics of the primary and not of the secondary market in terms of income. These entrepreneurs also prefer to hire individuals from their own ethnic group (in the process perhaps replicating relationships based on hierarchy, privilege, and exploitation among their own ethnic group), thus creating a social and labour network, which interacts as a group with the outside market. In so doing, the enclave has the solidarity and protection of numbers, and helps its members circumvent discrimination. It also skirts competition from the mainstream and majority. A large body of work by Marcel Fafchamps also focuses on the positive role that networks play especially in trading (see for example Fafchamps and Gubert 2007).

The important question for this chapter is whether the status of Indian minorities is analogous to that of ethnic minorities in the United States in terms of their participation in the labour market. Do Indian minorities also skirt a discriminatory 'primary' market to engage and excel in a 'secondary' labour market that is founded on their strengths and networks? With the data at our disposal, we cannot answer this question conclusively. But in building our hypothesis, and drawing on the conceptual work on ethnic enclaves, we believe that the idea can be extended to the larger context of religious and caste minorities, and we can, thus, expect to have 'minority enclaves' or 'minority labour markets'. Therefore, due to data limitations, rather than look at earnings in self-employment as the marker of minority enclaves, we look at entry into self-employment as that marker of enclaves.

Are Dalits and Muslims comparable? Indian academics are often startled at the comparison between Dalits and Muslims. The two minorities grew out of very different historical circumstances—one the product of an age-old ideology of caste and the other the product of waves of conversion and invasion, so complex that it is impossible to separate who was converted and when. There are other differences as well—those that play out in the present. The most important of these stems from Dalits as beneficiaries of a system of reserved quotas in public education and employment that allows them access to the salaried labour market (since the major part of this salaried market is in the public sector). A minor difference is that while there are large conclaves of Muslims in urban areas, Dalits reside mostly in rural areas. Finally, Muslims have strong elite and social networks that have allowed them to secure space in trading occupations, while Dalit networks, although strong politically, are weak in terms of garnering access to assets and markets. Yet, we argue that as sociologically conceptual categories, Dalits and Muslims have strong similarities that make them comparable entities for this analysis.

First, the numerical representation of Dalits and Muslims in our sample (and in the population as a whole) is roughly similar—18 per cent are Dalits and 13 per cent are Muslims. Second, perhaps the greatest social similarity between them is that there is an elaborate dominant religious ideology that 'excludes' them. The Brahmanical ideology that confers the status of the 'other' to these groups plays out also in the type of occupations they pursue. Third, while most social groups in India have historically and hierarchically determined occupations, the important similarity among Muslims and Dalits is that they are mostly landless.

## Key Hypothesis, Data, and Methods

Our main interest in this chapter is to find out what educated Muslims and educated Dalits do. We start from the assumption that for uneducated individuals, the casual labour market is the default option. But with some human capital—particularly secondary education and above—the chances of getting salaried jobs and better quality self-employment increase. For Dalits, reserved jobs in government should take care of some of the supply of educated labour from amongst them. The remainder of the educated persons ought to be in self-employment, since they should have the requisite skills. In the case of Muslims, since they have no quotas in government jobs, they would be more likely to be in self-employment than are Dalits. While we are unable to test if such engagement is better or worse for them than regular salaried work, disproportionate engagement in self-employment nevertheless could be an indication of their lack of options in the 'primary' or the more coveted market. Thus, as pointed out earlier, due to data limitations, rather than look at earnings in self-employment as the marker of minority enclaves, we look at entry into self-employment as that marker of enclaves.

Data for this analysis come from the Employment and Unemployment Schedule (Schedule 10) of the NSS 61st Round, conducted in 2004–5. All analysis is weighted and the multivariate analysis is conducted separately for urban and rural men in the age-group 15–59 years, excluding current students, and based on usual principal status activity only. The reason for excluding students is that in the age-group 15–25 years many are still students and this affects the labour force participation rates. If we take only those individuals who are available for employment, we can come to a more precise understanding of who is employed and who stays out of the labour market.

Our analytic sample includes 104,738 men in rural areas and 101,073 in urban areas. We first predict the probability of participating in the labour market at all and then proceed to understand what employment types these men would be allocated. Thus, for the first set of analyses, we report the odds ratios of a logistic regression model where the dependent variable is a dummy for participating in the labour market in the last 365 days.

For the second set of analyses we use a multinomial logistic regression model where the dependent variable has five categories that suggest a loose hierarchy of employment types to assess individuals' allocation to different employment types—viz. regular salaried, non-farm self-employed, farm-based self-employed, casual labour, and out of the labour force. We use regular salaried work as the comparison category, since this is the preferred form of employment for educated individuals and the employment type they aspire to—not merely due to its advantages in terms of wages but also in terms of job security, benefits, and status. We then estimate the likelihood of assignment of individuals to each of the employment categories simultaneously. Unlike Portes and others, we use entry into preferred employment categories, rather than earnings, to test our hypothesis.

The independent variables of interest are caste/religion and education (denoting ability to conduct successful self-employed ventures). Caste minorities are coded as three dummies—Dalit, Adivasi, with non-Dalit/Adivasi as the omitted reference category. Religious minorities are coded as three dummies as well—Muslim, other religions, with Hindu as the omitted reference category. While the two sets of minorities are, for the purposes of our social measurement, different, in that the comparison category for Muslims is Hindu and the comparison category for Dalits is non-Dalit (regardless of religion), yet conceptually the broad reference category is non-Dalit/Adivasi (or broadly 'upper caste') Hindu.

Education is coded as four dummies—some primary, primary completed, and post-primary, with uneducated as the omitted reference. We realize that post-primary education is a very broad category but when we run models for rural areas, the numbers of minorities with higher levels of education fall to such an extent that our analysis becomes untenable and so we conflate higher education into 'post-primary'.[1] Individual and household demographic and residence characteristics, including landownership, are controls. Land is an important determinant in India of the type of employment individuals are assigned, for not only is it a marker of social status but also of capital. Thus we expect land to be important even in self-employment at least in rural areas. In order to understand the effect of education with minority status, we add also interaction terms (education multiplied by caste and religious status) to the main model.

The coefficients of multinomial logistic models are based on a reference category dependent variable (in this case regular salaried work). The coefficients for each of the other dependent variables have to be interpreted in relation with the omitted category. This can sometimes become confusing. In order to have a clearer understanding of the coefficients, we calculate mean predicted probabilities for each dependent variable category with the main independent variables of interest (in this case Dalit and Muslim). For instance, we first calculate the mean predicted probability of being in formal employment for Muslims, then calculate the same probabilities if they were not Muslim but retained all other characteristics. The difference gives us the net effect of being Muslim for formal work. While we have undertaken the analysis separately for men and women, the focus is on men and we report only those results.

Finally, this analysis is a first step towards understanding the idea of minority enclaves. While some of its results are new and hitherto unexplored, there are also limitations arising from an analysis of aggregate data. For instance, we are not able to capture whether self-employment is a choice or a necessity since we cannot see returns to self-employment in the form of earnings and, hence, we do not know if minorities that build enclaves do so by choice. Therefore, we measure returns by entry into job types. Future analysis focusing on earnings would be able to address some of these more complex issues conclusively. Moreover, self-employment is a vast and heterogeneous category and some jobs may be lucrative while others may be 'disguised wage employment'. We cannot separate different types of self-employment and in the process miss out on the heterogeneity. Finally, we have no way of understanding the value of networks and other forms of 'entrepreneurial wherewithal' that is so important in building minority enclaves. We recommend that future studies focus on these themes to understand the barriers to self-employment better.

## Results

The descriptive and bivariate associations for this analysis are contained in Table 12.1. Tables 12.2 and 12.3 are predicted probabilities calculated from multinomial regressions and indicate the effects of being Dalit and being Muslim. Table A12.1 in the Annexure lays out the odds ratios of logistic regression models predicting the probability of labour force participation, while Tables A12.2 and A12.3 lay out the coefficients of the multinomial regression models in rural and urban areas respectively.

When we tabulate the allocation to employment types by religion in urban areas we find that 47 per cent of Muslim men and 37 per cent of men from other religions, including Hindus, are in non-farm self-employment. However, 25 per cent of Muslim men but 37 per cent of Hindu men are in salaried employment. In rural areas, where farming is the predominant form of employment for the majority of men, we find Muslims slightly less likely to be farmers and here too they are more likely to be self-employed in non-farm enterprises and less so in formal jobs. There seems to be little difference by religion among men who opt to stay out of the labour force or join casual labour (except that men from other minority religions are far less likely to be casual labourers and have generally much better employment outcomes than either Hindus or Muslims).

Tabulations by caste indicate that in urban areas, 'general category' men (or upper caste Hindu men) have an advantage, perhaps

TABLE 12.1: Where does Education Take Men in the Labour Market?

| Men | No education | Below primary | Completed primary | Post-primary | Total |
|---|---|---|---|---|---|
| | | | Proportion | | |
| | | Rural | | | |
| Regular | 0.05 | 0.07 | 0.09 | 0.22 | 0.14 |
| Non-farm self-employed | 0.21 | 0.25 | 0.26 | 0.26 | 0.25 |
| Self-employed farmers | 0.33 | 0.35 | 0.37 | 0.33 | 0.34 |
| Casual | 0.37 | 0.29 | 0.25 | 0.12 | 0.22 |
| Not in labour force | 0.05 | 0.04 | 0.04 | 0.07 | 0.06 |
| Total | 1.00 | 1.00 | 1.00 | 1.00 | 1.00 |
| | | Urban | | | |
| Regular | 0.18 | 0.25 | 0.28 | 0.42 | 0.35 |
| Non-farm self-employed | 0.37 | 0.39 | 0.38 | 0.37 | 0.37 |
| Self-employed farmers | 0.06 | 0.05 | 0.05 | 0.04 | 0.04 |
| Casual | 0.31 | 0.25 | 0.22 | 0.08 | 0.14 |
| Not in labour force | 0.09 | 0.07 | 0.07 | 0:09 | 0.08 |
| Total | 1.00 | 1.00 | 1.00 | 1.00 | 1.00 |

Source: Author's calculations based on NSS 61st Round for men age 15–59 years excluding students

Note: Numbers denote bivariate associations between education level and employment type 2004–5

TABLE 12.2: Dalit Effect on the Mean Predicted Probabilities of Various Employment Categories (Men Only)

| | Regular | Non-farm self-employed | Self-employed farmers | Casual workers | Out of the labour force |
|---|---|---|---|---|---|
| | | Dalit effect for rural males | | | |
| Non-dalit | 0.10 | 0.21 | 0.37 | 0.28 | 0.05 |
| Dalit | 0.09 | 0.15 | 0.19 | 0.52 | 0.05 |
| Dalit effect | −0.01 | −0.06 | −0.18 | 0.25 | 0.00 |
| | | Dalit effect for urban males | | | |
| Non-SC | 0.39 | 0.39 | 0.03 | 0.12 | 0.07 |
| SC | 0.38 | 0.27 | 0.02 | 0.23 | 0.10 |
| SC effect | −0.01 | −0.12 | −0.01 | 0.12 | 0.02 |

Source: Author's calculations based on multinomial logistic regression models—NSS 61st Round for men age 15–59 years excluding students

**TABLE 12.3: Muslim Effect on the Mean Predicted Probabilities of Various Employment Categories (Men Only)**

| | Regular | Non-darm self-employed | Self-employed farmers | Casual workers | Out of the labour force |
|---|---|---|---|---|---|
| *Muslim effect for rural males* | | | | | |
| Non-Muslim | 0.10 | 0.19 | 0.34 | 0.33 | 0.05 |
| Muslim | 0.07 | 0.29 | 0.26 | 0.32 | 0.06 |
| Muslim effect | −0.02 | 0.10 | −0.08 | 0.00 | 0.01 |
| *Muslim effect for urban males* | | | | | |
| | Regular | Non-darm self-employed | Self-employed farmers | Casual workers | Out of the labour force |
| Non-Muslim | 0.41 | 0.35 | 0.03 | 0.13 | 0.08 |
| Muslim | 0.27 | 0.48 | 0.02 | 0.15 | 0.08 |
| Muslim effect | −0.14 | 0.12 | 0.00 | 0.02 | 0.00 |

*Source*: Author's calculations based on multinomial logistic regression models—NSS 61st Round for men age 15–59 years Excluding students

because there are greater opportunities in these areas in the private sector, which does not have job quotas by caste. But this difference disappears in rural areas where formal jobs are limited and restricted to the public sector. Men from the 'general category' also have an advantage in non-farm employment, both in urban and rural areas. Dalit men in rural areas are distinct from other caste categories in having very low access to farm-based self-employment. Only 19 per cent of Dalit men as compared to 44 per cent Adivasi men, 32 per cent OBC men, and 35 per cent men from the 'general category' are self-employed farmers in rural areas. Perhaps as a result, Dalit men are more than twice as likely as other groups to be casual labourers. When we look at non-farm self-employment, our major employment type of interest, we find in rural areas that Dalits are slightly less likely than OBCs and general category men to be in such employment in rural areas, but this difference widens dramatically in urban areas. In cities and towns, 28 per cent of Dalit men but 44 per cent men from the general category and 39 per cent men from the OBC category are in self-employed ventures.

When we look at where education takes men in the Indian labour market (Table 12.1) we find results that seem to draw attention to the heterogeneity of self-employment. Increasing levels of education are associated with jobs in the salaried labour market and a dramatic decline in their representation in casual jobs. But education does not seem to increase the likelihood of being in either farm-based or non-farm self-employment. There seems to be roughly equal distribution of men from different educational categories in non-farm self-employment. In rural areas, education also does not seem to affect men's participation in farming and roughly one-third of men from every educational category are farmers. This probably points to the existence of both landowners and workers in farming.

The multivariate results for labour force participation are broadly in keeping with our analyses based on previous rounds of the NSS. Muslim status has no significant association with labour force participation for men (but it has huge effects for women) in either urban or rural areas. Dalit status is on the other hand associated with higher labour force participation in rural areas but has no effect in urban areas. Higher levels of education have a positive association with men's labour force participation (though not women's, as we have discussed elsewhere) and these effects are expectedly stronger in cities and towns than in villages since labour market opportunities are greater in the former. We have argued elsewhere that land is not merely an economic asset but also a marker of status and influences a number of outcomes. Here we find that owning land is associated not only with greater likelihood of labour force participation but also the likelihood of being in non-farm ventures.

The complexity of this analysis comes from the multinomial models, which estimate the probability of being in different employment categories compared to salaried work. Results from urban areas are more relevant than from rural areas when we look at self-employment. In rural areas, farming is still the major basis for employment and the non-farm sector is in its infancy. But in urban areas, where the real non-farm jobs are located, being Dalit means that men are ever so slightly disadvantaged even in regular salaried work, but hugely disadvantaged in self-employment. Dalit status makes urban men 12 per cent less likely to be self-employed. Of course, the real effects of being Dalit are felt in rural areas, since Dalits are disproportionately concentrated in villages. Here they have a 25 per cent greater likelihood of being casual labourers and a similar though slightly smaller likelihood of being out of self-employed farming.

Most insightful are the interaction effects between education level and Dalit or Muslim status. The multiplied effects of Dalit status and education show that Dalit men with post-primary education have distinctly lower returns in the form of formal jobs compared to other men. In that case, should educated Dalit men not set up small businesses and move to the next best alternative, because education gives them better skills and the formal labour market does not absorb them? It seems not, because they are even more disadvantaged in non-farm self-employment than they are in formal employment. In the wake of expanding education, once Dalit men do not get access to salaried jobs, they crowd into casual labour, or stay out of the labour force if they can afford to and this effect is present for both rural and urban Dalit men.

The picture that emerges for employment options for educated Dalit men is that they have an advantage in low-end formal jobs— ones that require primary education—but a glass ceiling or a system of rationing seems to be in existence that deters their entry into higher level jobs. It is also possible that there are more low-end jobs in the government than those that require higher education. These results also indicate that once reserved quotas are filled up (especially for Group A, B, and C jobs), Dalit candidates have no other avenue such as self-employment open to them. Expressed differently, job quotas create a system of rationing of regular salaried (public sector) jobs for Dalit men. A corollary of this is also the generation of an entrenched elite among Dalit men, who benefit from reservations across generations.

Being Muslim has large and significant positive effects for participation in self-employment in general but in urban areas there are almost equally large but negative effects of being in regular salaried jobs (Table 12.3). So being Muslim in a city or town makes men 12 per cent more likely to be self-employed and 14 per cent less likely to have a salaried job. In rural areas, Muslims, like Dalits, are not landowners and so being Muslim makes men 8 per cent less likely to be self-employed in farming—a disadvantage less pronounced than for Dalits. Again, the really vivid results are for the multiplied effects of Muslim and post-primary education. We would have expected that if they built 'enclave labour markets' from choice, that the more educated ones would be more likely to be self-employed, at least in urban areas. This is not borne out from NSS data. Post-primary education does not increase the likelihood of Muslim men to be self-employed. On the contrary, when compared to salaried work, post-primary educated Muslim men become more likely to engage in casual labour or stay out of the labour force. So, much like Dalit men, Muslim men too stay out of the labour market if they can afford to and, if they absolutely cannot, perhaps they join casual labour. The 'education penalty' also seems to be higher for Muslim men than for Dalit men.

## DISCUSSION

The minority enclaves hypothesis rests on the assumption that those who are excluded from or disadvantaged in formal employment (or the primary labour market) will set up alternative and lucrative 'enclaves' or 'minority labour markets' based on (non-farm) self-employment. In India, when we say formal employment we mean teachers, clerks, public sector medical providers, security personnel, and office attendants, mostly in the public sector—jobs that come with security, pension, and several important perquisites that confer social status particularly in rural areas but also in small towns and cities. While non-farm self-employed occupations are not necessarily high status and are highly heterogeneous, they are nonetheless the next best alternative to formal jobs. An important mediating factor in the push out of formal jobs is the effect of job quotas or affirmative action for Dalits.

The results from this analysis demonstrate that the 'minority enclave hypothesis' does not hold for Dalits but it does so over-whelmingly for Muslims. Dalits are highly unlikely to be in non-farm self-employment and are the least likely builders of minority enclaves. We do not a see a 'push' out of salaried work for Dalits in the same way as we do for Muslims. Perhaps reserved jobs in government work towards bringing them on a par with non-Dalits in the small pool of formal jobs. However, it is not because they have regular jobs that they do not build minority enclaves, but because they do not have the wherewithal to move into self-employment.

Several pieces of anecdotal evidence point to the exclusion of Dalits from the credit markets. Field studies and qualitative data also point to the possibility of small Dalit entrepreneurs, especially in rural areas, being prevented from moving out of caste-based occupations into self-employed ventures through social pressure and ostracism (see for instance Venkateswarlu 1990, cited in Thorat 2007) and in other ways being denied fair opportunities to participate in more lucrative trades. Therefore, Dalits in rural areas may be self-employed in a variety of low-end service trades like masonry and carpentry but moving out of these trades or expanding them may present significant barriers, as they are locked into a web of social relations based on these trades.

In urban areas, Dalits who do not get salaried jobs are actually just casual labourers. Here, in these 'melting pots', 'traditional' Dalit trades have little value and Dalits who may have wanted to enter self-employment do not have the 'entrepreneurial wherewithal' to do so. If Dalits had the requisite wherewithal in the form of networks, access to capital, markets, and raw material needed to start small self-employed ventures, indeed they would have done so. But since Dalits (and Adivasis) also are disproportionately poor, they lack the means to form minority enclaves, and thus they crowd into casual labour. Therefore, the second reason why they cannot build minority enclaves is because they do not have the requisite access to the inputs required to set up these businesses.

Muslim men seem to fit the minority enclave hypothesis to an extent. They do not get regular salaried jobs and the 'push' out of salaried work emerges clearly in our analysis, although some may argue that this is not a 'push' out of salaried jobs but a 'pull' into self-employment. Hence they end up highly likely to be self-employed in non-farm occupations. These effects are much more pronounced in urban areas, in spite of the fact that there are more salaried jobs. Muslims live and operate their businesses in geographical clusters within cities and towns, such as Crawford Market in Mumbai to cite a well-known example. Other cities with a substantial Muslim population, such as Hyderabad, Bhopal, Kolkata, and Patna, also have geographical enclaves, in much the same way as Portes and his colleagues (Wilson and Portes 1980; Portes and Jensen 1989, 1992) describe the business operations of Chinese and other Asian ethnic groups in US cities. Thus, for Muslims, it is fairly apparent that minority enclaves are a reality—one that plays out more intensely in urban areas due perhaps to the structure of opportunities and the absence of farm-related work.

The quality of the self-employed occupations Muslims pursue, however, leaves us in a quandary while asserting that Muslims are the builders of minority enclaves. Ideally, as we have pointed out, we would have liked to use earnings to look at returns to self-employment. But in the absence of that, we find that the interaction effects of Muslim with post-primary education in urban areas show that post-primary education confers almost a disadvantage: it does not seem to affect their allocation either to salaried work or to non-farm self-employment but does increase their likelihood of opting out of the labour force—and if they cannot afford to, they join the casual labour market.

Given that the multiplied effect of post-primary education and Muslim status makes Muslim men more likely to opt out of the labour force, or even to be casual labourers, what is the implication of their overwhelming concentration in self-employment? Perhaps Muslim men with lower levels of education enter into low-paying self-employed occupations in an effort to skirt the discriminatory formal labour market. But those with higher levels of education do not have access to higher-order self-employed occupations that are commensurate with their educational levels and they opt out of the labour force or wait out for other opportunities. Earlier analysis (Das 2002) indicates that half of all Muslim men are traders, merchants, and shopkeepers and the other half are in a range of petty occupations such as tailoring, weaving dyeing, transport, and in building activity as carpenters and masons.

The results of this study bring out some important issues for the employment outcomes of minorities in particular and the Indian labour market as a whole.

First, while reserved quotas may temper the disadvantage in

formal jobs for Dalit men, there are not enough of these jobs to keep even educated men out of casual labour. The effect of poverty and perhaps lack of networks and other 'entrepreneurial wherewithal' is felt most strongly by Dalits who cannot enter self-employment due to a variety of social and economic reasons. For Muslims, the lack of options in regular salaried jobs appears to push them to build minority enclaves. Thus the idea of ethnic enclaves in the Indian context applies to Muslim men.

Second, education seems to have counterintuitive effects on allocation to employment types.[2] In the absence of acceptable employment opportunities, educated minority men would rather opt out of the labour force if they can afford to, or else, undertake low status employment. The returns to education in the form of entry into preferred employment—regular salaried jobs—are lower for these groups compared to 'caste Hindus'.

Given our results and the limitations of our data, we venture a last tentative word on whether 'minority enclaves' are good or bad. For Muslims it appears that the 'push' out of salaried jobs combined with lack of access to land in rural areas has historically necessitated that they set up enclaves—it is likely that if we do have earnings, we may find that this employment strategy is a positive one; but in social terms, if enclave labour markets come into being due to a 'push', they are likely to have negative externalities in other areas.

What is puzzling about the results for Muslims is that education is not associated with either salaried work or with non-farm self-employment, but rather with casual work or with being out of the labour force. This seems to indicate that the returns to education for Muslims are low in the form of entry into coveted jobs. In that case, can the enclave labour markets they build be entirely positive? We cannot say for sure, but it appears as though we may be seeing discrimination in the labour market for educated Muslim men in much the same way as we see for Dalit men.

For Dalits, low availability of credit, being typed into caste-specific menial occupations, combined with a social pressure to stay in those occupations means that they do not have access to 'enclave labour markets' even if they are educated. So, while the salaried labour market absorbs some educated Dalits, clearly there are not enough of those jobs to absorb the growing pool of educated Dalits. What do they do? Rather than move into the next best strategy—of non-farm self-employment—they either stay out of the labour force or, as last resort, become casual labourers. Thus the builders of 'minority enclaves' in India are predominantly Muslims and they seem to act in much the same way as ethnic minorities in other countries do.

ANNEXURE

TABLE A12.1: Odds Ratios of Logistic Regression Models Predicting the Probability of Labour Force Participation

|  | Rural men | | | Urban men | | |
|---|---|---|---|---|---|---|
| Age | 1.242*** | 1.244*** | 1.243*** | 1.338*** | 1.339*** | 1.338*** |
|  | (0.019) | (0.019) | (0.019) | (0.029) | (0.029) | (0.029) |
| Age squared | 0.996*** | 0.996*** | 0.996*** | 0.995*** | 0.995*** | 0.995*** |
|  | (0.000) | (0.000) | (0.000) | (0.000) | (0.000) | (0.000) |
| Married | 2.753*** | 2.735*** | 2.725*** | 2.888*** | 2.886*** | 2.874*** |
|  | (0.088) | (0.089) | (0.089) | (0.132) | (0.132) | (0.133) |
| Household size | 1.012 | 1.014 | 1.015 | 1.015 | 1.014 | 1.015 |
|  | (0.012) | (0.012) | (0.012) | (0.015) | (0.015) | (0.015) |
| Below_prim | 1.512*** | 1.549*** | 1.559*** | 1.663*** | 1.671*** | 1.702*** |
|  | (0.093) | (0.094) | (0.094) | (0.167) | (0.168) | (0.171) |
| Prim_comp | 1.634*** | 1.682*** | 1.873*** | 2.492*** | 2.509*** | 2.517*** |
|  | (0.088) | (0.089) | (0.117) | (0.143) | (0.143) | (0.193) |
| Postpri | 1.952*** | 2.054*** | 2.241*** | 2.743*** | 2.782*** | 3.301*** |
|  | (0.076) | (0.079) | (0.095) | (0.107) | (0.112) | (0.142) |
| HH head | 3.233*** | 3.217*** | 3.226*** | 2.963*** | 2.942*** | 2.970*** |
|  | (0.105) | (0.106) | (0.106) | (0.141) | (0.141) | (0.142) |
| spouse | 0.065*** | 0.067*** | 0.066*** | 0.034*** | 0.033*** | 0.033*** |
|  | (0.267) | (0.263) | (0.262) | (0.420) | (0.420) | (0.422) |
| Land_poss | 1.274*** | 1.275*** | 1.277*** | 1.109** | 1.108** | 1.112** |
|  | (0.040) | (0.041) | (0.041) | (0.049) | (0.049) | (0.051) |
| North | 0.955 | 1.010 | 1.004 | 0.734** | 0.749** | 0.750** |
|  | (0.089) | (0.095) | (0.096) | (0.139) | (0.138) | (0.138) |
| South | 0.960 | 0.985 | 0.983 | 0.854 | 0.858 | 0.874 |
|  | (0.081) | (0.082) | (0.082) | (0.127) | (0.127) | (0.127) |

(Contd)

*(Table A12.1 contd)*

|  | Rural men | | | Urban men | | |
|---|---|---|---|---|---|---|
| East | 0.765*** | 0.756*** | 0.752*** | 1.027 | 1.023 | 1.037 |
|  | (0.085) | (0.085) | (0.085) | (0.167) | (0.166) | (0.166) |
| West | 0.952 | 0.951 | 0.955 | 0.770** | 0.776* | 0.783* |
|  | (0.105) | (0.105) | (0.105) | (0.132) | (0.131) | (0.130) |
| NE | 1.097 | 1.133 | 1.170 | 0.763 | 0.765 | 0.799 |
|  | (0.118) | (0.122) | (0.123) | (0.221) | (0.226) | (0.229) |
| Muslim |  | 0.921 | 0.968 |  | 1.016 | 1.112 |
|  |  | (0.090) | (0.116) |  | (0.120) | (0.199) |
| Otherel |  | 0.712*** | 0.715*** |  | 0.817 | 0.825 |
|  |  | (0.118) | (0.118) |  | (0.141) | (0.141) |
| SC |  | 1.238*** | 1.321*** |  | 0.996 | 1.346* |
|  |  | (0.078) | (0.102) |  | (0.115) | (0.180) |
| ST |  | 1.359*** | 1.687*** |  | 1.118 | 1.732* |
|  |  | (0.110) | (0.134) |  | (0.224) | (0.284) |
| SCprim_comp |  |  | 0.800 |  |  | 0.879 |
|  |  |  | (0.204) |  |  | (0.312) |
| SCpostpri |  |  | 0.926 |  |  | 0.547** |
|  |  |  | (0.176) |  |  | (0.239) |
| STprim_comp |  |  | 0.794 |  |  | 0.949 |
|  |  |  | (0.319) |  |  | (0.559) |
| STpostpri |  |  | 0.413*** |  |  | 0.434* |
|  |  |  | (0.242) |  |  | (0.443) |
| MUSprim_comp |  |  | 0.814 |  |  | 1.244 |
|  |  |  | (0.231) |  |  | (0.352) |
| MUSpostpri |  |  | 0.977 |  |  | 0.814 |
|  |  |  | (0.199) |  |  | (0.256) |

*Notes*: *** $p <= 0.001$
** $p <= 0.01$
* $p <= 0.05$
Standard deviations in parentheses
Uneducated, upper caste, Hindu, unmarried, central region are the omitted categories

TABLE A12.2: Coefficients of Multinomial Regression Models Predicting the Probability of Allocation to Various Employment Types for Rural Men (Age 15–59 Years Excluding Students)

| | Model 1: base model | | | | Model 2: base model + interaction terms | | | |
|---|---|---|---|---|---|---|---|---|
| | Non-farm self-employed v/s Regular salaried | Self-employed farmers v/s Regular salaried | Casual v/s Regular salaried | Not in labour force v/s Regular salaried | Non-farm self-employed v/s Regular salaried | Self-employed farmers v/s Regular salaried | Casual v/s Regular salaried | Not in labour force v/s Regular salaried |
| Age | 0.018 | −0.052*** | −0.059*** | −0.242*** | 0.018 | −0.052*** | −0.058*** | −0.242*** |
| | (0.009) | (0.009) | (0.009) | (0.011) | (0.009) | (0.009) | (0.009) | (0.011) |
| Age squared | −0.000** | 0.001*** | 0.000* | 0.004*** | −0.000** | 0.001*** | 0.000* | 0.004*** |
| | (0.000) | (0.000) | (0.000) | (0.000) | (0.000) | (0.000) | (0.000) | (0.000) |
| Married | 0.014 | 0.121** | 0.063 | −1.037*** | 0.011 | 0.120** | 0.058 | −1.037*** |
| | (0.043) | (0.042) | (0.042) | (0.057) | (0.043) | (0.042) | (0.042) | (0.057) |
| Household size | 0.062*** | 0.009 | 0.029*** | 0.010 | 0.062*** | 0.009 | 0.028*** | 0.009 |
| | (0.006) | (0.006) | (0.006) | (0.008) | (0.006) | (0.006) | (0.006) | (0.008) |
| Below-prim | −0.122* | −0.404*** | −0.521*** | −0.675*** | −0.122* | −0.410*** | −0.533*** | −0.686*** |
| | (0.055) | (0.054) | (0.052) | (0.074) | (0.055) | (0.054) | (0.052) | (0.074) |
| Prim. comp | −0.393*** | −0.634*** | −1.057*** | −1.057*** | −0.328*** | −0.659*** | −1.103*** | −1.165*** |
| | (0.048) | (0.047) | (0.046) | (0.066) | (0.061) | (0.060) | (0.060) | (0.087) |
| Postpri | −1.131*** | −1.573*** | −2.486*** | −1.469*** | −1.069*** | −1.592*** | −2.648*** | −1.587*** |
| | (0.038) | (0.037) | (0.037) | (0.051) | (0.047) | (0.046) | (0.047) | (0.064) |
| HH head | −0.014 | −0.051 | −0.000 | −1.532*** | −0.015 | −0.052 | −0.005 | −1.535*** |
| | (0.042) | (0.041) | (0.041) | (0.067) | (0.042) | (0.041) | (0.041) | (0.067) |

(Contd)

(Table A12.2 contd)

| | Model 1: base model | | | | Model 2: base model + interaction terms | | | |
|---|---|---|---|---|---|---|---|---|
| | Non-farm self-employed v/s Regular salaried | Self-employed farmers v/s Regular salaried | Casual v/s Regular salaried | Not in labour force v/s Regular salaried | Non-farm self-employed v/s Regular salaried | Self-employed farmers v/s Regular salaried | Casual v/s Regular salaried | Not in labour force v/s Regular salaried |
| Land poss | 0.167*** | 0.699*** | −0.807*** | −0.051* | 0.167*** | 0.697*** | −0.808*** | −0.052* |
| | (0.015) | (0.014) | (0.019) | (0.023) | (0.015) | (0.014) | (0.019) | (0.023) |
| North | −0.960*** | −1.101*** | −0.952*** | −0.662*** | −0.954*** | −1.100*** | −0.946*** | −0.657*** |
| | (0.043) | (0.040) | (0.042) | (0.064) | (0.043) | (0.040) | (0.042) | (0.064) |
| South | −0.001 | −1.891*** | 0.239*** | −0.201*** | 0.008 | −1.889*** | 0.239*** | −0.201*** |
| | (0.036) | (0.040) | (0.036) | (0.053) | (0.036) | (0.040) | (0.036) | (0.053) |
| East | −0.104* | −0.225*** | 0.067 | 0.396*** | −0.105* | −0.222*** | 0.076 | 0.404*** |
| | (0.045) | (0.043) | (0.044) | (0.059) | (0.045) | (0.043) | (0.044) | (0.059) |
| West | −0.977*** | −0.986*** | 0.188*** | −0.430*** | −0.972*** | −0.985*** | 0.190*** | −0.432*** |
| | (0.044) | (0.040) | (0.040) | (0.063) | (0.044) | (0.040) | (0.040) | (0.064) |
| NE | −0.685*** | −0.191** | −0.551*** | −0.045 | −0.678*** | −0.191** | −0.557*** | −0.057 |
| | (0.067) | (0.060) | (0.067) | (0.091) | (0.068) | (0.060) | (0.068) | (0.091) |
| Muslim | 0.478*** | −0.222*** | 0.085 | 0.144* | 0.719*** | −0.185* | 0.171* | 0.142 |
| | (0.045) | (0.047) | (0.046) | (0.063) | (0.085) | (0.086) | (0.084) | (0.108) |
| Otherel | 0.086 | −0.193*** | −0.080 | 0.300*** | 0.078 | −0.190*** | −0.085 | 0.295*** |
| | (0.054) | (0.054) | (0.052) | (0.074) | (0.054) | (0.054) | (0.052) | (0.074) |
| SC | −0.216*** | −0.429*** | 0.640*** | 0.051 | −0.218*** | −0.509*** | 0.408*** | −0.163* |
| | (0.034) | (0.034) | (0.032) | (0.047) | (0.064) | (0.062) | (0.059) | (0.082) |

| | Model 1: Base Model | | | | Model 2: Base Model+Interaction Terms | | | |
| --- | --- | --- | --- | --- | --- | --- | --- | --- |
| | Non-farm self-employed f/s Regular salaried | Self-employed farmers v/s Regular salaried | Casual v/s Regular salaried | Not in labour force v/s Regular salaried | Non-farm self-employed v/s Regular salaried | Self-employed farmers v/s Regular salaried | Casual v/s Regular salaried | Not in labour force v/s Regular salaried |
| Land possessed | 0.203*** | 0.569*** | −0.231*** | 0.089* | 0.203*** | 0.571*** | −0.232*** | 0.086* |
| | (0.020) | (0.023) | (0.050) | (0.034) | (0.020) | (0.023) | (0.051) | (0.035) |
| North | −0.328*** | −0.843*** | −0.746*** | −0.197** | −0.328*** | −0.856*** | −0.736*** | −0.200*** |
| | (0.033) | (0.084) | (0.054) | (0.061) | (0.033) | (0.084) | (0.054) | (0.061) |
| South | −0.174*** | −1.203*** | 0.595*** | −0.036 | −0.171*** | −1.272*** | 0.580*** | −0.046 |
| | (0.030) | (0.088) | (0.042) | (0.054) | (0.030) | (0.089) | (0.042) | (0.054) |
| East | 0.015 | −0.726*** | 0.449*** | 0.380*** | 0.019 | −0.728*** | 0.444*** | 0.373*** |
| | (0.039) | (0.111) | (0.054) | (0.064) | (0.039) | (0.111) | (0.054) | (0.064) |
| West | −0.401*** | −1.201*** | 0.019 | −0.165** | −0.400*** | −1.212*** | 0.001 | −0.173** |
| | (0.030) | (0.086) | (0.045) | (0.055) | (0.031) | (0.086) | (0.045) | (0.055) |
| NE | −0.147 | 0.220 | −0.190 | 0.415** | −0.132 | 0.107 | −0.174 | 0.391** |
| | (0.086) | (0.165) | (0.143) | (0.141) | (0.086) | (0.169) | (0.143) | (0.142) |
| Muslim | 0.401*** | −0.388*** | 0.193*** | 0.159*** | 0.356*** | −1.041*** | 0.002 | −0.138 |
| | (0.031) | (0.088) | (0.044) | (0.055) | (0.063) | (0.143) | (0.072) | (0.105) |
| otherel | 0.234*** | −0.190 | 0.365*** | 0.429*** | 0.239*** | −0.206 | 0.372*** | 0.431*** |
| | (0.043) | (0.139) | (0.063) | (0.069) | (0.043) | (0.140) | (0.063) | (0.069) |
| SC | −0.412*** | −0.653*** | 0.503*** | 0.212*** | −0.219*** | −0.905*** | 0.391*** | 0.014 |
| | (0.031) | (0.096) | (0.037) | (0.049) | (0.064) | (0.145) | (0.066) | (0.103) |

*(Contd)*

(Table A12.3 contd)

| | Model 1: Base Model | | | | Model 2: Base Model+Interaction Terms | | | |
|---|---|---|---|---|---|---|---|---|
| | Non-farm self-employed f/s Regular salaried | Self-employed farmers v/s Regular salaried | Casual v/s Regular salaried | Not in labour force v/s Regular salaried | Non-farm self-employed v/s Regular salaried | Self-employed farmers v/s Regular salaried | Casual v/s Regular salaried | Not in labour force v/s Regular salaried |
| ST | -0.626*** | 0.646*** | 0.398*** | -0.214 | -0.451** | -0.318 | 0.483*** | -0.675* |
| | (0.071) | (0.118) | (0.079) | (0.114) | (0.142) | (0.262) | (0.131) | (0.264) |
| SCprim_comp | | | | | -0.220* | -0.423 | -0.220* | 0.137 |
| | | | | | (0.098) | (0.305) | (0.104) | (0.167) |
| SCpostpri | | | | | -0.301*** | 0.627** | 0.406*** | 0.269* |
| | | | | | (0.077) | (0.204) | (0.085) | (0.119) |
| STprim_comp | | | | | 0.432 | 0.422 | -0.149 | 0.480 |
| | | | | | (0.222) | (0.452) | (0.228) | (0.422) |
| STpostpri | | | | | -0.428* | 1.464*** | -0.238 | 0.586* |
| | | | | | (0.171) | (0.297) | (0.188) | (0.297) |
| MUSprim comp | | | | | 0.074 | 0.418 | -0.026 | 0.174 |
| | | | | | (0.097) | (0.253) | (0.117) | (0.181) |
| MUSpostpri | | | | | 0.059 | 1.185*** | 0.450*** | 0.423*** |
| | | | | | (0.074) | (0.187) | (0.098) | (0.124) |
| _cons | -0.959*** | -0.490 | 1.401*** | 3.527*** | -0.992*** | -0.330 | 1.455*** | 3.660*** |
| | (0.132) | (0.334) | (0.172) | (0.185) | (0.135) | (0.337) | (0.174) | (0.189) |

Notes: ***  $p <= 0.001$, ** $p <= 0.01$, * $p <= 0.05$
Uneducated, upper caste, Hindu, unmarried, central region are the omitted categories
Standard deviations in parentheses

## Notes

1   In urban areas it may be possible to break education down into finer categories but for the sake of comparison this chapter keeps to the broad 'post-primary' category for both rural and urban areas.

2   We have found this in previous analysis as well (see Das 2006).

## References

Béteille, André (1991), *Society and Politics in India: Essays in a Comparative Perspective*, London School of Economics Monographs on Social Anthropology, New Delhi: Oxford University Press.

Bonacich, Edna (1972), 'A Theory of Ethnic Antagonism: The Split Labor Market', *American Sociological Review*, vol. 37, no. 5. October, pp. 547–59.

Clark, Kenneth and Stephen Drinkwater (1999). 'Pushed Out or Pulled in Self Employment among Ethnic Minorities in England and Wales', Annual Conference of the Royal Economic Society, Nottingham, England.

Das, Maitreyi Bordia (2002), 'Employment and Social Inequality in India: How Much do Caste and Religion Matter?', PhD Thesis, College Park: University of Maryland.

—— (2005), 'Self-Employed or Unemployed: Muslim Women's Low Labor-Force Participation in India', in Zoya Hasan and Ritu Menon (eds), *The Diversity of Muslim Women's Lives in India,* New Brunswick, New Jersey: Rutgers University Press, pp. 135–69.

—— (2006), *Do Traditional Axes of Exclusion Affect Labor Market Outcomes in India?* South Asia Social Development Discussion Paper No. 3. Washington DC: The World Bank.

Das, Maitreyi Bordia and Sonalde Desai (2003), 'Are Educated Women Less Likely to be Employed in India?', Social Protection Discussion Paper No. 313, Washington DC: The World Bank.

Das, Maitreyi Bordia and Puja Vasudeva Dutta (2008), 'Does Caste Matter for Wages in the Indian Labor Market?', Paper presented at the Third IZA/World Bank Conference on Employment and Development, Rabat, Morocco, May.

Deshpande, Ashwini and Katherine S. Newman (2007), 'Where the Path Leads: The Role of Caste in Post-University Employment Expectations', *Economic and Political Weekly,* vol. 42, no. 41, pp. 4133–40.

Evans, M.D.R. (1989), 'Immigrant Entrepreneurship: Effects of Ethnic Market Size and Isolated Labor Pool', *American Sociological Review*, vol. 54, pp. 950–62.

Fafchamps, Marcel and Flores Gubert (2007), 'Risksharing and Network Formation', *American Economic Review Papers and Proceedings*, (forthcoming).

Government of India (2006), 'Social, Economic and Educational Status of the Muslim Community of India', Report of the Prime Minister's High Level Committee, Cabinet Secretariat, New Delhi.

Jodhka, Surinder S. and Katherine S. Newman (2007), 'In the Name of Globalisation: Meritocracy, Productivity and the Hidden Language of Caste', *Economic and Political Weekly*, vol. 42, no. 41, pp. 4125–32.

Light, Ivan, Georges Sabagh, Mehdi Bozorgmehr, and Claudia Der-Martirosian (1994), 'Beyond the Ethnic Enclave Economy', *Social Problems*, vol. 41, no. 1, Special Issue on Immigration, Race, and Ethnicity in America, February, pp. 65–80.

Madheswaran, S. and Paul Attewell (2007), 'Caste Discrimination in the Indian Urban Labour Market: Evidence from the National Sample Survey', *Economic and Political Weekly*, vol. 42, no. 41, pp. 4146–54.

Massey, Garth, Randy Hodson, and Dusko Sekulic (1999), 'Ethnic Enclaves and Intolerance: The Case of Yugoslavia', *Social Forces*, vol. 78, no. 2, December, pp. 669–93.

Polanyi, Karl (1944), *The Great Transformation*, Boston: Beacon Hill.

Portes, Alejandro and Leif Jensen (1989), 'The Enclave and the Entrants: Patterns of Ethnic Enterprise in Miami before and after Mariel', *American Sociological Review*, vol. 54, no. 6, December, pp. 929–49.

—— (1992), 'Disproving the Enclave Hypothesis: Reply', *American Sociological Review*, vol. 57, no. 3, pp. 418–20.

Sanders, Jimy, M. and Victor Nee (1987), 'Limits of Ethnic Solidarity in the Enclave Economy', *American Sociological Review*, vol. 52, no. 6, pp. 745–73.

—— (1992), 'Problems in Resolving the Enclave Economy Debate', *American Sociological Review*, vol. 57, no. 3, pp. 415–18.

Semyonov, Moshe (1988), 'Bi-Ethnic Labor Markets, Mono-Ethnic Labor Markets, and Socioeconomic Inequality', *American Sociological Review*, vol. 53, no. 2, April, pp. 256–66.

Thorat, Sukhadeo (undated mimeo), 'Remedies against Market Discrimination: Lessons from International Experience for Reservation Policy in Private Sector in India', http://www.dalit.de/details/dsid_codeofconduct_thorat0404.pdf, accessed 2 October 2007.

Thorat, Sukhadeo (2007), 'Economic Exclusion and Poverty: Indian Experience of Remedies against Exclusion', prepared for Policy Forum on Agricultural and Rural Development for Reducing Poverty and Hunger in Asia: In Pursuit of Inclusive and Sustainable Growth,

Manila, August, Draft, http://www.ifpri.org/ 2020China Conference/ pdf/manilac_Thorat.pdf, accessed 2 October 2007.

Thorat, Sukhadeo and Paul Attewell (2007), 'The Legacy of Social Exclusion: A Correspondence Study of Job Discrimination in India', *Economic and Political Weekly*, vol. 42, no. 41, pp. 4141–45.

Thorat, Sukhadeo and R.S. Deshpande (1999), 'Caste and Labour Market Discrimination', *Indian Journal of Labour Economics,* vol. 42, no. 4, October–December, pp. 841–54.

Venkateswarlu, D. (1990), 'Harijan—Upper Class Conflict', *Discovery,* Delhi.

Wilson, Kenneth L. and Alejandro Portes (1980), 'Immigrant Enclaves: An Analysis of the Labor Market Experiences of Cubans in Miami', *American Journal of Sociology*, vol. 86, no. 2, September, pp. 295–319.

Wilson, Kenneth L. and W. Allen Martin (1982), 'Ethnic Enclaves: A Comparison of the Cuban and Black Economies in Miami', *American Sociological Review*, vol. 88, no. 1, pp. 135–60.

Zhou, Min and John R. Logan (1989), 'Returns on Human Capital in Ethic Enclaves: New York City's Chinatown', *American Sociological Review*, vol. 54, no. 5, October, pp. 809–20.

# 13

# Caste, Ethnicity, and Religion[*]
## Linkages with Unemployment and Poverty

*Smita Das*

## BACKGROUND

This chapter attempts to evaluate the impact of a person's caste and religion on poverty status in the Indian context during 1993–4 and 2004. Deprivation in any society has a social as well as an economic dimension; more often than not they tend to overlap and reinforce one another. Bhalla and Lapeyre (1999) rightly argue that poverty and social exclusion are interrelated and draw attention to the multidimensional character of deprivation. On a similar note the *World Development Report* observed,

Poverty outcomes are also greatly affected by social norms, values and customary practices that, within the family, the community, or the market lead to exclusion of women, ethnic and racial groups, or the socially disadvantaged. (World Bank 2000: 3)

The relationship between poverty and social exclusion is particularly relevant in India given its unique socio-cultural structure whereby race, caste, and religion-based discrimination has defined social relations for several thousand years. The Scheduled Castes (SC) and Scheduled Tribes (ST) have been the two most deprived groups traditionally, even though for different reasons. The STs or 'Adivasis' lived in remote and isolated areas away from mainstream society while the SCs, the lowest caste under the caste system, suffered a denial of basic rights, including economic rights. The association between

* This essay is based on my PhD Thesis. I sincerely thank Vani Borooah and Siddquer Osmani for their support and guidance while writing my thesis. I am also grateful to Amaresh Dubey for providing me the data for the study.

hierarchy and the deplorable condition of these population groups has constantly been the focus of recent poverty studies in India. For example, Dubey and Gangopadhyay (1998), in a poverty study among the SCs, STs, and 'Others', that is non-STs/SCs, conclude that poverty incidence among the STs and the SCs was much higher when compared to that of 'Others'. Similarly, Meenakshi and others (2000), estimating the poverty incidence among the SCs, STs, and female headed households for the year 1993–4, find that relative deprivation is higher than otherwise among the STs and SCs. Deshpande (2000) recognized inter-caste disparity to be a major factor underlying the overall disparity. Mutatkar (2005) observed that difference in the levels of living of STs, SCs, and Others are the result of the discrimination faced by these groups historically.

Caste division aside, the religious denomination of a person in India also has significant bearing on his/her economic standing. Among religious groups, minority Muslims emerge as the disadvantaged group. John and Mutatkar (2005) observed wide gap in the economic status of the population belonging to different religious groups and found high incidence of poverty among the Muslims compared to Hindus in urban areas. A recent study on the socio-economic and educational status of the Muslim community of India (Government of India [GoI] 2006) observed that although the situation of Muslims on the whole was slightly better than that of SCs and STs, they were relatively more deprived compared to other religious groups, particularly in urban areas.

## DATA-RELATED ISSUES

In assessing poverty in relation to social exclusion, it is, therefore, imperative to consider religious denomination along with caste division. This chapter investigates the employment and poverty status of seven mutually exclusive caste and religious groups based on an individual's caste and religion in 1993–4 and 2004–5 and attempts to bring out the variations among them. On the basis of information from the National Sample Survey Organisation (NSSO), seven mutually exclusive socio-religious groups have been identified for the study, namely SC, ST, non-ST/SC Hindu, non-ST/SC Muslim, non-ST/SC Christian, non-ST/SC Sikh, and All Others.[1] The analysis in this chapter is based on the 50th Round (1993-4) and the most recent 61st Round (2004–5) of quinquennial survey carried out by the NSSO of the GOI. Both consumption expenditure and employment–unemployment data have been used for the study.

The Foster and others (1984) measure has been used to capture poverty incidence. The Foster, Greer, and Thorbecke (FGT) Index is measured as:

$$\text{FGT} = \frac{1}{n.z^{\alpha}} \sum_{i=1}^{q} (z - y_i)^{\alpha} \qquad \alpha = 2 \qquad (13.1)$$

where $z$ is the poverty norm, $n$ the total population, and $y$ the income or expenditure. The FGT degenerates to Head Count Ratio (HCR) and Poverty Gap Index (PGI) depending on the value of the parameter '$\alpha$'. For $\alpha = 0$, FGT equals HCR, and for $\alpha = 1$, FGT equals PGI (Borooah 1991). The poverty lines of the Planning Commission of India[2] have been used to identify the population below the poverty line. The analysis in this chapter has been carried out at the country level for each of the seven socio-religious groups mentioned above, further disaggregated by place of residence (rural and urban sectors).

## PRIMARY OCCUPATION

Table 13.1 reports the primary source of income of households by socio-religious groups. Clearly, from the data of 2004–5, the rural sector has a very large fraction of the ST and SC households making a living from some form of manual labour. For example, in 2004–5 the main source of income of about 35 per cent of ST households and 43 per cent of SC households was agricultural labour. Another 10 to 15 per cent of ST/SC households earn their livelihood from other types of labour. The next most important source of livelihood for these two groups (about 39 per cent of ST and 19 per cent of SC households) is self-employment in agriculture. Among the non-ST/SC Muslims as well, one or the other form of labour appears to be the main income source for about 32 per cent of households followed by self-employment in agriculture (27 per cent) and self-employment in non-agriculture (28 per cent). The primary source of income of 43 per cent of non-ST/SC Hindu households and 51

### TABLE 13.1: Primary Source of Income of Households, 2004–5

(in per cent)

| Socio-religious group | Rural | | | | | Urban | | | |
|---|---|---|---|---|---|---|---|---|---|
| | Self-employed in non-agriculture | Agricultural lab | Other lab | Self-employed in agriculture | Others | Self-employed | Regular wage and salary | Casual lab | Others |
| ST | 6.66 | 34.87 | 10.88 | 38.49 | 9.10 | 22.86 | 41.15 | 21.53 | 14.46 |
| SC | 14.17 | 42.52 | 15.17 | 19.18 | 8.97 | 28.79 | 41.91 | 22.08 | 7.22 |
| Hindu (non-ST/SC) | 15.64 | 20.59 | 8.65 | 42.92 | 12.19 | 37.16 | 43.97 | 8.66 | 10.21 |
| Muslim (non-ST/SC) | 27.93 | 21.34 | 10.82 | 26.56 | 13.35 | 51.94 | 26.17 | 13.76 | 8.13 |
| Christian (non-ST/SC) | 15.47 | 17.26 | 24.21 | 25.62 | 17.43 | 24.48 | 46.78 | 10.12 | 18.62 |
| Sikh (non-ST/SC) | 16.17 | 10.64 | 8.79 | 50.96 | 13.45 | 53.19 | 34.03 | 1.31 | 11.47 |
| All others | 36.93 | 10.90 | 7.17 | 34.28 | 10.72 | 60.65 | 22.50 | 0.50 | 16.34 |
| Total | 15.63 | 26.75 | 10.71 | 35.54 | 11.36 | 37.62 | 40.90 | 11.64 | 9.85 |

*Source*: 61st Round Consumer Expenditure data

per cent of non-ST/SC Sikh households, on the other hand, is self-employment in agriculture. Although about 30 per cent and 20 per cent of Hindu and Sikh households as well earn their livelihood from labour-based activities, this proportion is much lower than that for ST, SC, Muslim, or Christian households.

In the urban sector, regular wage and salary is the main source of income of the majority of ST, SC, and Hindu households but this proportion is higher in the case of the Hindus; 41 per cent of ST/SC households and 44 per cent of Hindu households reported their main source of income to be regular salaried employment in 2004–5. We also see that 22 per cent of ST and SC households earn their livelihood from casual labour in the urban sector against 9 per cent of Hindu households. The majority of Muslim (52 per cent) and Sikh (53 per cent) households, on the other hand, earn their livelihood from self-employment activities.

Thus the main income source of the majority of households in the rural sector is labour-based activities. For the Hindus, however, the main income source is mostly self-employment. In the urban sector, the main income source is usually regular wage but a very large fraction of ST/SC households are also engaged as casual labour. The Muslims, on the other hand, are mostly self-employed.

## Employment Level

Table 13.2 reports the unemployment rates of individuals in the age-group of 15–59 years (both inclusive) by socio-religious group and place of residence based on the usual principal status. The unemployment rate is highest among non-ST/SC Christians, also the educationally most advanced group, and has amplified over the years. The STs, on the other hand, have the least number of unemployed. The unemployment rate for most groups is lower in the rural sector than in the urban sector. The fact that households in the rural sector are mostly engaged in family-based agricultural activities appears to be a prime factor concealing the extent of disguised unemployment prevailing in the rural sector. The unemployment rate for the SCs and STs also works out to be high because it is based on usual principal status which attempts to capture their employment situation around the year. Their employment appears to be higher because they have no alternative except to participate in any work irrespective of the level of employment and wage earning. If we estimate unemployment based on current weekly and current daily status the unemployment rate turns out to be much higher, particularly among the SCs. Thorat has observed higher rates of employment based on current weekly and current daily status (Thorat *et al.* 2006).

TABLE 13.2: Unemployment Rates, 1993–4 and 2004–5
(Principal Status)

(in per cent)

| Socio-religious group | Rural | Urban | Total | Rural | Urban | Total |
|---|---|---|---|---|---|---|
| | | 1993–4 | | | 2004–5 | |
| ST | 0.87 | 4.87 | 1.15 | 1.35 | 4.54 | 1.61 |
| SC | 1.59 | 5.29 | 2.19 | 2.97 | 7.24 | 3.84 |
| Hindu (non-ST/SC) | 2.12 | 5.62 | 3.02 | 2.78 | 5.69 | 3.60 |
| Muslim (non-ST/SC) | 2.87 | 4.02 | 3.28 | 3.86 | 5.25 | 4.36 |
| Christian (non-ST/SC) | 7.96 | 10.90 | 9.03 | 11.61 | 10.58 | 11.22 |
| Sikh (non-ST/SC) | 1.45 | 5.86 | 2.64 | 6.85 | 5.70 | 6.53 |
| All others | 1.67 | 5.50 | 2.89 | 0.59 | 4.22 | 3.07 |
| Total | 1.97 | 5.47 | 2.78 | 2.88 | 5.93 | 3.66 |

*Source*: 50th and 61st Round Employment and Unemployment data
50th round Employment and Unemployment data

## POVERTY INCIDENCE AND RISK OF POVERTY

This section examines the extent of and changes in the poverty incidence of the socio-religious groups between 1993 and 2004 based on the FGT index of poverty. This group of poverty indices is 'additively decomposable' and 'subgroup consistent' and can, therefore, be expressed as the weighted average of the subgroup values. Using this property, we further decompose overall poverty by socio-religious group, thereby identifying the groups most at risk of running into poverty, besides capturing the contribution of each of these groups to aggregate poverty. The poverty risk of each of the caste/religious groups considered, thus, is the ratio of the group's share in total poverty to its share in total population (Borooah 2006). Thus, if '$P_k$' represents the poverty share of group 'k' and '$W_k$' the population share; poverty risk '$R_k$' can then be defined as,

$$R_k = \frac{P_k}{W_k}$$ (13.2)

Taking the poverty risk norm as unity, $R_k > 1$ would imply a higher poverty risk for the group members and *vice versa*.

In Tables 13.3 and 13.4, poverty incidence by sector and socio-religious group for the two years under study has been reported for all the three poverty measures. On the head count index, which gives the percentage of population below the poverty line, 27.48 per cent of the total population is poor, even in 2004–5. The rural sector exhibits a higher incidence of poverty (28.04 per cent) as compared to the urban sector (25.81 per cent). In the same year, the STs (43.80 per cent) report the highest incidence of poverty followed by SCs (37.44 per cent) and non-ST/SC Muslims (35.62 per cent). Christians (11.20 per cent) have the lowest poverty incidence next only to Sikhs (4.45 per cent). Of the Hindus 20.57 per cent were below the poverty line

| TABLE 13.3: Poverty Ratio, FGT ($\alpha$) × 100, 1993–4 | | | | | | | | |
|---|---|---|---|---|---|---|---|---|
| *Socio-religious group* | *Rural* | | | *Urban* | | | *Total* | | |
| | $\alpha = 0$ | $\alpha = 1$ | $\alpha = 2$ | $\alpha = 0$ | $\alpha = 1$ | $\alpha = 2$ | $\alpha = 0$ | $\alpha = 1$ | $\alpha = 2$ |
| ST | 50.22 | 12.28 | 4.32 | 42.88 | 12.43 | 4.96 | 49.57 | 12.29 | 4.38 |
| SC | 48.33 | 11.76 | 4.08 | 49.72 | 13.76 | 5.42 | 48.58 | 12.12 | 4.32 |
| Hindu (non-ST/SC) | 29.55 | 6.28 | 2.00 | 26.24 | 6.26 | 2.20 | 28.64 | 6.28 | 2.05 |
| Muslim (non-ST/SC) | 45.04 | 10.24 | 3.32 | 47.73 | 12.23 | 4.42 | 45.96 | 10.92 | 3.69 |
| Christian (non-ST/SC) | 27.11 | 5.76 | 1.82 | 20.74 | 4.94 | 1.74 | 24.79 | 5.47 | 1.79 |
| Sikh (non-ST/SC) | 4.40 | 0.59 | 0.13 | 7.57 | 1.05 | 0.26 | 5.21 | 0.71 | 0.16 |
| All others | 17.99 | 2.97 | 0.61 | 11.90 | 2.10 | 0.48 | 13.92 | 2.39 | 0.52 |
| Total | 36.87 | 8.38 | 2.79 | 32.77 | 8.26 | 3.01 | 35.85 | 8.35 | 2.84 |

*Source*: 50th Round Consumer Expenditure data

TABLE 13.4: Poverty Ratio, FGT ($\alpha$) × 100, 2004–5

| Socio-religious group | Rural | | | Urban | | | Total | | |
|---|---|---|---|---|---|---|---|---|---|
| | $\alpha = 0$ | $\alpha = 1$ | $\alpha = 2$ | $\alpha = 0$ | $\alpha = 1$ | $\alpha = 2$ | $\alpha = 0$ | $\alpha = 1$ | $\alpha = 2$ |
| ST | 44.69 | 10.66 | 3.69 | 34.24 | 10.87 | 4.68 | 43.80 | 10.68 | 3.77 |
| SC | 37.13 | 7.51 | 2.23 | 40.86 | 10.39 | 3.79 | 37.88 | 8.09 | 2.55 |
| Hindu (non-ST/SC) | 21.21 | 3.80 | 1.04 | 18.89 | 4.13 | 1.35 | 20.57 | 3.89 | 1.13 |
| Muslim (non-ST/SC) | 33.01 | 6.02 | 1.66 | 40.65 | 10.41 | 3.67 | 35.52 | 7.46 | 2.32 |
| Christian (non-ST/SC) | 11.20 | 2.17 | 0.66 | 11.19 | 2.12 | 0.65 | 11.20 | 2.15 | 0.65 |
| Sikh (non-ST/SC) | 5.71 | 0.87 | 0.20 | 1.20 | 0.19 | 0.05 | 4.45 | 0.68 | 0.16 |
| All others | 9.86 | 2.04 | 0.57 | 5.60 | 0.87 | 0.21 | 6.94 | 1.23 | 0.32 |
| Total | 28.04 | 5.50 | 1.63 | 25.81 | 6.21 | 2.16 | 27.48 | 5.68 | 1.76 |

Source: 61st Round Consumer Expenditure data

in 2004–5. On the head count index of poverty, again the STs in the urban sector seem to have fared better than the SCs and Muslims. Nevertheless, the other two measures indicate that the intensity and severity of poverty is highest for the STs in both the sectors. All the three poverty measures suggest an evident fall in the poverty ratio of each of the groups considered from 1993 to 2004. However, this fall on all three poverty measures was largest for the SCs in both rural and urban sectors. The Sikhs in the rural sector, on the other hand, have marked a small increase in their poverty ratio. The SCs in the urban sector were more severely deprived than the STs in 1993–4 but the situation in 2004–5 appears to have reversed.

Coming to the next set of Tables, Tables 13.5 and 13.6 report the population share, poverty share, and poverty risk of the various socio-religious groups by their place of residence for the respective years. Clearly, in both the years and on all measures of poverty, the share of STs, SCs, and Muslims in aggregate poverty was higher than their share in the total population. Also, these three groups are seen to be most vulnerable to poverty with poverty risk significantly above the norm. At the country level, STs in 2004–5 account for nearly 9 per cent of the total population whereas their share in aggregate poverty

### TABLE 13.5: Decomposition of Poverty in India, Rural, 1993–4

(in per cent)

| Socio-religious group | Population share | Poverty share | | | Poverty risk | | |
|---|---|---|---|---|---|---|---|
| | | $\alpha=0$ | $\alpha=1$ | $\alpha=2$ | $\alpha=0$ | $\alpha=1$ | $\alpha=2$ |
| ST | 10.79 | 14.69 | 15.80 | 16.73 | 1.36 | 1.46 | 1.55 |
| SC | 21.11 | 27.67 | 29.61 | 30.92 | 1.31 | 1.40 | 1.46 |
| Hindu (non-ST/SC) | 55.79 | 44.71 | 41.81 | 39.96 | 0.80 | 0.75 | 0.72 |
| Muslim (non-ST/SC) | 9.68 | 11.83 | 11.82 | 11.52 | 1.22 | 1.22 | 1.19 |
| Christian (non-ST/SC) | 1.19 | 0.88 | 0.82 | 0.78 | 0.74 | 0.69 | 0.65 |
| Sikh (non-ST/SC) | 1.29 | 0.15 | 0.09 | 0.06 | 0.12 | 0.07 | 0.05 |
| All others | 0.16 | 0.08 | 0.06 | 0.03 | 0.49 | 0.35 | 0.22 |

*Source*: 50th Round Consumer Expenditure data

### TABLE 13.6: Decomposition of Poverty in India, Rural, 2004–5

(in per cent)

| Socio-religious group | Population share | Poverty share | | | Poverty risk | | |
|---|---|---|---|---|---|---|---|
| | | $\alpha=0$ | $\alpha=1$ | $\alpha=2$ | $\alpha=0$ | $\alpha=1$ | $\alpha=2$ |
| ST | 10.57 | 16.85 | 20.50 | 23.99 | 1.59 | 1.94 | 2.27 |
| SC | 20.92 | 27.71 | 28.58 | 28.73 | 1.32 | 1.37 | 1.37 |
| Hindu (non-ST/SC) | 54.84 | 41.48 | 37.93 | 35.17 | 0.76 | 0.69 | 0.64 |
| Muslim (non-ST/SC) | 11.26 | 13.26 | 12.33 | 11.48 | 1.18 | 1.10 | 1.02 |
| Christian (non-ST/SC) | 1.03 | 0.41 | 0.41 | 0.42 | 0.40 | 0.39 | 0.40 |
| Sikh (non-ST/SC) | 1.25 | 0.25 | 0.20 | 0.15 | 0.20 | 0.16 | 0.12 |
| All others | 0.14 | 0.05 | 0.05 | 0.05 | 0.35 | 0.37 | 0.35 |

*Source*: 61st Round Consumer Expenditure data

is nearly 14 per cent—5 points above their share in population. Similarly, nearly 20 per cent and 13 per cent of the total population in 2004–5 is SC and Muslim respectively, but their share in total poverty is 27 per cent and 16 per cent respectively. On the other hand, the share of non-ST/SC Hindus, Christians, and Sikhs in total poverty is much lower than their share in the total population. We further note that the poverty risk of STs, SCs, and Muslims was respectively 59 per cent, 38 per cent, and 29 per cent above the norm in 2004–5.

During the same year the poverty risk of a non-ST/SC Hindu, Christian, and Sikh respectively, was 25 per cent, 59 per cent, and 84 per cent below the norm (Tables 13.7 and 13.8). The condition of these three groups in this regard has unquestionably deteriorated during this span of 10 years. We see that the poverty risk of an ST has increased by 21 percentage points from 1993 to 2004; that of an SC and a Muslim has increased by three percentage points and one percentage point respectively. The backwardness of these groups with respect to education, possibly more dependents in the household, and inadequate assets in terms of landholding and also the amount of land cultivated are probably some of the key factors responsible for the higher poverty risk of these groups. However, when it comes to the STs, coupled with the above-mentioned factors, lack of mobility could also possibly explain higher poverty risk of this group. The STs have traditionally lived isolated (geographically) from the rest of society and in closed communities. As a result, this section of population fails to have a well-developed social network that is conducive to migration. To a large extent, even today, this group is concentrated in certain parts of the country and lacks incentive to migrate. We also see that among the well-off groups, it is the Sikhs and Christians who perform relatively better.

Taking the rural and urban sectors separately, we observe that the STs have a higher poverty risk in the rural sector than in the

**TABLE 13.7: Decomposition of Poverty in India, Urban, 1993–4**

(in per cent)

| Socio-religious group | Population share | Poverty share | | | Poverty risk | | |
|---|---|---|---|---|---|---|---|
| | | $\alpha = 0$ | $\alpha = 1$ | $\alpha = 2$ | $\alpha = 0$ | $\alpha = 1$ | $\alpha = 2$ |
| ST | 3.20 | 4.18 | 4.81 | 5.26 | 1.31 | 1.50 | 1.65 |
| SC | 13.77 | 20.89 | 22.94 | 24.75 | 1.52 | 1.67 | 1.80 |
| Hindu (non-ST/SC) | 63.51 | 50.85 | 48.14 | 46.25 | 0.80 | 0.76 | 0.73 |
| Muslim (non-ST/SC) | 15.19 | 22.13 | 22.48 | 22.29 | 1.46 | 1.48 | 1.47 |
| Christian (non-ST/SC) | 2.06 | 1.30 | 1.23 | 1.19 | 0.63 | 0.60 | 0.58 |
| Sikh (non-ST/SC) | 1.34 | 0.31 | 0.17 | 0.12 | 0.23 | 0.13 | 0.09 |
| All others | 0.94 | 0.34 | 0.24 | 0.15 | 0.36 | 0.25 | 0.16 |

Source: 50th Round Consumer Expenditure data

TABLE 13.8: Decomposition of Poverty in India, Urban, 2004–5

(in per cent)

| Socio-religious group | Population share | Poverty share | | | Poverty risk | | |
|---|---|---|---|---|---|---|---|
| | | $\alpha = 0$ | $\alpha = 1$ | $\alpha = 2$ | $\alpha = 0$ | $\alpha = 1$ | $\alpha = 2$ |
| ST | 2.92 | 3.88 | 5.12 | 6.33 | 1.33 | 1.75 | 2.17 |
| SC | 15.64 | 24.76 | 26.16 | 27.41 | 1.58 | 1.67 | 1.75 |
| Hindu (non-ST/SC) | 61.16 | 44.77 | 40.72 | 38.03 | 0.73 | 0.67 | 0.62 |
| Muslim (non-ST/SC) | 16.25 | 25.59 | 27.24 | 27.60 | 1.57 | 1.68 | 1.70 |
| Christian (non-ST/SC) | 1.72 | 0.75 | 0.59 | 0.51 | 0.43 | 0.34 | 0.30 |
| Sikh (non-ST/SC) | 1.42 | 0.07 | 0.04 | 0.03 | 0.05 | 0.03 | 0.02 |
| All others | 0.89 | 0.19 | 0.12 | 0.09 | 0.22 | 0.14 | 0.10 |

Source: 61st Round Consumer Expenditure data

urban sector. In case of the SCs and Muslims, on the other hand, the opposite holds; the poverty risk of the SCs and non-ST/SC Muslims in the urban sector is higher than of those in the rural sector. For example, in 2004–5 the poverty risk of the STs is 59 per cent above the norm in the rural sector and 33 per cent above the norm in the urban sector. Similarly, the poverty risk of the SCs is 32 per cent and 58 per cent above the norm, while that of Muslims is 18 per cent and 57 per cent above the norm in the rural and urban sectors respectively. Among the well-off groups the poverty risk of non-ST/SC Hindus in the rural sector is marginally higher than of those in the urban sector on all measures of poverty. Christians and Sikhs, however, are comparatively better off in the rural sector. We further note that the increase in the poverty risk of the SCs in both the sectors has been modest and balanced during the period between 1993 and 2004. In the case of the STs and Muslims, however, the change appears to be more erratic. The poverty risk of Muslims in the rural sector fell from 22 per cent in 1993–4 to 18 per cent in 2004–5 and that in the urban sector rose from 46 per cent to 57 per cent above the norm during this period. In the case of the STs, the poverty risk in the rural sector increased from 36 per cent to 59 per cent; in the urban sector, the poverty risk of this group increased only marginally from 31 per cent to 33 per cent.

To reiterate, we find that among the socio-religious groups the STs, SCs, and Muslims are particularly prone to poverty and deprivation in India. The contribution of these three groups to total poverty and also their poverty risk is much higher when compared to the remaining groups. Between the STs and SCs again, the STs in the rural sector are more vulnerable than the STs in the urban sector whereas the SCs are more vulnerable in the urban sector. The non-ST/SC Hindus, Christians, and Sikhs, on the other hand, manage to have a poverty risk much below the norm in both the sectors, in both years and on all measures of poverty. Also, between 1993–4 and 2004–5 the poverty risk of the STs, SCs, and Muslims has increased; this increase is significant and sharp in the case of the STs, especially in the rural sector, and the Muslims in the urban sector.

## SUMMING UP

This chapter analysed poverty status on the basis of caste and religion during 1993–4 and 2004–5. The STs, SCs, non-ST/SC Hindus, non-ST/SC Christians, non-ST/SC Muslims, non-ST/SC Sikhs, and All Others are the seven mutually exclusive population groups under study. Both in the rural and urban sectors, a very large fraction of the STs and SCs are casual labourers; the percentage of those employed in regular jobs is much lower than that of the Hindus and Christians.

In terms of levels of poverty as well, the STs, SCs, and non-ST/SC Muslims turn out to be the most deprived groups, in that order. Their poverty levels are higher than the poverty levels of the remaining four groups in both the years, even with a fall in poverty between 1993 and 2004. Thus, the STs, even in 2004–5, are the poorest on all measures of poverty, followed by the SCs and the non-ST/SC Muslims. Notably, the poverty risk of these three groups has increased during this period, particularly in the case of the STs in the rural sector and Muslims in the urban sector.

## NOTES

1.  In the absence of information on Other Backward Classes in 1993–4, this social group has been merged with 'Others' in 2004–5 for comparison between years.

2. In defining the poverty line, the Planning Commission accepts the normative calorie intake for fourteen age-sex-activity categories, as worked out by the Task Force (1979) based on the recommendation of the Nutrition Expert Group (1968). Average daily calorie intakes of 2435 and 2095 per person were recommended for the rural and urban areas respectively, which in monetary terms worked out to be Rs 49 per person per month for the rural areas and Rs 57 for urban areas at 1973–4 prices. Thereafter, these poverty lines have been updated periodically at current prices to correct for inflation.

## REFERENCES

Borooah, Vani K. (1991), *Regional Income Inequality and Poverty in the United Kingdom*, England: Dartmouth Publishing Company.
—— (2006), 'China and India: Income Inequality and Poverty North and South of the Himalayas', *Journal of Asian Economics*, vol. 17, pp. 797–817.
Bhalla, Ajit S. and Frederic Lapeyre (1999), *Poverty and Exclusion in a Global World*, London: Macmillan Press.
Das, M.B. (2003), 'Ethnicity and Social Exclusion in Job Outcomes in India: Summary of Research Findings', Washington, DC: World Bank, Social Protection Unit.
De Haan, A. and A. Dubey (2003), 'Extreme Deprivation in Remote Areas in India: Social Exclusion as Explanatory Concept', Paper for Chronic Poverty and Development Policy Conference, Manchester, University of Manchester, held from 7–9 April.
Deshpande, A. (2000), 'Does Caste Still Define Disparity? A Look at Inequality in Kerala, India', *The American Economic Review*, vol. 90, no. 2, pp. 322–5.
Dubey, Amaresh and Shubhashis Gangopadhyay (1998), 'Counting the Poor: Where are the Poor in India?', Sarvekshana Analytical Report No. 1, Department of Statistics, Government of India, New Delhi.
Foster, J.E. and A.F. Shorrocks (1991), 'Subgroup Consistent Poverty Indices', *Econometrica*, vol. 59, no. 3, pp. 687–709.
Foster, J., J. Greer, and E. Thorbecke (1984), 'A Class of Decomposable Poverty Measures', *Econometrica*, vol. 52, no. 3, pp. 761–6.
Government of India (2006), 'Social, Economic and Educational Status of the Muslim Community in India: A Report', Prime Minister's High Level Committee, New Delhi.
John, R.M. and R. Mutatkar (2005), 'Statewise Estimates of Poverty among

Religious Groups in India', *Economic and Political Weekly*, vol. 40, no. 13, pp. 1337–44.

Meenakshi, J.V., R. Ray, and S. Gupta (2000), 'Estimates of Poverty for SC, ST and Female-Headed Households', *Economic and Political Weekly*, vol. 35, no. 31, pp. 2748–54.

Mutatkar, R. (2005), 'Social Group Disparities and Poverty in India', Working Paper Series No. WP-2005–4, Indira Gandhi Institute of Development Research, Mumbai.

Thorat, S.K., M. Mahamallik, and S.Venkatesan (2006), 'Human Poverty and Socially Disadvantage Groups in India', Discussion Paper, UNDP, Human Development Resource Centre, Delhi.

The World Bank (2000), *World Development Report 2000/2001: Attacking Poverty*, New York: Oxford University Press.

# Select Bibliography

Ahmed, Ausaf (1993), *Indian Muslims: Issues in Social and Economic Development*, New Delhi: Khama Publishers.

Ahmed, Imtiaz (ed.) (1973/8), *Caste and Social Stratification Among the Muslims in India*, New Delhi: Manohar.

Allport, Gordon W. (1954), *The Nature of Prejudice*, Cambridge: Addison-Wesley.

Ambedkar, B.R. (1979) [1916], 'Castes in India', in Vasant Moon (ed.), *Dr. Babasaheb Ambedkar: Writings and Speeches*, vol. 1, Education Department, Government of Maharashtra, pp. 3–22.

—— (1979) [1919], 'Evidence before the Southborough Committee on Franchise', in Vasant Moon (ed.), *Dr. Babasaheb Ambedkar: Writings and Speeches*, vol. 1, Education Department Government of Maharashtra, pp. 245–77.

—— (1979) [1935], 'Annihilation of Caste', in Vasant Moon (ed.), *Dr. Babasaheb Ambedkar: Writings and Speeches*, vol. 1, Education Department, Government of Maharashtra, pp. 25–96.

—— (1979) [1945], 'Communal Deadlock and How to Solve It', in Vasant Moon (ed.), *Dr. Babasaheb Ambedkar: Writings and Speeches*, vol. 1, Education Department, Government of Maharashtra, pp. 335–79.

—— (1982) [1930], 'Proceedings of Round Table Conference: (1) In the Plenary Session—Fifth Sitting—20th November 1930, Need for Political Power for Depressed Classes. (2) In Sub-Committee No. III (Minorities) Second Sitting, Government of India', in Vasant Moon (ed.), *Dr. Babasaheb Ambedkar: Writings and Speeches*, vol. 2, Education Department, Government of Maharashtra, pp. 502–9, 528–45.

—— (1982) [1931], 'Proceedings of the Round Table Conference: (1) Plenary Session—Ninth Sitting—October 1931, Provisions for a Settlement of the Communal Problem Put Forward Jointly by Muslims, Depressed Classes etc.'—Appendix to the Report in the Monorities Committee', in Vasant Moon (ed.), *Dr. Babasaheb Ambedkar: Writings and Speeches*, vol. 2, Education Department, Government of Maharashtra, pp. 659–63, 664–9.

Ambedkar, B.R. (1989) [1946], 'Essays on Untouchables and Untouchablity: Social-Political-Religious', in Vasant Moon (ed.), *Dr. Babasaheb Ambedkar: Writings and Speeches*, vol. 5, Education Department, Government of Maharashtra, pp. 1–445.

—— (1990) [1932], 'Poona Pact Correspondence with Gandhi and Others', in Vasant Moon (ed.), *Dr. Babasaheb Ambedkar: Writings and Speeches*, vol. 9, Education Department, Government of Maharashtra, pp. 74–91.

—— (1990) [1947], 'States and Minorities: What are Their Rights and How to Secure Them in the Constitution of Free India, Memorandum Submitted on Behalf of All India Scheduled Castes Federation', in Vasant Moon (ed.), *Dr. Babasaheb Ambedkar: Writings and Speeches*, vol. 9, Education Department, Government of Maharashtra, pp. 391–450.

—— (1994) [1948], 'The Untouchables: Who Were They and Why They Become Untouchables?', in Vasant Moon (ed.), *Dr. Babasaheb Ambedkar: Writings and Speeches*, vol. 7, Education Department, Government of Maharashtra, pp. 239–381.

America, Richard F. and Rao Bahadur R. Srinivasan (1982) [1930], 'A Scheme of Political Safeguards for the Protection of the Depressed Classes in the Future Constitution of Self-Governing India—Appendix to Report of Sub-Committee No. III (Minorities)', in Vasant Moon (ed), *Dr. Babasaheb Ambedkar: Writings and Speeches*, vol. 2, Education Department, Government of Maharashtra, pp. 546–56.

America, Richard F. (ed.) (1990), *The Wealth of Races: The Present Value of Benefits from Past Injustices*, Westport: Greenwood Press.

Angel, Ronald and William Gronfein (1988), 'The Use of Subjective Information in Statistical Models', *American Sociological Review*, vol. 53, June, pp. 464–73.

Becker, Gary S. (1957), *The Economics of Discrimination*, Chicago: University of Chicago Press.

—— (1971), *The Economics of Discrimination*, second edition, Chicago: University of Chicago.

Behrman, J.R., A. Gaviria, and M. Szekely (eds) (2003), *Who's In and Who's Out: Social Exclusion in Latin America*, Washington, DC: Inter-American Development Bank.

Bennett, Lynn (2003), 'Empowerment and Social Inclusion: A Social Development Perspective on the Cultural and Institutional Foundations of Poverty Reduction', Mimeo, Washington, DC: World Bank.

Bhalla, Ajit and Frederic Lapeyere (1997), 'Social Exclusion: Towards an Analytical and Operational Framework', *Development and Change*, vol. 28, no. 2, pp. 413–34.

Burden, Tom and Trica Hamm (2000), 'Responding to Socially Excluded Groups', in Janie Percy-Smith (ed.), *Policy Responses to Social Exclusion: Towards Inclusion?*, Buckingham: Open University Press, pp. 100–14.

Buvinic, Mayra and Jacqeline Mazza, with Ruthanne Deutsch (2007), *Social Inclusion and Economic Development in Latin America*, Inter-American Development Bank.

Conrad, Cecilia A. (1993), 'A Different Approach to the Measurement of Racial Inequality', *Review of Black Political Economy*, vol. 22, no. 1, Summer, pp. 19–31.

Darity Jr, William A. (1975), 'Economic Theory and Racial Economic Inequality', *Review of Black Political Economy*, vol. 5, no. 3, pp. 225–48.

—— (1987), 'Equal Opportunity, Equal Results and Social Hierarchy', *Praxis International*, vol. 7, no. 2, p. 180.

—— (1989), 'What's Left of the Economic Theory of Discrimination?', in Steven Shulman and William Darity, Jr. (eds), *The Question of Discrimination: Racial Inequality in the U.S. Labor Market*, Middletown: Wesleyan University Press, pp. 335–74.

—— (1991), 'Underclass and Overclass: Race, Class and Economic Inequality in the Managerial Age', in Emily P. Hoffman (ed.), *Essays on the Economics of Discrimination*, Kalamazoo, MI: The Upjohn Institute, pp. 67–84.

—— (1992), *Racial Earnings Inequality: Trends and Prospects*, Minneapolis: University of Minnesota.

Darity Jr, A. William and Rhonda M. Williams (1985), 'Peddlers Forever? Culture, Competition, and Discrimination', *American Economic Review*, vol. 75, no. 2, May, pp. 256–61.

Darity Jr, A. William and Samuel L. Myers Jr (1998), *Persistent Disparity*, Northhamption, USA: Edward Elgar.

Deshi, Autar Singh and Harbhajan Singh (1995), 'Education, Labour Market Distortions and Relative Earning of Different Religion Caste Categories in India', *Canadian Journal of Development Studies*, 21 December, pp. 78–104.

Deshpande, Satish and Yogendra Yadav (2006), 'Regarding Affirmative Action-Caste and Benefits in Higher Education', *Economic and Political Weekly*, vol. 17, pp. 2419–24.

Durlauf, Steven (2001), 'The Memberships Theory of Poverty: The Role of Group Affiliations in Determining Socioeconomic Outcomes', in Sheldon Danziger and Robert Haveman (eds), *Understanding Poverty*, Cambridge: Harvard University Press, pp. 96–115.

European Commission (1988), *The Social Dimension of the Internal Market: Social Europe*, Special edition, Brussels.

European Comission (1993), Medium-Term Action Programme to Combat Exclusion and Promote Solidarity, and Report on the Implementation of the Community Programme (1989–1994)', COM (93) 435 final, Brussels.

—— (2002), Joint Report on Social Inclusion, Luxembourg.

Evers, H.D. and H. Schrader (1993), *The Moral Economy of Trade: Ethnicity and Developing Markets*, London: Routledge.

Falrie, Robert W. and William A. Sundstrom (1997), 'The Racial Unemployment Gap in Long-Run Perspective', AEA Papers and Proceedings, May.

Figueroa, A. (2001), 'Social Exlcusion as Distribution Theory', in E. Gacitua, C. Sojo, and S.H. Davis (eds), *Social Exclusion and Poverty Reduction in Latin America and the Caribbean*, Washington, DC: World Bank.

Fix, Michael, George C. Galster, and Raymond J. Struyk (1993), 'An Overview of Auditing for Discrimination', in Michael Fix and Raymond J. Struyk (eds), *Clear and Convincing Evidence: Measurement of Discrimination in America*, Washington, DC: Urban Institute Press, pp. 1–67.

Forbes, Ian and Geoffrey Mead (1992), *Measure for Measure: A Comparative Analysis of Measures to Combat Racial Discrimination in the Member Countries of the European Community*, Equal Opportunity Studies Group, University of Southampton.

Fuller, C. (ed.) (1996), *Caste Today*, New Delhi: Oxford University Press.

Galanter, Marc (1984), *Competing Equalities: Law and the Backward Classes in India*, Berkeley: University of California Press.

Gooptu, N. (2001), *The Urban Poor and the Politics of Class, Community and Nation: Uttar Pradesh between the Two World Wars*, Cambridge: Cambridge University Press.

Gordon, D., A. Adelman, K. Ashworth, J. Bradshaw, R. Levitas, S. Middleton, C. Pantazis, D. Patsios, S. Payne, P. Townsend, and I. Williams (2000), *Poverty and Social Exclusion in Britain*, York: Joseph Rowntree Foundation.

Gore, C. (1995), 'Introduction: Markets, Citizenship and Social Exclusion', in G. Rodgers, C. Gore, and J.B. Figueiredo (eds), *Social Exclusion: Rhetoric Reality Responses*, Geneva: International Institute for Labour Studies, pp. 1–10.

Goyal, S. (1990), 'Social Background of Indian Corporate Executives', in F.R. Frankel and M.S.A. Rao (ed.), *Dominance and State Power in Modern India*, vol. 1, New Delhi: Oxford University Press.

Harriss White, Barbara (2005), *India's Market Society: Three Essays in Political Economy*, Delhi: Three Essays Collective.

Harriss White, Barbara (1981), *Transitional Trade and Rural Development*, New Delhi: Vikas.

—— (1984), *State and Market*, New Delhi: Concept.

—— (1996), *A Political Economy of Agricultural Markets in South India*, New Delhi: Sage.

Inter-American Development Bank (2001), *Action Plan for Combating Social Exclusion due to Race or Ethnic Background*, Washington, DC: Inter-American Development Bank.

Jaffrelott Christophe (2003), *India's Silent Revolution: The Rise of Low Castes in Indian Politics*, Delhi: Permanent Black.

Jayaram, N. (1996), 'Caste and Hinduism: Changing Protean Relationship', in M.N. Srinivas (ed.), *Caste: Its Modern Avatar*, New Delhi: Viking.

Jaynes, Gerald D. and Robin M. Williams, Jr (eds) (1989), *A Common Destiny: Blacks and American Society*, Washington, DC: National Academy Press.

Johnson, G. David and Marc Matre (1991),'Race and Religiosity: An Empirical Evaluation of a Causal Model', *Review of Religious Research*, vol. 32, pp. 252–66.

Joly, Daniele (1998), *Scapegoats and Social Actors: The Exclusion and Integration of Minorities in Western and Eastern Europe*, Basingstoke: Macmillan.

Jomol K.S. and Ishak Shari (1986), *Development Policies and Income Incquality in Peninsular Malaysia*, Kuala Lumpur: Institute of Advanced Studies.

Kahn, Lawrence M. (1991), 'Customer Discrimination and Affirmative Action', *Economic Inquiry*, vol. 29, pp. 555–71.

Kimenyi, Mwangi S. (1991), 'Rational Choice, Culture of Poverty, and the Intergenerational Transmission of Welfare Dependency', *Southern Economic Journal*, vol. 57, pp. 947–60.

Kotz, D.M., T. McDonough, and M. Reich (1994), *Social Structures of Accumulation: The Political Economy of Growth and Crisis*, Cambridge: Cambridge University Press.

Krueger, Anne O. (1963), 'The Economics of Discrimination', *Journal of Political Economy*, vol. 71, no. 5, pp. 481–6.

Lieten, George K. (1979), 'Caste in Class Politics', *Economic and Political Weekly*, Annual Issue, February, pp. 67–79.

MacEwen, Martin (1995), *Tackling Racism in Europe*, Oxford: Berg.

—— (ed.) (1997), *Anti-Discrimination Law Enforcement: A Comparative Perspective*, Aldershot: Avebury.

Mason, Patrick L. (1992), 'The Divide-and-Conquer and Employer/Employee Models of Discrimination: Neoclassical Competition as a Familial Defect', *Review of Black Political Economy*, vol. 20, no. 4, pp. 73–89.

Mason, Patrick L. and Rhonda M. Williams (1997), *Race Markets, and Social Outcomes*, Boston: Kluwer Academic Publishers.

Mendelsohn, Oliver and Marica Vicziany (1988), *The Untouchables: Subordination, Poverty and the State in Modern India*, Cambridge: Cambridge University Press.

Mincy, Ronald B. (1993), 'The Urban Institute Audit Studies: Their Research and Policy Context', in Michael Fix and Raymond J. Struyk (eds), *Clear and Convincing Evidence: Measurement of Discrimination in America*, Washington: Urban Institute Press, pp. 165–86.

Patrinos, H.A. (2000), 'The Costs of Discrimination in Latin America', Working Paper, World Bank, Human Capital Development and Operations Policy, Washington, DC.

Perner, D. and G.L. Porter (1998), 'Creating Inclusive Schools: Changing Roles and Strategies', in A. Hilton and R. Ringlaben (eds), *Best and Promising Practices Developmental Disabilities*, Austin, Texas: Pro-ed.

Reiniche, M.L. (1996), 'The Urban Dynamics of Caste: A Case Study from Tamil Nadu', in C. Fuller (ed.), *Caste Today*, New Delhi: Oxford University Press.

Rodrigues, Valerian (2002), *The Essential Writings of B.R. Ambedkar*, New Delhi: Oxford University Press.

Roemer, John E. (1979), 'Divide and Computer: Microfoundations of a Marxian Theory of Wage Discrimination', *Bell Journal of Economics*, vol. 10, no. 2, pp. 695–705.

Ruhm, Christopher J. (1998), 'When "Equal Opportunity" Is Not Enough: Training Costs and Intergenerational Inequality', *Journal of Human Resources*, vol. 23, no. 2, pp. 155–72.

Saenger, Gerhart (1953), *The Social Psychology of Prejudice*, New York: Harper & Bros.

Scalera, Domenico and Alberto Zazzaro (2001), 'Group Reputation and Persistent (or Permanent) Discrimination in Credit Markets', *Journal of Multinational Financial Management*, vol. 11, pp. 483–96.

Schiller, Bradley R. (1989), *The Economics of Poverty and Discrimination*, New York: Prentice Hall.

Shulman, S. and William Darity, Jr (eds), *The Question of Discrimination: Racial Inequality in the US Labor Market*, Middleton, CT: Wesleyan University.

Simms, Margaret (ed.) (1995), *Economic Perspectives on Affirmatives Action*, Washington, DC: Joint Center for Political and Economic Studies.

Simms, Margaret and Samuel L. Mysers, Jr (eds) (1998), *The Economics of Race and Crime*, New Brunswick, NJ: Transaction Books.

Srinivas, M.N. (ed.) (1996), *Caste: Its Modern Avatar*, New Delhi: Viking.

Stewart, James B. (1997), 'Recent Perspectives on African in Post Industrial Labour Markets', AEA Papers and Proceedings.

Stiglitz, Joseph E. (1973), 'Approaches to the Economics of Discrimination', *American Economic Review*, vol. 63, no. 2, pp. 287–95.

Thurow, Lester (1969), *Poverty and Discrimination*, Washington DC: Brookings.

Torero, M., Jamie Saavedra, Hugo Nopo, and Javier Escobal (2002), 'The Economics of Social Exclusion in Peru: An Invisible Wall?', Working Paper, GRADE, Lima.

Yinger, John (1986), 'Measuring Racial Discrimination with Fair Housing Audits: Caught in the Act', *American Economic Review*, vol. 76, no. 5, December, pp. 881–93.

Zoninsein, J. (1995), 'The Economic Cost of Discrimination Against Black Americans', in Margaret Simmons (ed.), *Economic Perspectives on Affirmative Action*, Washington, DC: Joint Center for Political and Economic Studies, pp. 57–70.

# Contributors

SANGHAMITRA S. ACHARYA is Associate Professor at the Centre of Social Medicine and Community Health, School of Social Sciences, Jawaharlal Nehru University, New Delhi. Her research interests include reproductive morbidity, women's empowerment, adolescent and youth, and discrimination and social exclusion in health.

PAUL ATTEWELL is Professor of Sociology at the Graduate Center of the City University of New York, USA. He is an expert on the sociology of higher education.

KAUSHIK BASU is Chief Economic Advisor, Ministry of Finance, Government of India, and Professor of Economics and C. Marks Professor of International Studies, Cornell University, USA.

MAITREYI BORDIA DAS works on social protection issues at the World Bank in Washington DC. She focuses on the role of social inequality in a range of development outcomes, related policy, and institutional reform, primarily in India, Bangladesh, and Nepal.

VANI K. BOROOAH is Professor of Applied Economics at the University of Ulster, Northern Ireland. His work has been mainly in the areas of unemployment, inequality, poverty, and development.

CECILY DARDEN ADAMS is pursuing her graduation from the Department of Sociology, University of Maryland, USA.

SMITA DAS is Senior Research Analyst–Economist, Monster.com India Pvt Ltd., and former Fellow, Institute for Human Development, Delhi. Her area of interest is poverty by social and religious groups.

SONALDE DESAI is Professor of Sociology at the University of Maryland. She is a social demographer whose research focuses on caste, class, and gender inequality in human development.

ASHWINI DESHPANDE is Professor of Economics at the Delhi School of Economics, University of Delhi, India. Her research focuses on the economics of discrimination and affirmative action issues, aspects of the Chinese economy, role of FDI in the reform process, regional disparities, and gender discrimination.

AMARESH DUBEY is Professor of Economics in the Centre for the Study of Regional Development, Jawaharlal Nehru University, New Delhi. His research interest includes poverty assessment, education, and labour markets.

SURINDER S. JODHKA is Professor of Sociology at the Centre for the Study of Social Systems in the School of Social Sciences, Jawaharlal Nehru University, New Delhi, and former Director of Indian Institute of Dalit Studies, New Delhi. He has published widely on 'agrarian change' and the 'Indian Village'. More recently he has been working on 'caste' and 'religious communities' in the contemporary Indian context.

DEBOLINA KUNDU is an Associate Professor at the Institute of Public Finance and Policy, India. She has vast professional experience in the field of development studies.

JOEL LEE is pursuing doctoral research at Columbia University in New York. He has worked with numerous well-known Dalit human rights organizations in India.

S. MADHESWARAN is Professor of Economics at the Institute of Social and Economic Change, India. His area of research is environmental economics and economic of labour market discrimination.

M. MAHAMALLIK is Assistant Professor at Institute of Development Studies, Jaipur. He has been working in the area of 'social exclusion' for many years. His areas of interests are land rights and livelihood, social movements, and political economy of agrarian distress.

GEETHA B. NAMBISSAN is Professor of Sociology of Education at the Zakir Husain Centre for Educational Studies, Jawaharlal Nehru University, New Delhi. Her research has focused on exclusion and inclusion in education with a focus on marginal groups.